S⋅A

Special A

Hikari age 5 and Atsushi age 6.

Volume 10

Story & Art by
Maki Minami

STORY

★At the tender age of 6, carpenter's daughter Hikari Hanazono suffered her first loss to the wealthy Kei Takishima in a wrestling match. Now the hardworking Hikari has followed Kei to the most elite school for the rich just to beat him! I call this story "Overthrow Takishima! Rise Above Perpetual Second Place!!" It's the story of Hikari's sweat, tears and passion, with a little bit of love thrown in!

★During a party at Sakura's villa, Hikari and Kei get stuck for the night on a deserted island. While they are alone, Kei confesses his love for Hikari. Now how will Hikari respond?

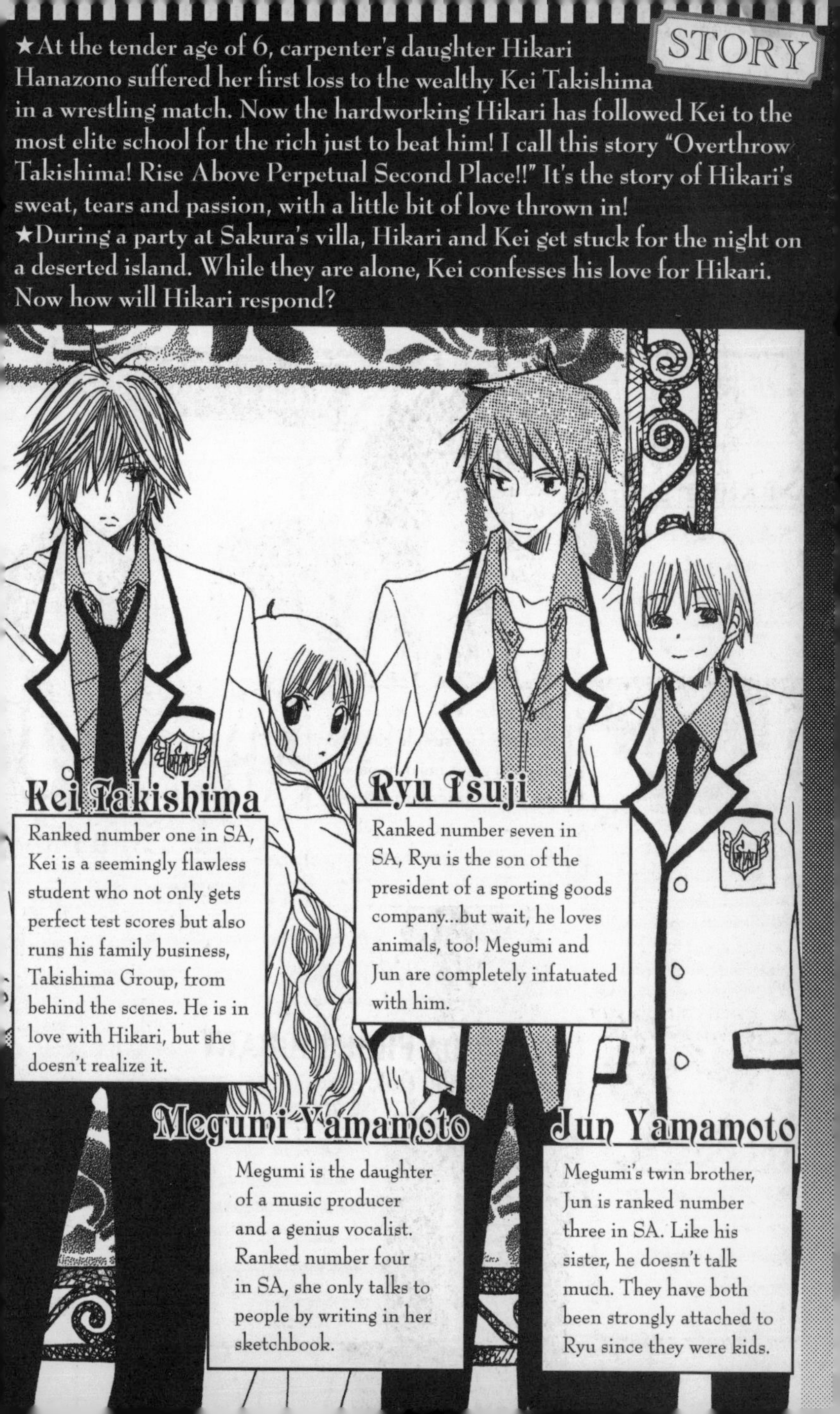

Kei Takishima

Ranked number one in SA, Kei is a seemingly flawless student who not only gets perfect test scores but also runs his family business, Takishima Group, from behind the scenes. He is in love with Hikari, but she doesn't realize it.

Ryu Tsuji

Ranked number seven in SA, Ryu is the son of the president of a sporting goods company...but wait, he loves animals, too! Megumi and Jun are completely infatuated with him.

Megumi Yamamoto

Megumi is the daughter of a music producer and a genius vocalist. Ranked number four in SA, she only talks to people by writing in her sketchbook.

Jun Yamamoto

Megumi's twin brother, Jun is ranked number three in SA. Like his sister, he doesn't talk much. They have both been strongly attached to Ryu since they were kids.

S·A CHARACTERS

What is "Special A"?

Hikari goes to an elite school called Hakusenkan High School. This school divides each grade level into groups A through F, according to the students' test scores. Group A includes only the top seven students in each class. Then the top seven students from all grades' A-groups are put into a group called Special A, which is considered much higher than all others. Known as SA, they are "the elite among the elite."

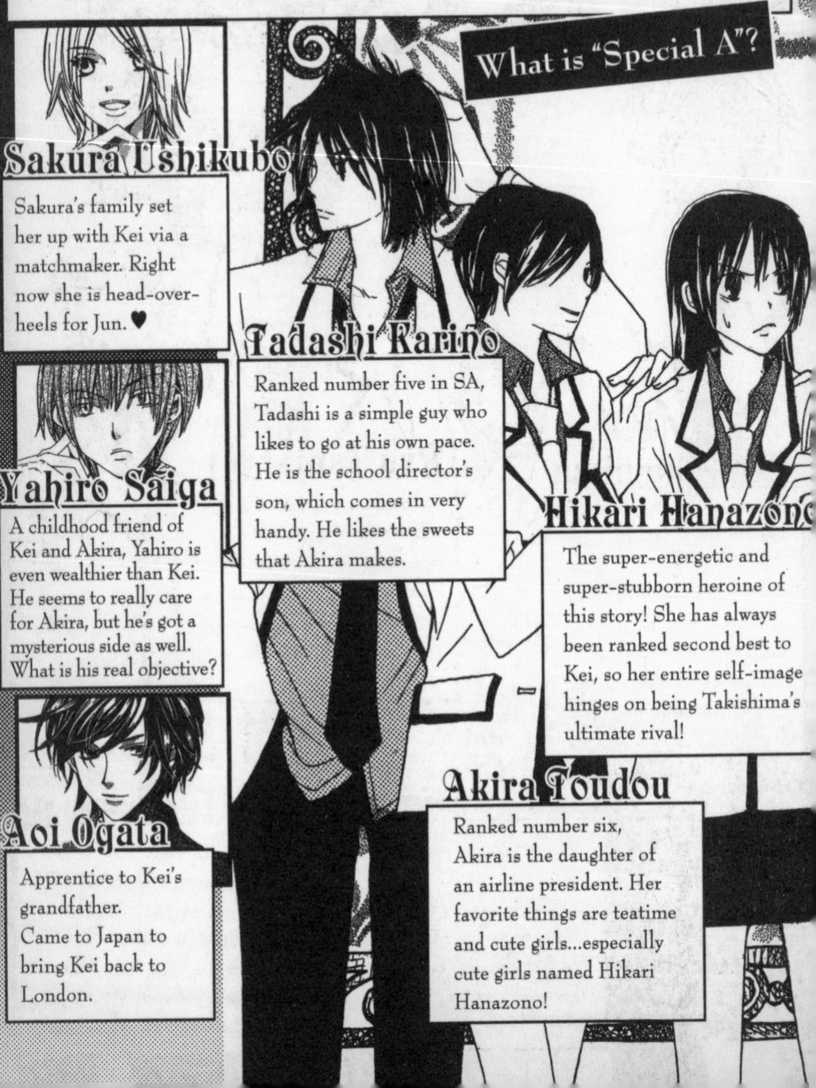

Sakura Ushikubo

Sakura's family set her up with Kei via a matchmaker. Right now she is head-over-heels for Jun. ♥

Tadashi Karino

Ranked number five in SA, Tadashi is a simple guy who likes to go at his own pace. He is the school director's son, which comes in very handy. He likes the sweets that Akira makes.

Hikari Hanazono

The super-energetic and super-stubborn heroine of this story! She has always been ranked second best to Kei, so her entire self-image hinges on being Takishima's ultimate rival!

Yahiro Saiga

A childhood friend of Kei and Akira, Yahiro is even wealthier than Kei. He seems to really care for Akira, but he's got a mysterious side as well. What is his real objective?

Aoi Ogata

Apprentice to Kei's grandfather.
Came to Japan to bring Kei back to London.

Akira Toudou

Ranked number six, Akira is the daughter of an airline president. Her favorite things are teatime and cute girls...especially cute girls named Hikari Hanazono!

Contents

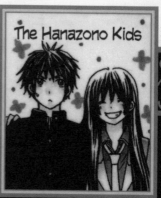

The Hanazono Kids

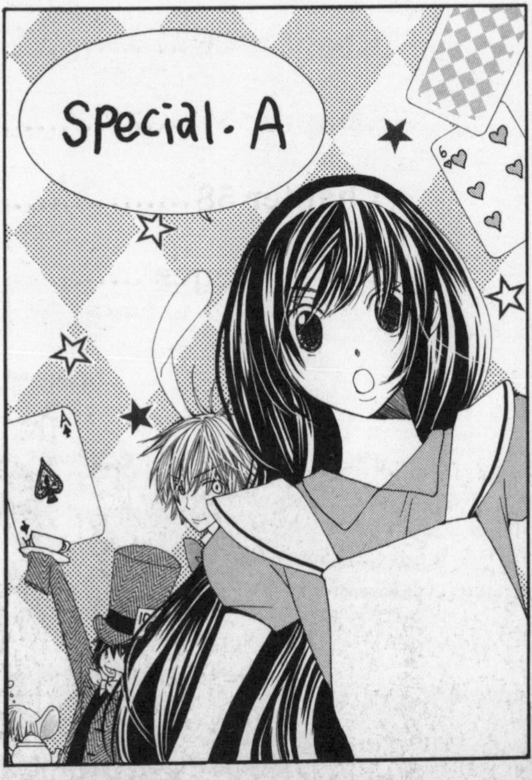
Special・A

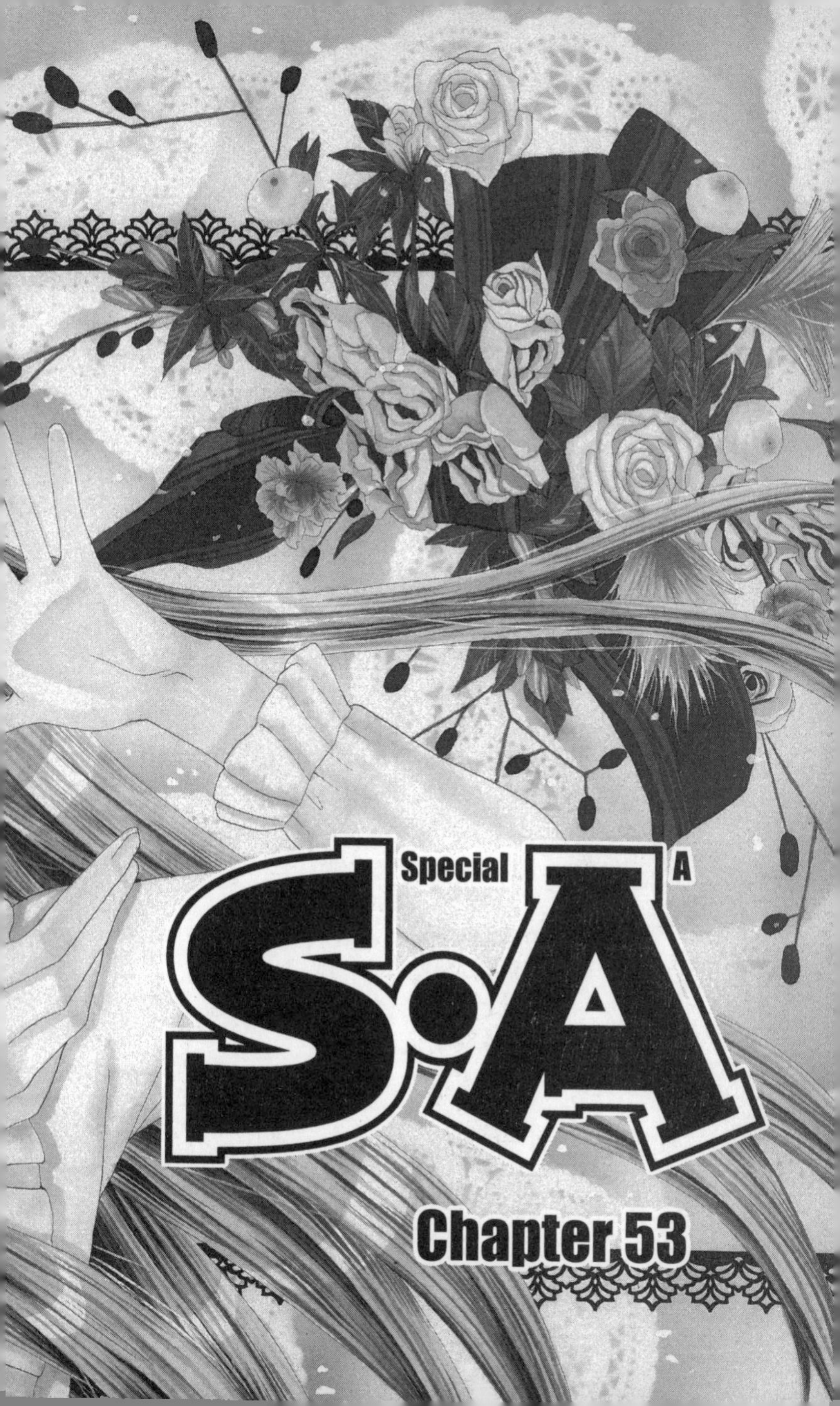
Special A
S.A
Chapter 53

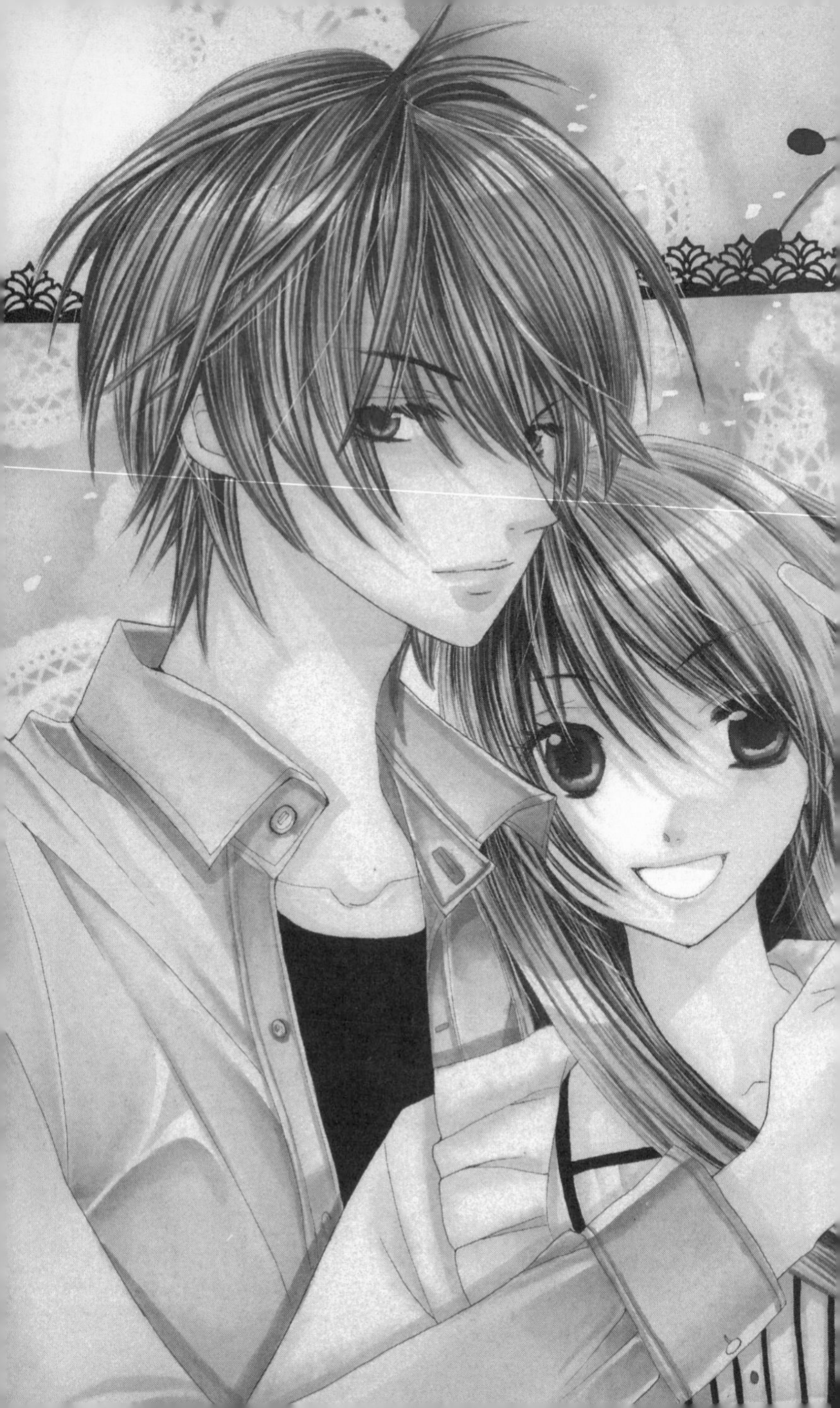

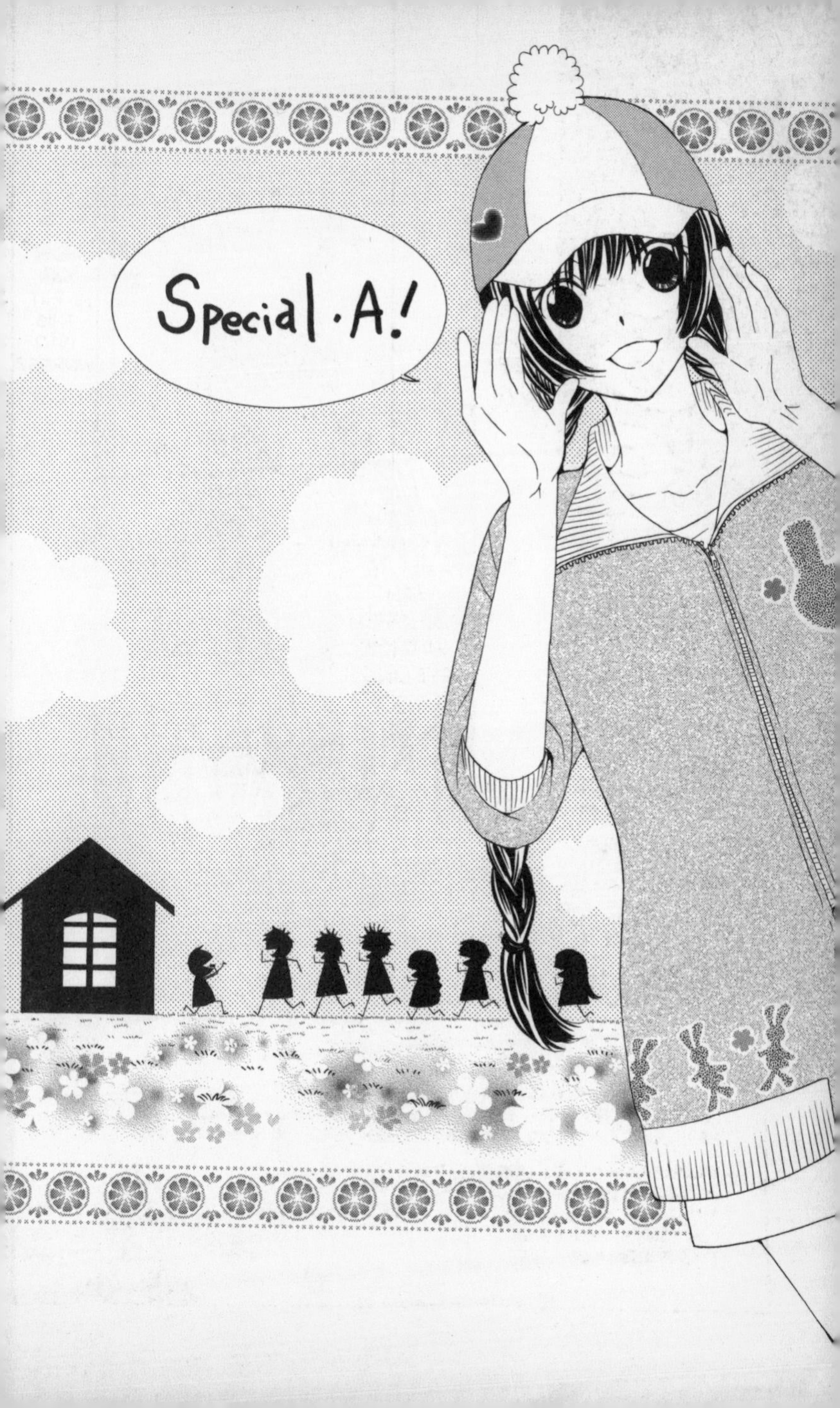
Special·A!

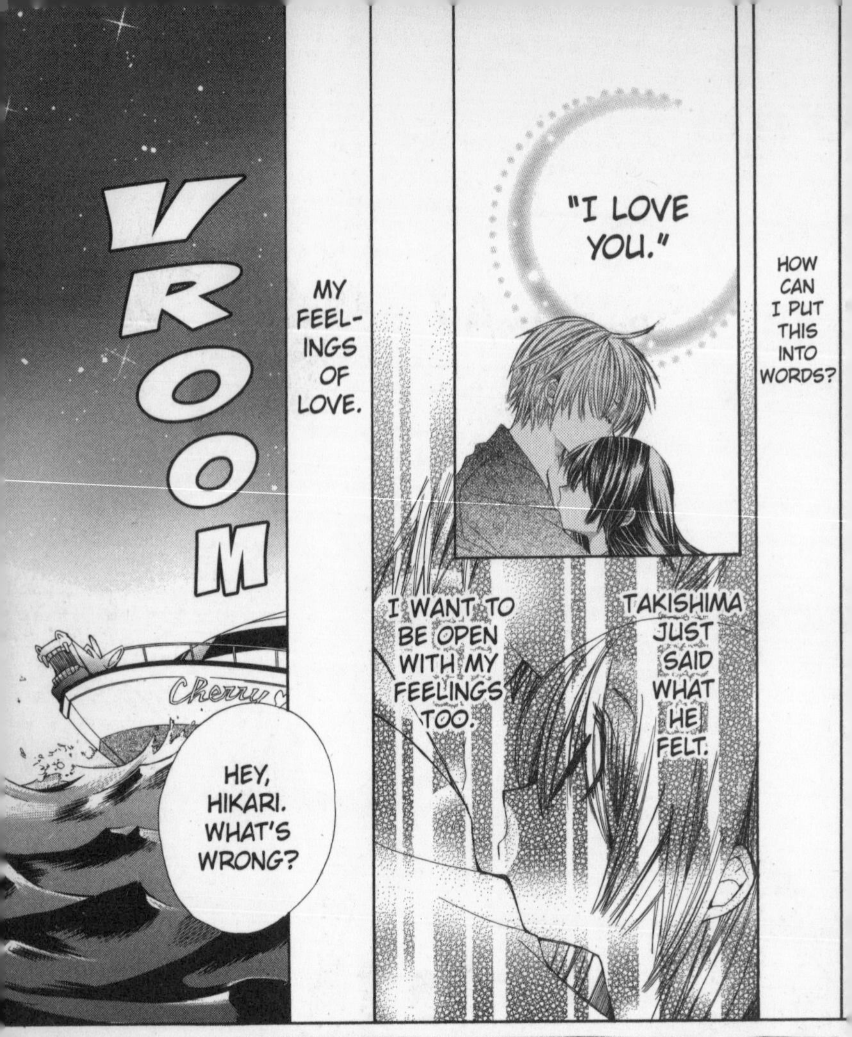
HOW CAN I PUT THIS INTO WORDS?
"I LOVE YOU."
MY FEEL-INGS OF LOVE.
TAKISHIMA JUST SAID WHAT HE FELT.
I WANT TO BE OPEN WITH MY FEELINGS TOO.
VROOM
Cherry
HEY, HIKARI. WHAT'S WRONG?

• THE COVER, ETC. •

- THIS TIME HIKARI AND HER BROTHER ARE ON THE COVER, EVEN THOUGH HER BROTHER ALMOST NEVER APPEARS. HIS NAME IS ATSUSHI HANAZONO. HE'S JUST A NORMAL GUY, BUT I THINK HE'S THE BEST BROTHER.
- THANK YOU FOR SUGGESTING THE QUARTER-PAGE ILLUSTRATIONS, ♡ Love! THE FILLER ART AND IDEAS FOR TADASHI'S PAGES! I LOVE DRAWING THEM!

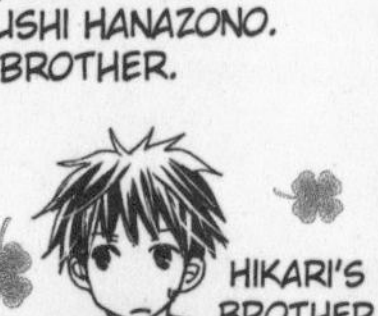

HIKARI'S BROTHER

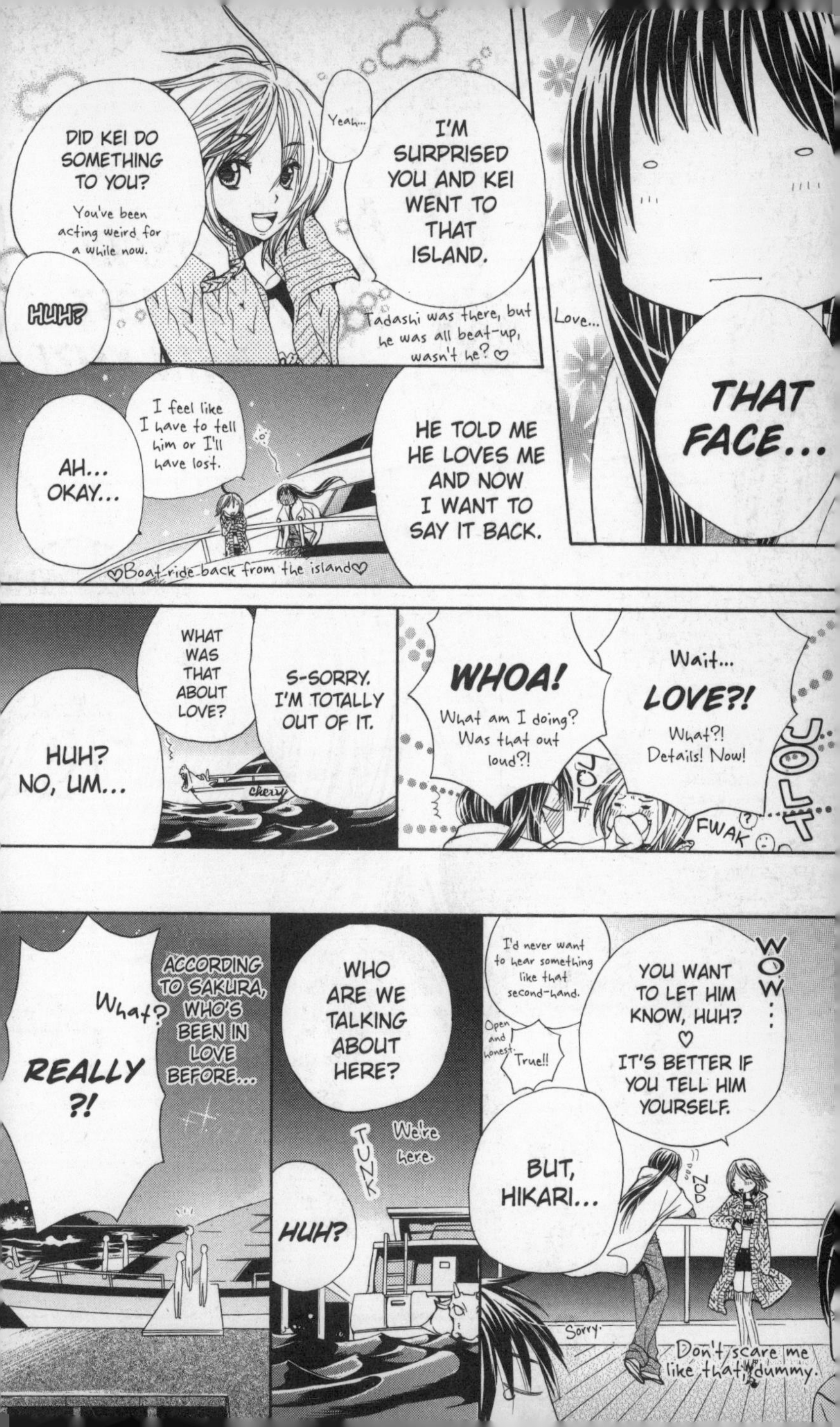

Love...
THAT FACE...
Yeah...
I'M SURPRISED YOU AND KEI WENT TO THAT ISLAND.
Tadashi was there, but he was all beat-up, wasn't he? ♡
DID KEI DO SOMETHING TO YOU?
You've been acting weird for a while now.
HUH?
HE TOLD ME HE LOVES ME AND NOW I WANT TO SAY IT BACK.
I feel like I have to tell him or I'll have lost.
AH... OKAY...
♡Boat-ride back from the island♡
JOLT
Wait...
LOVE?!
What?! Details! Now!
WHOA!
What am I doing? Was that out loud?!
FWAK
S-SORRY. I'M TOTALLY OUT OF IT.
WHAT WAS THAT ABOUT LOVE?
HUH? NO, UM...
Cherry
WOW...
YOU WANT TO LET HIM KNOW, HUH? ♡
IT'S BETTER IF YOU TELL HIM YOURSELF.
I'd never want to hear something like that second-hand.
Open and honest.
True!!
BUT, HIKARI...
NOD
Sorry.
Don't scare me like that, dummy.
WHO ARE WE TALKING ABOUT HERE?
TUNK
We're here.
HUH?
ACCORDING TO SAKURA, WHO'S BEEN IN LOVE BEFORE...
What?
REALLY?!

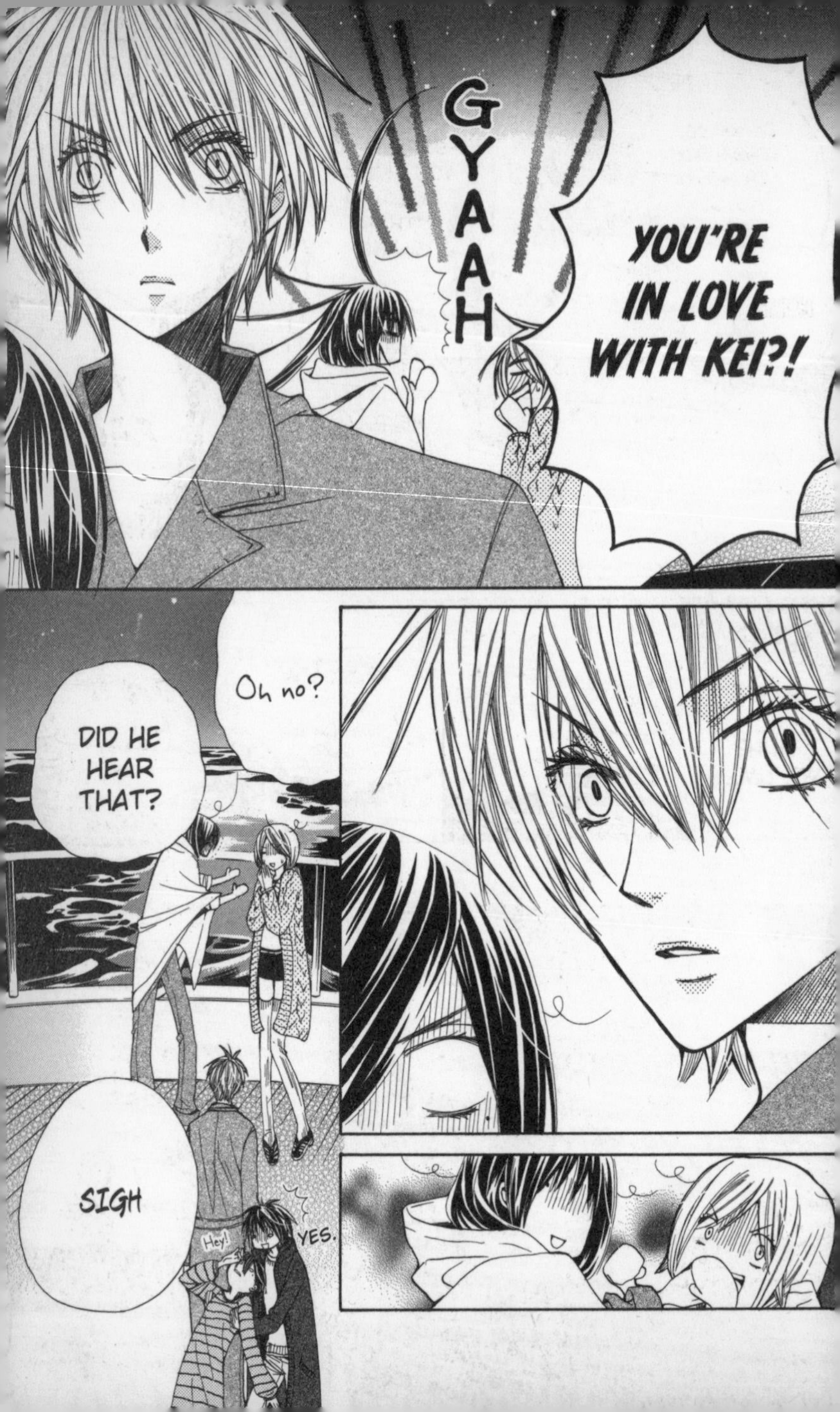
YOU'RE IN LOVE WITH KEI?!
GYAAH
Oh no?
DID HE HEAR THAT?
YES.
Hey!
SIGH

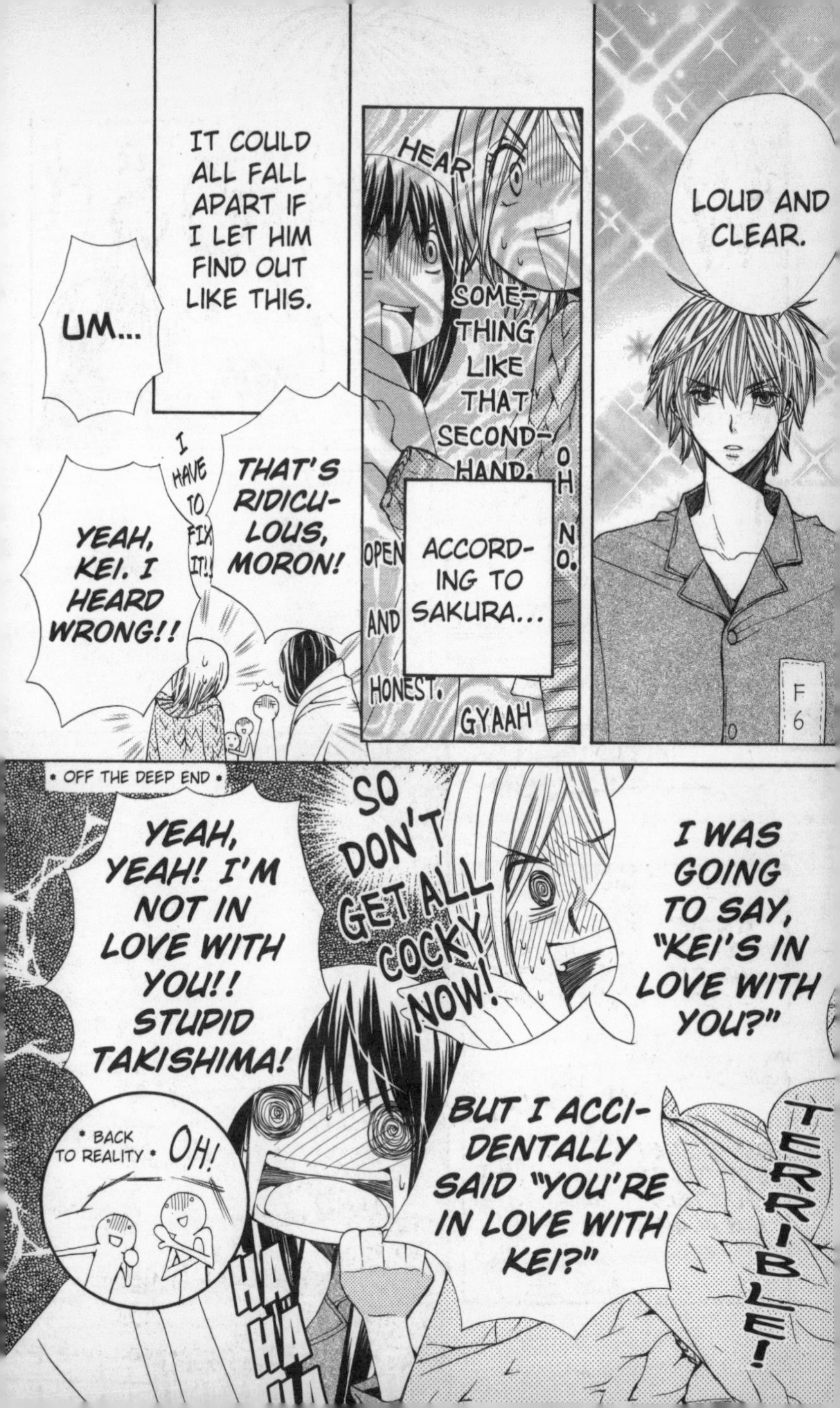

LOUD AND CLEAR.
HEAR SOMETHING LIKE THAT SECOND-HAND.
OH NO.
ACCORDING TO SAKURA...
OPEN AND HONEST.
GYAAH
IT COULD ALL FALL APART IF I LET HIM FIND OUT LIKE THIS.
UM...
THAT'S RIDICULOUS, MORON!
I HAVE TO FIX IT!!
YEAH, KEI. I HEARD WRONG!!
* OFF THE DEEP END *
I WAS GOING TO SAY, "KEI'S IN LOVE WITH YOU?"
SO DON'T GET ALL COCKY NOW!
YEAH, YEAH! I'M NOT IN LOVE WITH YOU!! STUPID TAKISHIMA!
TERRIBLE!
BUT I ACCIDENTALLY SAID "YOU'RE IN LOVE WITH KEI?"
OH!
* BACK TO REALITY *
HA HA HA

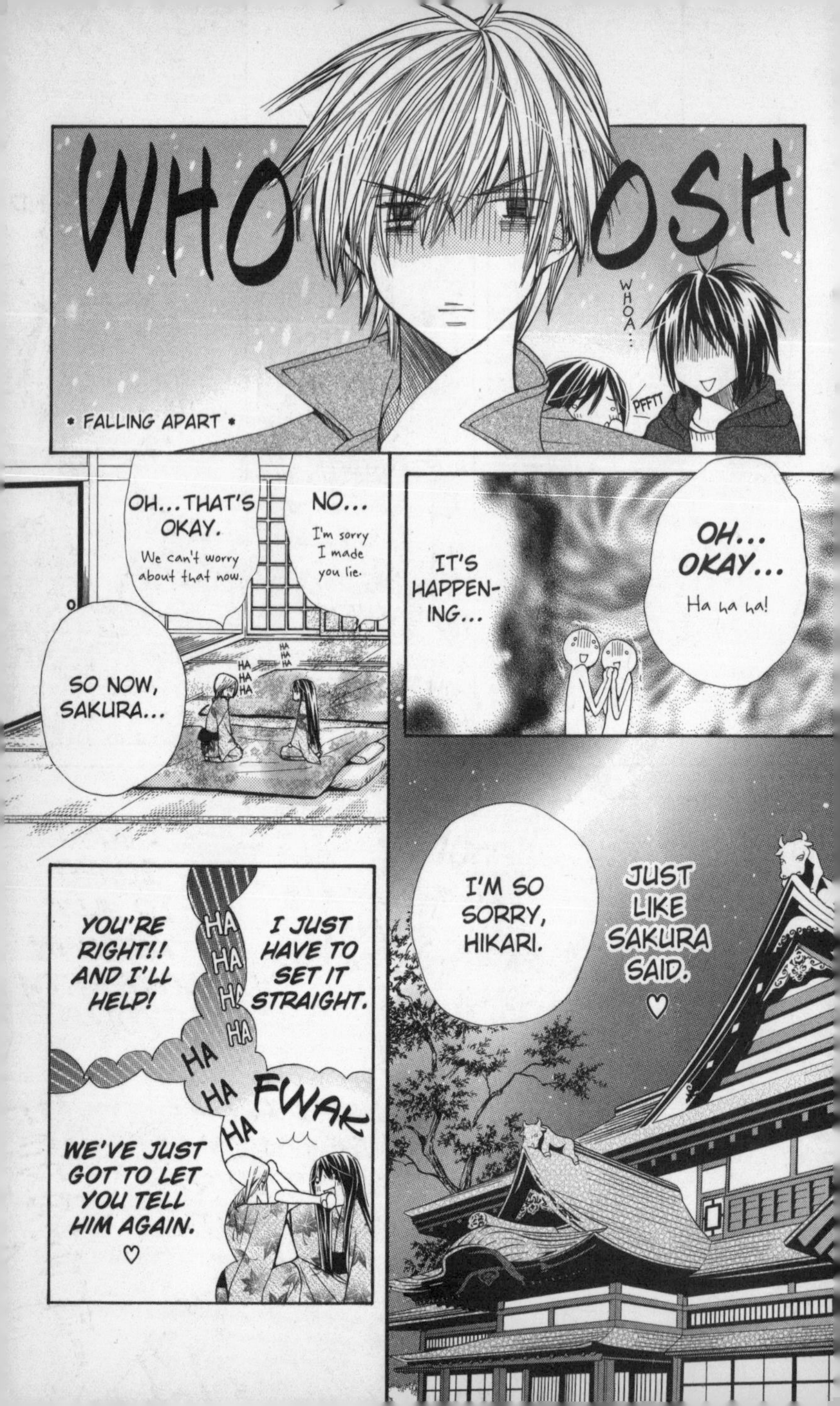
WHOOSH
WHOA...
PFFTT
• FALLING APART •
OH... OKAY... Ha ha ha!
IT'S HAPPENING...
NO... I'm sorry I made you lie.
OH...THAT'S OKAY. We can't worry about that now.
HA HA HA
HA HA HA
SO NOW, SAKURA...
JUST LIKE SAKURA SAID. ♡
I'M SO SORRY, HIKARI.
I JUST HAVE TO SET IT STRAIGHT.
HA HA HA HA HA HA HA
YOU'RE RIGHT!! AND I'LL HELP!
FWAK
WE'VE JUST GOT TO LET YOU TELL HIM AGAIN. ♡

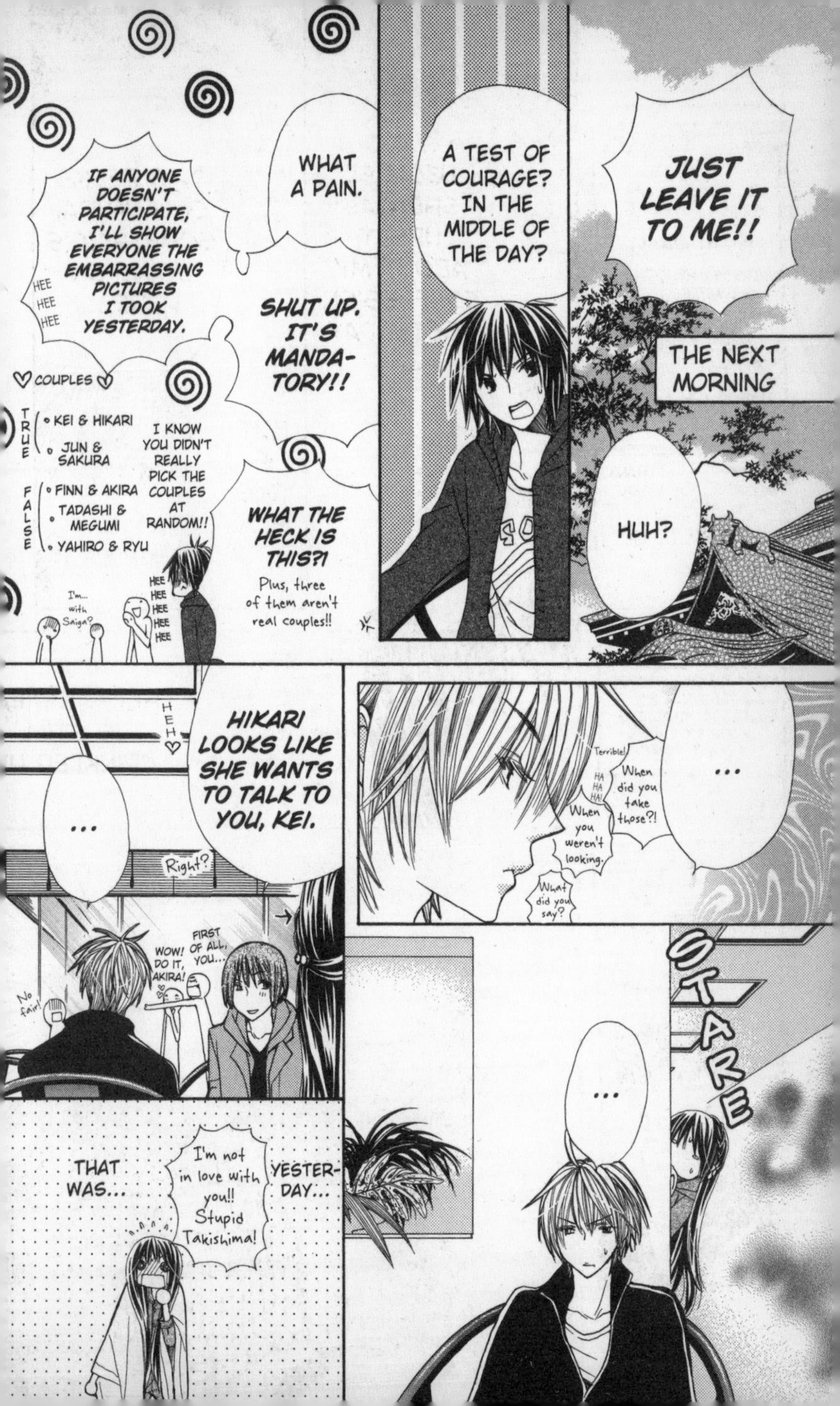
JUST LEAVE IT TO ME!!
THE NEXT MORNING
HUH?
A TEST OF COURAGE? IN THE MIDDLE OF THE DAY?
WHAT A PAIN.
IF ANYONE DOESN'T PARTICIPATE, I'LL SHOW EVERYONE THE EMBARRASSING PICTURES I TOOK YESTERDAY.
HEE HEE HEE
SHUT UP. IT'S MANDATORY!!
♡COUPLES♡
TRUE
• KEI & HIKARI
• JUN & SAKURA
FALSE
• FINN & AKIRA
• TADASHI & MEGUMI
• YAHIRO & RYU
I KNOW YOU DIDN'T REALLY PICK THE COUPLES AT RANDOM!!
WHAT THE HECK IS THIS?!
Plus, three of them aren't real couples!!
HEE HEE HEE HEE HEE
I'm... with Saiga?
...
Terrible!
When did you take those?!
HA HA HA!
When you weren't looking.
What did you say?
HIKARI LOOKS LIKE SHE WANTS TO TALK TO YOU, KEI.
HEH♡
...
Right?
FIRST OF ALL, YOU...
WOW! DO IT, AKIRA!
No fair!
STARE
...
YESTER-DAY...
I'm not in love with you!! Stupid Takishima!
THAT WAS...

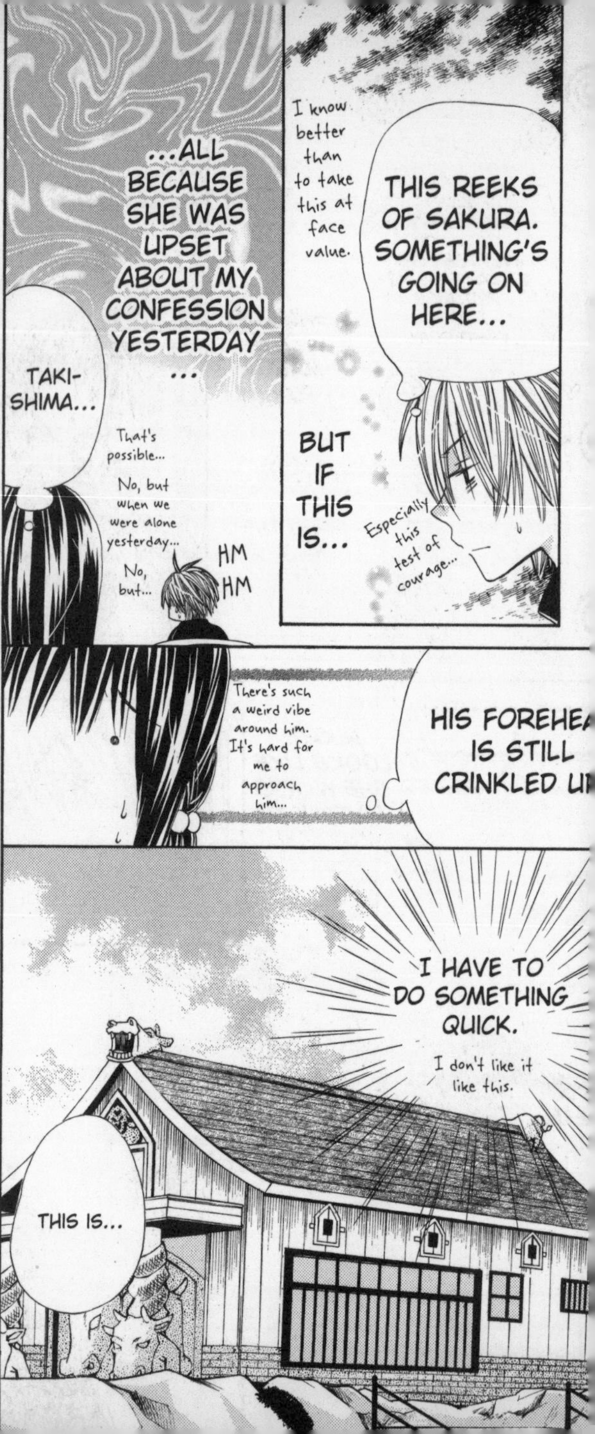
I know better than to take this at face value.
THIS REEKS OF SAKURA. SOMETHING'S GOING ON HERE...
BUT IF THIS IS...
Especially this test of courage...
...ALL BECAUSE SHE WAS UPSET ABOUT MY CONFESSION YESTERDAY...
TAKI-SHIMA...
That's possible...
No, but when we were alone yesterday...
No, but...
HM HM
HIS FOREHEA IS STILL CRINKLED U
There's such a weird vibe around him. It's hard for me to approach him...
I HAVE TO DO SOMETHING QUICK.
I don't like it like this.
THIS IS...

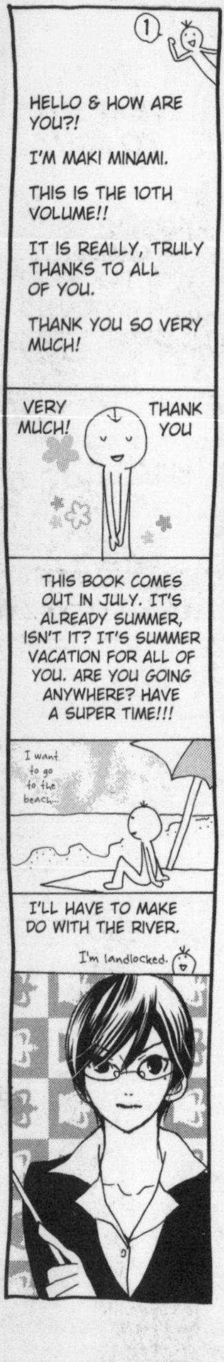
1
HELLO & HOW ARE YOU?!
I'M MAKI MINAMI.
THIS IS THE 10TH VOLUME!!
IT IS REALLY, TRULY THANKS TO ALL OF YOU.
THANK YOU SO VERY MUCH!
THANK YOU
VERY MUCH!
THIS BOOK COMES OUT IN JULY. IT'S ALREADY SUMMER, ISN'T IT? IT'S SUMMER VACATION FOR ALL OF YOU. ARE YOU GOING ANYWHERE? HAVE A SUPER TIME!!!
I want to go to the beach...
I'LL HAVE TO MAKE DO WITH THE RIVER.
I'm landlocked.

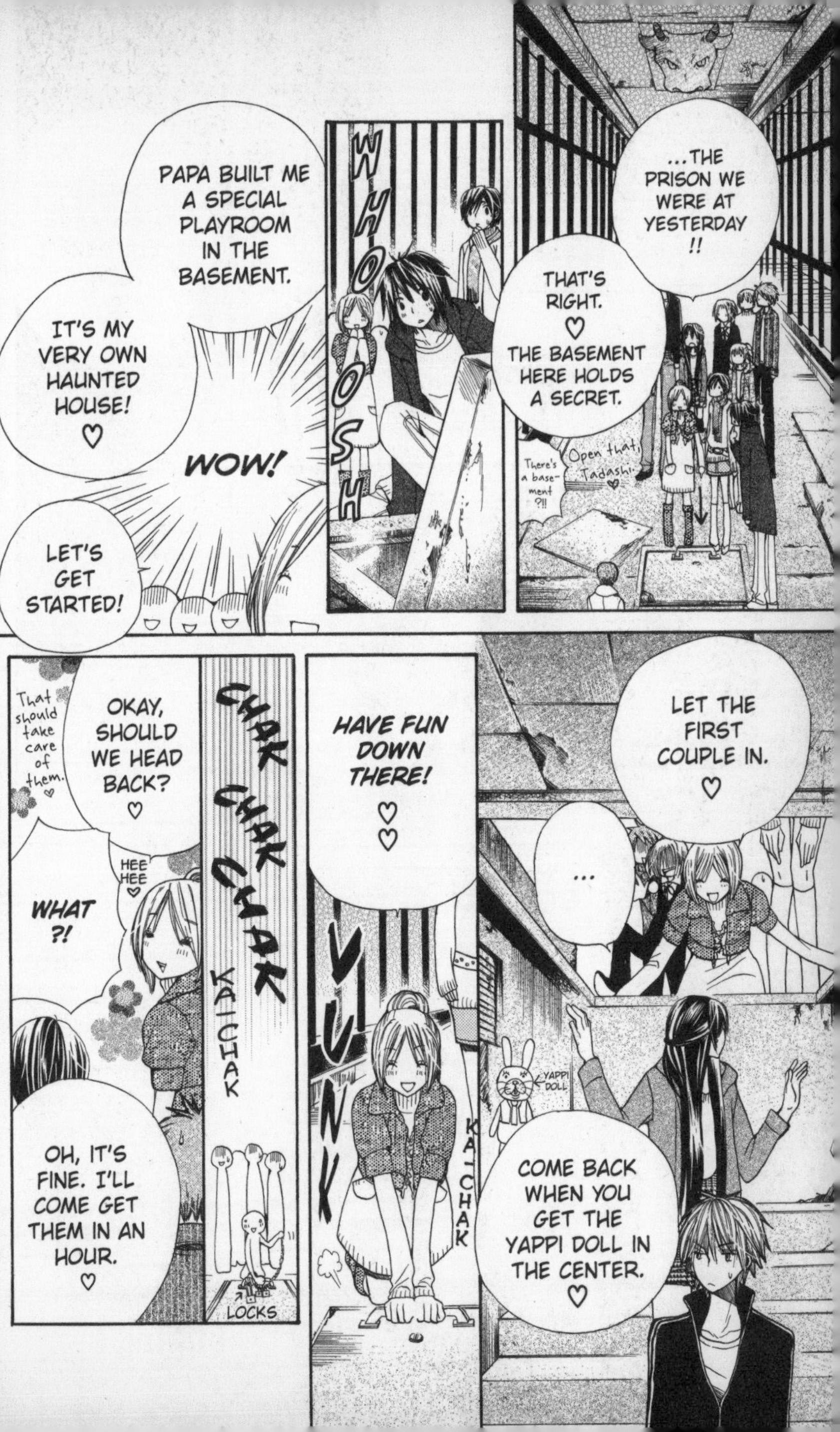
...THE PRISON WE WERE AT YESTERDAY !!
THAT'S RIGHT. ♡ THE BASEMENT HERE HOLDS A SECRET.
Open that, Tadashi. ♡
There's a basement ?!!
WHOOSH
PAPA BUILT ME A SPECIAL PLAYROOM IN THE BASEMENT.
IT'S MY VERY OWN HAUNTED HOUSE! ♡
WOW!
LET'S GET STARTED!
LET THE FIRST COUPLE IN. ♡
...
YAPPI DOLL
COME BACK WHEN YOU GET THE YAPPI DOLL IN THE CENTER. ♡
HAVE FUN DOWN THERE! ♡ ♡
VUNK
KA-CHAK
CHAK CHAK CHAK
KA-CHAK
LOCKS
OKAY, SHOULD WE HEAD BACK? ♡
That should take care of them. ♡
HEE HEE ♡
WHAT ?!
OH, IT'S FINE. I'LL COME GET THEM IN AN HOUR. ♡

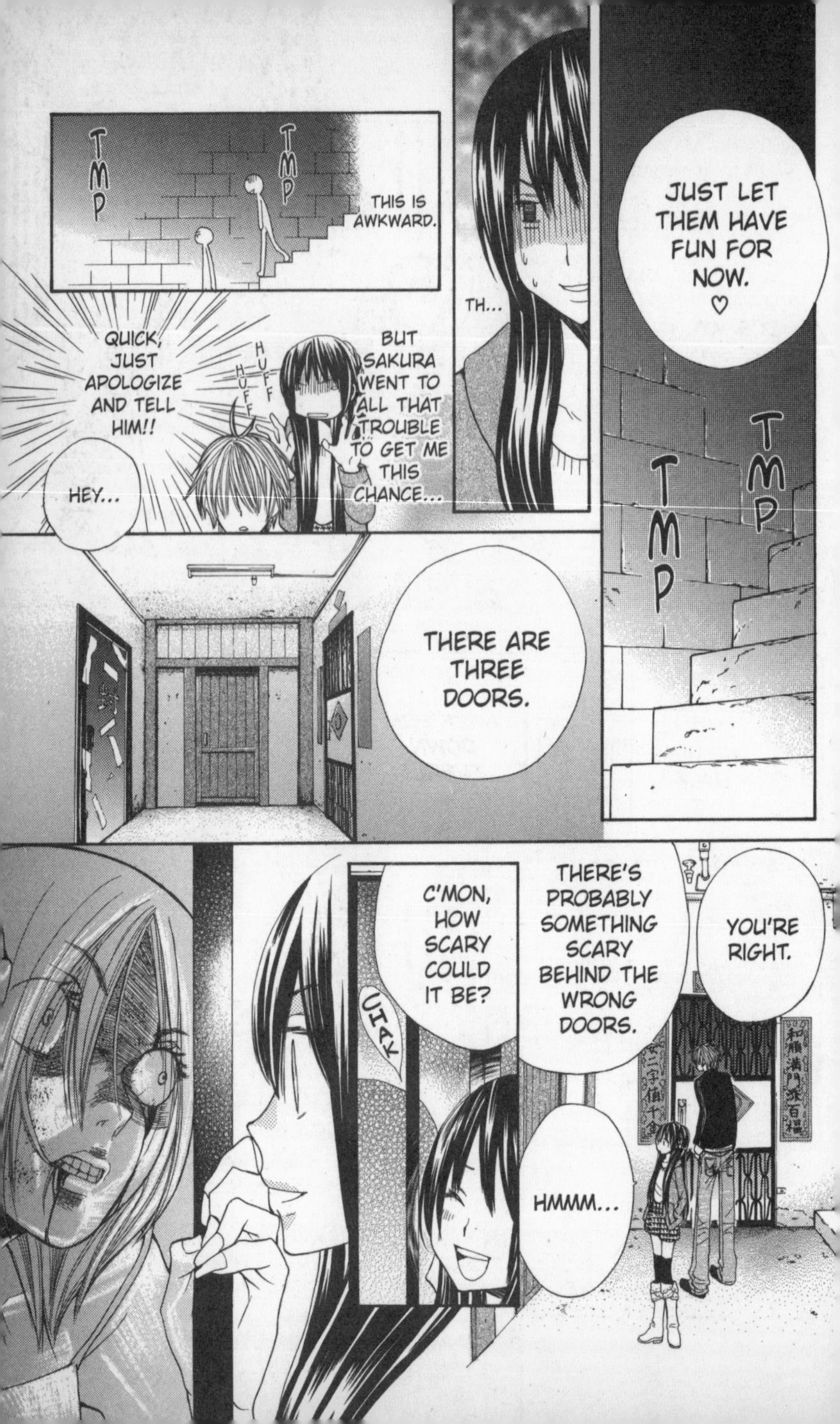
JUST LET THEM HAVE FUN FOR NOW. ♡
TMP TMP
TH...
TMP TMP
THIS IS AWKWARD.
BUT SAKURA WENT TO ALL THAT TROUBLE TO GET ME THIS CHANCE...
HUFF HUFF
QUICK, JUST APOLOGIZE AND TELL HIM!!
HEY...
THERE ARE THREE DOORS.
YOU'RE RIGHT.
THERE'S PROBABLY SOMETHING SCARY BEHIND THE WRONG DOORS.
HMMM...
C'MON, HOW SCARY COULD IT BE?
CHAK

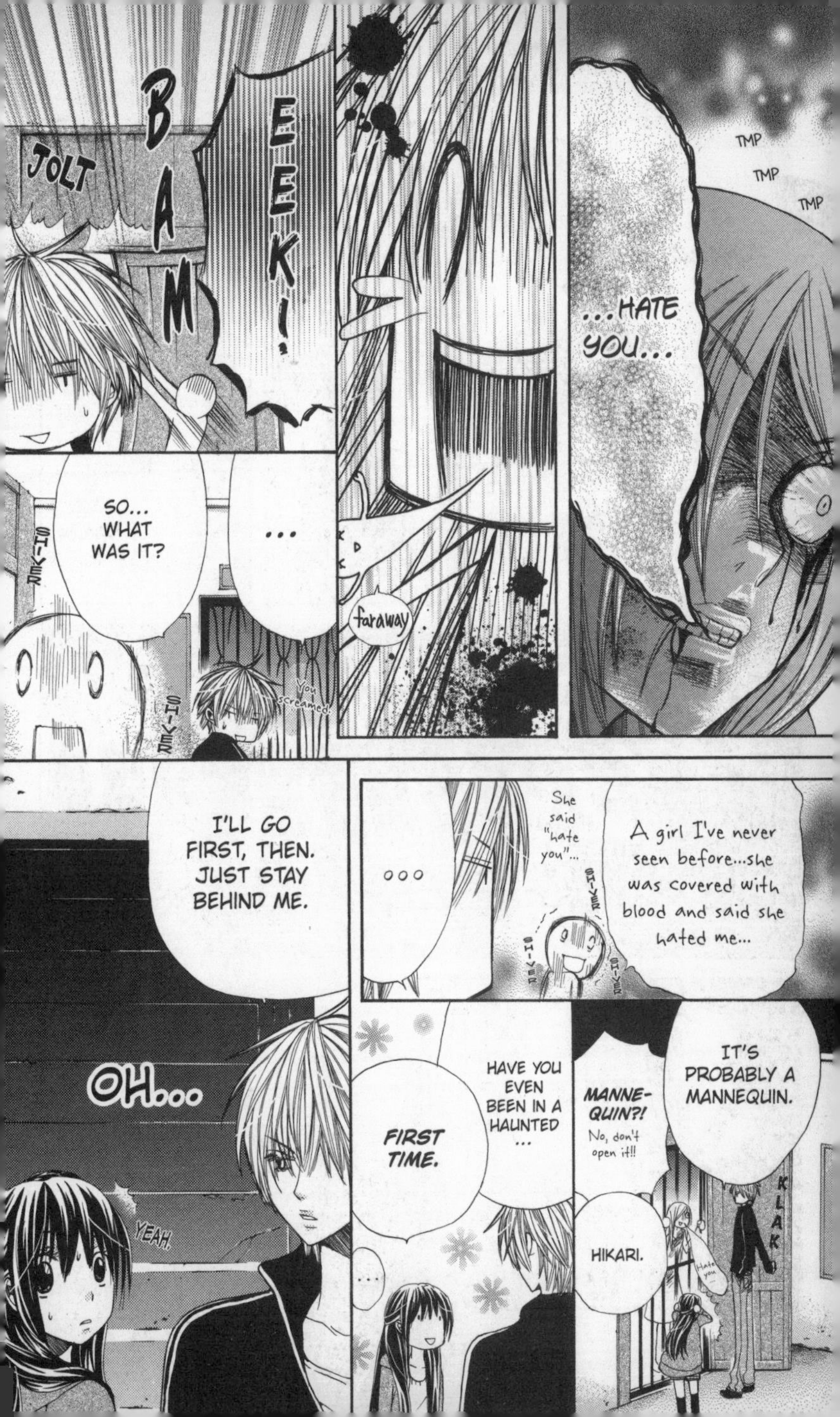
TMP
TMP
TMP
...HATE YOU...
faraway
JOLT
BAM
EEEK!
...
SO... WHAT WAS IT?
You screamed.
SHIVER
SHIVER
SHIVER
A girl I've never seen before...she was covered with blood and said she hated me...
She said "hate you"...
SHIVER
SHIVER
SHIVER
ooo
IT'S PROBABLY A MANNEQUIN.
KLAK
MANNE-QUIN?!
No, don't open it!!
Hate you
HIKARI.
HAVE YOU EVEN BEEN IN A HAUNTED ...
FIRST TIME.
...
I'LL GO FIRST, THEN. JUST STAY BEHIND ME.
OH...
YEAH.

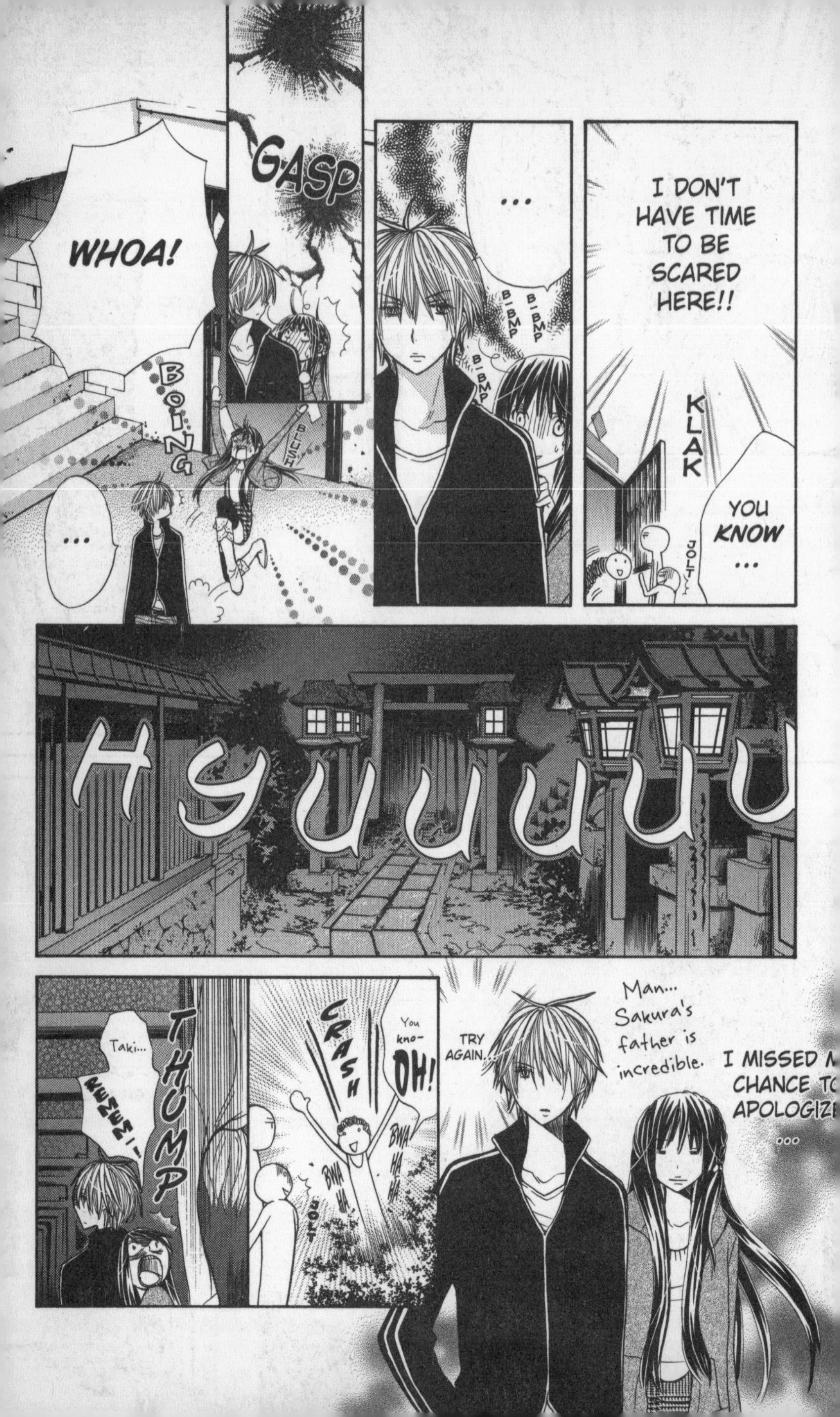
I DON'T HAVE TIME TO BE SCARED HERE!!
KLAK
YOU KNOW ...
JOLT
...
B-BMP
B-BMP
B-BMP
GASP
WHOA!
BOING
BLUSH
...
HYUUUUU
Man... Sakura's father is incredible.
I MISSED M
CHANCE TO
APOLOGIZ
TRY AGAIN...
You kno-
OH!
CRASH
BWA HA HA!
BWA HA
JOLT
Taki...
THUMP

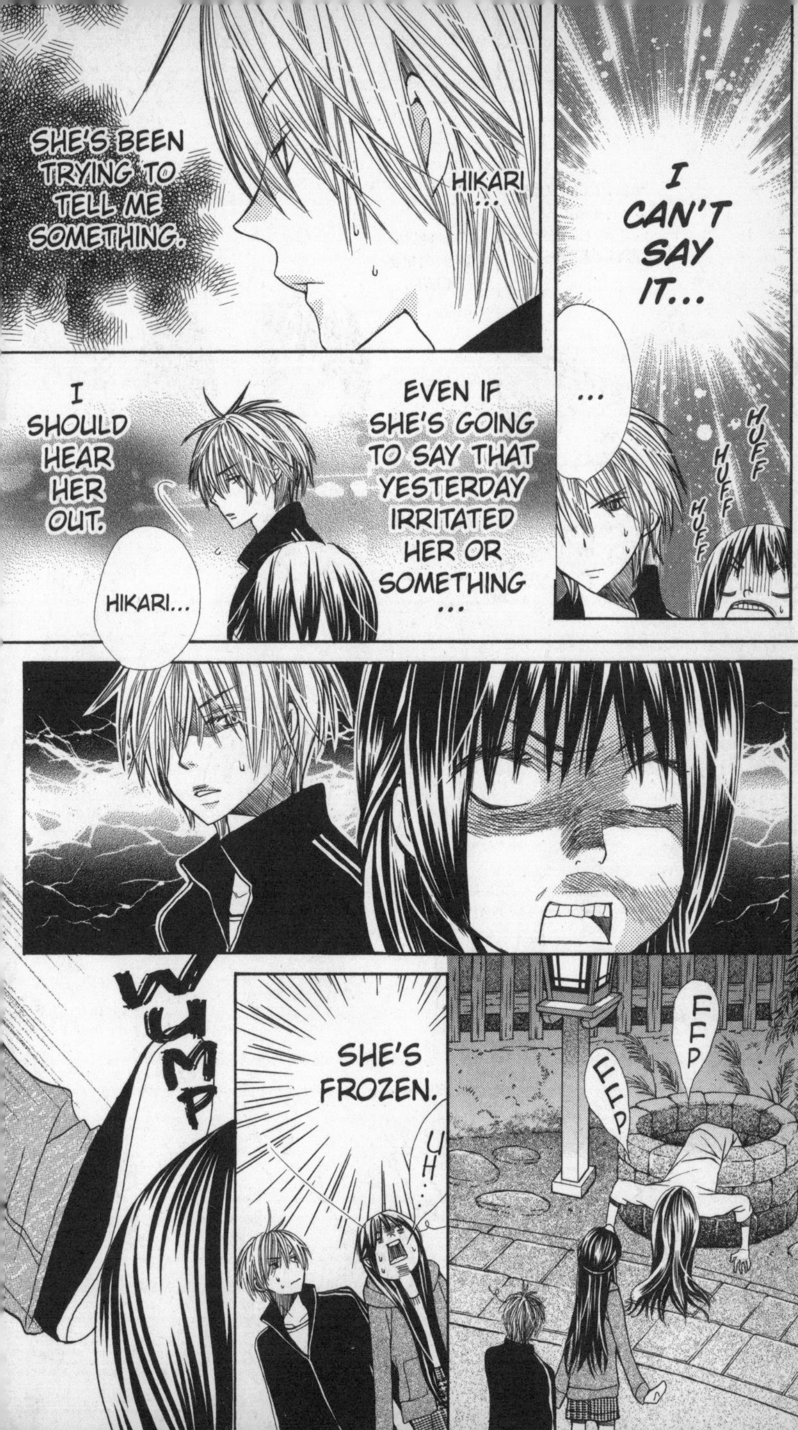
I CAN'T SAY IT...
...
HUFF HUFF HUFF
HIKARI ...
SHE'S BEEN TRYING TO TELL ME SOMETHING.
EVEN IF SHE'S GOING TO SAY THAT YESTERDAY IRRITATED HER OR SOMETHING ...
I SHOULD HEAR HER OUT.
HIKARI...
FFP
FFP
SHE'S FROZEN.
UH...
WUMP

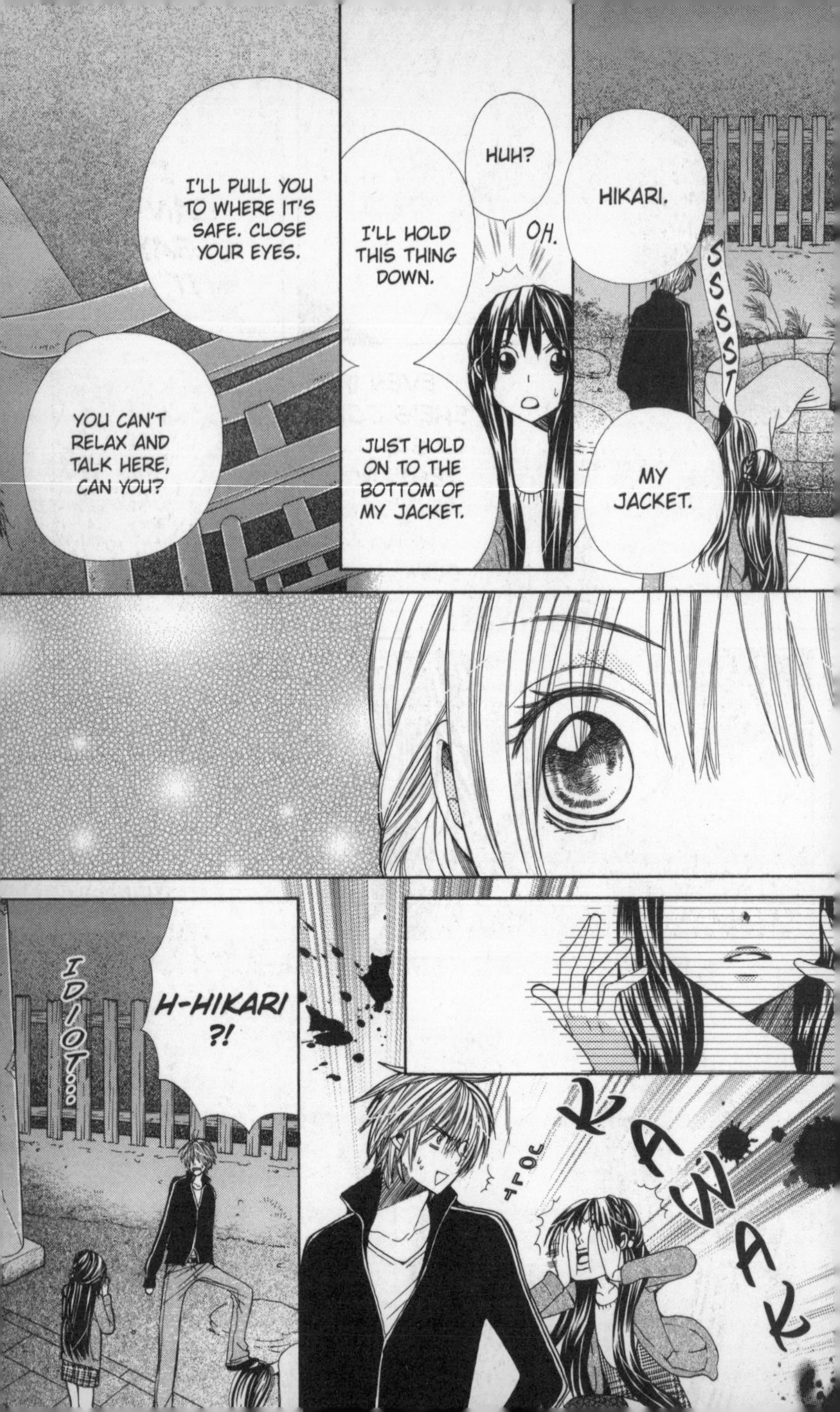

HIKARI.
SSSST
MY JACKET.
HUH?
OH.
I'LL HOLD THIS THING DOWN.
JUST HOLD ON TO THE BOTTOM OF MY JACKET.
I'LL PULL YOU TO WHERE IT'S SAFE. CLOSE YOUR EYES.
YOU CAN'T RELAX AND TALK HERE, CAN YOU?
KAWAK
TROC
H-HIKARI ?!
IDIOT...

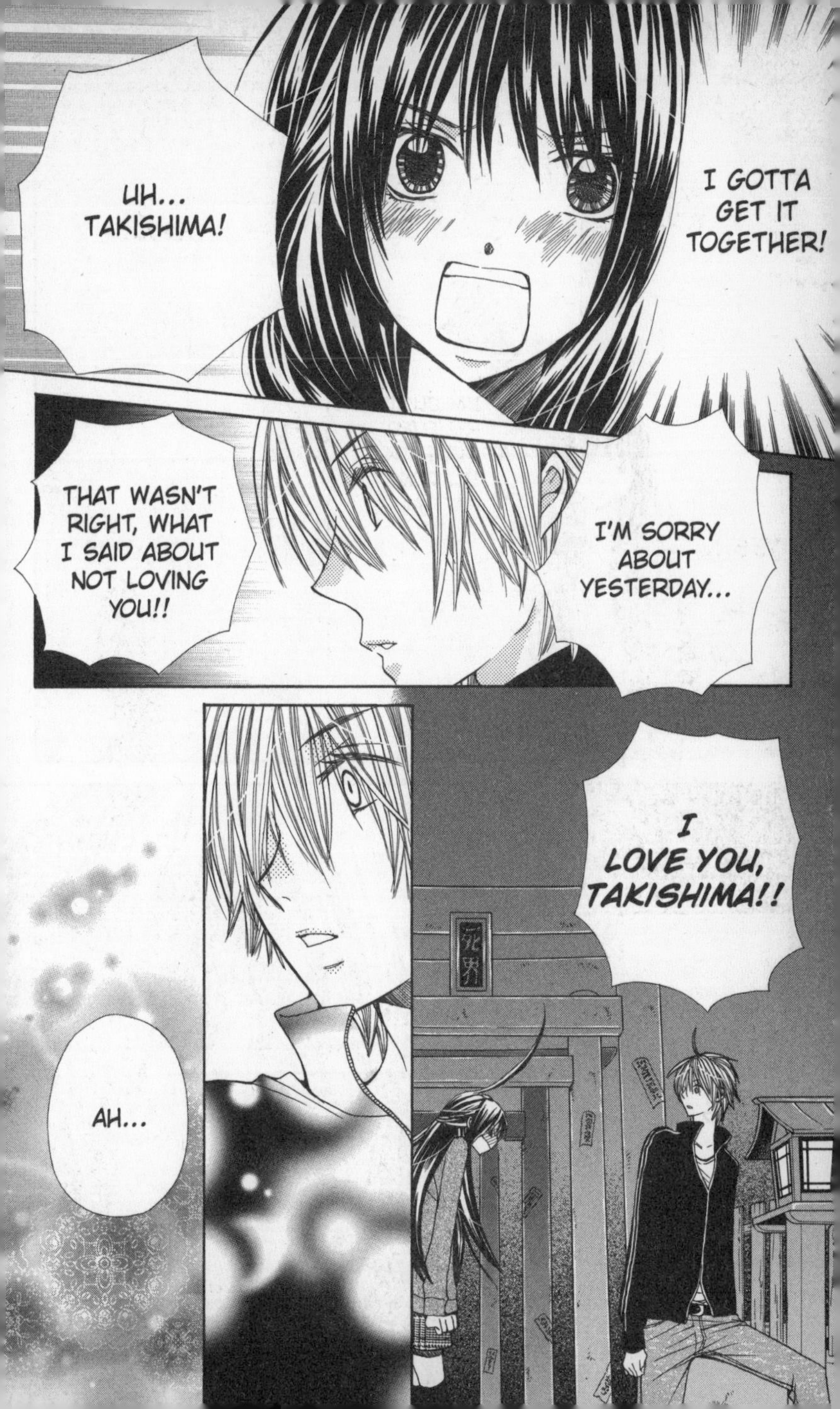
I GOTTA GET IT TOGETHER!
UH... TAKISHIMA!
I'M SORRY ABOUT YESTERDAY...
THAT WASN'T RIGHT, WHAT I SAID ABOUT NOT LOVING YOU!!
I LOVE YOU, TAKISHIMA!!
AH...

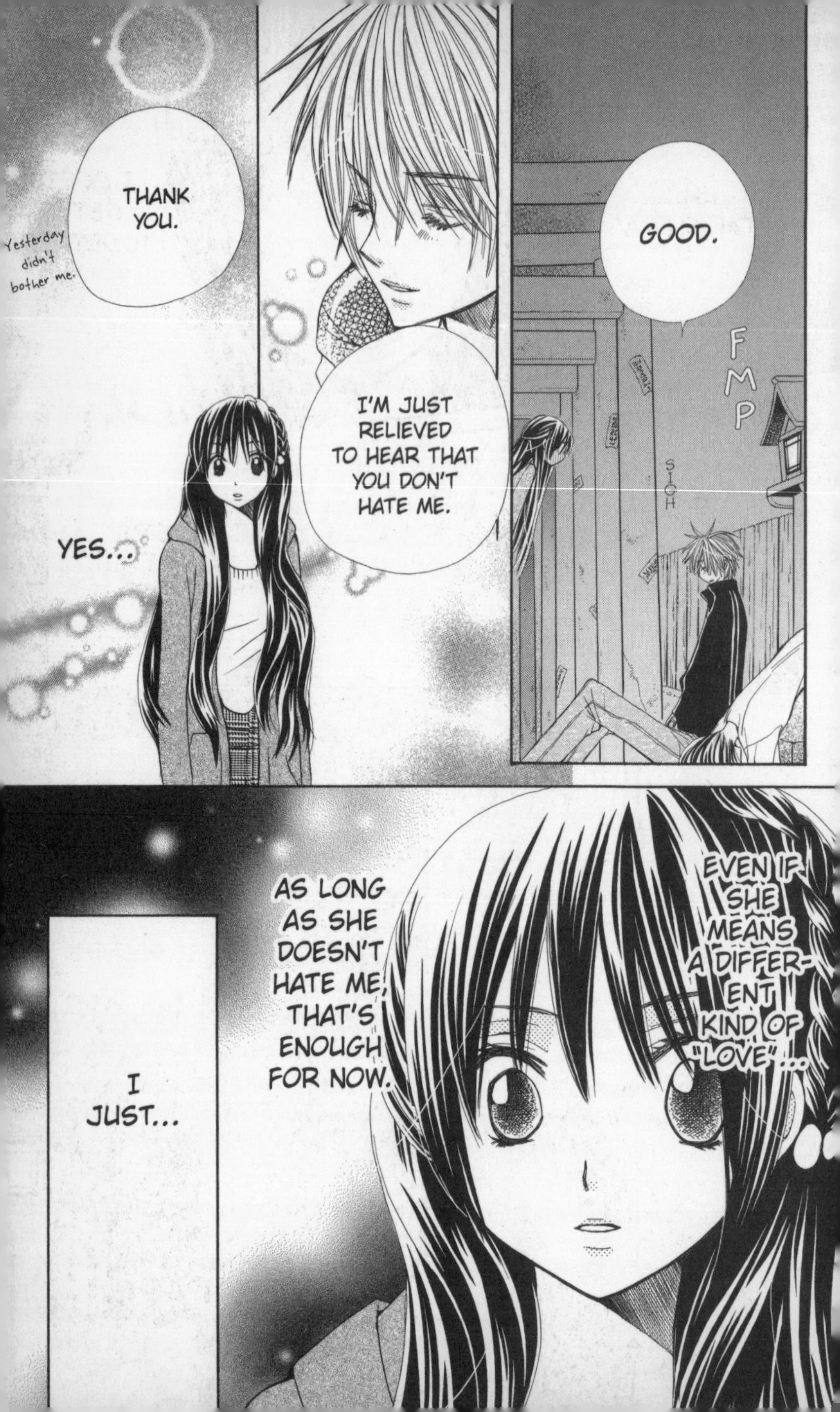
GOOD.
FMP
SIGH
I'M JUST RELIEVED TO HEAR THAT YOU DON'T HATE ME.
THANK YOU.
Yesterday didn't bother me.
YES...
EVEN IF SHE MEANS A DIFFERENT KIND OF "LOVE"...
AS LONG AS SHE DOESN'T HATE ME, THAT'S ENOUGH FOR NOW.
I JUST...

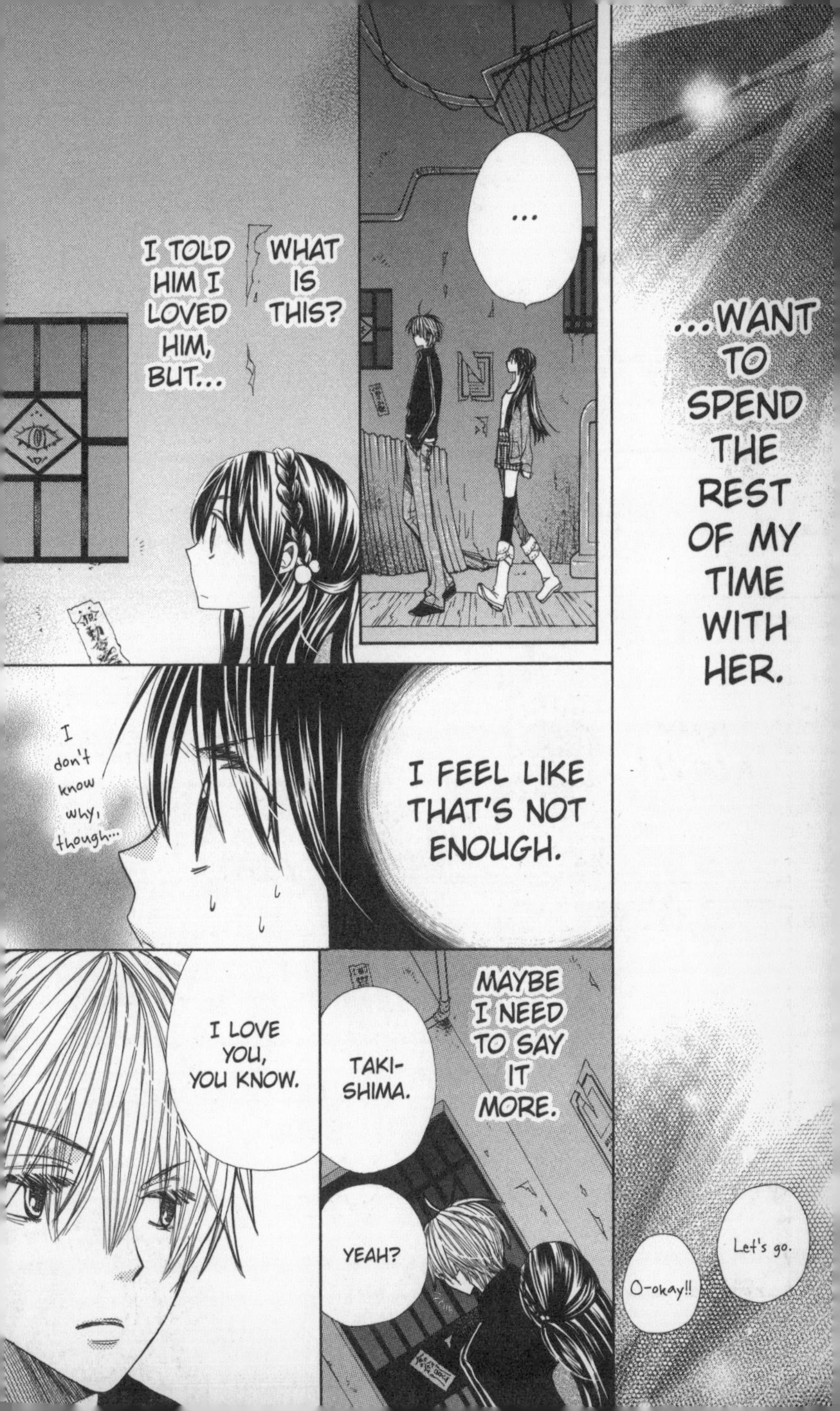
...WANT TO SPEND THE REST OF MY TIME WITH HER.
Let's go.
O-okay!!
...
WHAT IS THIS?
I TOLD HIM I LOVED HIM, BUT...
I FEEL LIKE THAT'S NOT ENOUGH.
I don't know why, though...
MAYBE I NEED TO SAY IT MORE.
TAKI-SHIMA.
YEAH?
I LOVE YOU, YOU KNOW.

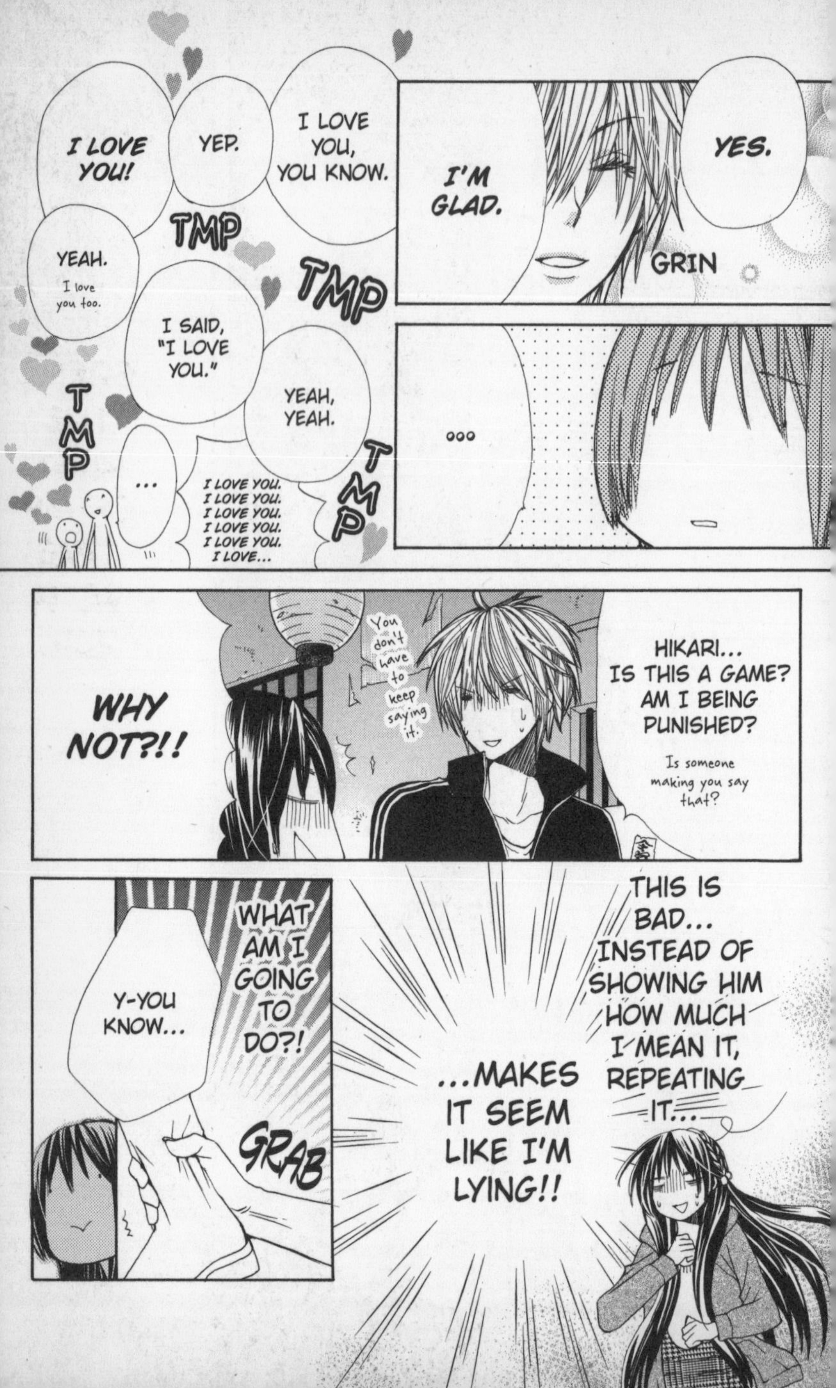
YES.
I'M GLAD.
GRIN
...
I LOVE YOU, YOU KNOW.
YEP.
I LOVE YOU!
TMP
TMP
YEAH.
I love you too.
I SAID, "I LOVE YOU."
YEAH, YEAH.
TMP
I LOVE YOU. I LOVE YOU. I LOVE YOU. I LOVE YOU. I LOVE YOU. I LOVE...
...
TMP
HIKARI... IS THIS A GAME? AM I BEING PUNISHED?
Is someone making you say that?
You don't have to keep saying it.
WHY NOT?!!
THIS IS BAD... INSTEAD OF SHOWING HIM HOW MUCH I MEAN IT, REPEATING IT...
...MAKES IT SEEM LIKE I'M LYING!!
WHAT AM I GOING TO DO?!
Y-YOU KNOW...
GRAB

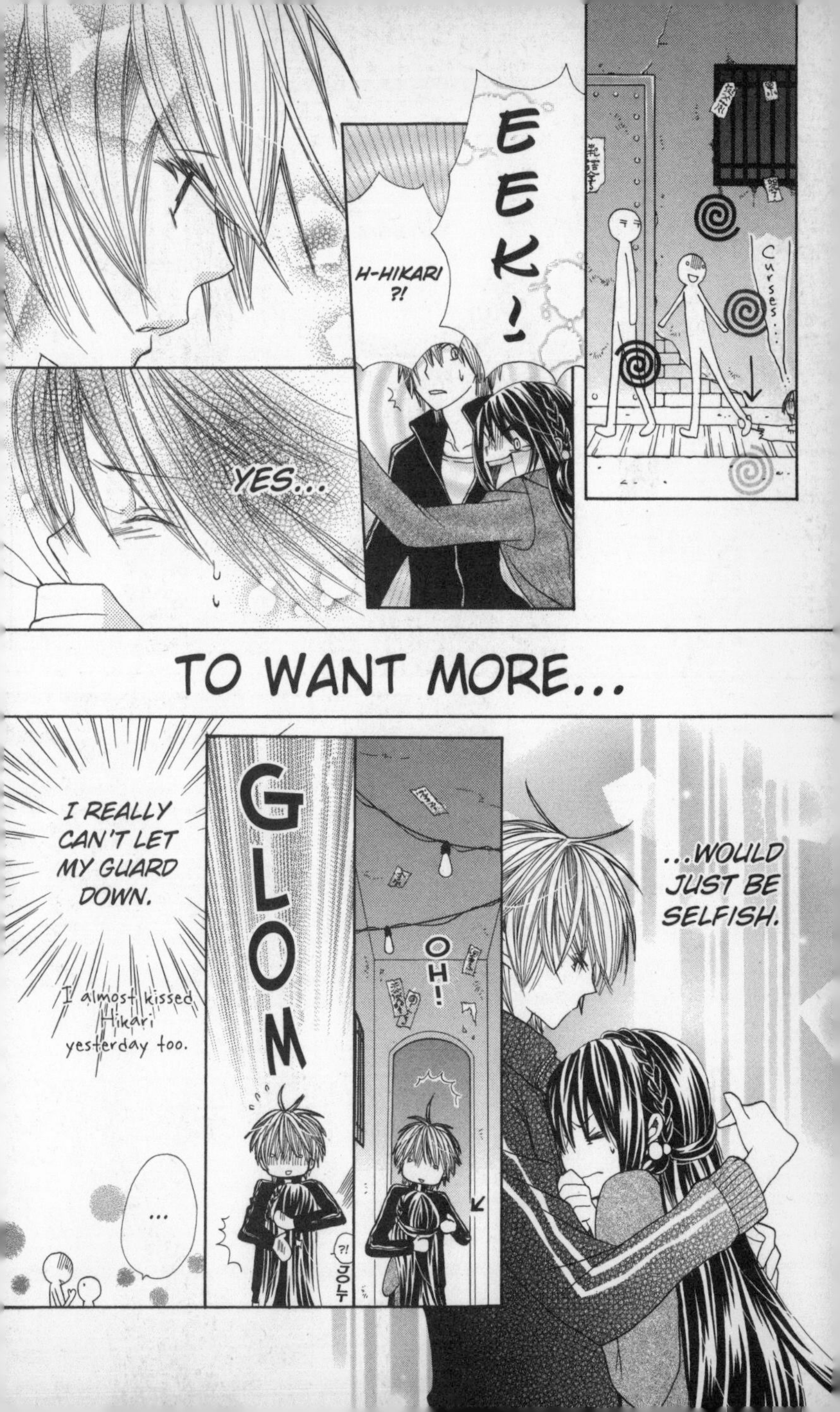

Curses...
EEK!
H-HIKARI ?!
YES...
TO WANT MORE...
...WOULD JUST BE SELFISH.
OH!
?!
JOLT
GLOM
I REALLY CAN'T LET MY GUARD DOWN.
I almost kissed Hikari yesterday too.
...

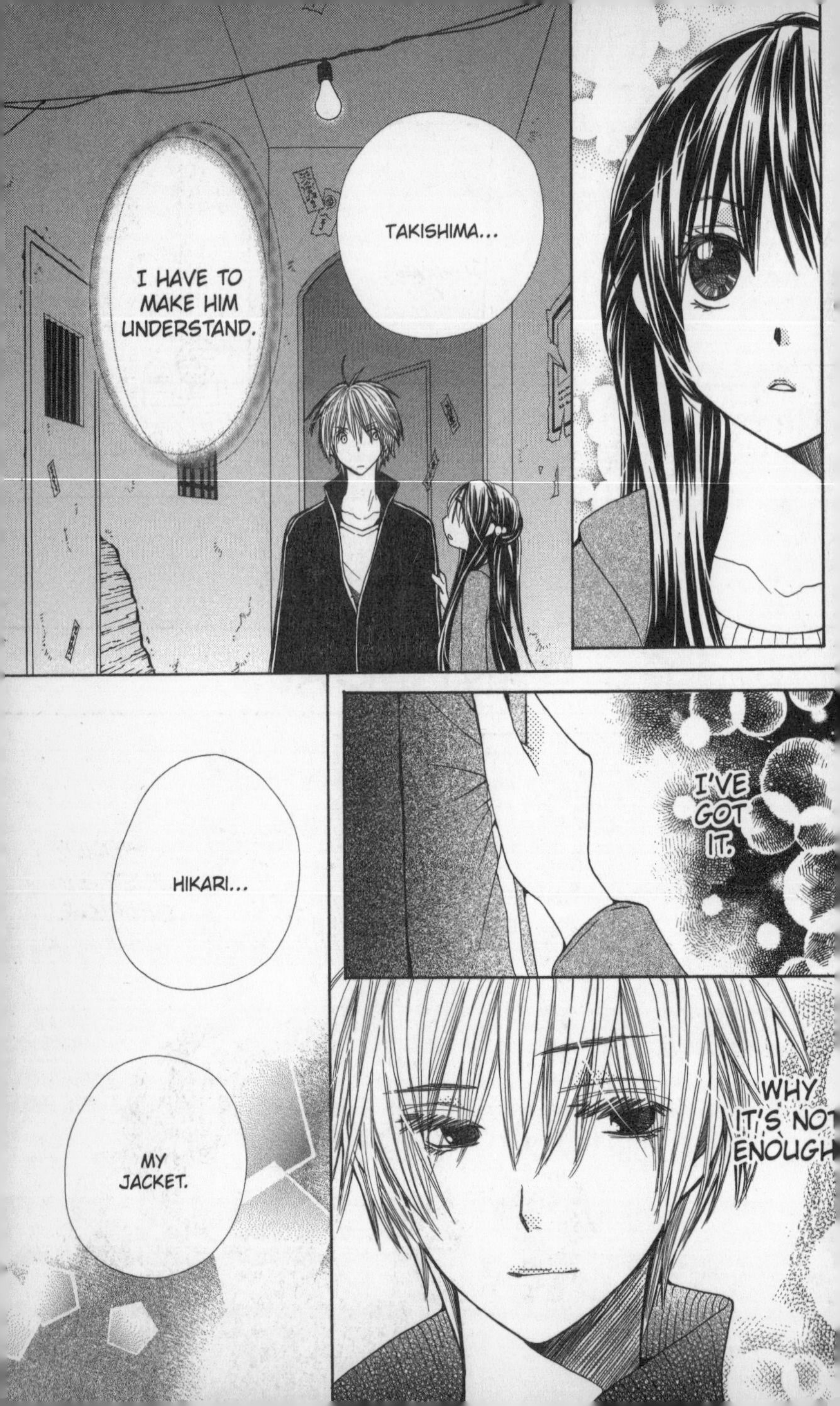
TAKISHIMA...
I HAVE TO MAKE HIM UNDERSTAND.
I'VE GOT IT.
WHY IT'S NOT ENOUGH
HIKARI...
MY JACKET.

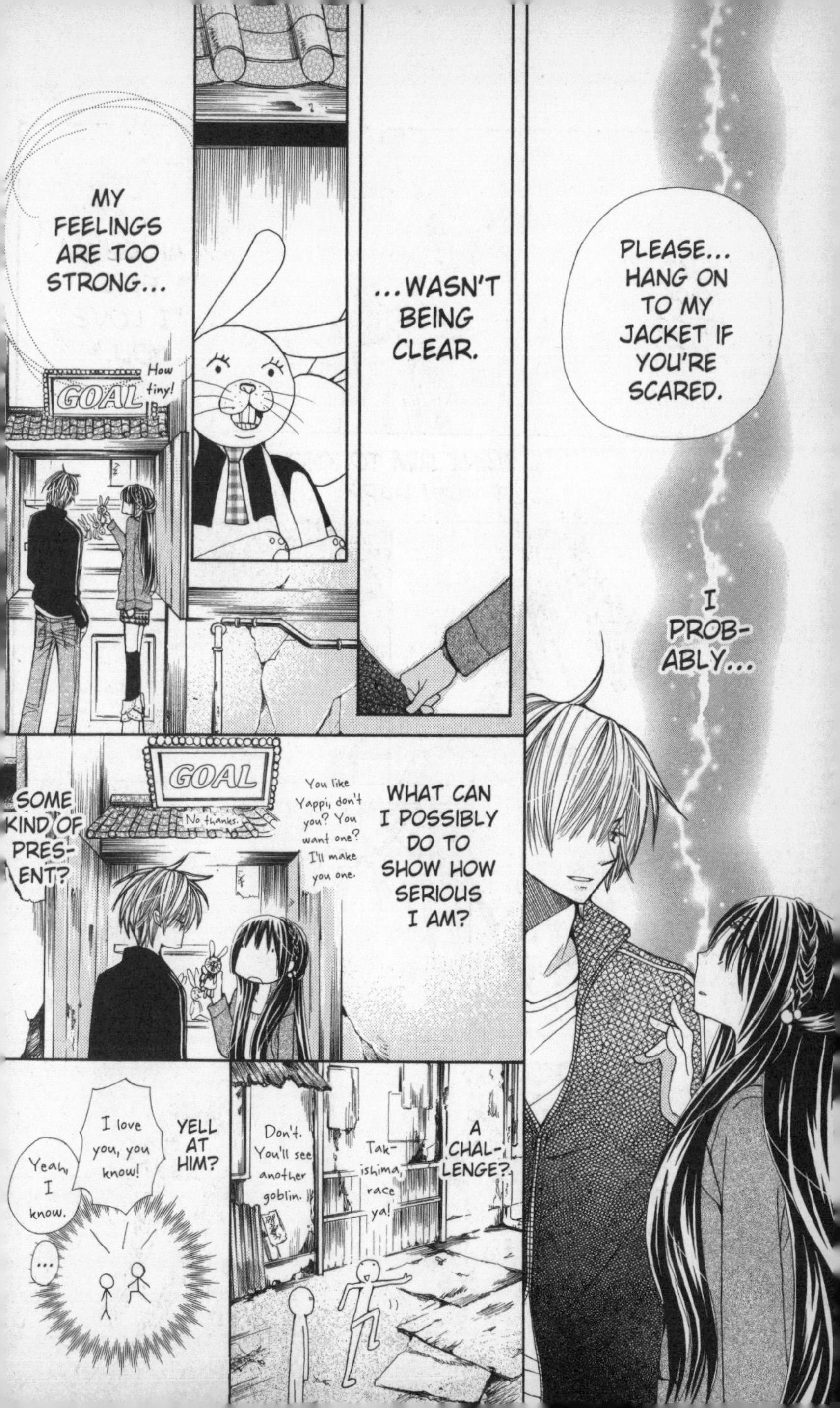
PLEASE... HANG ON TO MY JACKET IF YOU'RE SCARED.
I PROBABLY...
...WASN'T BEING CLEAR.
MY FEELINGS ARE TOO STRONG...
GOAL
How tiny!
WHAT CAN I POSSIBLY DO TO SHOW HOW SERIOUS I AM?
You like Yappi, don't you? You want one? I'll make you one.
GOAL
No thanks.
SOME KIND OF PRES-ENT?
A CHAL-LENGE?
Tak-ishima, race ya!
Don't. You'll see another goblin.
YELL AT HIM?
I love you, you know!
Yeah, I know.
...

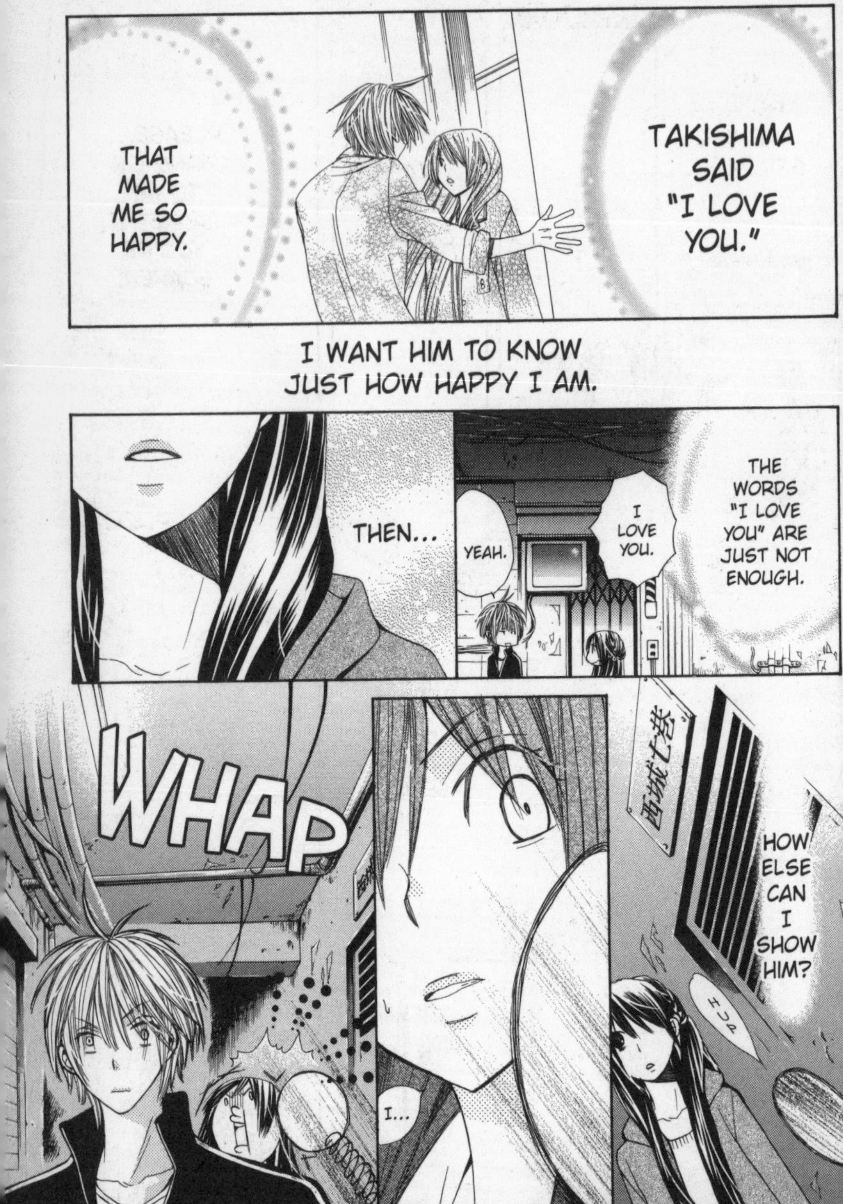
TAKISHIMA SAID "I LOVE YOU."
THAT MADE ME SO HAPPY.
I WANT HIM TO KNOW JUST HOW HAPPY I AM.
THE WORDS "I LOVE YOU" ARE JUST NOT ENOUGH.
I LOVE YOU.
YEAH.
THEN...
HOW ELSE CAN I SHOW HIM?
HUP
I...
WHAP

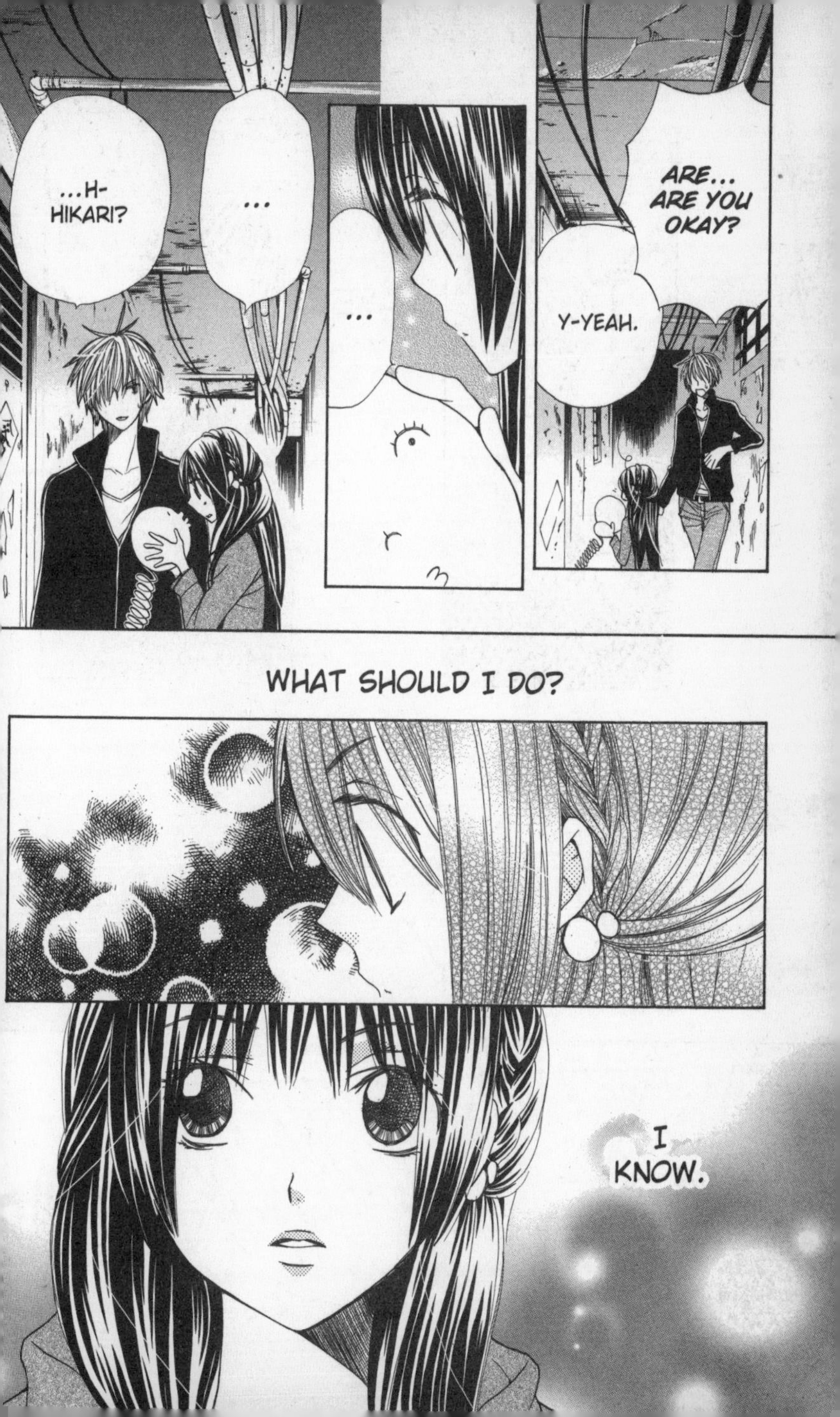
ARE... ARE YOU OKAY?
Y-YEAH.
...
...
...H-HIKARI?
WHAT SHOULD I DO?
I KNOW.

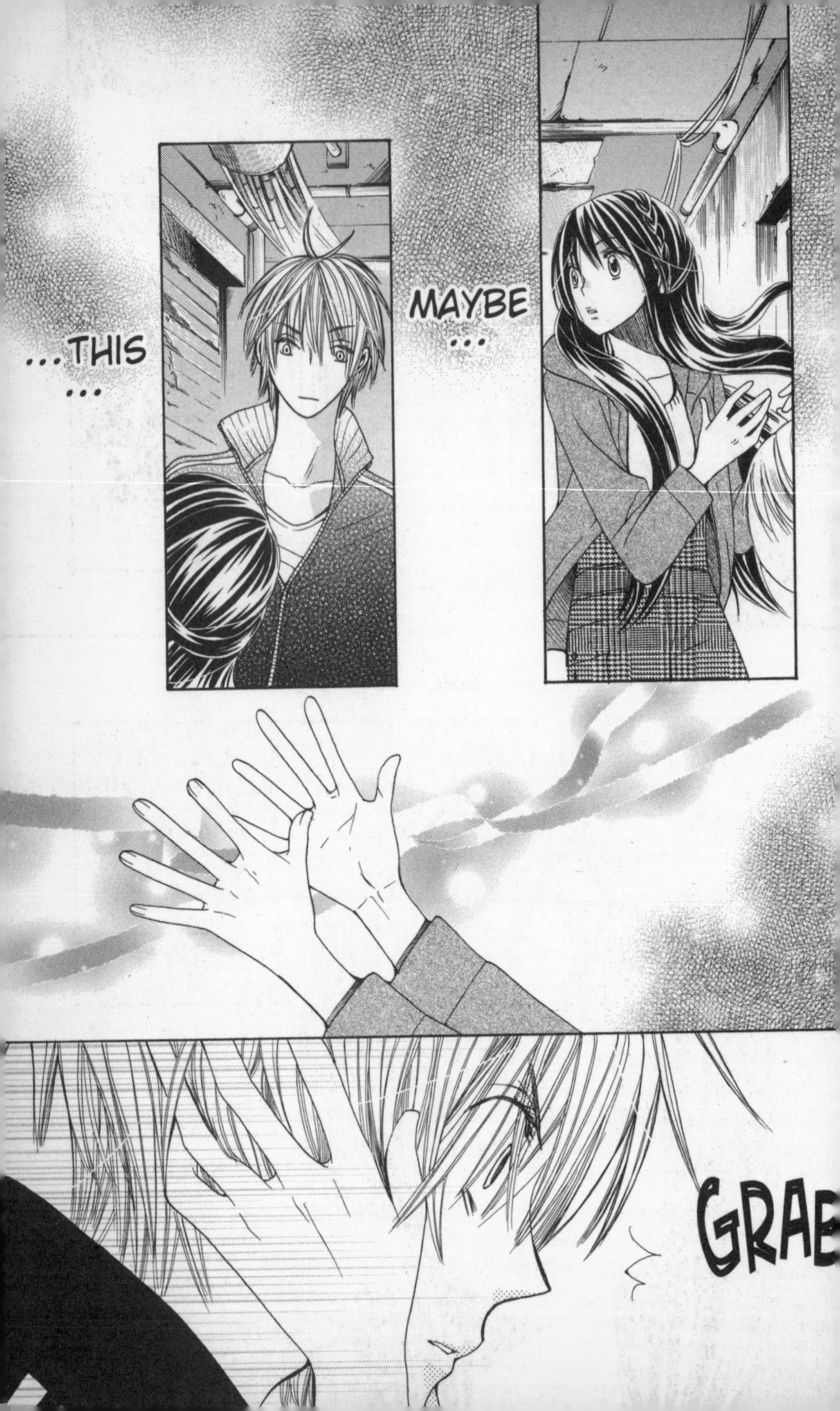
MAYBE ...
... THIS ...
GRAB

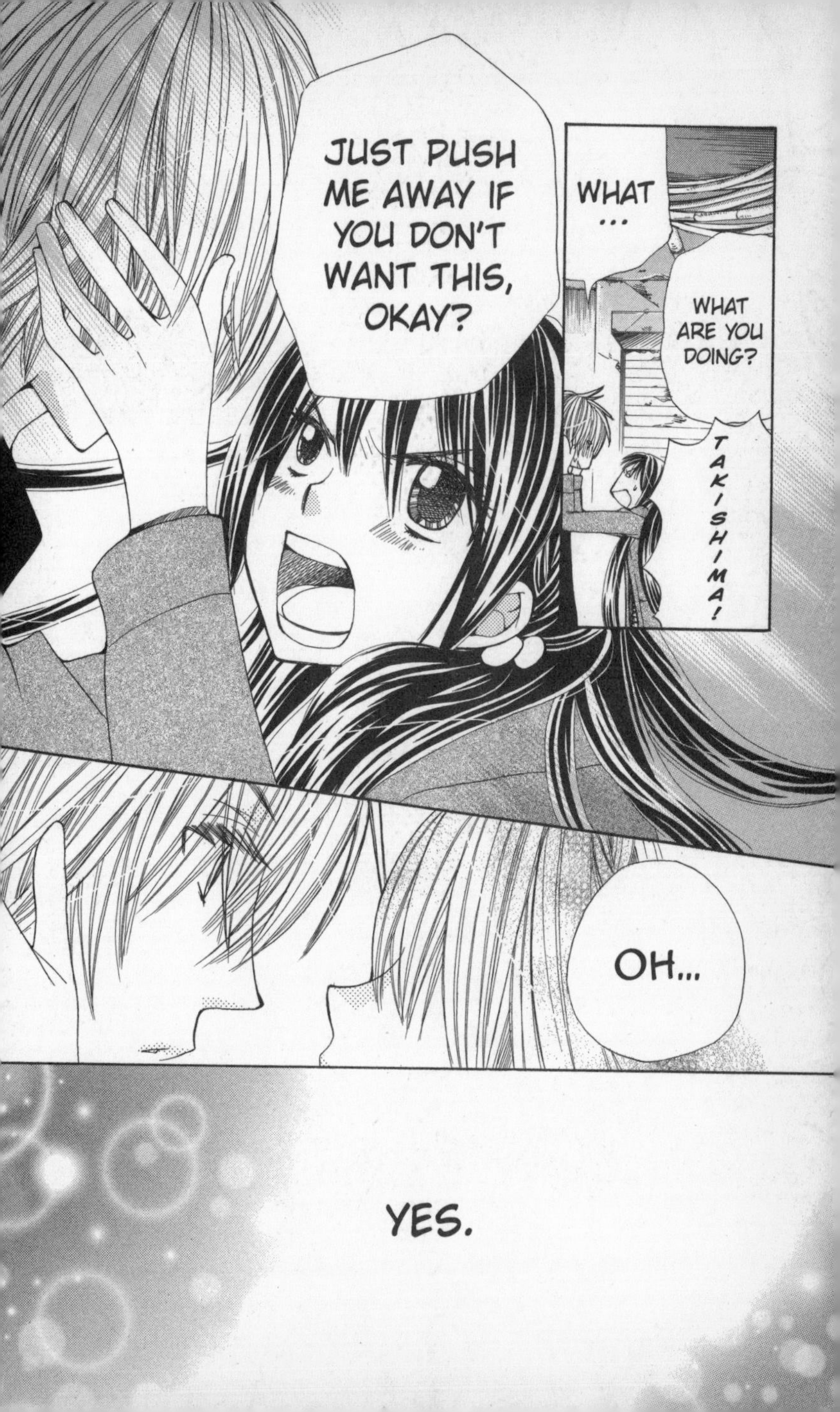
WHAT ...
WHAT ARE YOU DOING?
TAKISHIMA!
JUST PUSH ME AWAY IF YOU DON'T WANT THIS, OKAY?
OH...
YES.

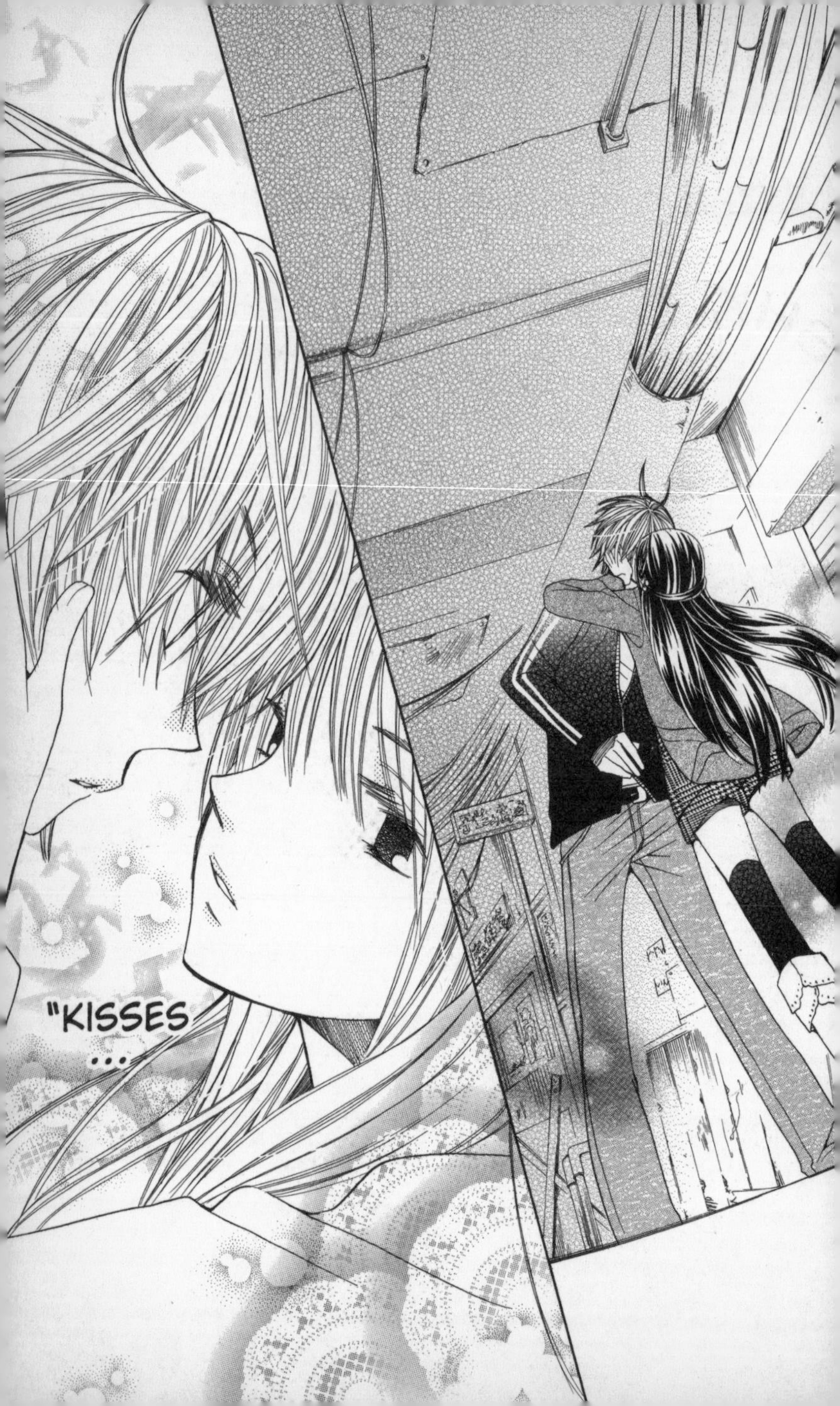
"KISSES
...

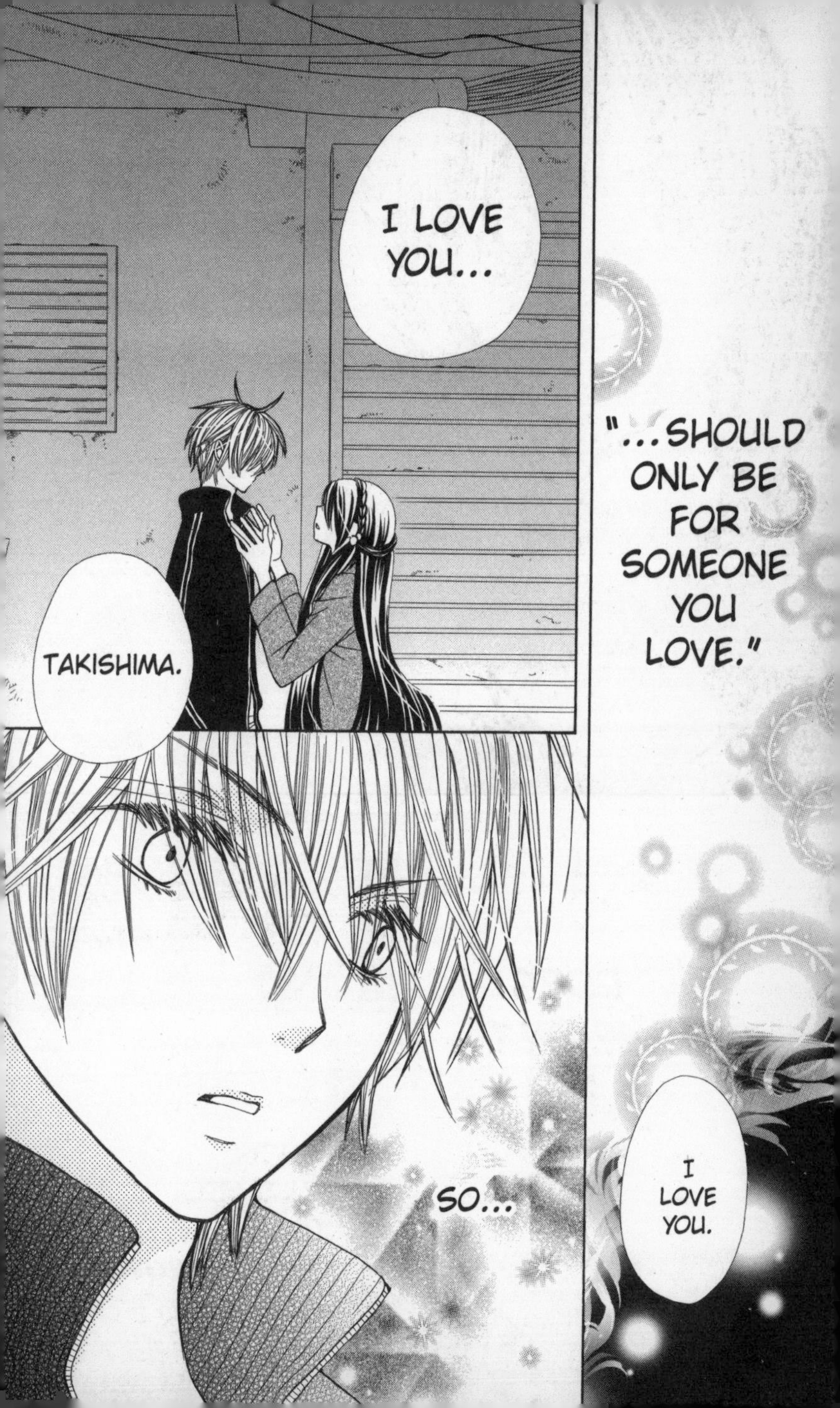
"...SHOULD ONLY BE FOR SOMEONE YOU LOVE."
I LOVE YOU.
I LOVE YOU...
TAKISHIMA.
SO...

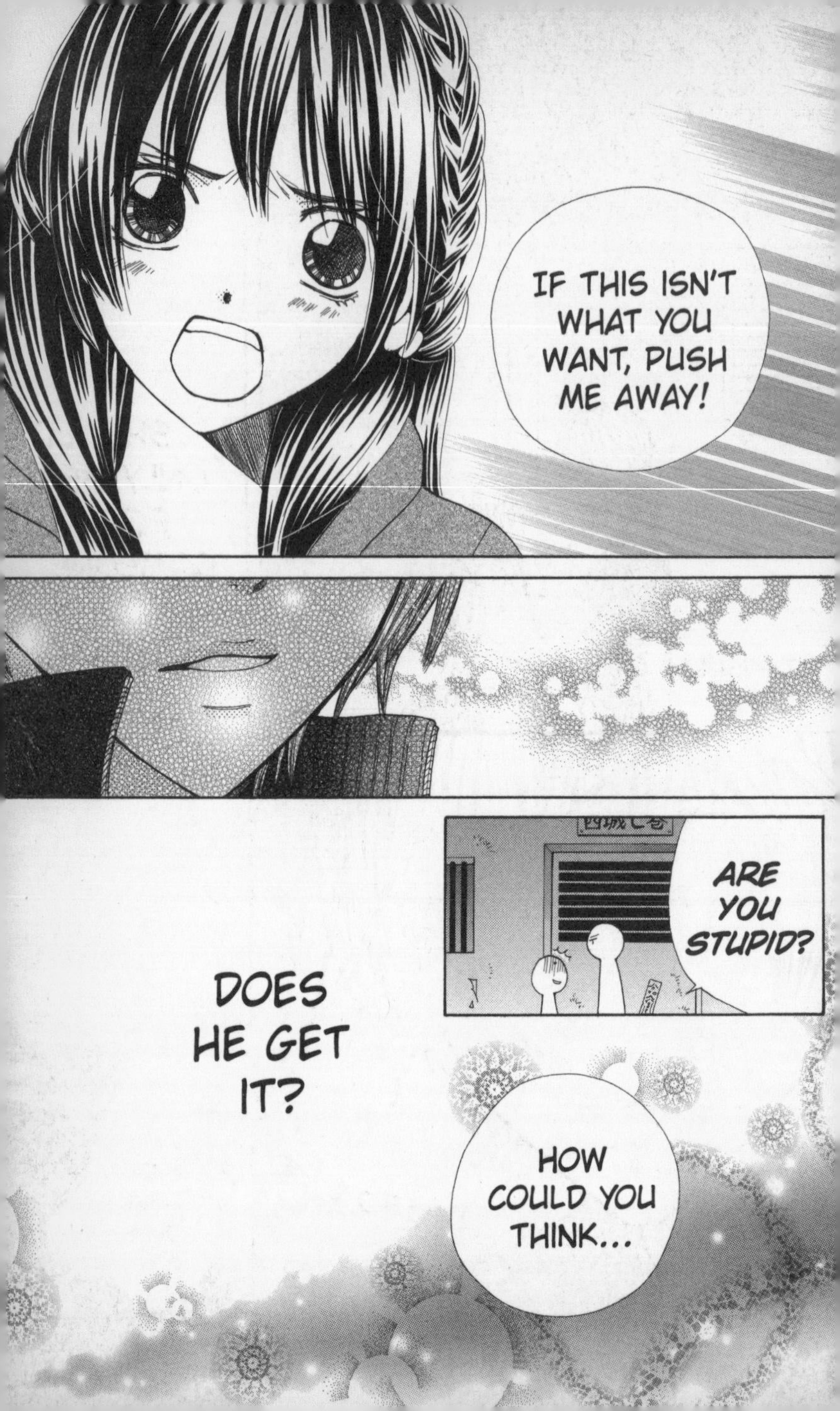
IF THIS ISN'T WHAT YOU WANT, PUSH ME AWAY!
ARE YOU STUPID?
DOES HE GET IT?
HOW COULD YOU THINK...

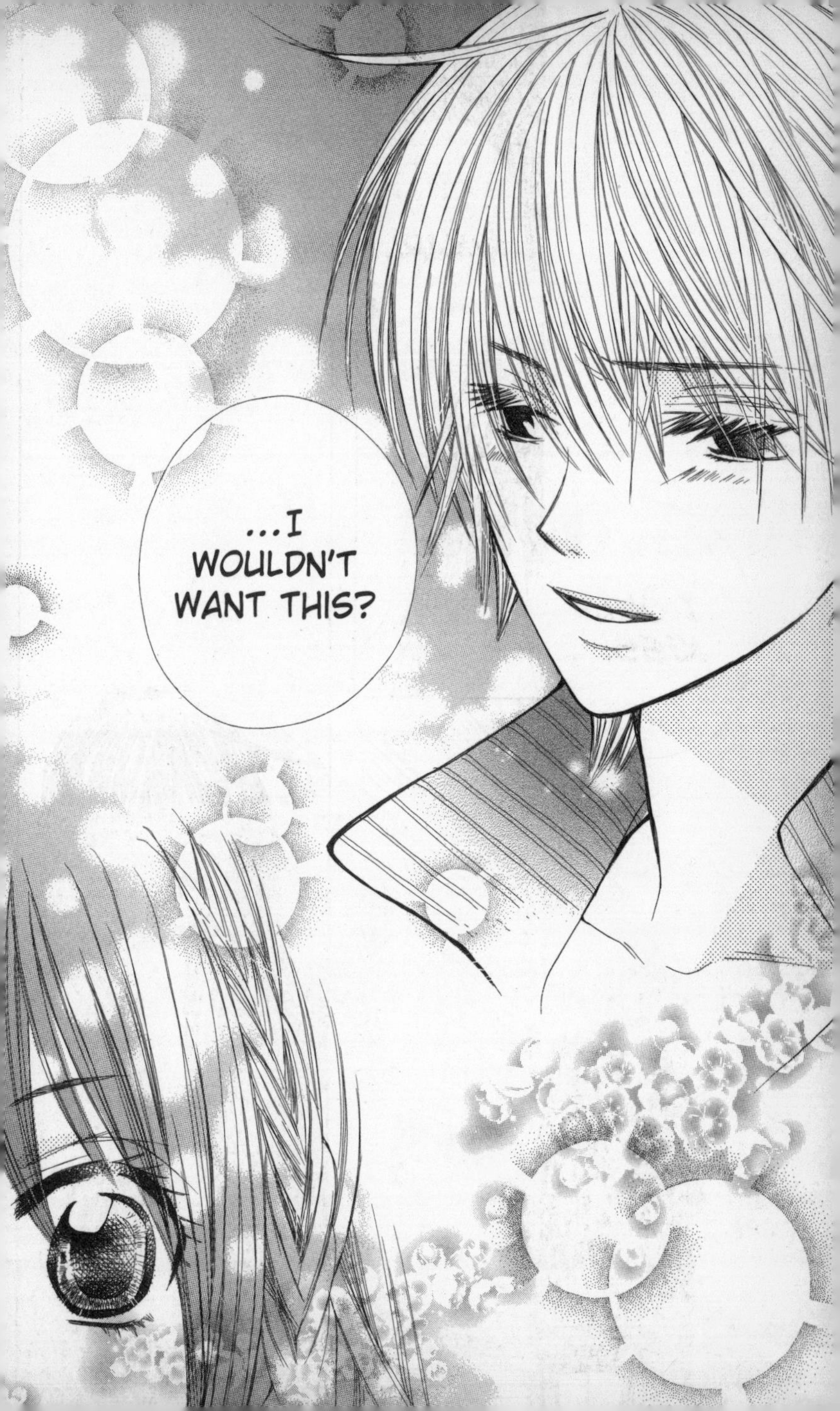
...I WOULDN'T WANT THIS?

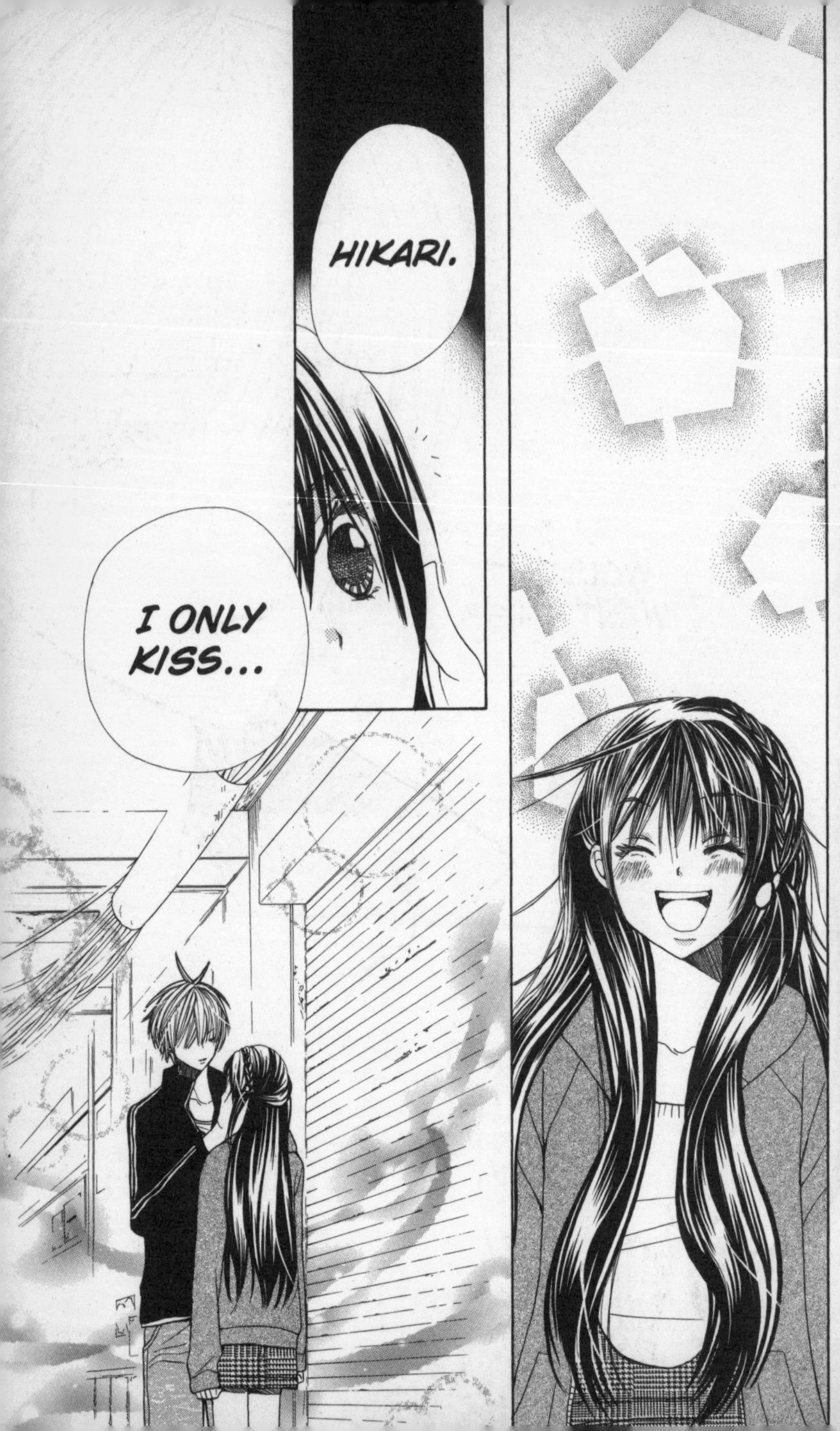
HIKARI.
I ONLY KISS...

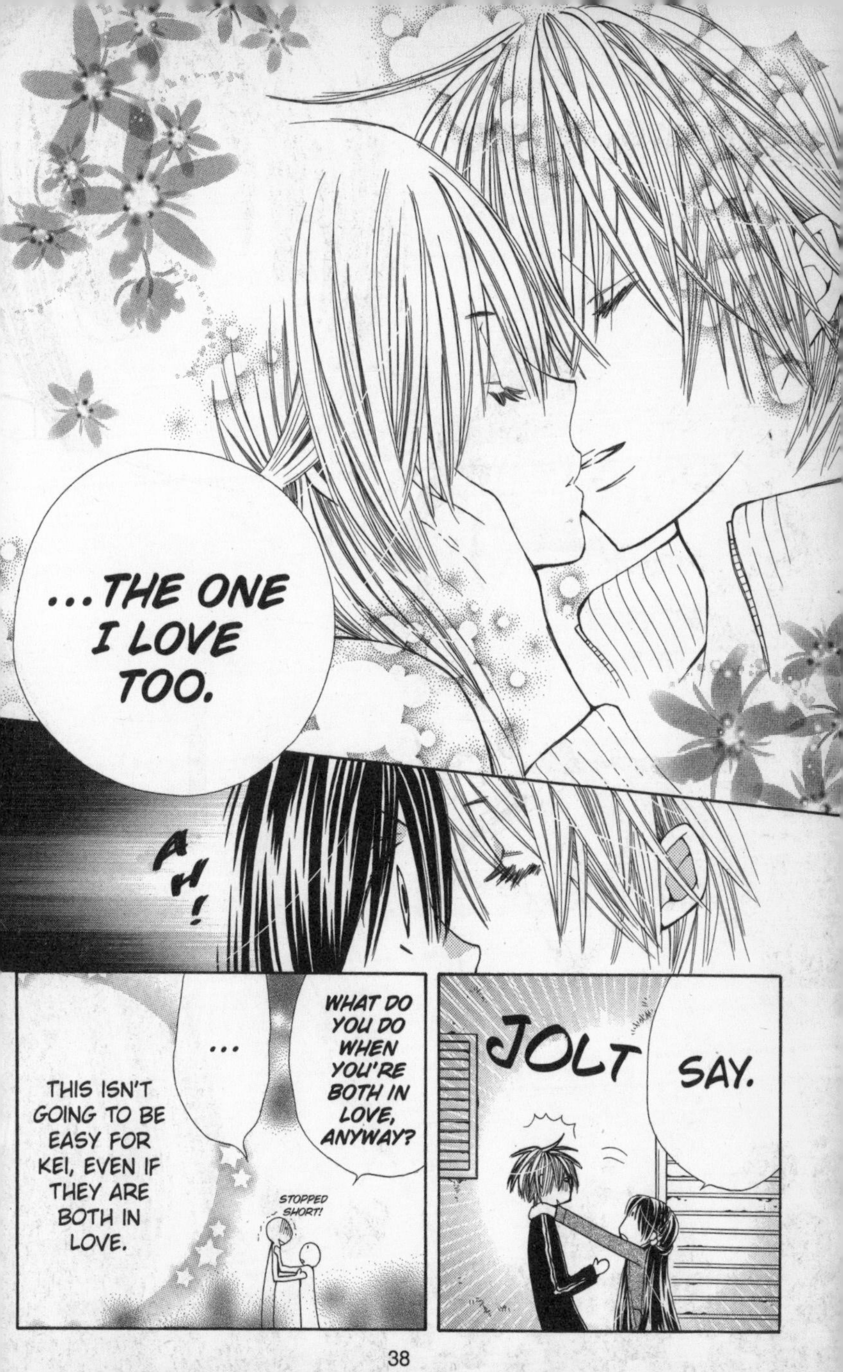
...THE ONE I LOVE TOO.
AH!
SAY.
JOLT
WHAT DO YOU DO WHEN YOU'RE BOTH IN LOVE, ANYWAY?
...
THIS ISN'T GOING TO BE EASY FOR KEI, EVEN IF THEY ARE BOTH IN LOVE.
STOPPED SHORT!

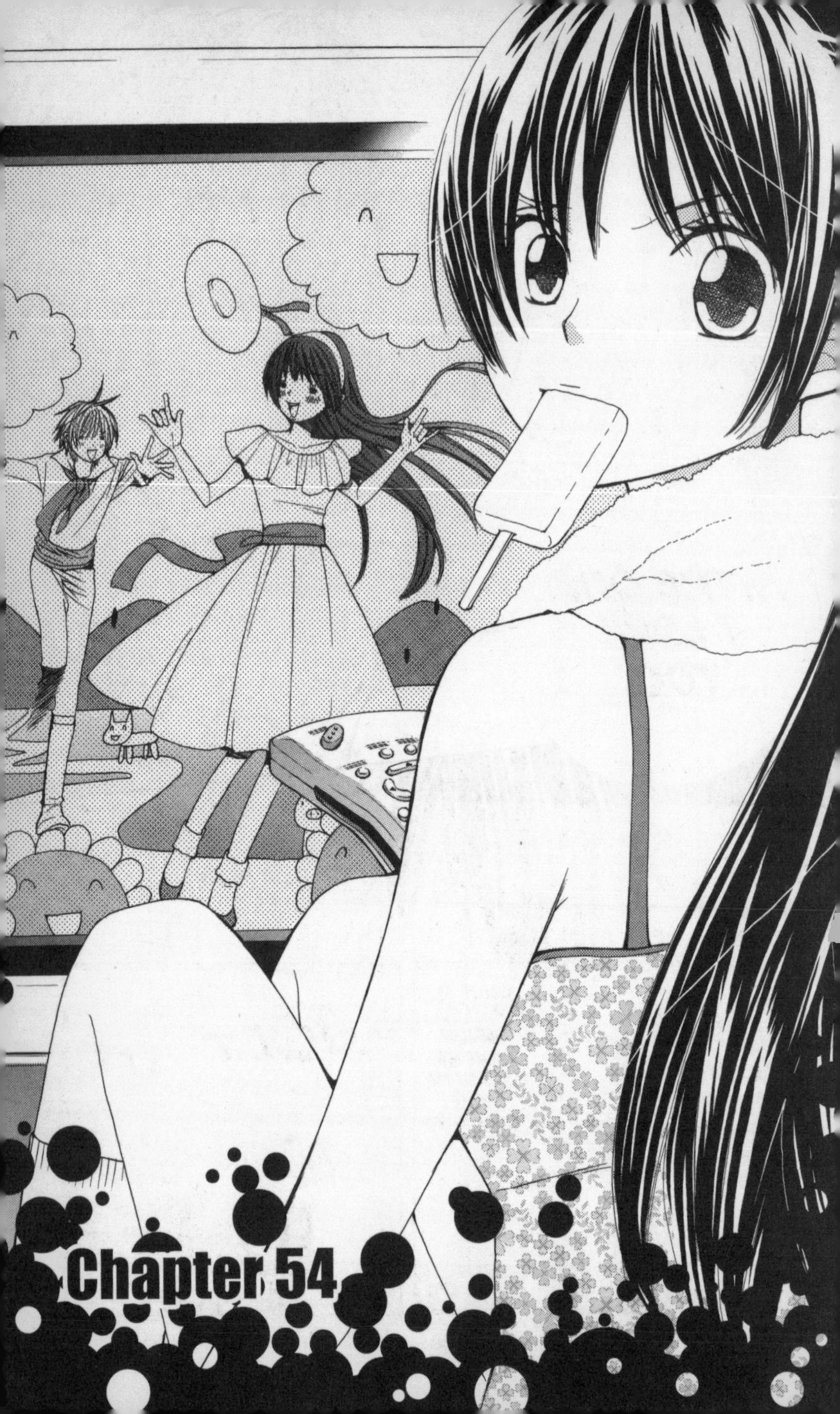
Chapter 54

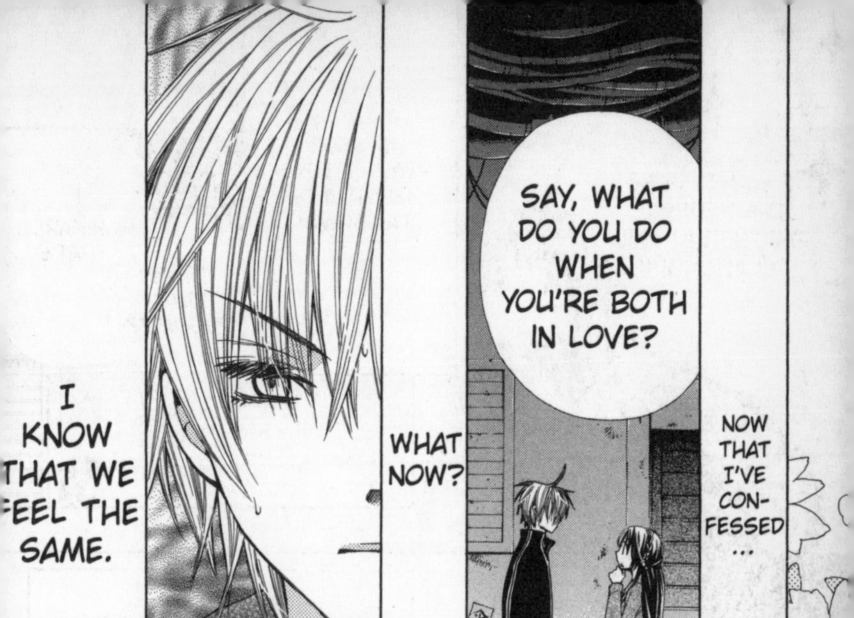
NOW THAT I'VE CON-FESSED...
SAY, WHAT DO YOU DO WHEN YOU'RE BOTH IN LOVE?
WHAT NOW?
...
I KNOW THAT WE FEEL THE SAME.

• SING AND DANCE •

MY ASSISTANTS AND I SING AND DANCE WHILE WE WORK (NOT ALL THE TIME, YOU KNOW). THEY ARE WONDERFUL PEOPLE AND ALWAYS PUMP ME UP. THE OTHER DAY WHEN WE FINISHED OUR WORK, WE WENT TO SING KARAOKE AND ONE OF MY ASSISTANTS MADE A SONGBOOK.

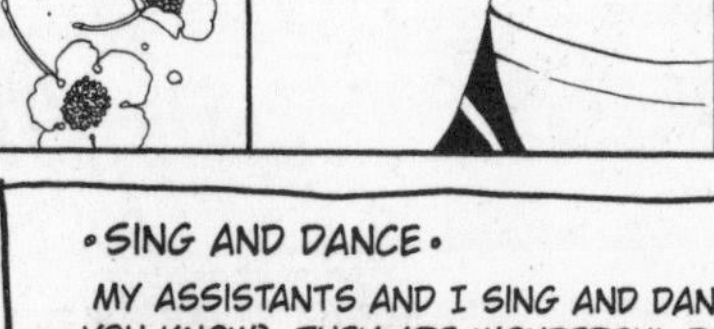
I MADE SONG-BOOKS ♡ for every-body!
WHAT GUSTO!!!
WOW

I LOVE MY ASSISTANTS! SORRY TO BORE YOU WITH MY PERSONAL LIFE... THANK YOU FOR ALWAYS GIVING ME ENERGY!!

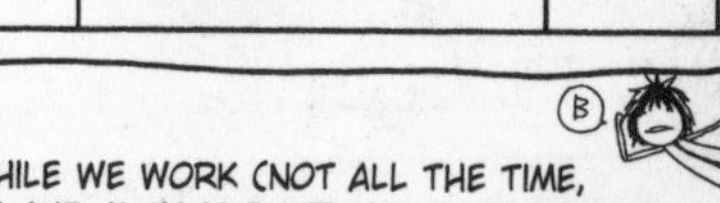
HEE HEE HEE HEE ♡

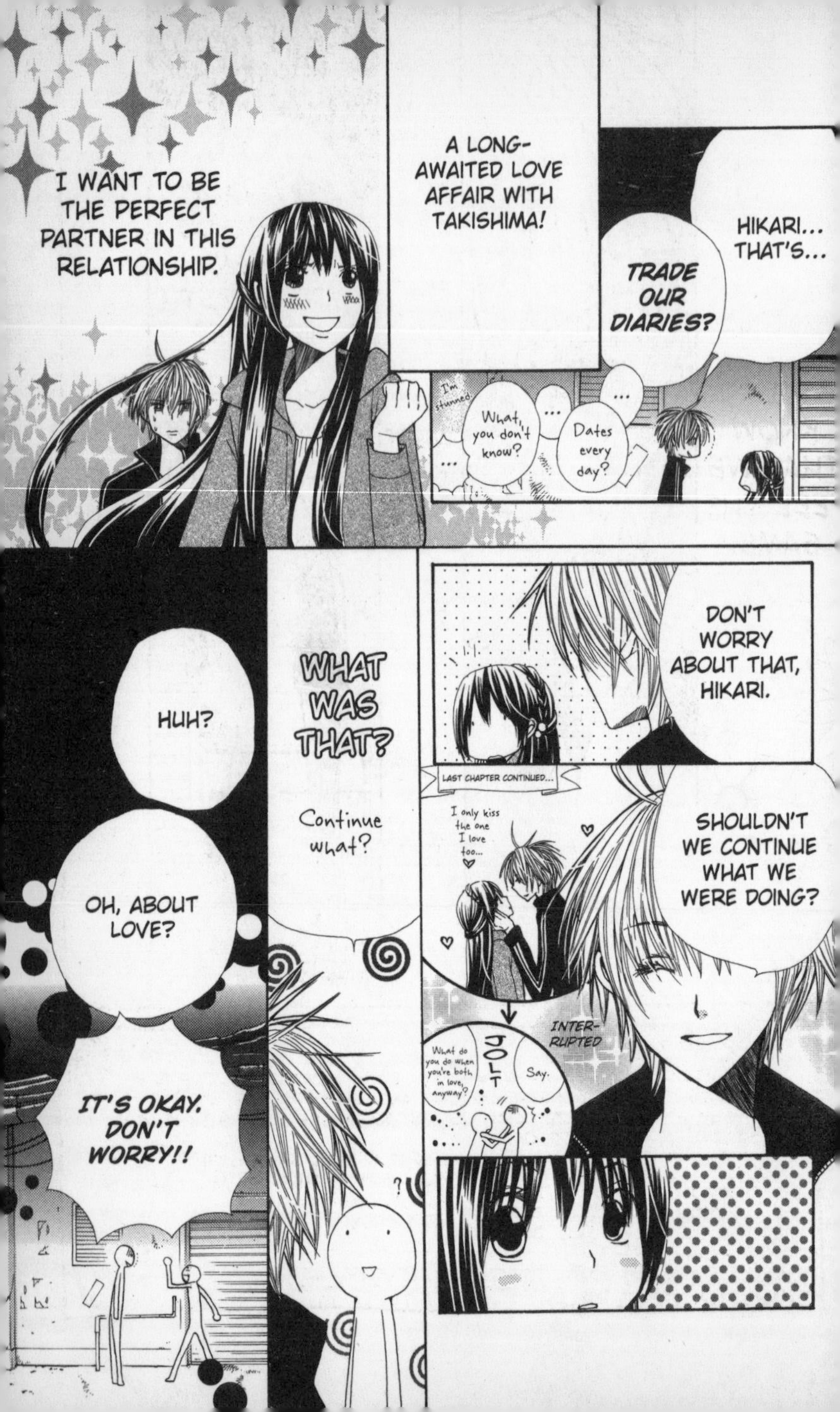
HIKARI... THAT'S...
TRADE OUR DIARIES?
...
Dates every day?
...
What, you don't know?
I'm stunned
...
A LONG-AWAITED LOVE AFFAIR WITH TAKISHIMA!
I WANT TO BE THE PERFECT PARTNER IN THIS RELATIONSHIP.
DON'T WORRY ABOUT THAT, HIKARI.
LAST CHAPTER CONTINUED...
SHOULDN'T WE CONTINUE WHAT WE WERE DOING?
I only kiss the one I love too...
INTERRUPTED
JOLT
Say.
What do you do when you're both in love, anyway?
WHAT WAS THAT?
Continue what?
?
HUH?
OH, ABOUT LOVE?
IT'S OKAY. DON'T WORRY!!

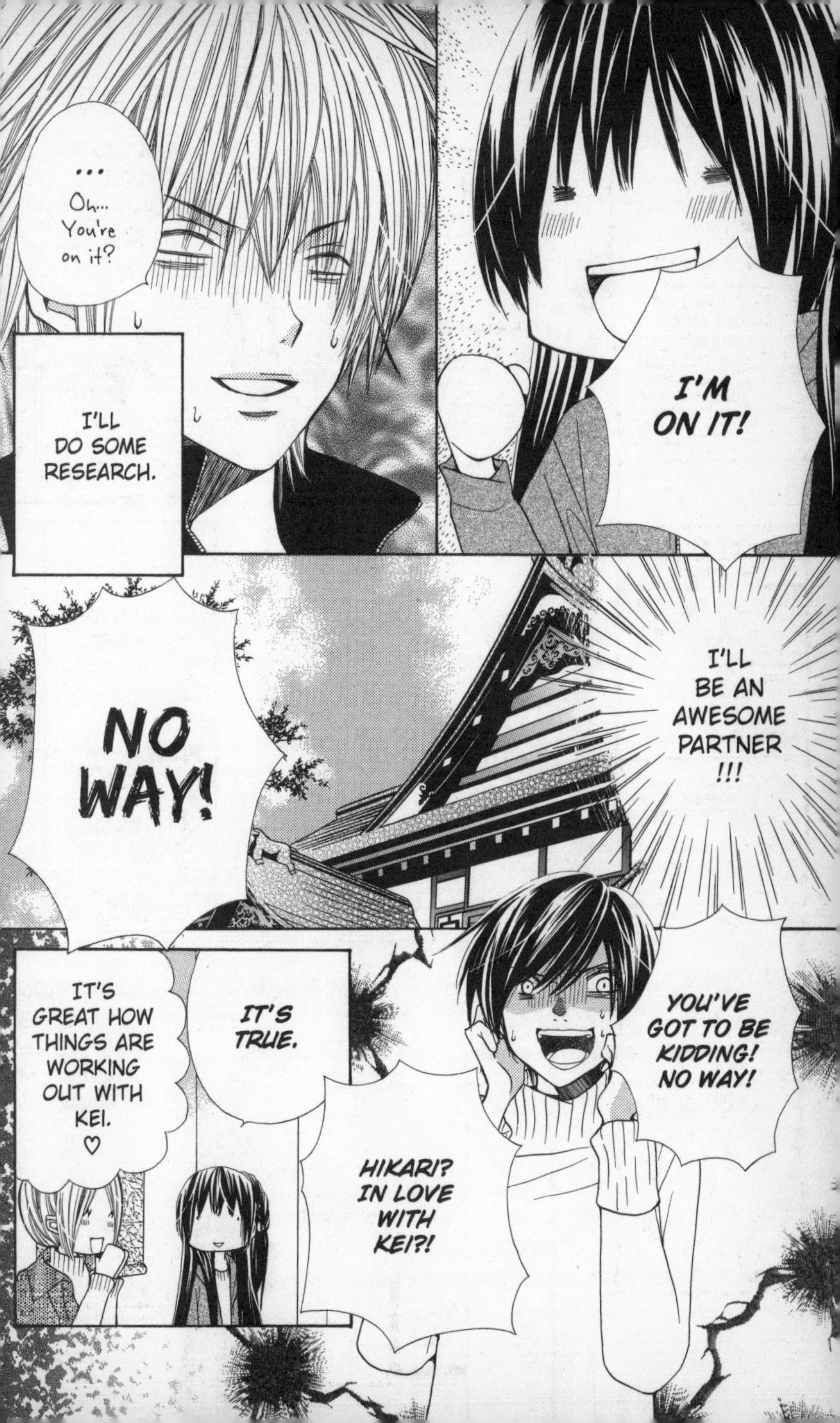
I'M ON IT!
...
Oh... You're on it?
I'LL DO SOME RESEARCH.
I'LL BE AN AWESOME PARTNER!!!
NO WAY!
YOU'VE GOT TO BE KIDDING! NO WAY!
HIKARI? IN LOVE WITH KEI?!
IT'S TRUE.
IT'S GREAT HOW THINGS ARE WORKING OUT WITH KEI. ♡

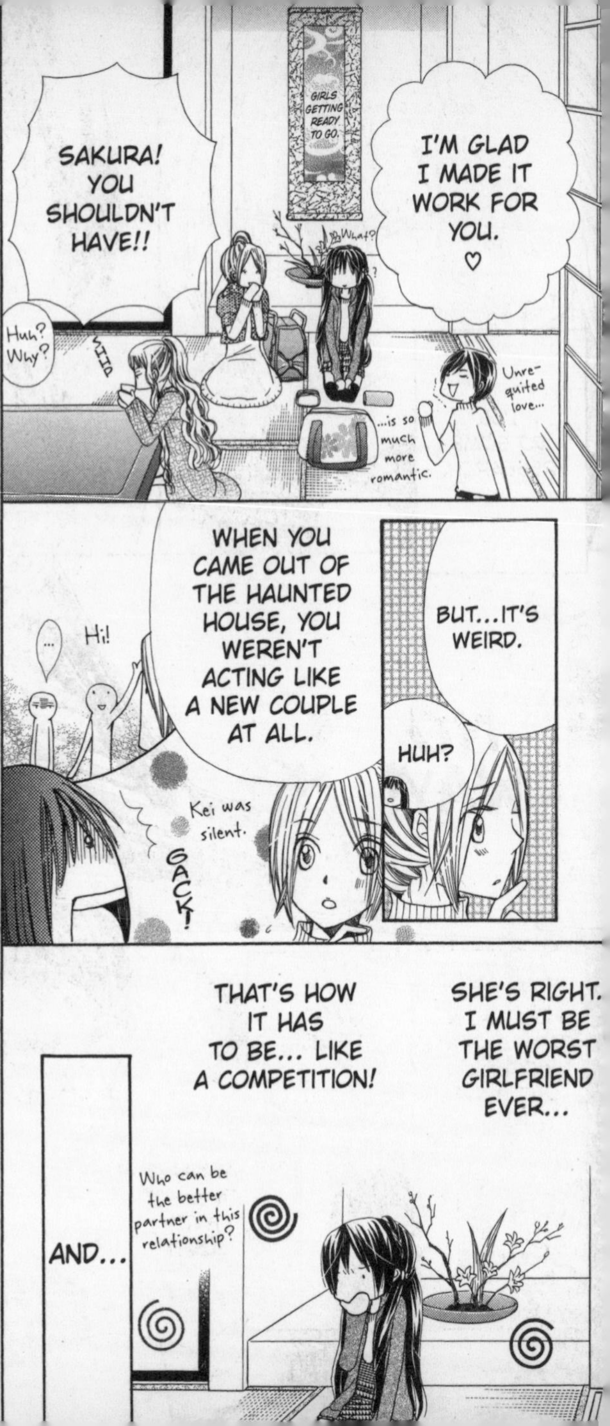
I'M GLAD I MADE IT WORK FOR YOU. ♡
Unrequited love...
...is so much more romantic.
GIRLS GETTING READY TO GO.
What?
?
SAKURA! YOU SHOULDN'T HAVE!!
WHIP
Huh? Why?
BUT...IT'S WEIRD.
HUH?
WHEN YOU CAME OUT OF THE HAUNTED HOUSE, YOU WEREN'T ACTING LIKE A NEW COUPLE AT ALL.
Hi!
...
Kei was silent.
GACK!
SHE'S RIGHT. I MUST BE THE WORST GIRLFRIEND EVER...
THAT'S HOW IT HAS TO BE... LIKE A COMPETITION!
AND...
Who can be the better partner in this relationship?

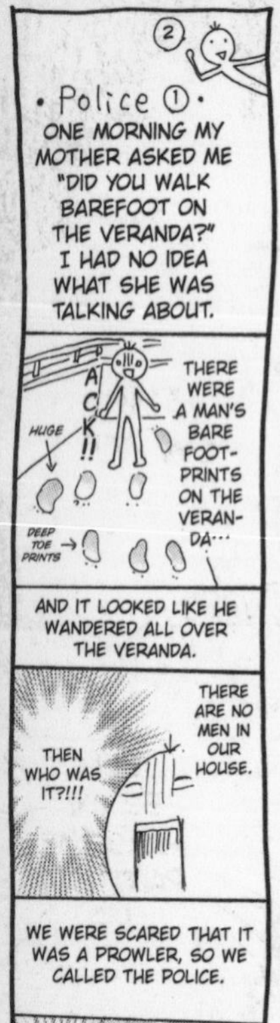
2
• Police ① •
ONE MORNING MY MOTHER ASKED ME "DID YOU WALK BAREFOOT ON THE VERANDA?" I HAD NO IDEA WHAT SHE WAS TALKING ABOUT.
THERE WERE A MAN'S BARE FOOTPRINTS ON THE VERANDA...
ACK!!
HUGE
DEEP TOE PRINTS
AND IT LOOKED LIKE HE WANDERED ALL OVER THE VERANDA.
THERE ARE NO MEN IN OUR HOUSE.
THEN WHO WAS IT?!!!
WE WERE SCARED THAT IT WAS A PROWLER, SO WE CALLED THE POLICE.
SIX MEN FROM THE PREFECTURE'S STATION CAME!!
THEY LOOKED SUPER!!
SNAP
CONTINUED IN 2

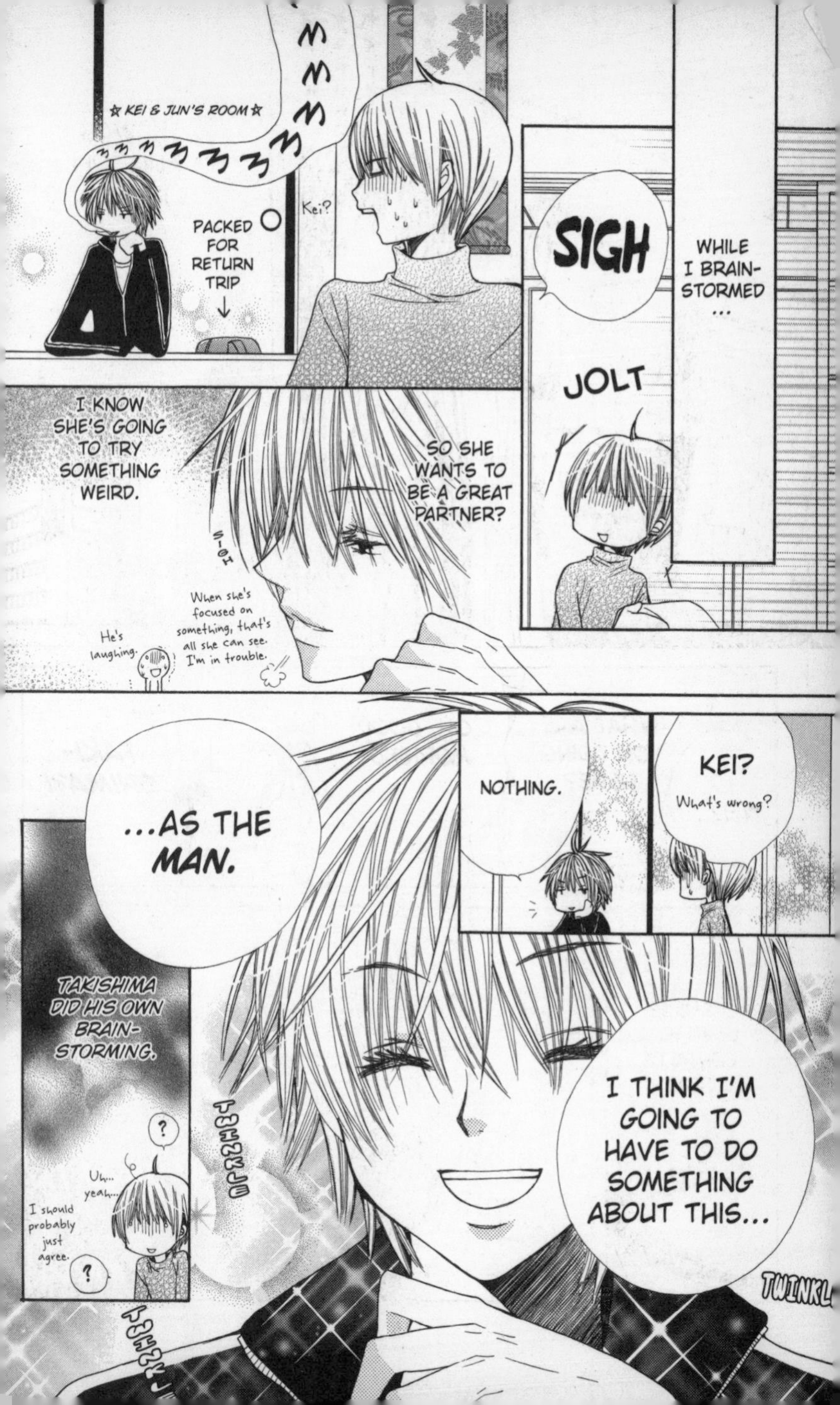
WHILE I BRAIN-STORMED...
SIGH
JOLT
☆KEI & JUN'S ROOM☆
Kei?
PACKED FOR RETURN TRIP ↓
SO SHE WANTS TO BE A GREAT PARTNER?
I KNOW SHE'S GOING TO TRY SOMETHING WEIRD.
SIGH
When she's focused on something, that's all she can see. I'm in trouble.
He's laughing.
KEI?
What's wrong?
NOTHING.
...AS THE MAN.
I THINK I'M GOING TO HAVE TO DO SOMETHING ABOUT THIS...
TAKISHIMA DID HIS OWN BRAIN-STORMING.
TWINKLE
?
Uh... yeah...
I should probably just agree.
?
TWINKLE
TWINKL

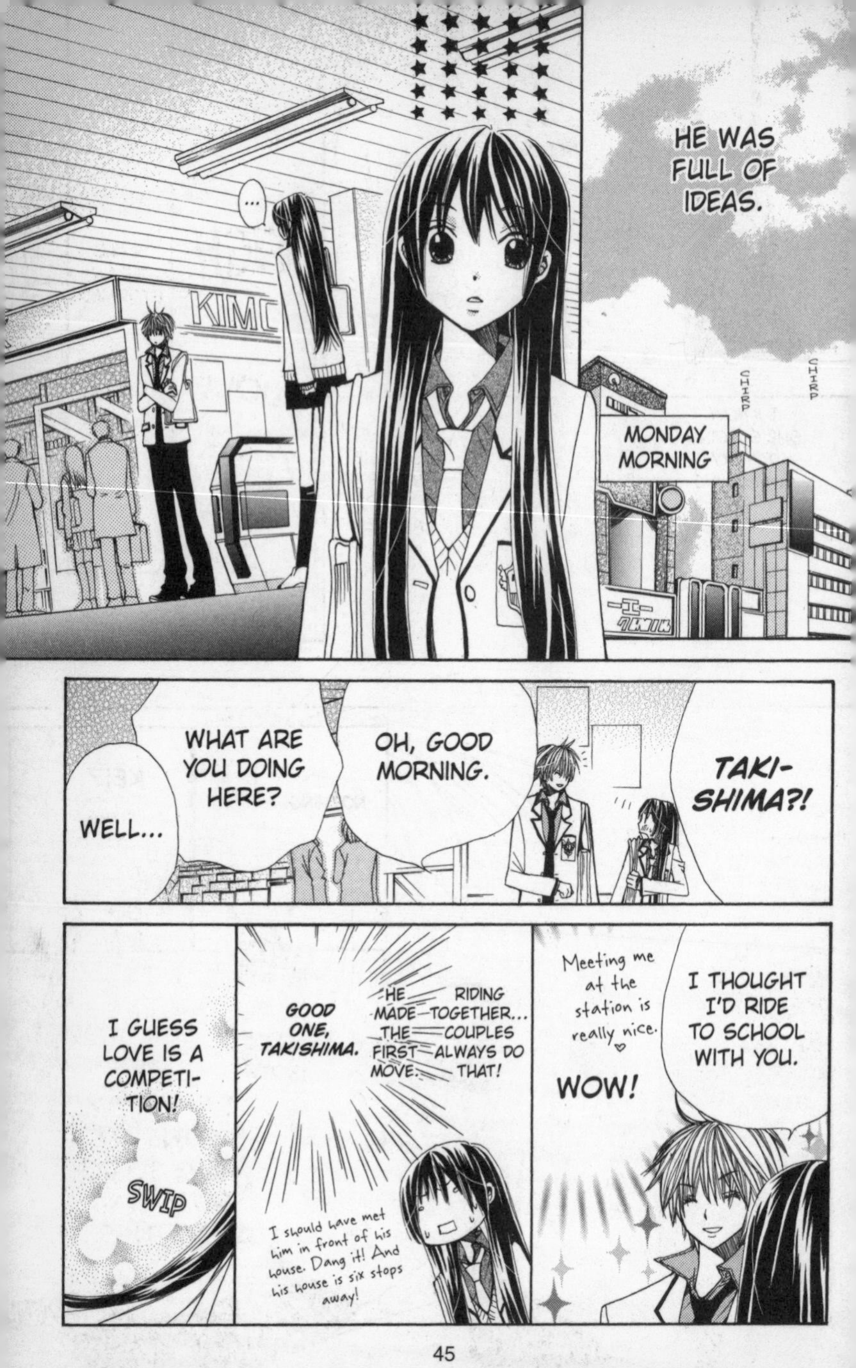
HE WAS FULL OF IDEAS.
CHIRP
CHIRP
MONDAY MORNING
...
TAKI-SHIMA?!
OH, GOOD MORNING.
WHAT ARE YOU DOING HERE?
WELL...
I THOUGHT I'D RIDE TO SCHOOL WITH YOU.
Meeting me at the station is really nice.
WOW!
RIDING TOGETHER... COUPLES ALWAYS DO THAT!
HE MADE THE FIRST MOVE.
GOOD ONE, TAKISHIMA.
I should have met him in front of his house. Dang it! And his house is six stops away!
I GUESS LOVE IS A COMPETI-TION!
SWIP

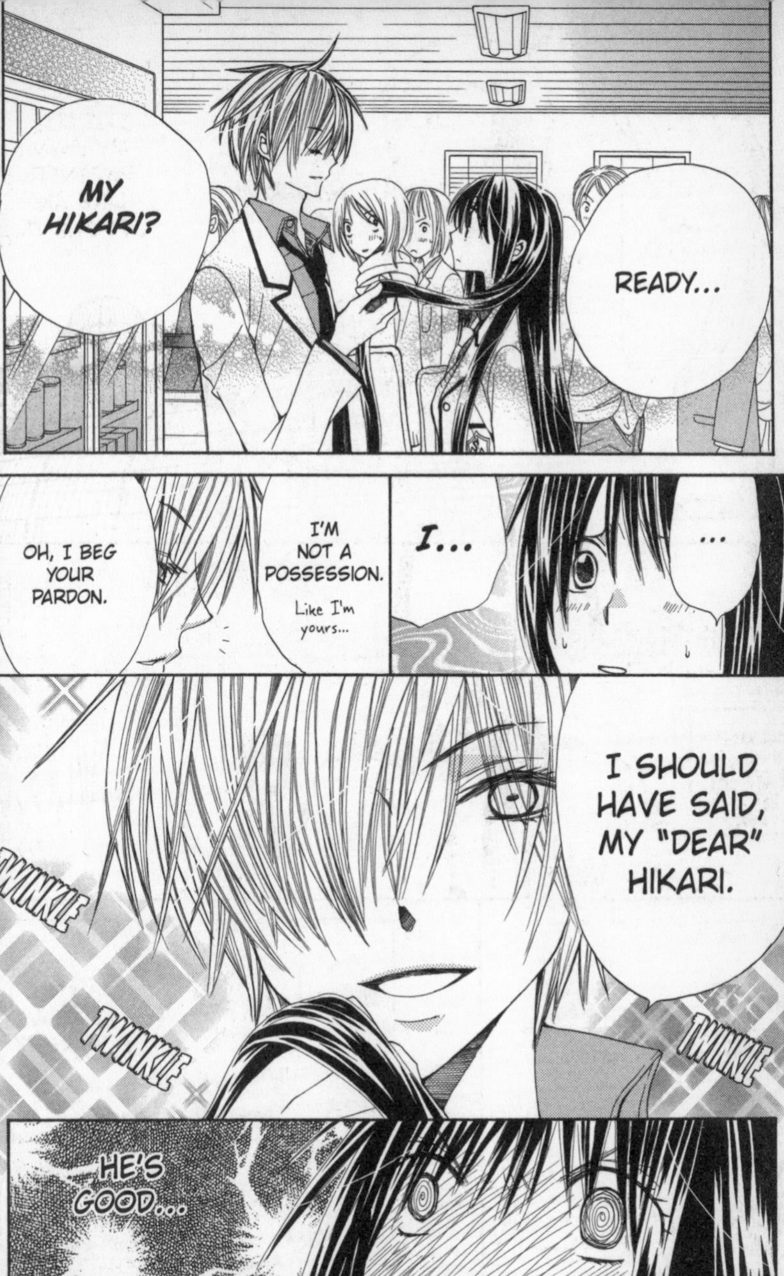
READY...
MY HIKARI?
...
I...
I'M NOT A POSSESSION.
Like I'm yours...
OH, I BEG YOUR PARDON.
I SHOULD HAVE SAID, MY "DEAR" HIKARI.
TWINKLE
TWINKLE
TWINKLE
HE'S GOOD...

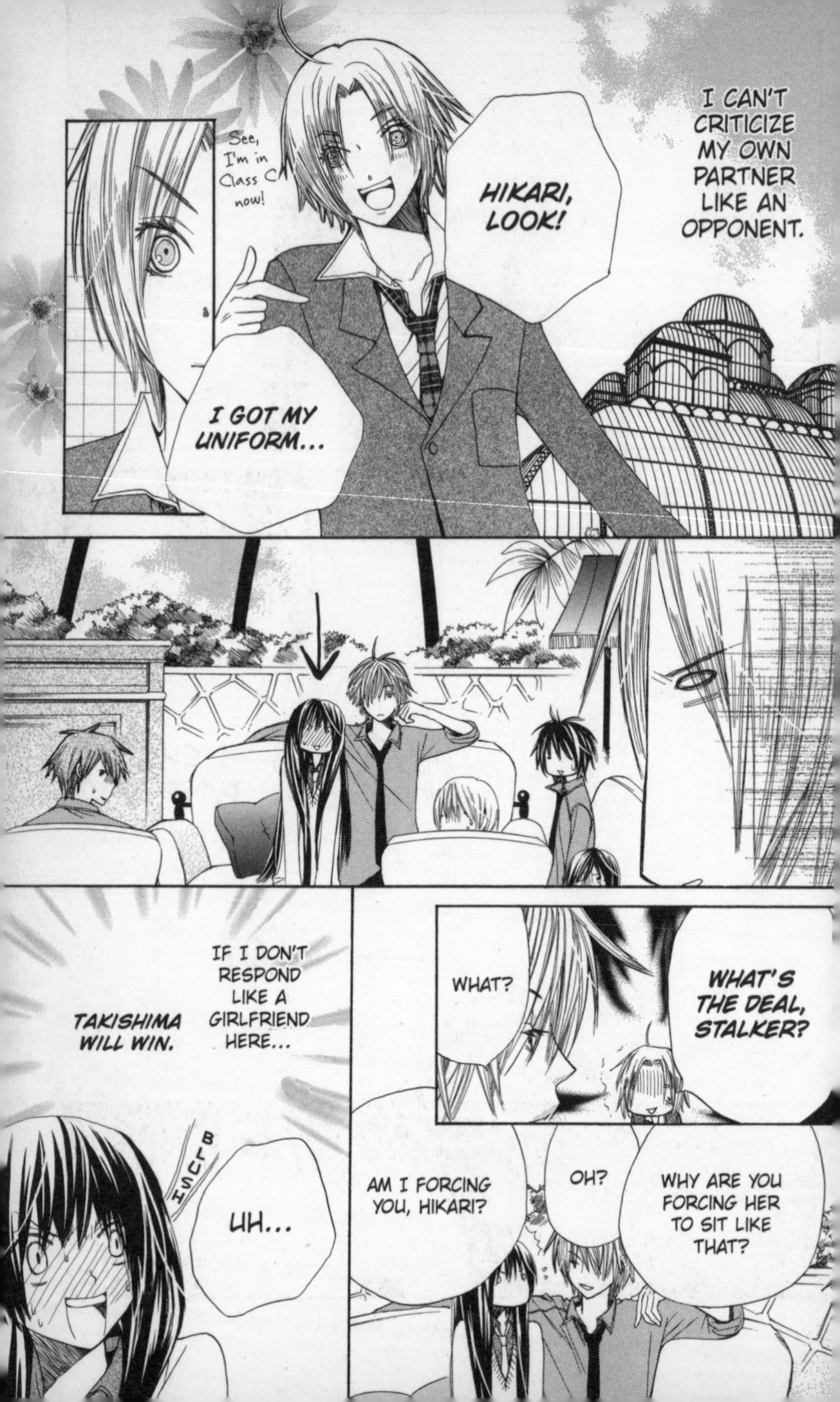
I CAN'T CRITICIZE MY OWN PARTNER LIKE AN OPPONENT.
HIKARI, LOOK!
See, I'm in Class C now!
I GOT MY UNIFORM...
WHAT'S THE DEAL, STALKER?
WHAT?
WHY ARE YOU FORCING HER TO SIT LIKE THAT?
OH?
AM I FORCING YOU, HIKARI?
IF I DON'T RESPOND LIKE A GIRLFRIEND HERE...
TAKISHIMA WILL WIN.
BLUSH
UH...

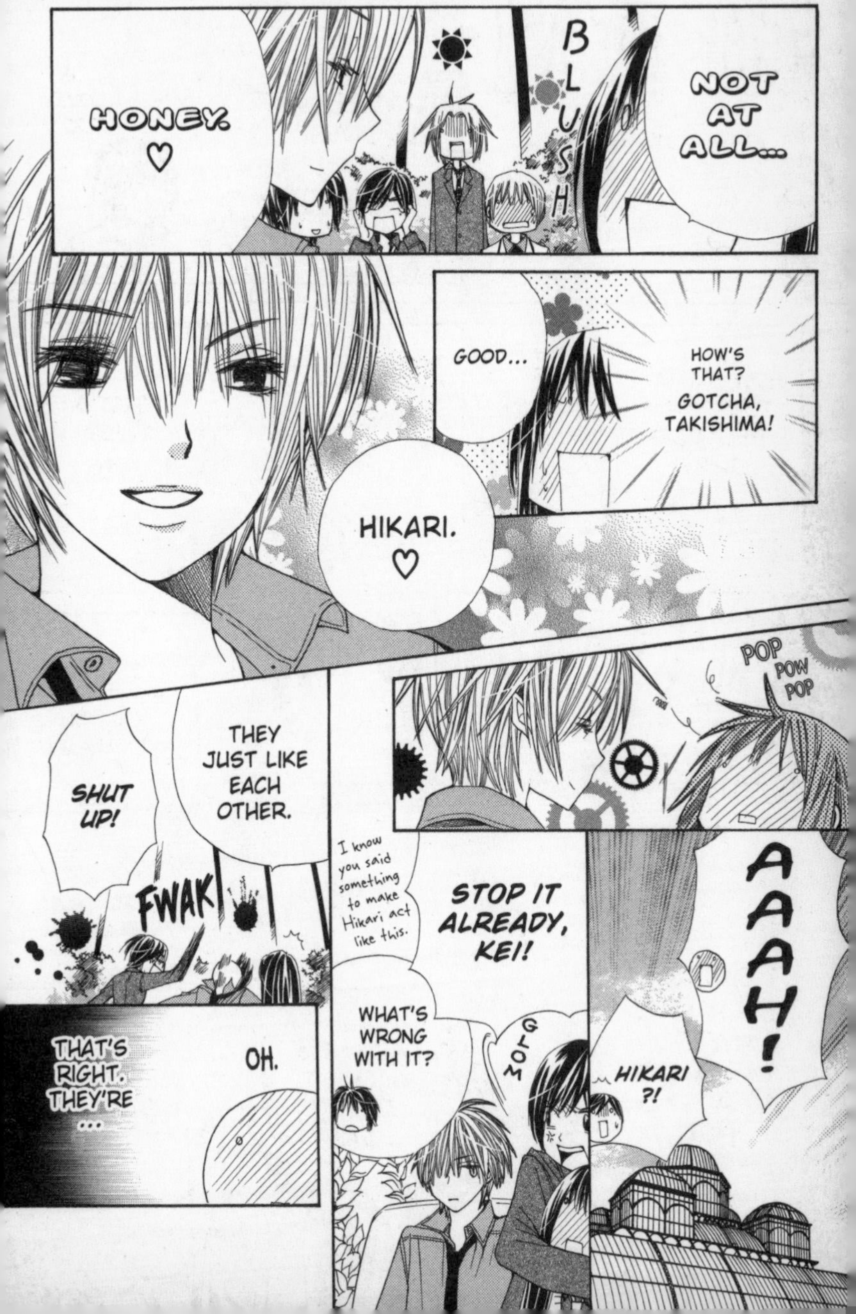
NOT AT ALL...
BLUSH
HONEY. ♡
HOW'S THAT? GOTCHA, TAKISHIMA!
GOOD...
HIKARI. ♡
POP POW POP
THEY JUST LIKE EACH OTHER.
SHUT UP!
FWAK
AAAAH!
HIKARI ?!
STOP IT ALREADY, KEI!
I know you said something to make Hikari act like this.
GLOM
WHAT'S WRONG WITH IT?
OH.
THAT'S RIGHT. THEY'RE ...

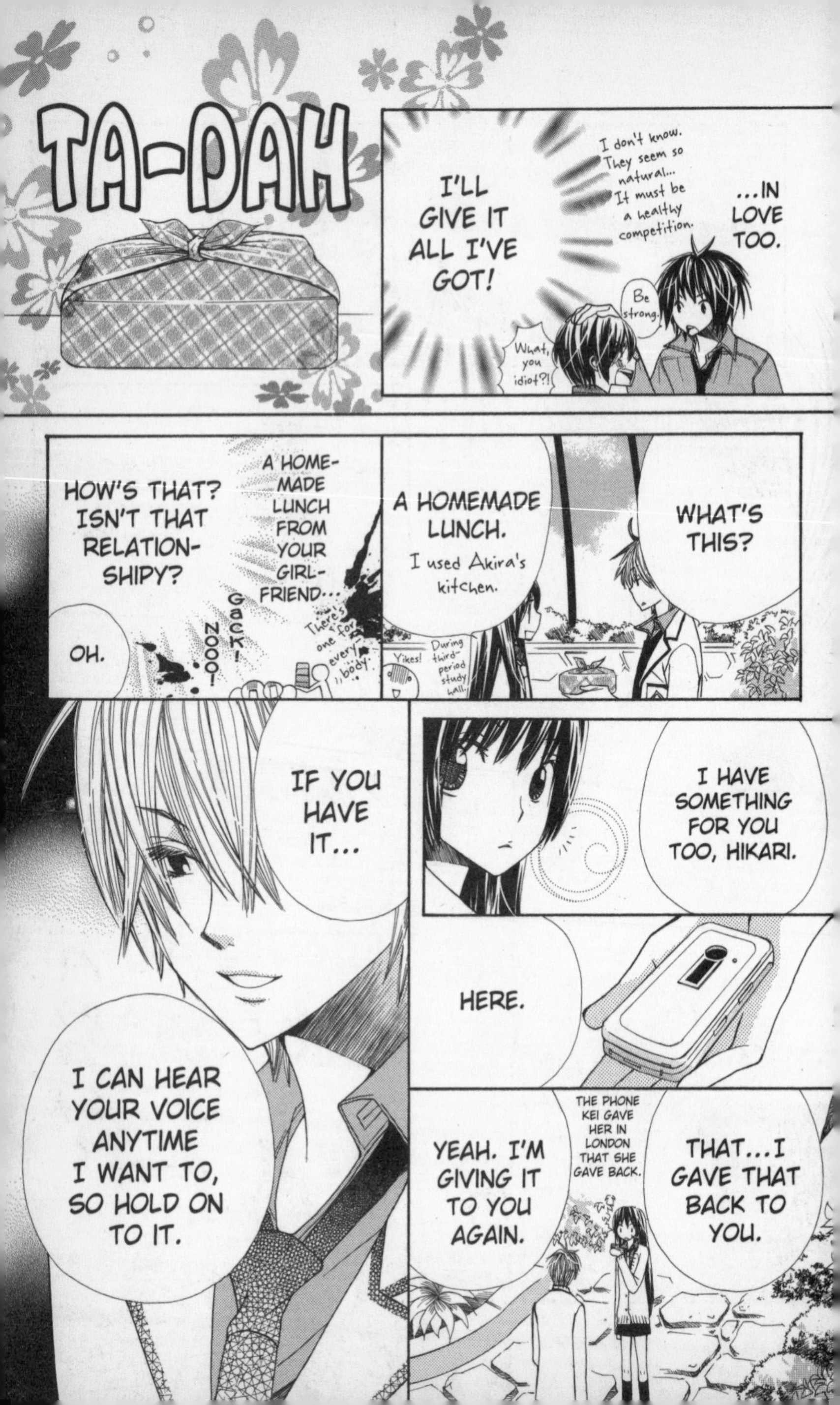
...IN LOVE TOO.
I don't know. They seem so natural... It must be a healthy competition.
I'LL GIVE IT ALL I'VE GOT!
Be strong.
What, you idiot?!
TA-DAH
WHAT'S THIS?
A HOMEMADE LUNCH.
I used Akira's kitchen.
During third-period study hall.
Yikes!
A HOME-MADE LUNCH FROM YOUR GIRL-FRIEND...
HOW'S THAT? ISN'T THAT RELATION-SHIPY?
GACK!
NOOO!
There's one for every-body.
OH.
I HAVE SOMETHING FOR YOU TOO, HIKARI.
HERE.
THAT...I GAVE THAT BACK TO YOU.
THE PHONE KEI GAVE HER IN LONDON THAT SHE GAVE BACK.
YEAH. I'M GIVING IT TO YOU AGAIN.
IF YOU HAVE IT...
I CAN HEAR YOUR VOICE ANYTIME I WANT TO, SO HOLD ON TO IT.

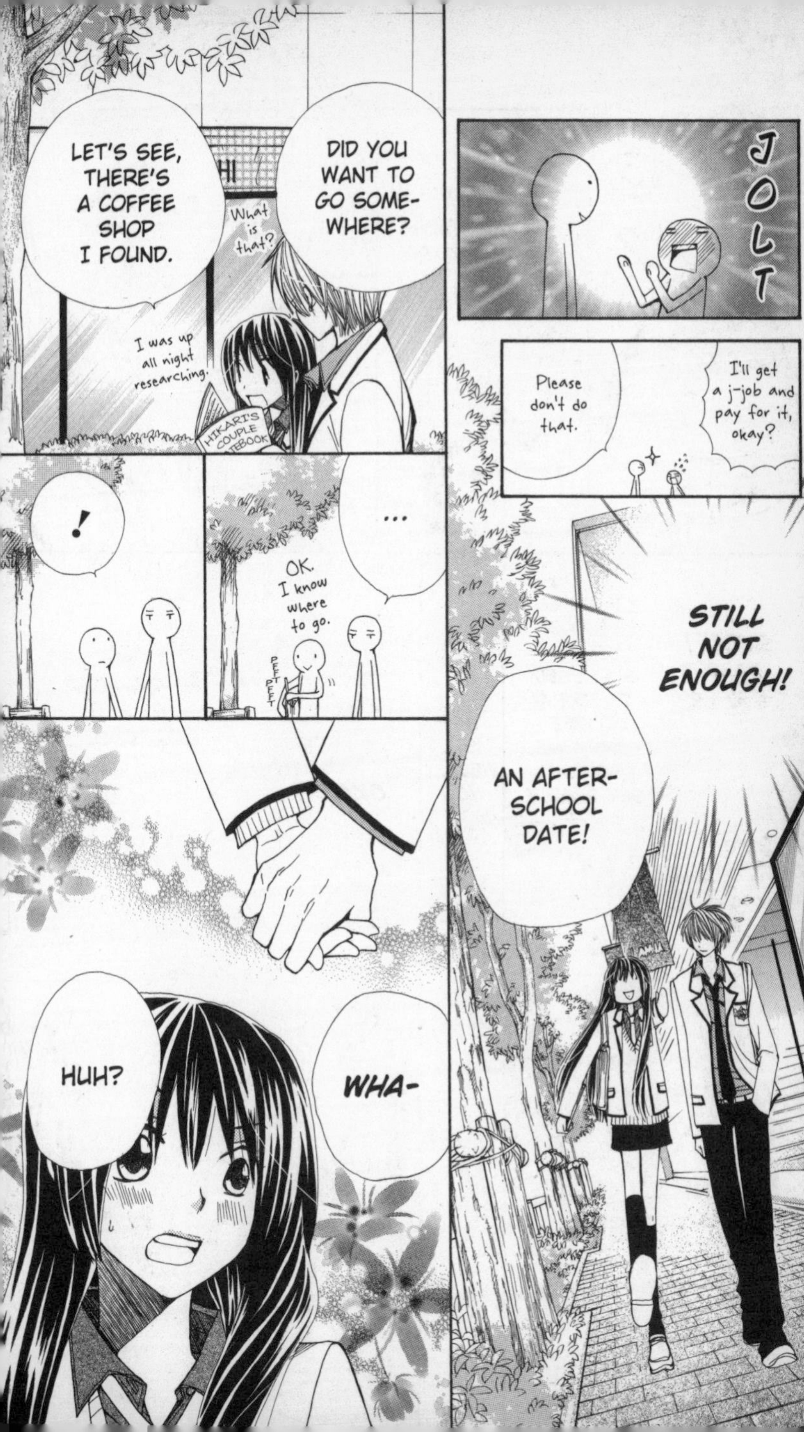
JOLT
I'll get a j-job and pay for it, okay?
Please don't do that.
STILL NOT ENOUGH!
AN AFTER-SCHOOL DATE!
DID YOU WANT TO GO SOMEWHERE?
What is that?
LET'S SEE, THERE'S A COFFEE SHOP I FOUND.
I was up all night researching.
HIKARI'S COUPLE TEBOOK
...
OK. I know where to go.
PFFT PFFT
!
WHA-
HUH?

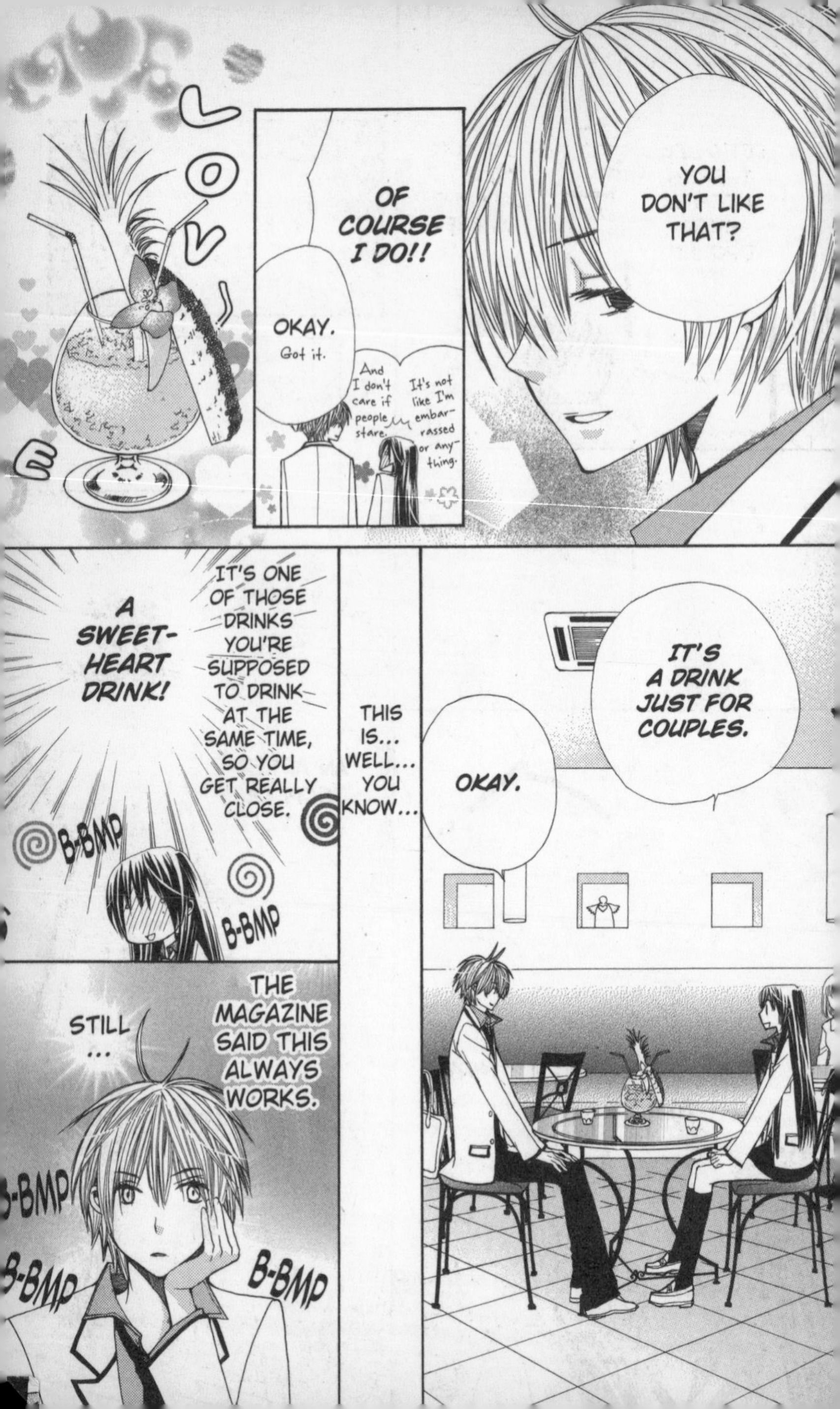
YOU DON'T LIKE THAT?
OF COURSE I DO!!
OKAY.
Got it.
It's not like I'm embarrassed or anything.
And I don't care if people stare.
LOVE
IT'S A DRINK JUST FOR COUPLES.
OKAY.
THIS IS... WELL... YOU KNOW...
IT'S ONE OF THOSE DRINKS YOU'RE SUPPOSED TO DRINK AT THE SAME TIME, SO YOU GET REALLY CLOSE.
A SWEETHEART DRINK!
B-BMP
B-BMP
THE MAGAZINE SAID THIS ALWAYS WORKS.
STILL ...
B-BMP
B-BMP
B-BMP

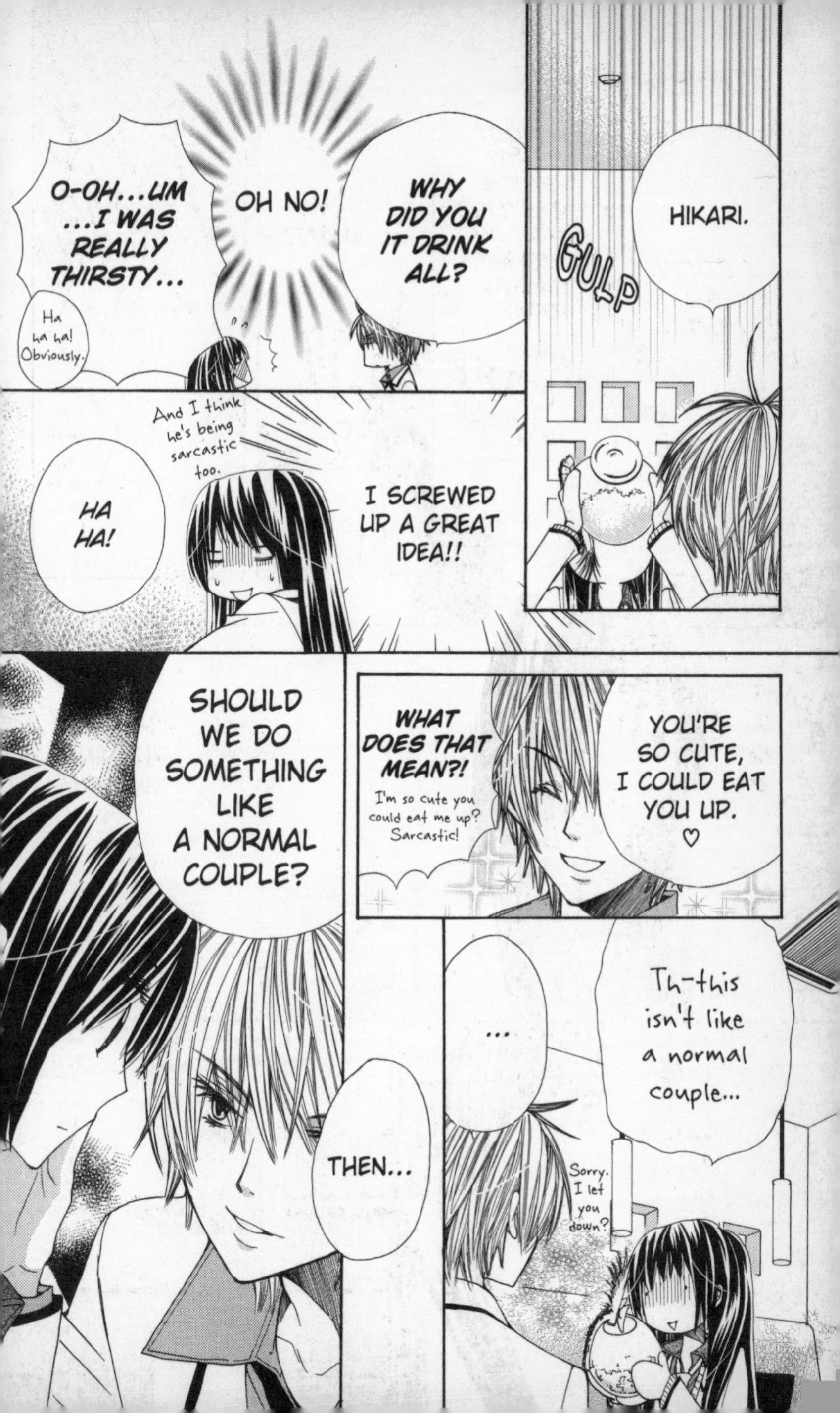
HIKARI.
GULP
WHY DID YOU IT DRINK ALL?
OH NO!
O-OH...UM ...I WAS REALLY THIRSTY...
Ha ha ha! Obviously.
I SCREWED UP A GREAT IDEA!!
And I think he's being sarcastic too.
HA HA!
YOU'RE SO CUTE, I COULD EAT YOU UP. ♡
WHAT DOES THAT MEAN?!
I'm so cute you could eat me up? Sarcastic!
Th-this isn't like a normal couple...
...
Sorry. I let you down?
SHOULD WE DO SOMETHING LIKE A NORMAL COUPLE?
THEN...

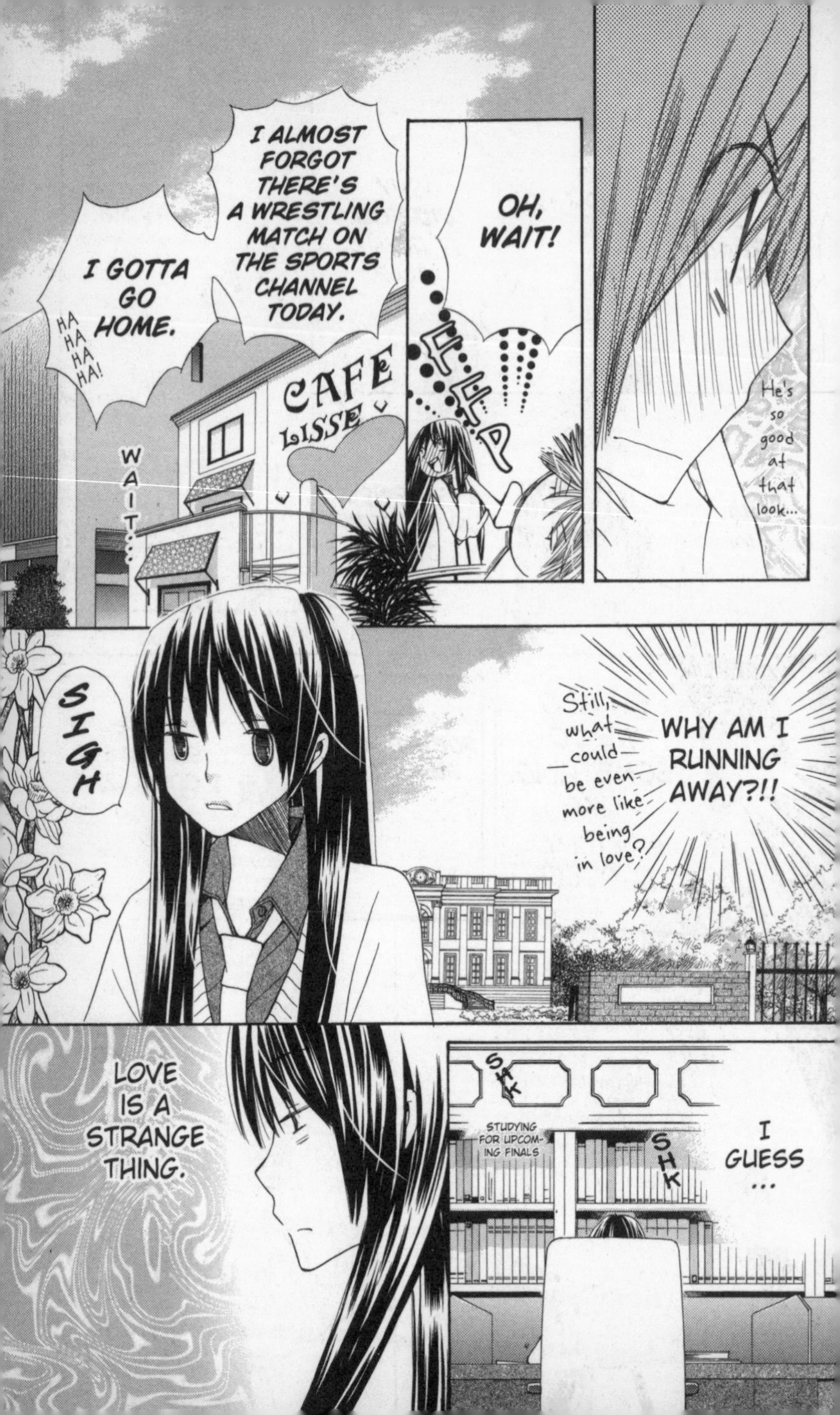
He's so good at that look...
OH, WAIT!
FFFP
I ALMOST FORGOT THERE'S A WRESTLING MATCH ON THE SPORTS CHANNEL TODAY.
I GOTTA GO HOME.
HA HA HA HA HA!
CAFE LISSE
WAIT...
WHY AM I RUNNING AWAY?!!
Still, what could be even more like being in love?
SIGH
I GUESS ...
SHK
SHK
STUDYING FOR UPCOMING FINALS
LOVE IS A STRANGE THING.

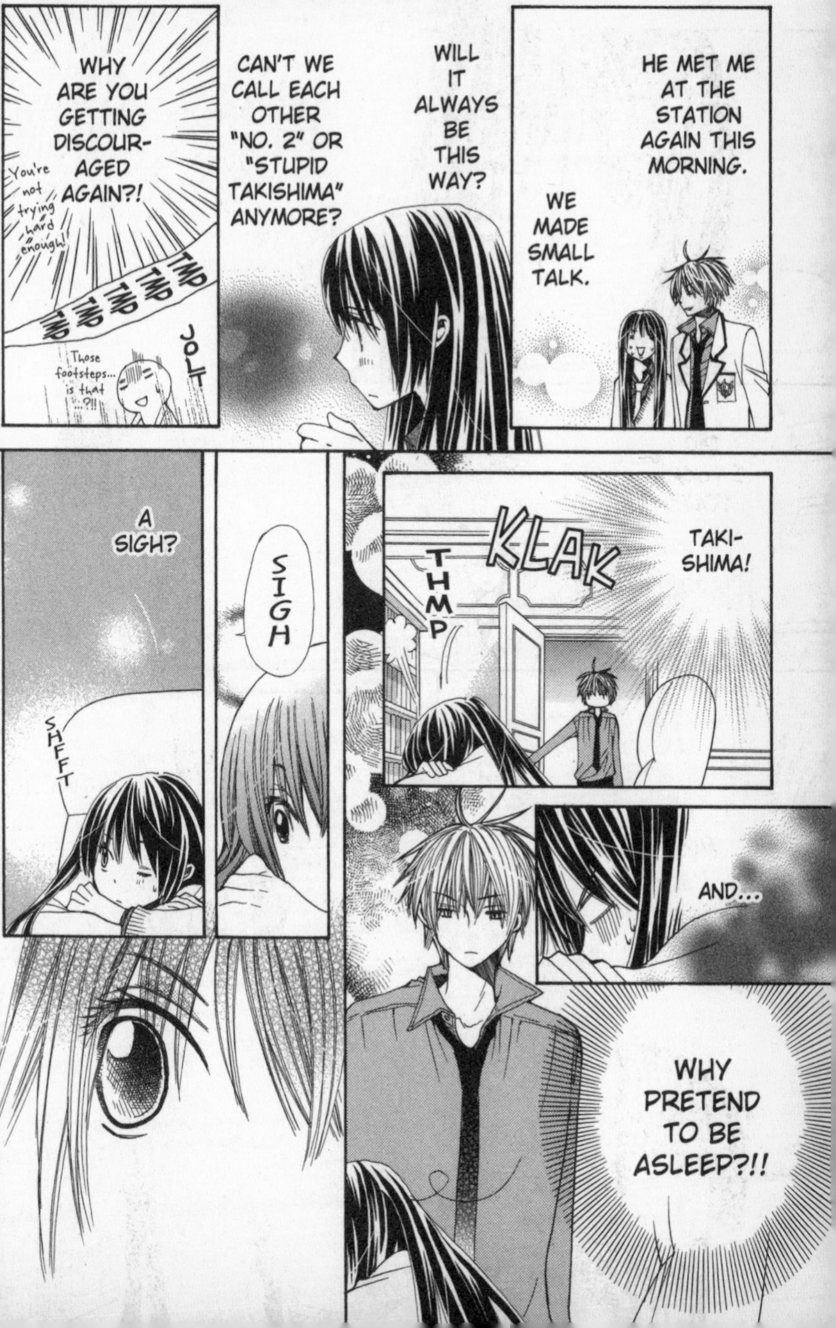
HE MET ME AT THE STATION AGAIN THIS MORNING.
WE MADE SMALL TALK.
WILL IT ALWAYS BE THIS WAY?
CAN'T WE CALL EACH OTHER "NO. 2" OR "STUPID TAKISHIMA" ANYMORE?
WHY ARE YOU GETTING DISCOUR-AGED AGAIN?!
You're not trying hard enough!
TMP TMP TMP TMP
JOLT
Those footsteps... is that ...?!!
KLAK
THMP
TAKI-SHIMA!
AND...
SIGH
A SIGH?
SHFFT
WHY PRETEND TO BE ASLEEP?!!

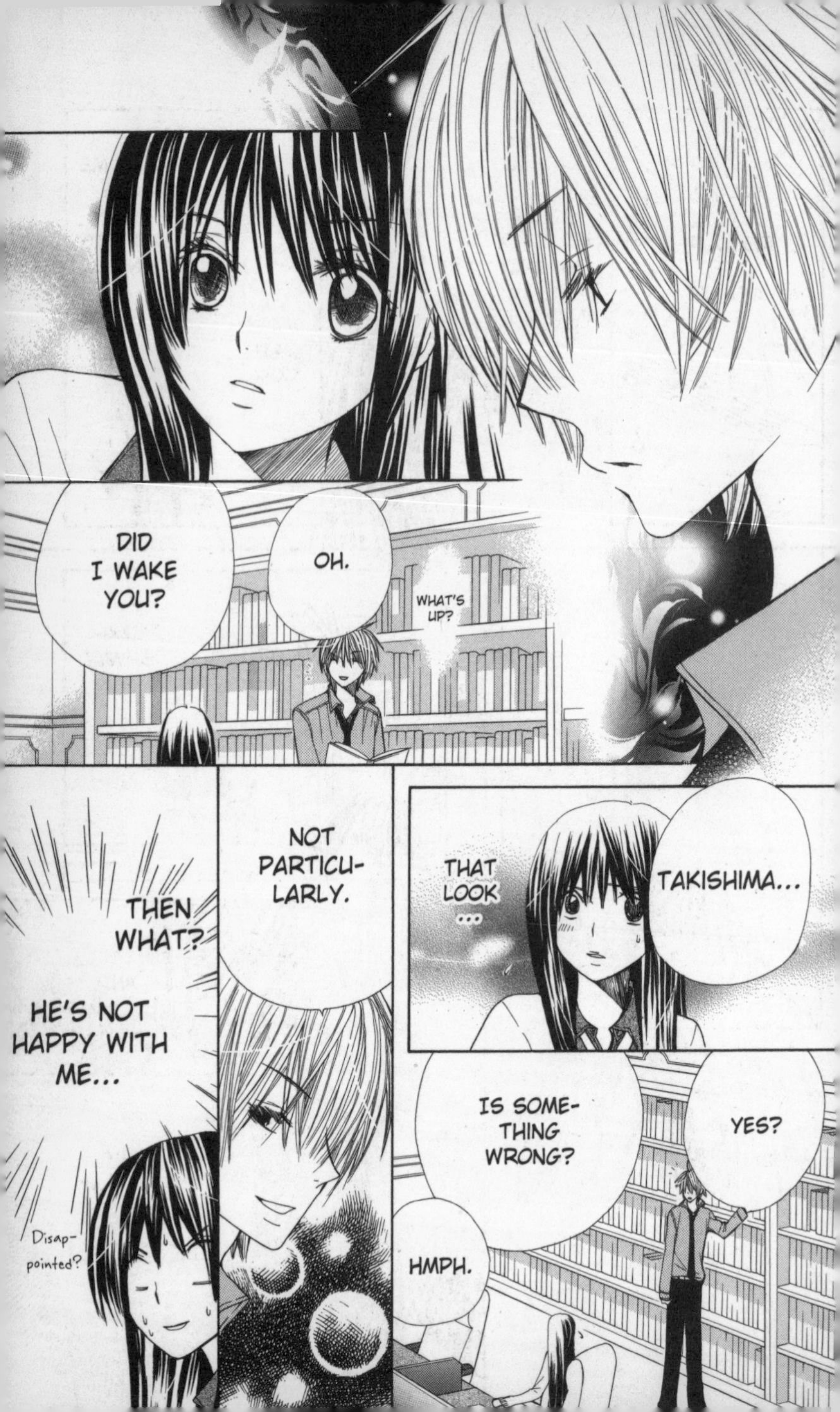
OH.
WHAT'S UP?
DID I WAKE YOU?
TAKISHIMA...
THAT LOOK...
YES?
IS SOME-THING WRONG?
HMPH.
NOT PARTICU-LARLY.
THEN WHAT?
HE'S NOT HAPPY WITH ME...
Disap-pointed?

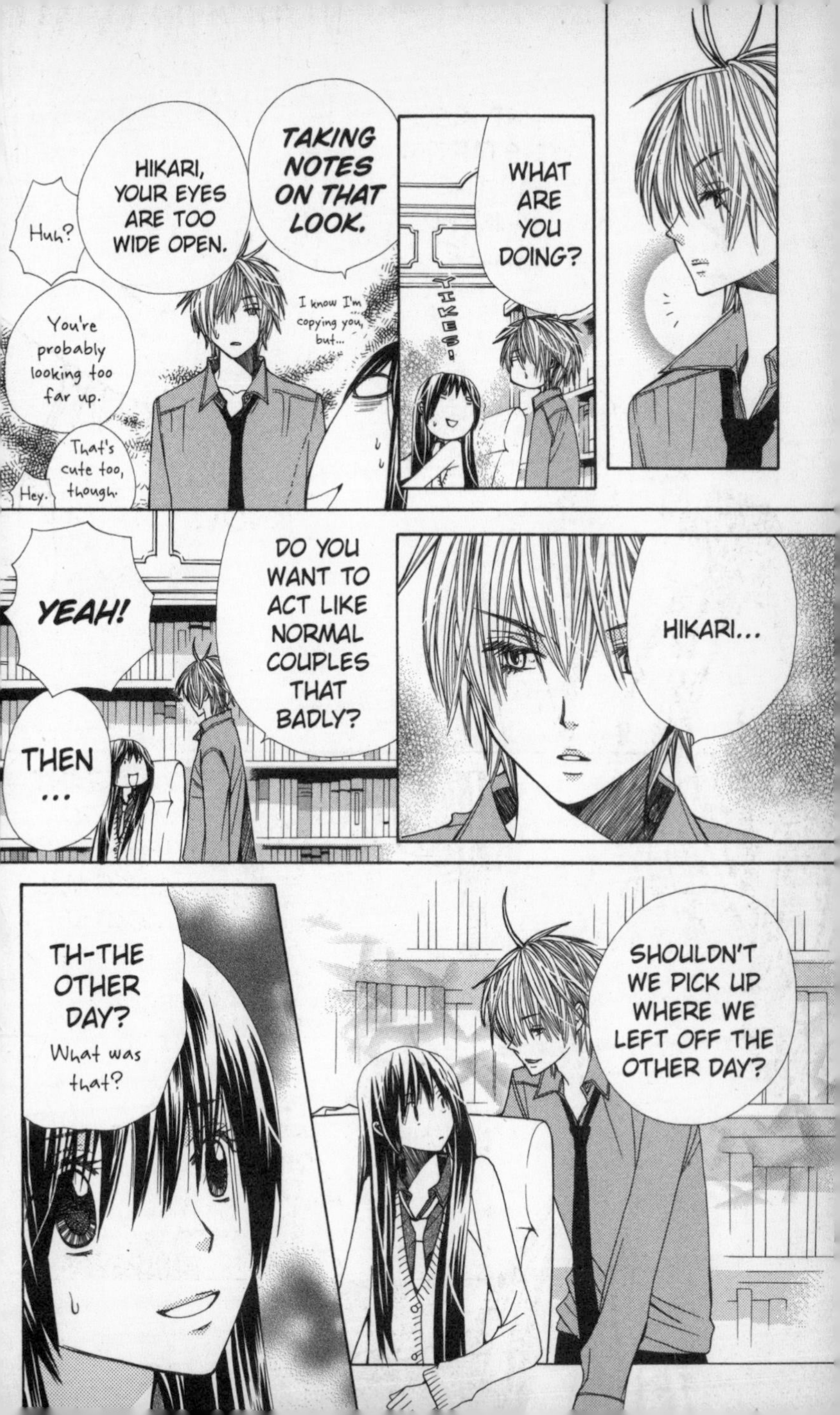
WHAT ARE YOU DOING?
YIKES!
TAKING NOTES ON THAT LOOK.
I know I'm copying you, but...
HIKARI, YOUR EYES ARE TOO WIDE OPEN.
Huh?
You're probably looking too far up.
That's cute too, though.
Hey.
HIKARI...
DO YOU WANT TO ACT LIKE NORMAL COUPLES THAT BADLY?
YEAH!
THEN ...
SHOULDN'T WE PICK UP WHERE WE LEFT OFF THE OTHER DAY?
TH-THE OTHER DAY?
What was that?

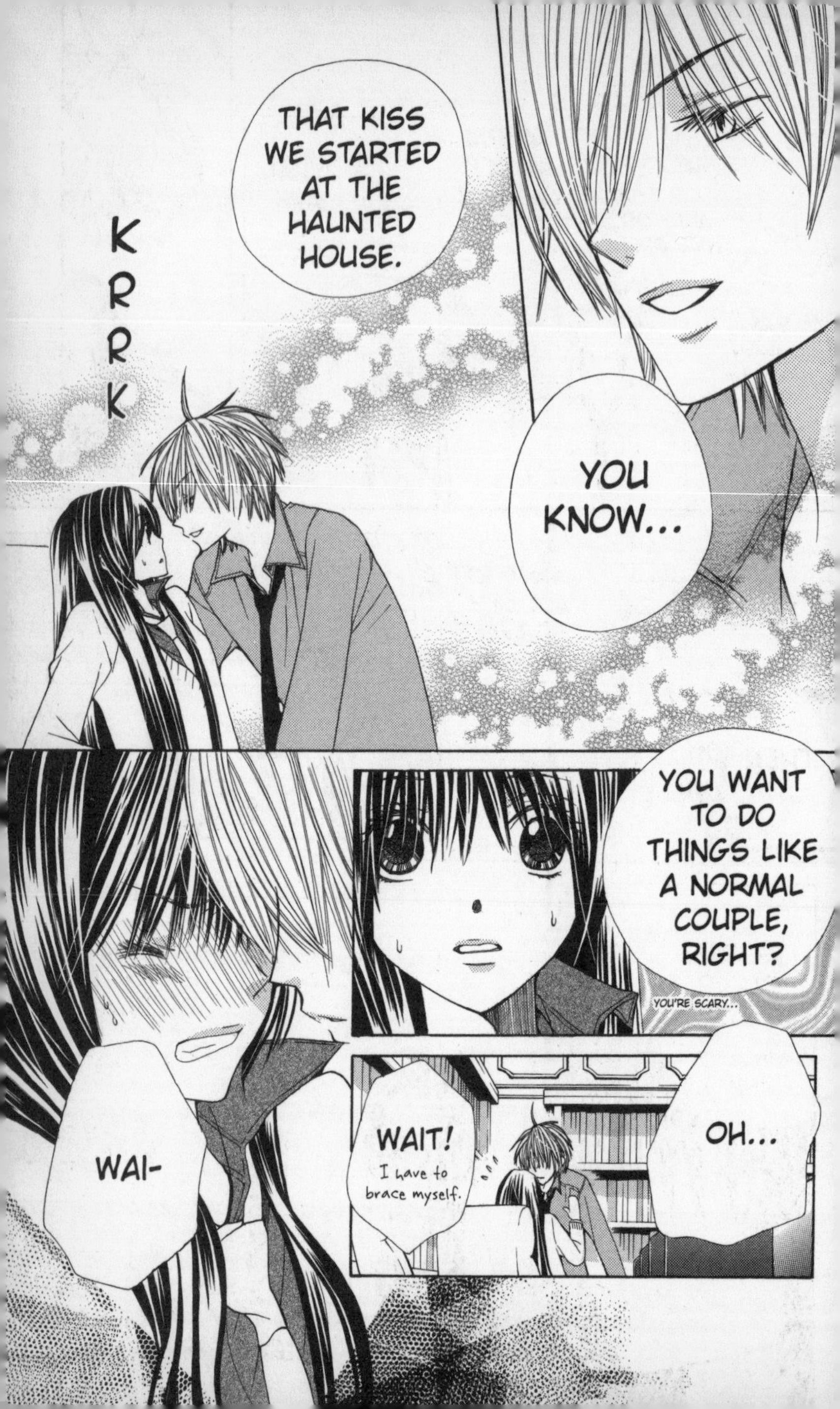
YOU KNOW...
THAT KISS WE STARTED AT THE HAUNTED HOUSE.
KRRK
YOU WANT TO DO THINGS LIKE A NORMAL COUPLE, RIGHT?
YOU'RE SCARY...
OH...
WAIT! I have to brace myself.
WAI-

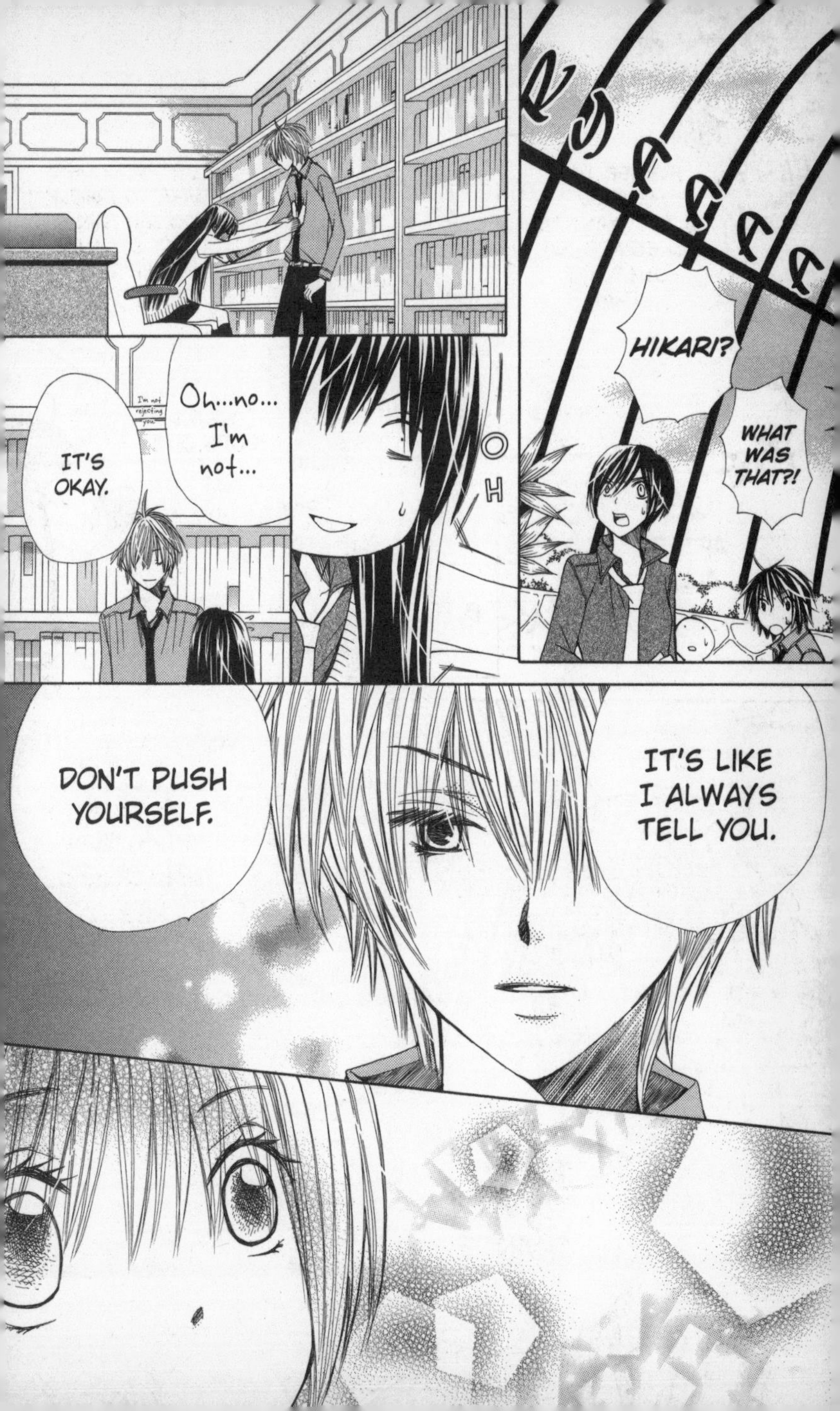
KYAAAA
HIKARI?
WHAT WAS THAT?!
OH
Oh...no... I'm not...
I'm not rejecting you.
IT'S OKAY.
IT'S LIKE I ALWAYS TELL YOU.
DON'T PUSH YOURSELF.

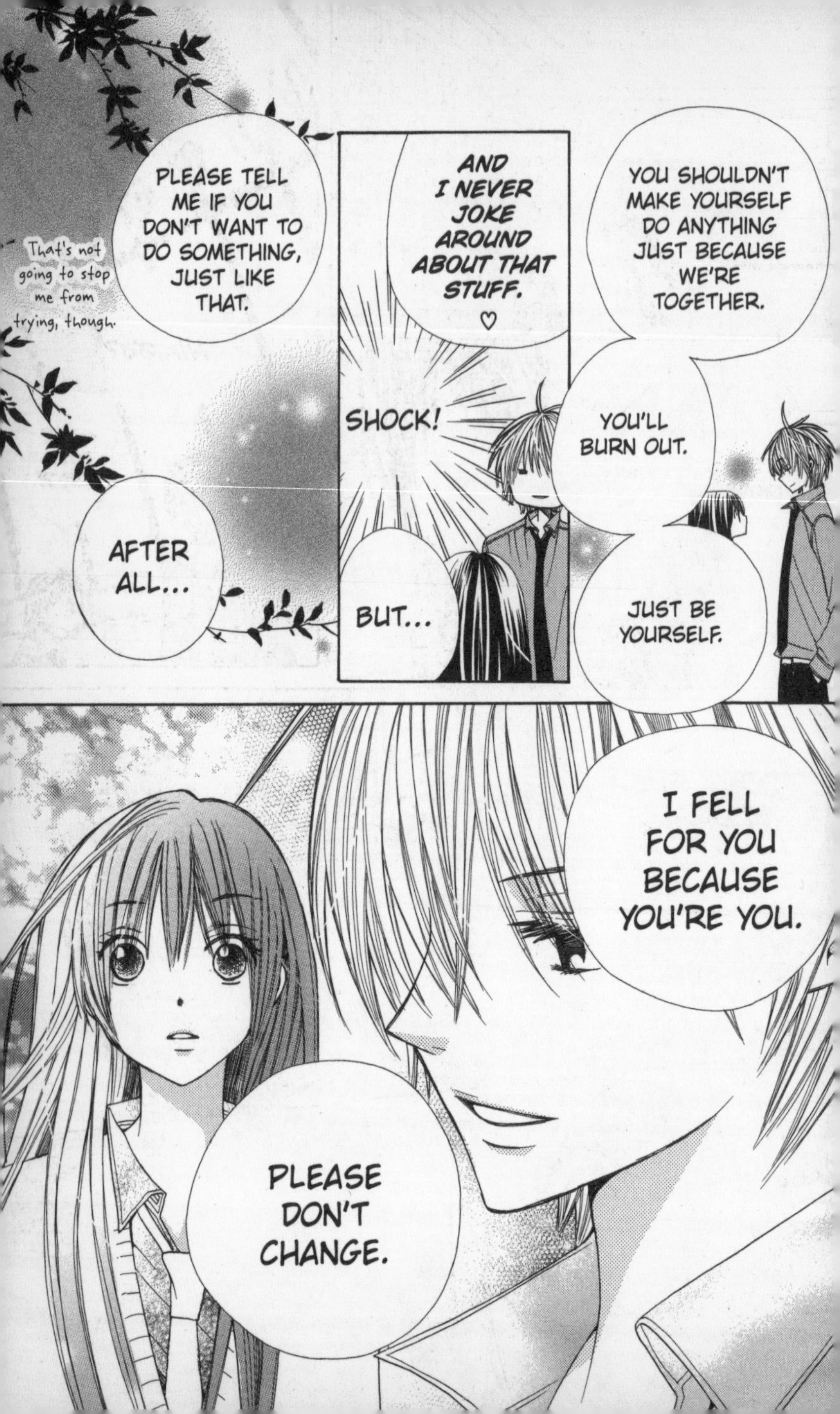
AND I NEVER JOKE AROUND ABOUT THAT STUFF. ♡
SHOCK!
BUT...
YOU SHOULDN'T MAKE YOURSELF DO ANYTHING JUST BECAUSE WE'RE TOGETHER.
YOU'LL BURN OUT.
JUST BE YOURSELF.
PLEASE TELL ME IF YOU DON'T WANT TO DO SOMETHING, JUST LIKE THAT.
That's not going to stop me from trying, though.
AFTER ALL...
I FELL FOR YOU BECAUSE YOU'RE YOU.
PLEASE DON'T CHANGE.

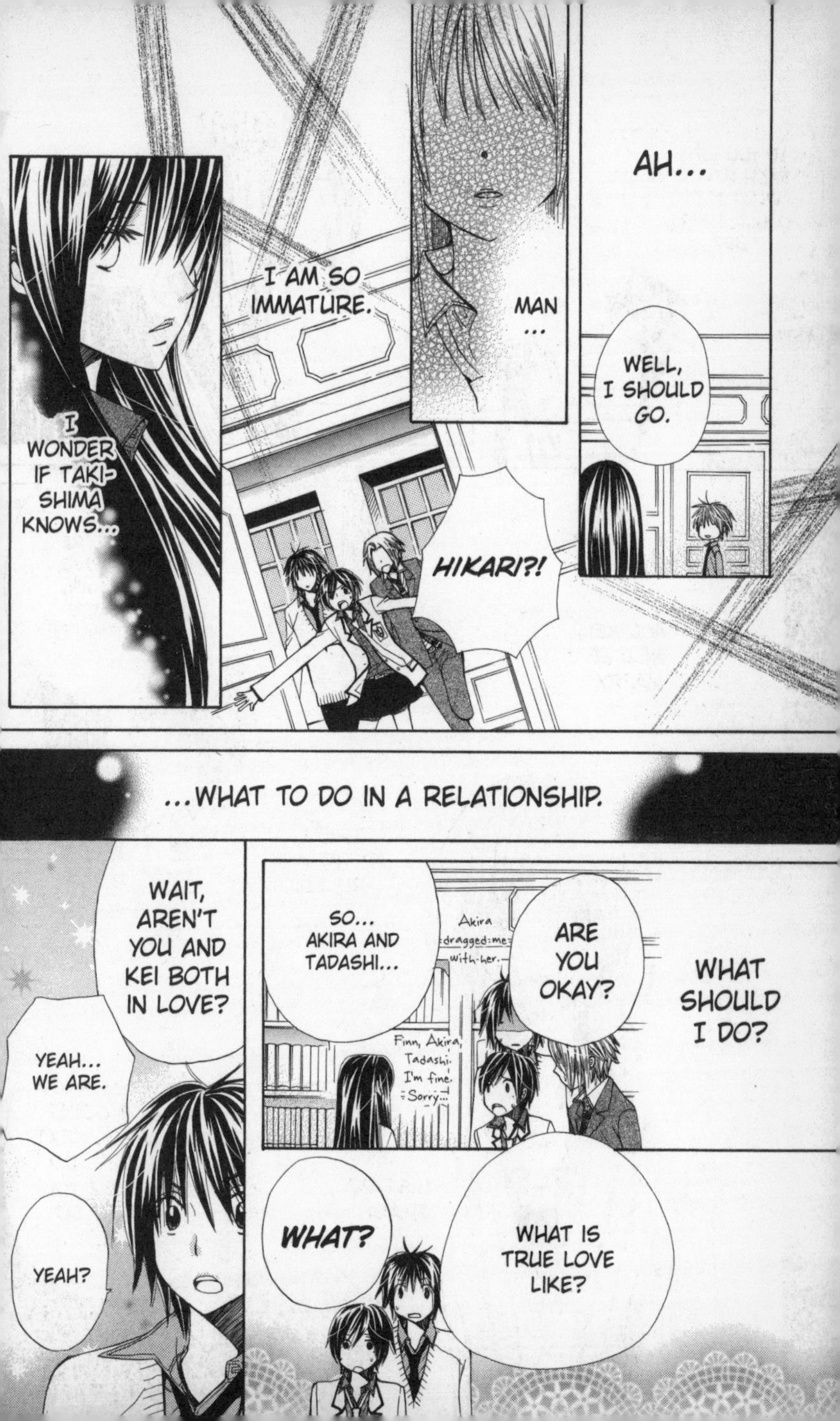

AH...
MAN ...
WELL, I SHOULD GO.
I AM SO IMMATURE.
HIKARI?!
I WONDER IF TAKI-SHIMA KNOWS...
...WHAT TO DO IN A RELATIONSHIP.
WHAT SHOULD I DO?
ARE YOU OKAY?
Akira dragged me with her.
SO... AKIRA AND TADASHI...
Finn, Akira, Tadashi. I'm fine. Sorry...
WHAT IS TRUE LOVE LIKE?
WHAT?
WAIT, AREN'T YOU AND KEI BOTH IN LOVE?
YEAH... WE ARE.
YEAH?

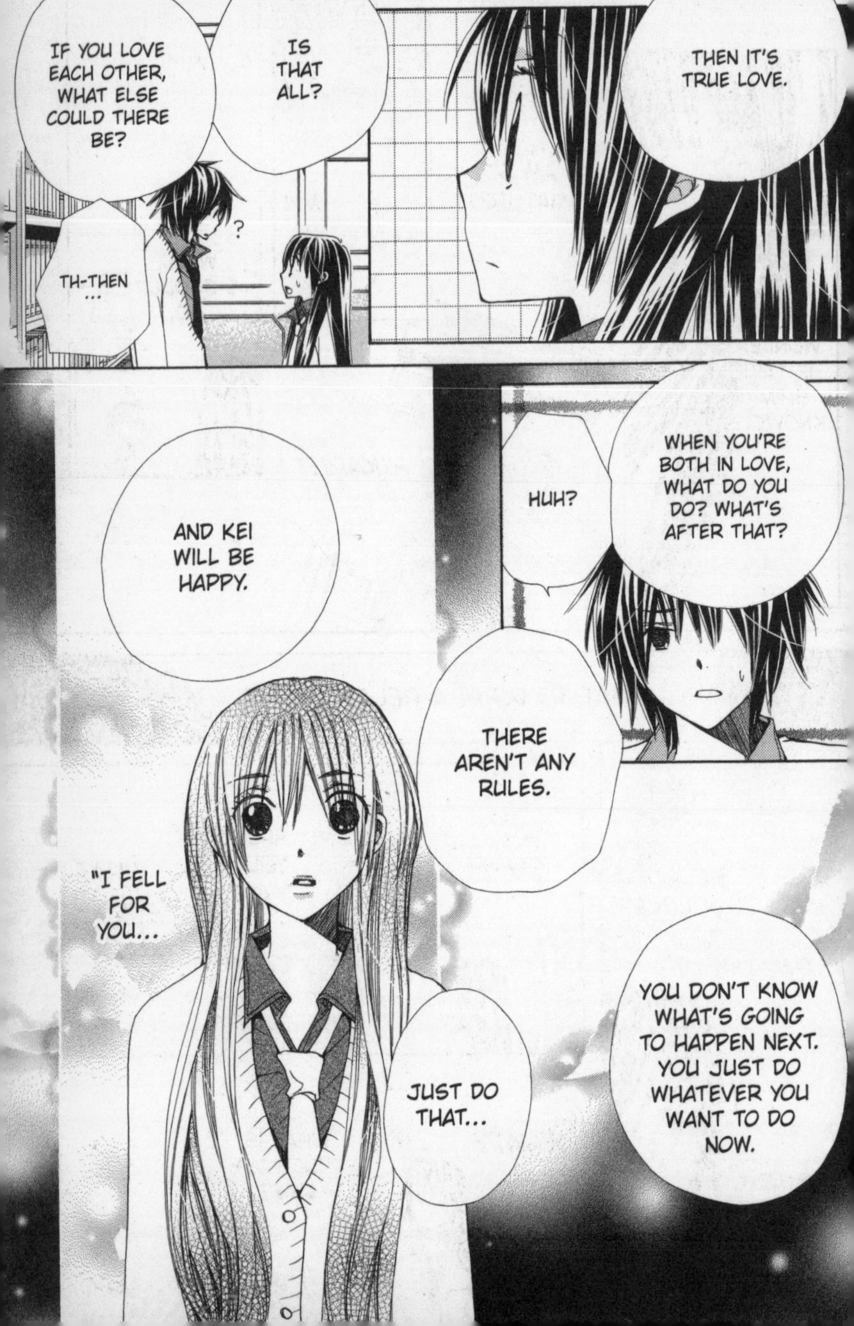
THEN IT'S TRUE LOVE.
IS THAT ALL?
IF YOU LOVE EACH OTHER, WHAT ELSE COULD THERE BE?
?
TH-THEN ...
WHEN YOU'RE BOTH IN LOVE, WHAT DO YOU DO? WHAT'S AFTER THAT?
HUH?
THERE AREN'T ANY RULES.
YOU DON'T KNOW WHAT'S GOING TO HAPPEN NEXT. YOU JUST DO WHATEVER YOU WANT TO DO NOW.
JUST DO THAT...
AND KEI WILL BE HAPPY.
"I FELL FOR YOU...

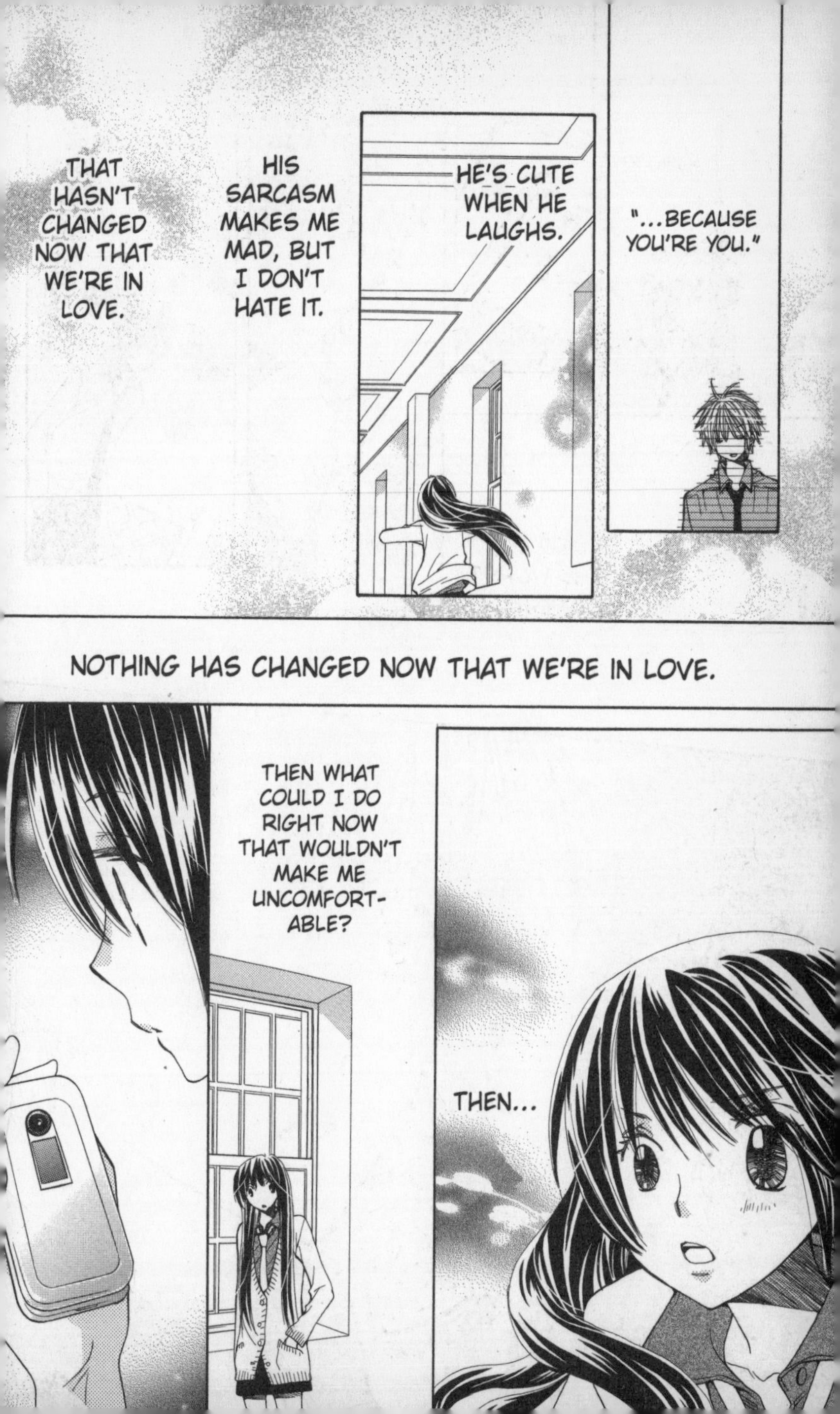
"...BECAUSE YOU'RE YOU."
HE'S CUTE WHEN HE LAUGHS.
HIS SARCASM MAKES ME MAD, BUT I DON'T HATE IT.
THAT HASN'T CHANGED NOW THAT WE'RE IN LOVE.
NOTHING HAS CHANGED NOW THAT WE'RE IN LOVE.
THEN...
THEN WHAT COULD I DO RIGHT NOW THAT WOULDN'T MAKE ME UNCOMFORT-ABLE?

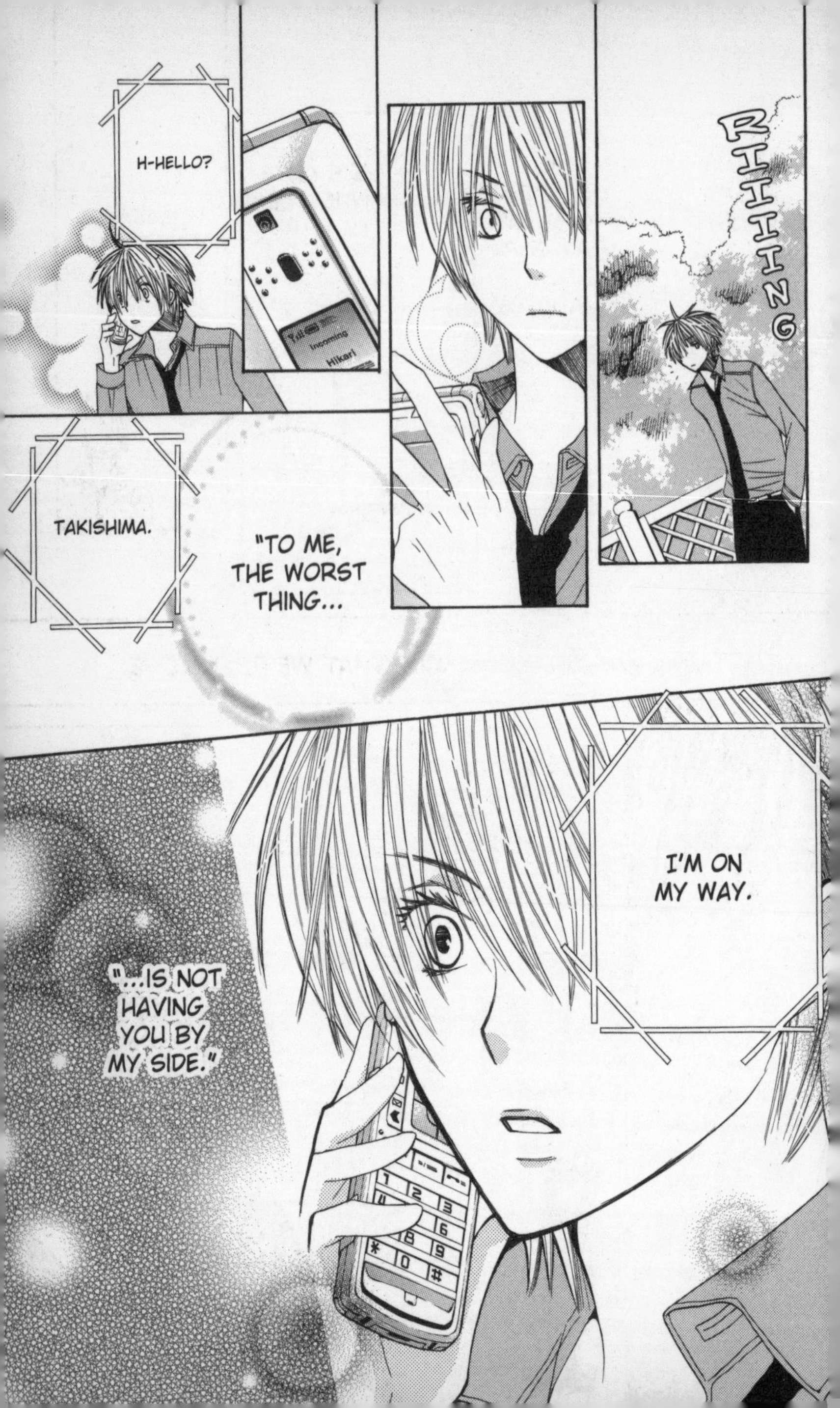
RIIIING
Incoming
Hikari
H-HELLO?
"TO ME, THE WORST THING...
TAKISHIMA.
I'M ON MY WAY.
"...IS NOT HAVING YOU BY MY SIDE."

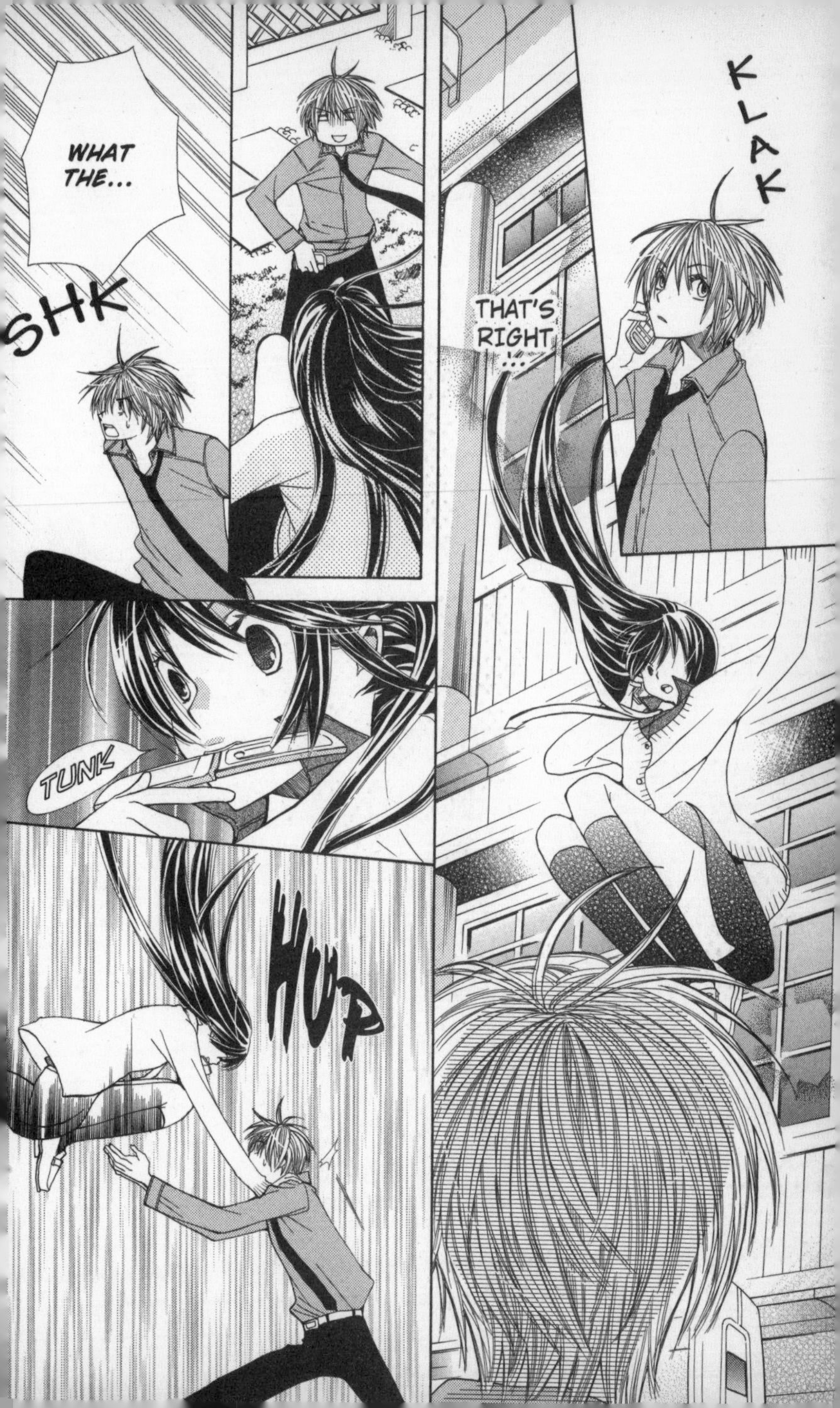
KLAK
THAT'S RIGHT ...!
WHAT THE...
SHK
TUNK
HUP

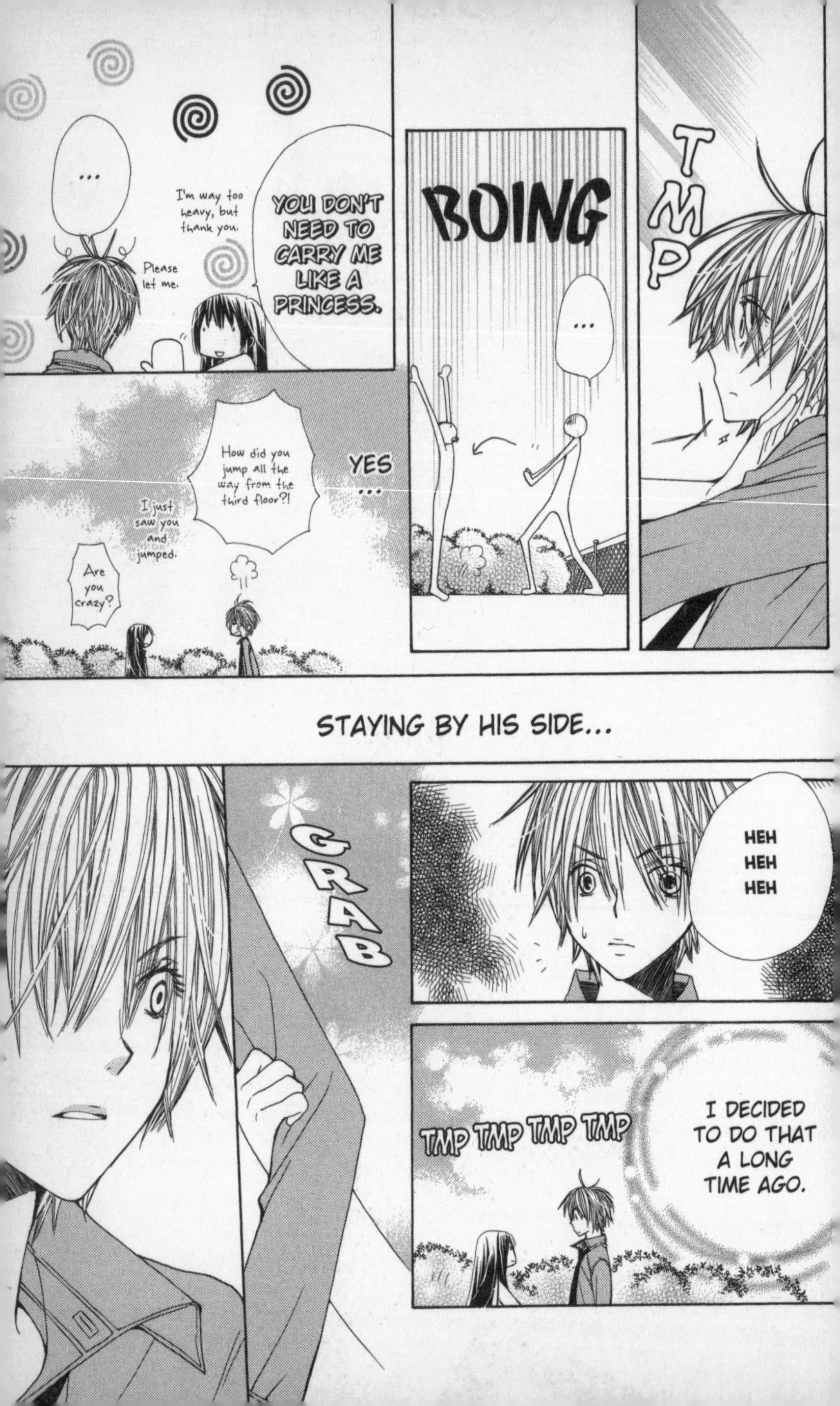
TMP
BOING
...
YOU DON'T NEED TO CARRY ME LIKE A PRINCESS.
I'm way too heavy, but thank you.
...
Please let me.
YES...
How did you jump all the way from the third floor?!
I just saw you and jumped.
Are you crazy?
STAYING BY HIS SIDE...
HEH HEH HEH
I DECIDED TO DO THAT A LONG TIME AGO.
TMP TMP TMP TMP
GRAB

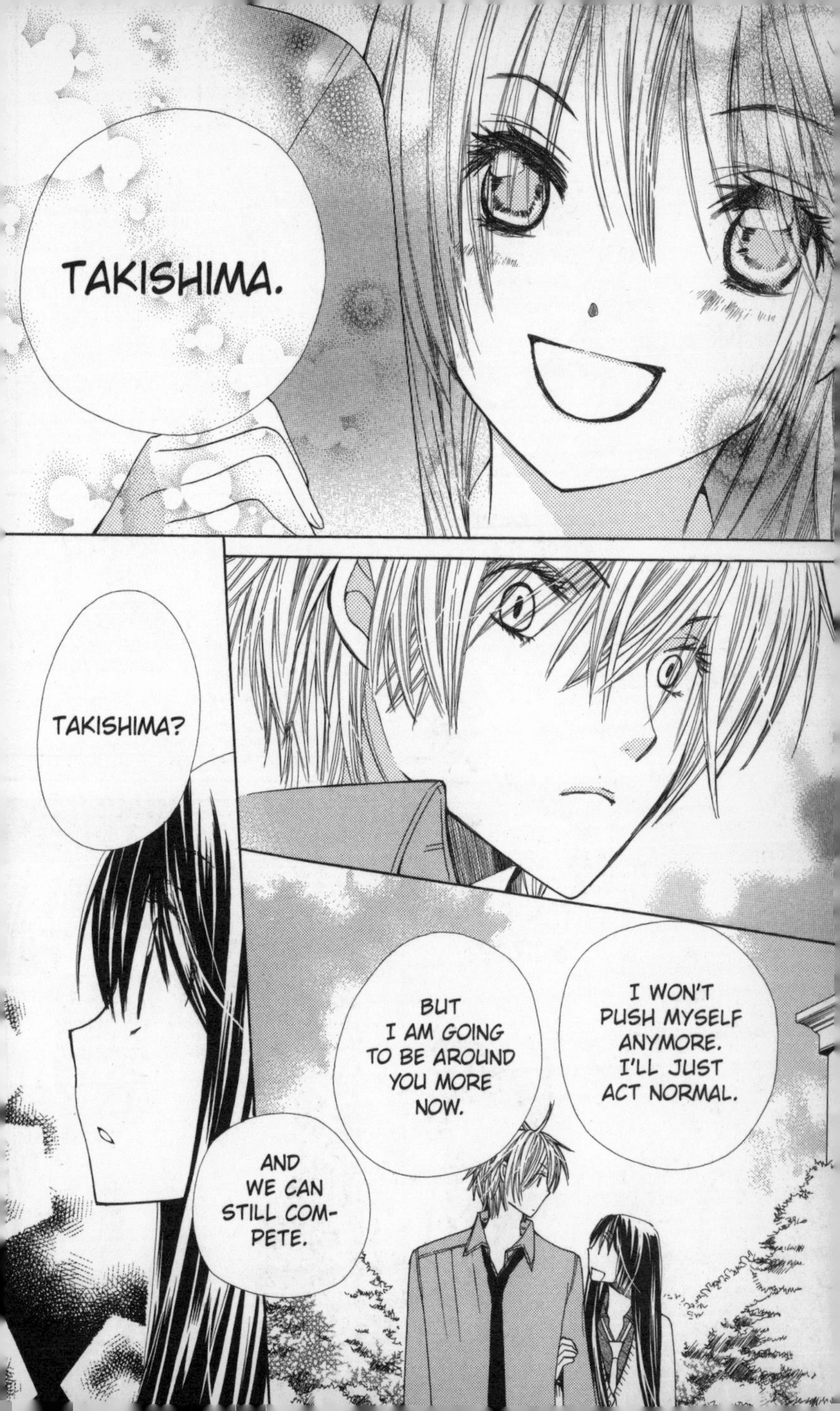
TAKISHIMA.
TAKISHIMA?
I WON'T PUSH MYSELF ANYMORE. I'LL JUST ACT NORMAL.
BUT I AM GOING TO BE AROUND YOU MORE NOW.
AND WE CAN STILL COM-PETE.

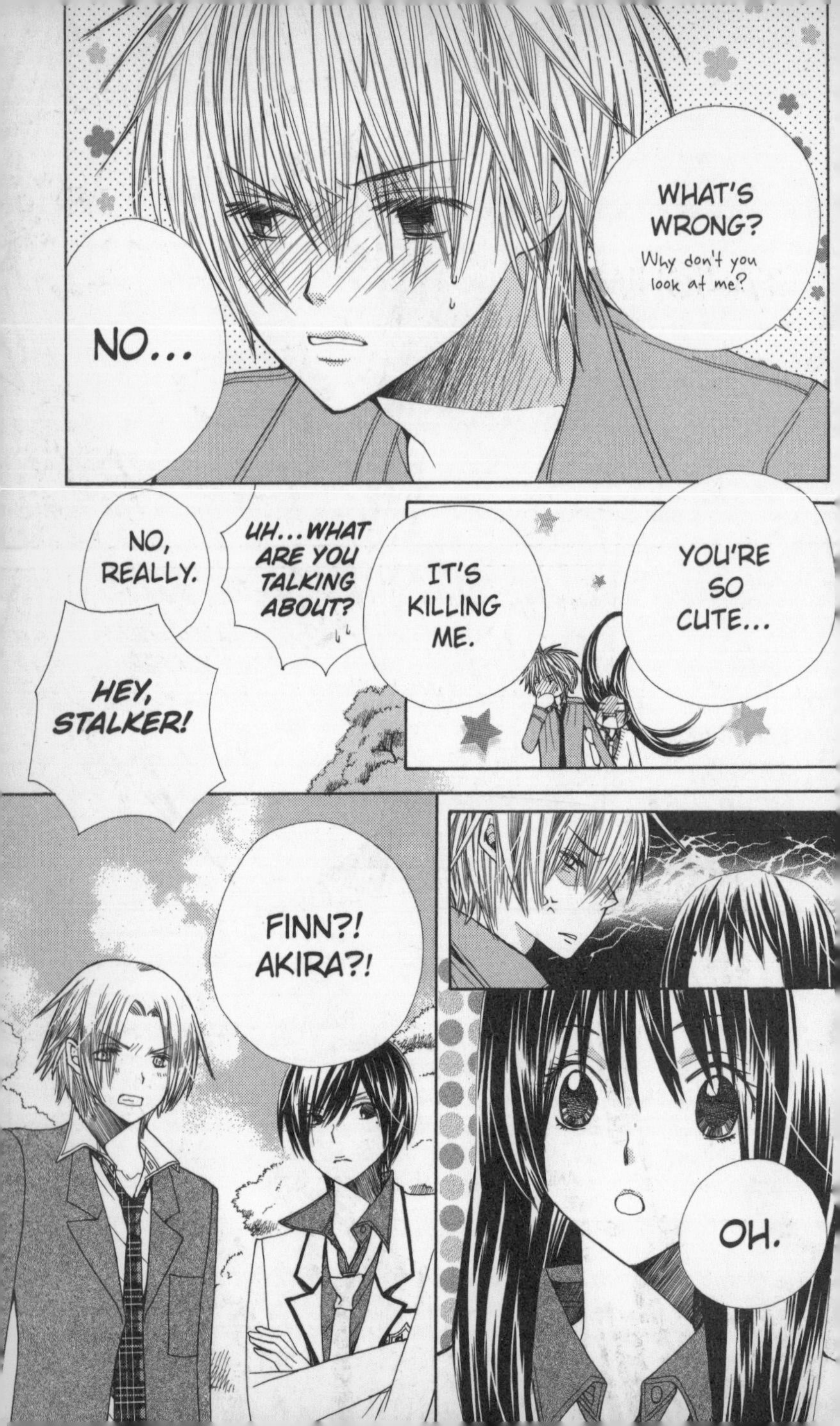
WHAT'S WRONG?
Why don't you look at me?
NO...
YOU'RE SO CUTE...
IT'S KILLING ME.
UH...WHAT ARE YOU TALKING ABOUT?
NO, REALLY.
HEY, STALKER!
OH.
FINN?! AKIRA?!

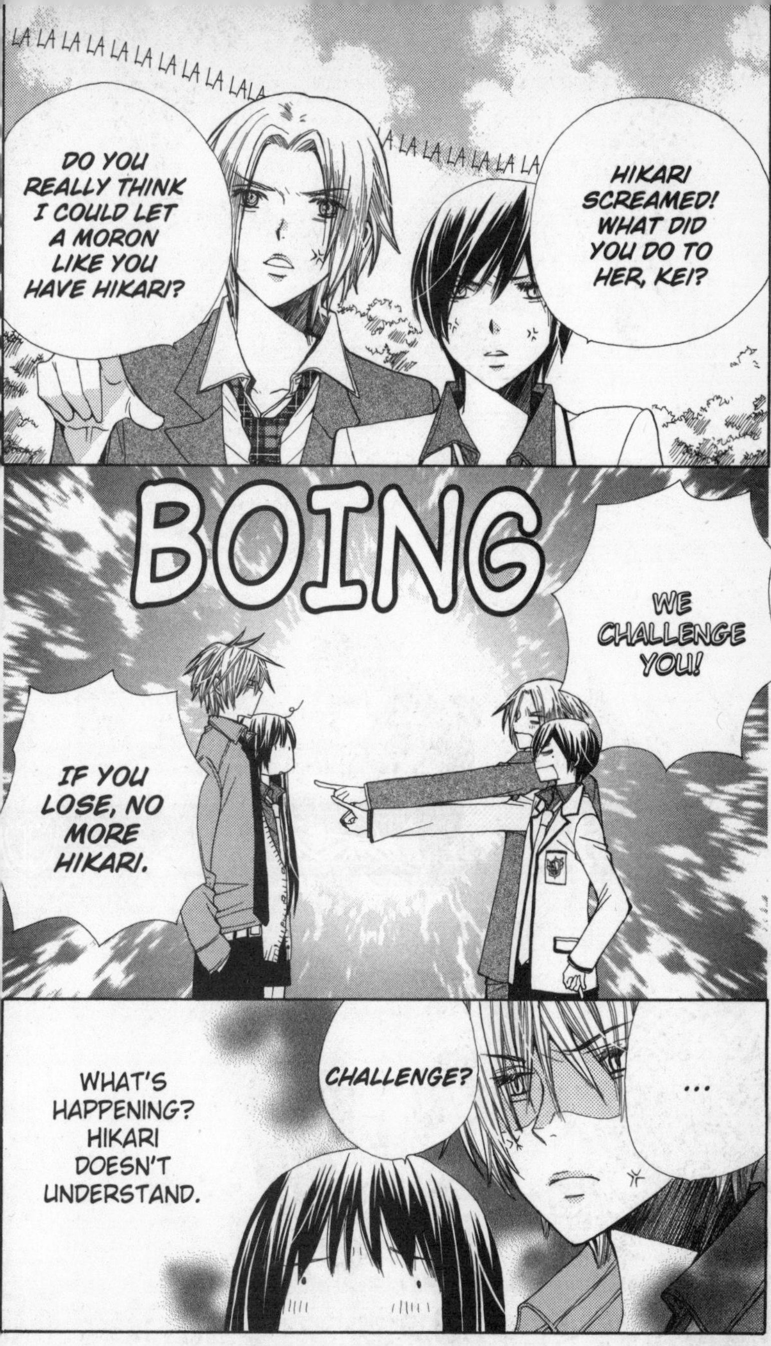
HIKARI SCREAMED! WHAT DID YOU DO TO HER, KEI?
LA LA LA LA LA LA LA LA LA LA LA LA LA
LA LA LA LA LA LA LA
DO YOU REALLY THINK I COULD LET A MORON LIKE YOU HAVE HIKARI?
BOING
WE CHALLENGE YOU!
IF YOU LOSE, NO MORE HIKARI.
...
CHALLENGE?
WHAT'S HAPPENING? HIKARI DOESN'T UNDERSTAND.

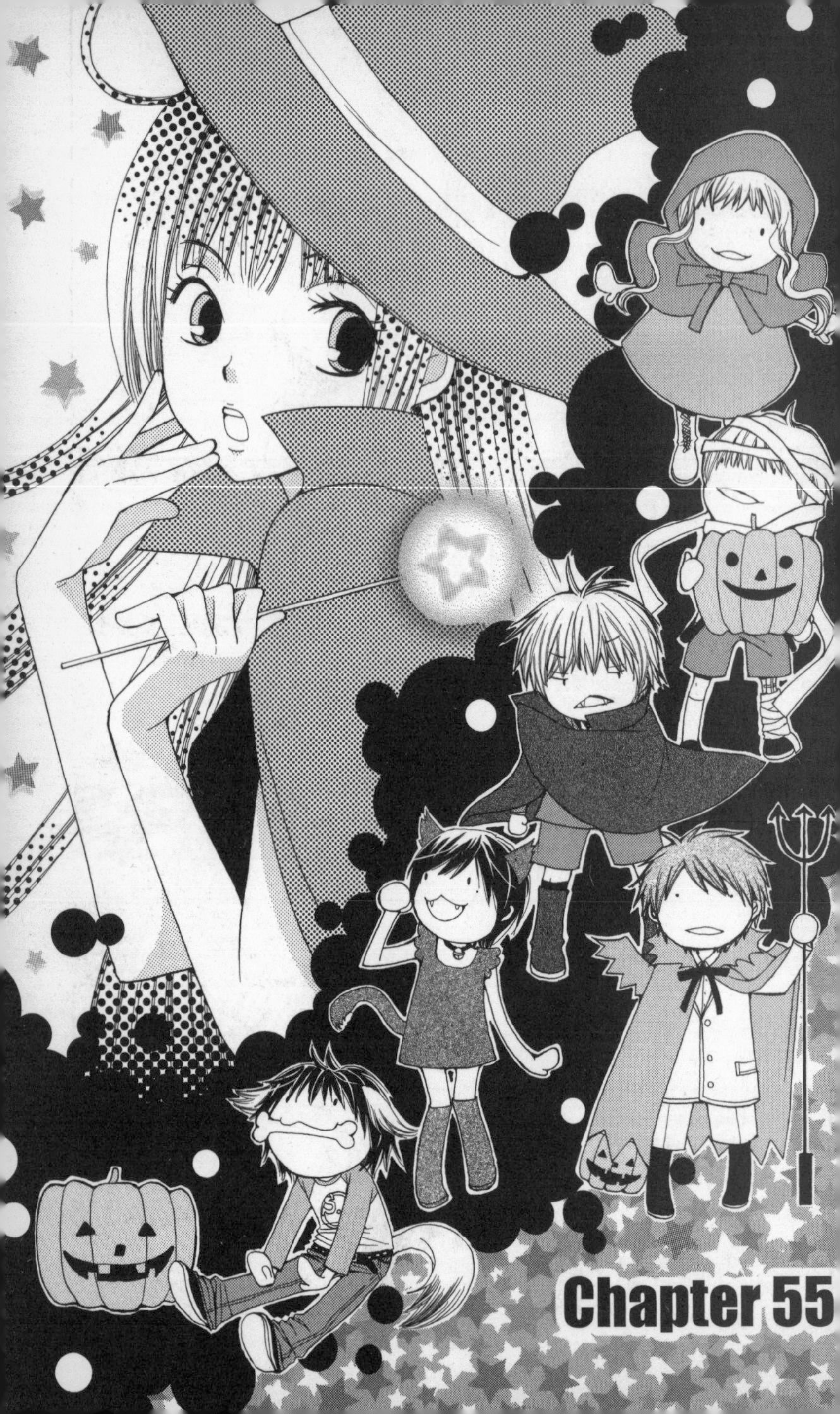
Chapter 55

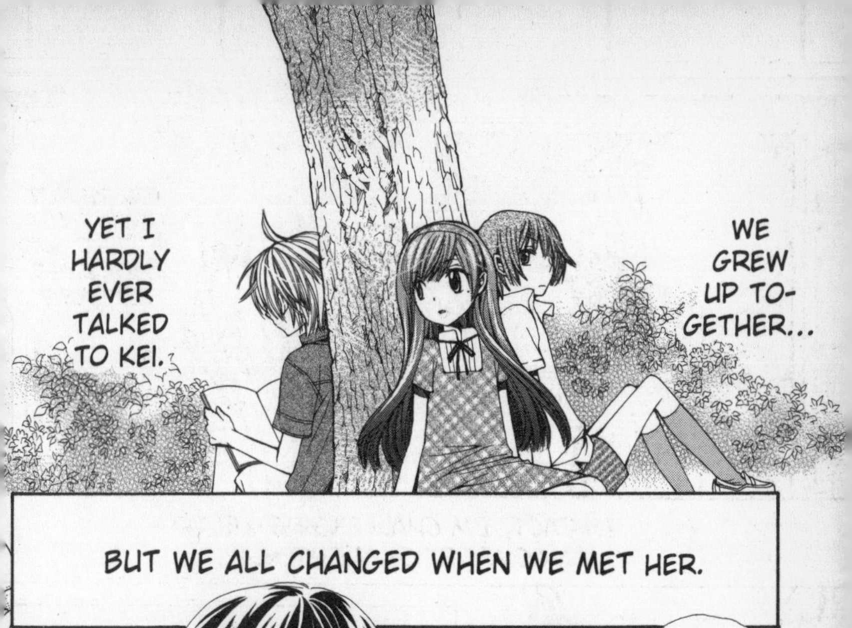
WE GREW UP TO-GETHER...
YET I HARDLY EVER TALKED TO KEI.
BUT WE ALL CHANGED WHEN WE MET HER.
OH!
STILL ...
KEI!

• BIKES •

WHEN I CAN'T COME UP WITH A NAME OR I DON'T HAVE ANY IDEAS, I RIDE LIKE A MANIAC ON MY BICYCLE. THE WIND FEELS GREAT AND REFRESHES ME. AFTER A WILD RIDE, I USUALLY END UP AT THE MALL. THERE'S A GREAT BAKERY THERE. I BUY. I EAT.

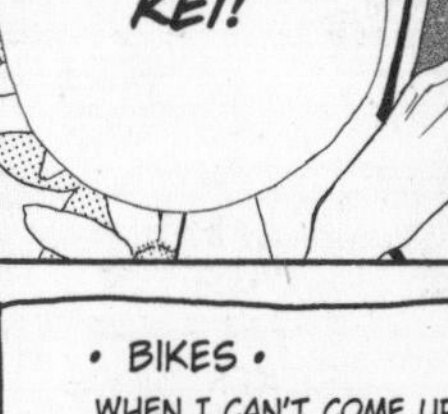
WHOOSH
RWAR!! MY GREAT...
...BIKE.
weee!

BIKES ARE G-R-E-A-T ♡

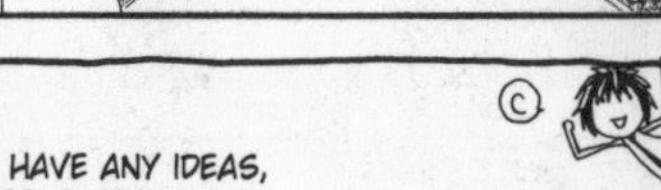
YEAH!

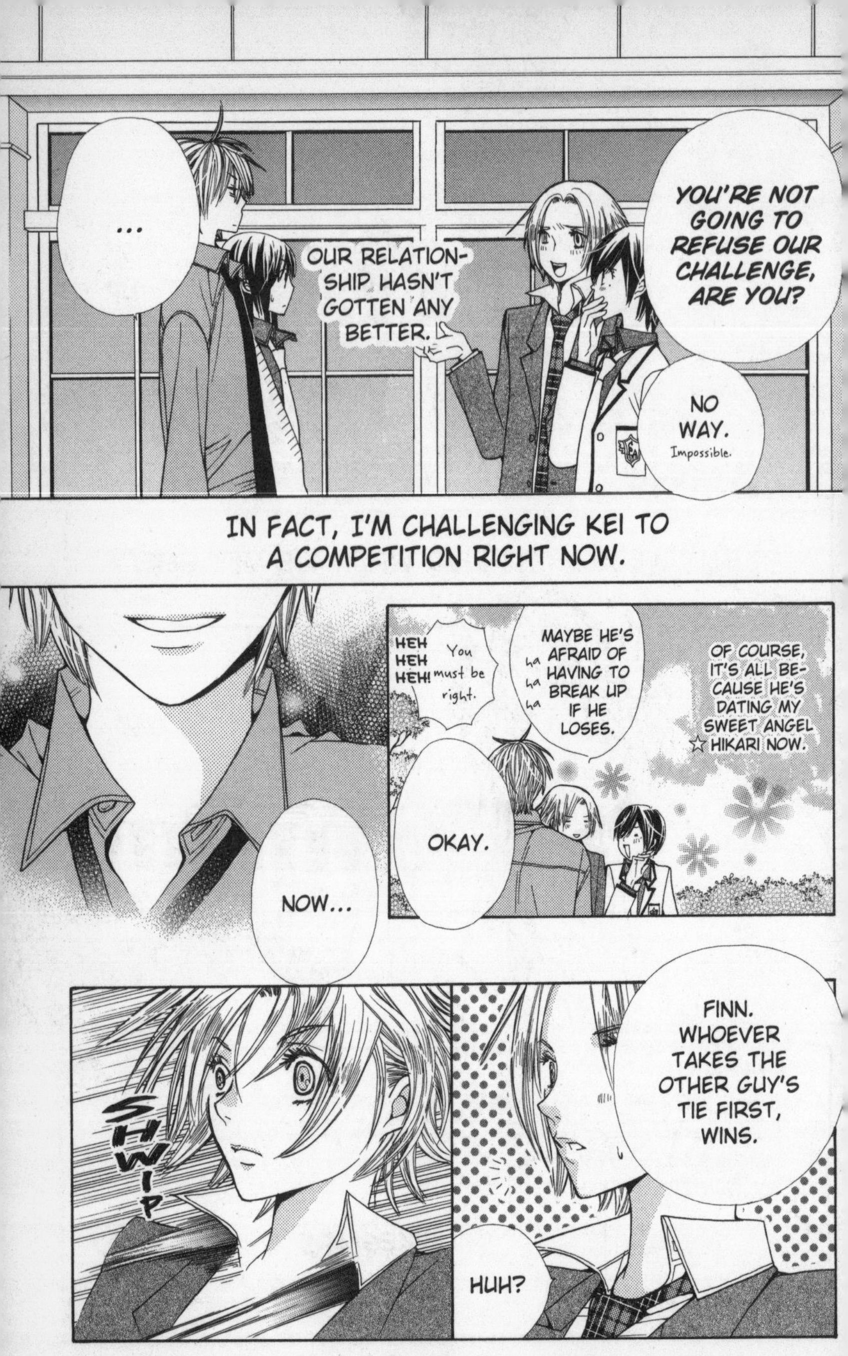
YOU'RE NOT GOING TO REFUSE OUR CHALLENGE, ARE YOU?
NO WAY.
Impossible.
OUR RELATION-SHIP HASN'T GOTTEN ANY BETTER.
...
IN FACT, I'M CHALLENGING KEI TO A COMPETITION RIGHT NOW.
OF COURSE, IT'S ALL BE-CAUSE HE'S DATING MY SWEET ANGEL ☆ HIKARI NOW.
MAYBE HE'S AFRAID OF HAVING TO BREAK UP IF HE LOSES.
ha ha ha
HEH HEH HEH!
You must be right.
OKAY.
NOW...
FINN. WHOEVER TAKES THE OTHER GUY'S TIE FIRST, WINS.
HUH?
SHWIP

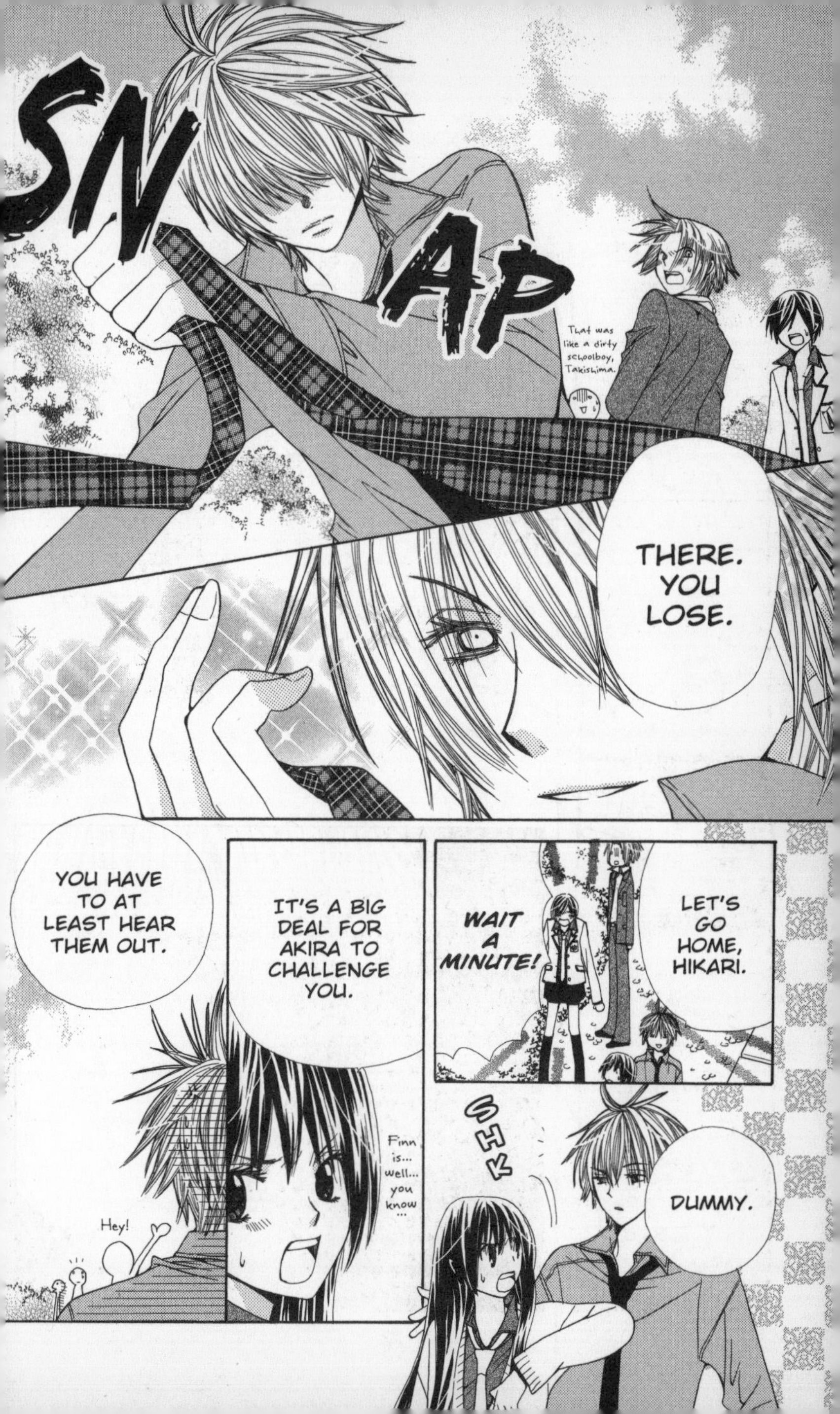
SNAP
That was like a dirty schoolboy, Takishima.
THERE. YOU LOSE.
LET'S GO HOME, HIKARI.
WAIT A MINUTE!
IT'S A BIG DEAL FOR AKIRA TO CHALLENGE YOU.
YOU HAVE TO AT LEAST HEAR THEM OUT.
SHK
DUMMY.
Finn is... well... you know ...
Hey!

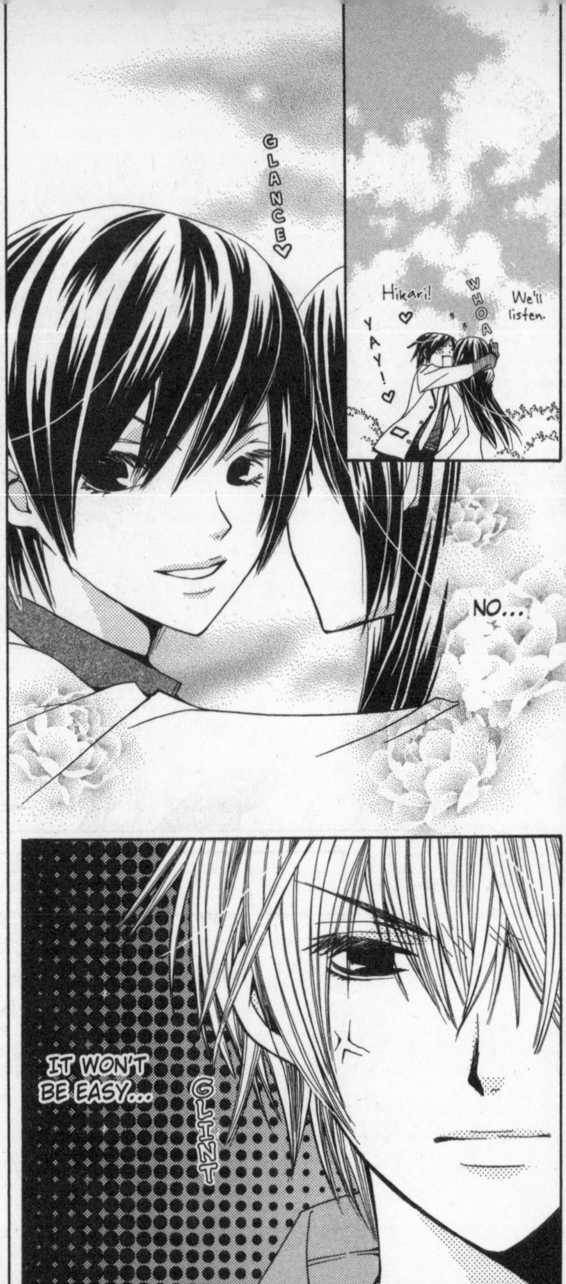
We'll listen.
WHOA
Hikari! ♡
YAY! ♡
GLANCE♡
NO...
GLINT
IT WON'T BE EASY...

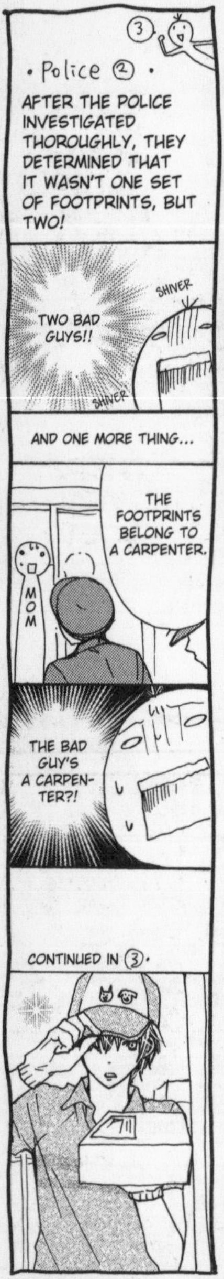
③
• Police ② •
AFTER THE POLICE INVESTIGATED THOROUGHLY, THEY DETERMINED THAT IT WASN'T ONE SET OF FOOTPRINTS, BUT TWO!
SHIVER
TWO BAD GUYS!!
SHIVER
AND ONE MORE THING...
THE FOOTPRINTS BELONG TO A CARPENTER.
MOM
THE BAD GUY'S A CARPENTER?!
CONTINUED IN ③.

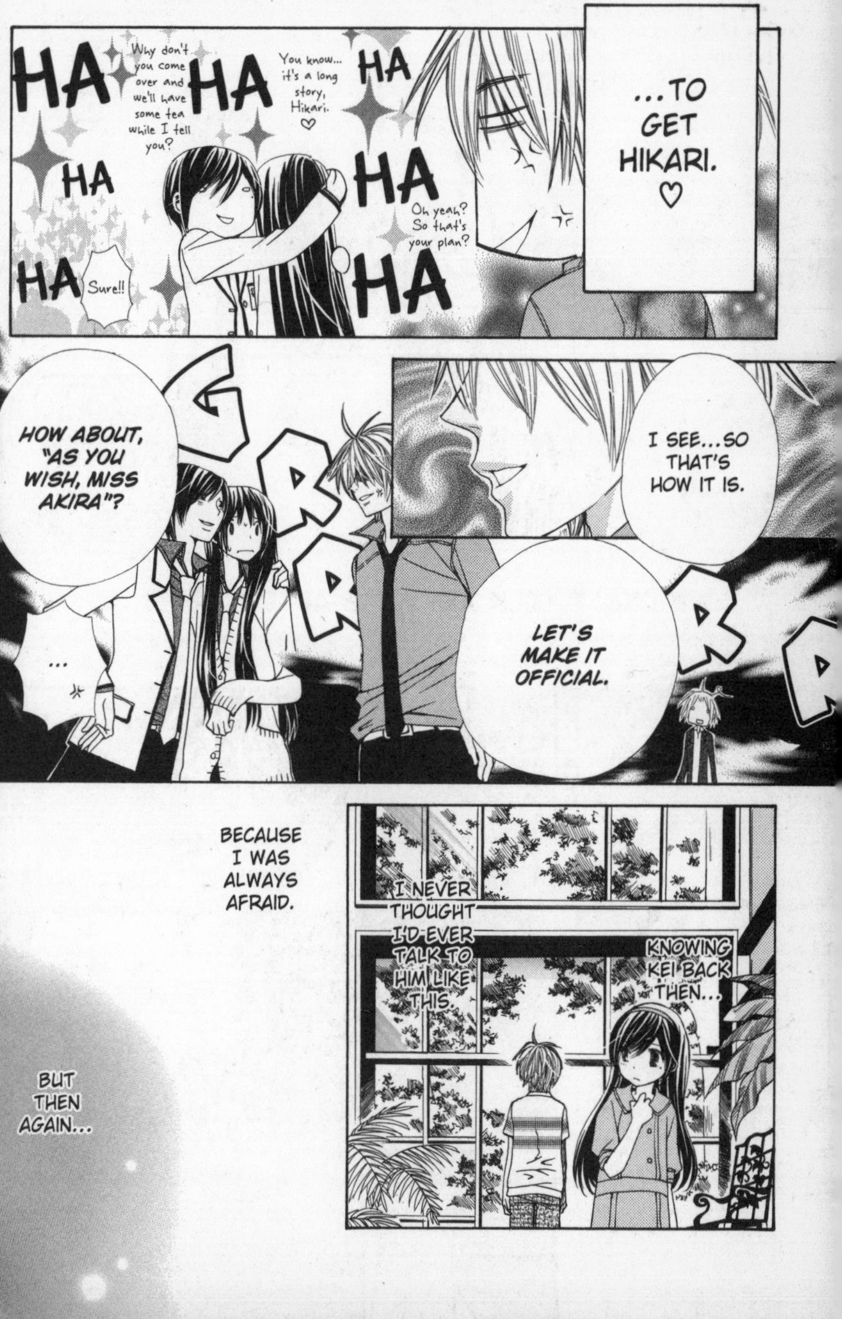
...TO GET HIKARI. ♡
Oh yeah? So that's your plan?
HA HA HA
You know... it's a long story, Hikari. ♡
HA
Why don't you come over and we'll have some tea while I tell you?
HA HA HA
Sure!!
I SEE...SO THAT'S HOW IT IS.
LET'S MAKE IT OFFICIAL.
GRRRR
HOW ABOUT, "AS YOU WISH, MISS AKIRA"?
...
KNOWING KEI BACK THEN...
I NEVER THOUGHT I'D EVER TALK TO HIM LIKE THIS.
BECAUSE I WAS ALWAYS AFRAID.
BUT THEN AGAIN...

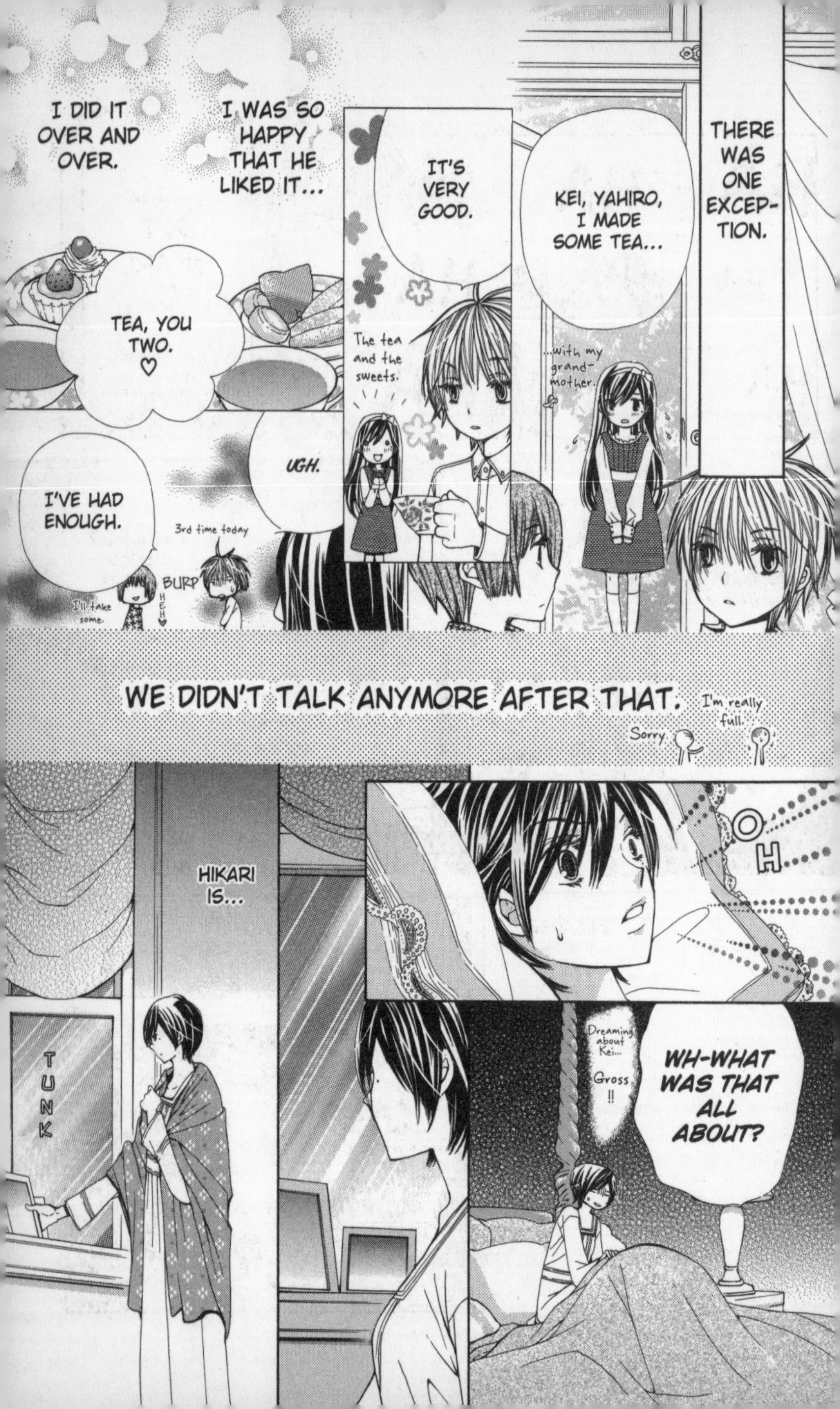
THERE WAS ONE EXCEPTION.
KEI, YAHIRO, I MADE SOME TEA...
...with my grandmother.
IT'S VERY GOOD.
The tea and the sweets.
I WAS SO HAPPY THAT HE LIKED IT...
I DID IT OVER AND OVER.
TEA, YOU TWO. ♡
UGH.
3rd time today
BURP
HEH♥
I'VE HAD ENOUGH.
I'll take some.
WE DIDN'T TALK ANYMORE AFTER THAT.
I'm really full.
Sorry.
OH
WH-WHAT WAS THAT ALL ABOUT?
Dreaming about Kei... Gross!!
HIKARI IS...
TUNK

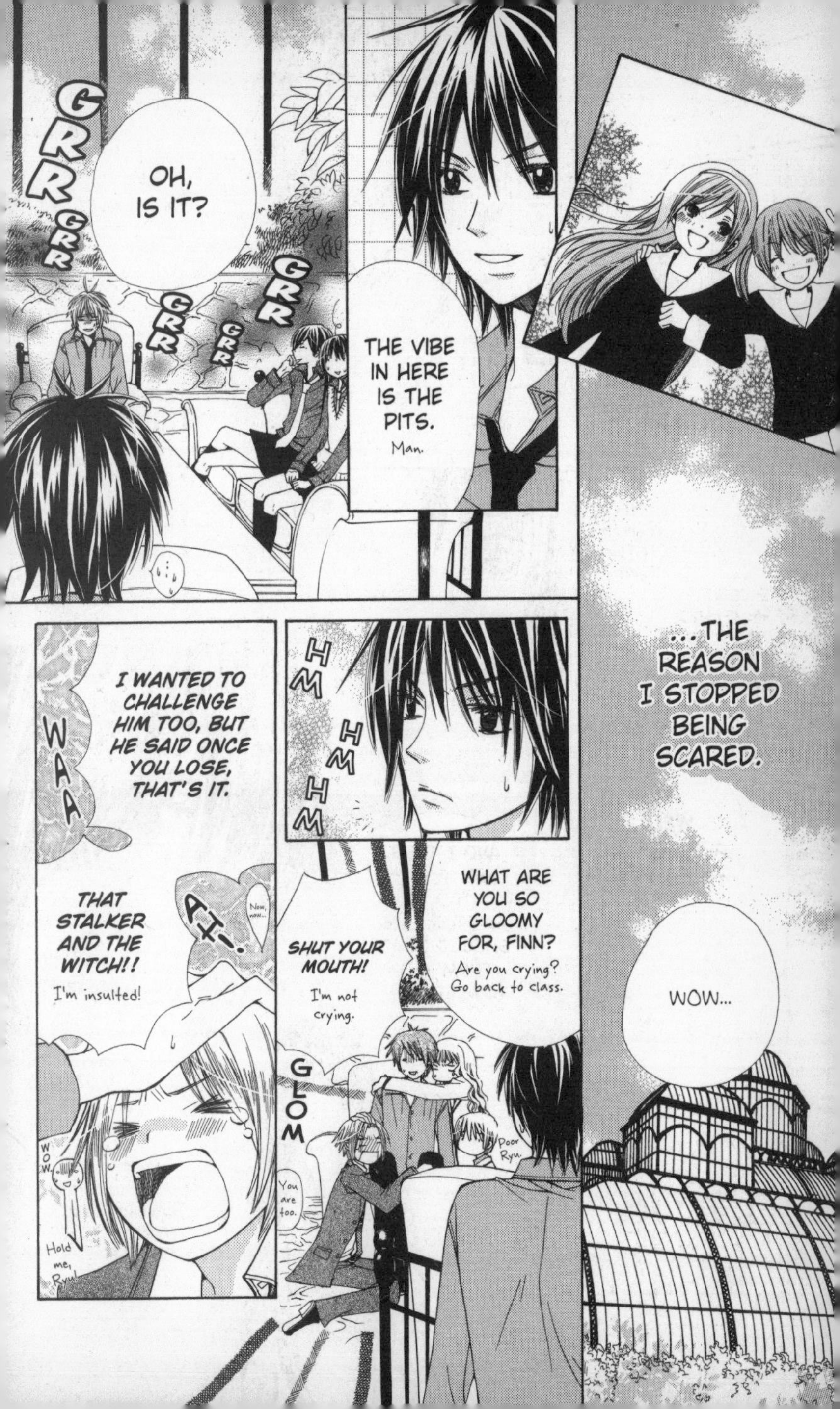
THE VIBE IN HERE IS THE PITS.
Man.
OH, IS IT?
GRR GRR GRR
GRR GRR GRR
...
...THE REASON I STOPPED BEING SCARED.
WOW...
HM HM HM HM
I WANTED TO CHALLENGE HIM TOO, BUT HE SAID ONCE YOU LOSE, THAT'S IT.
WAA
WHAT ARE YOU SO GLOOMY FOR, FINN?
Are you crying? Go back to class.
SHUT YOUR MOUTH!
I'm not crying.
GLOM
Poor Ryu.
You are too.
THAT STALKER AND THE WITCH!!
I'm insulted!
AI-.
Now, now...
WOW.
Hold me, Ryu!

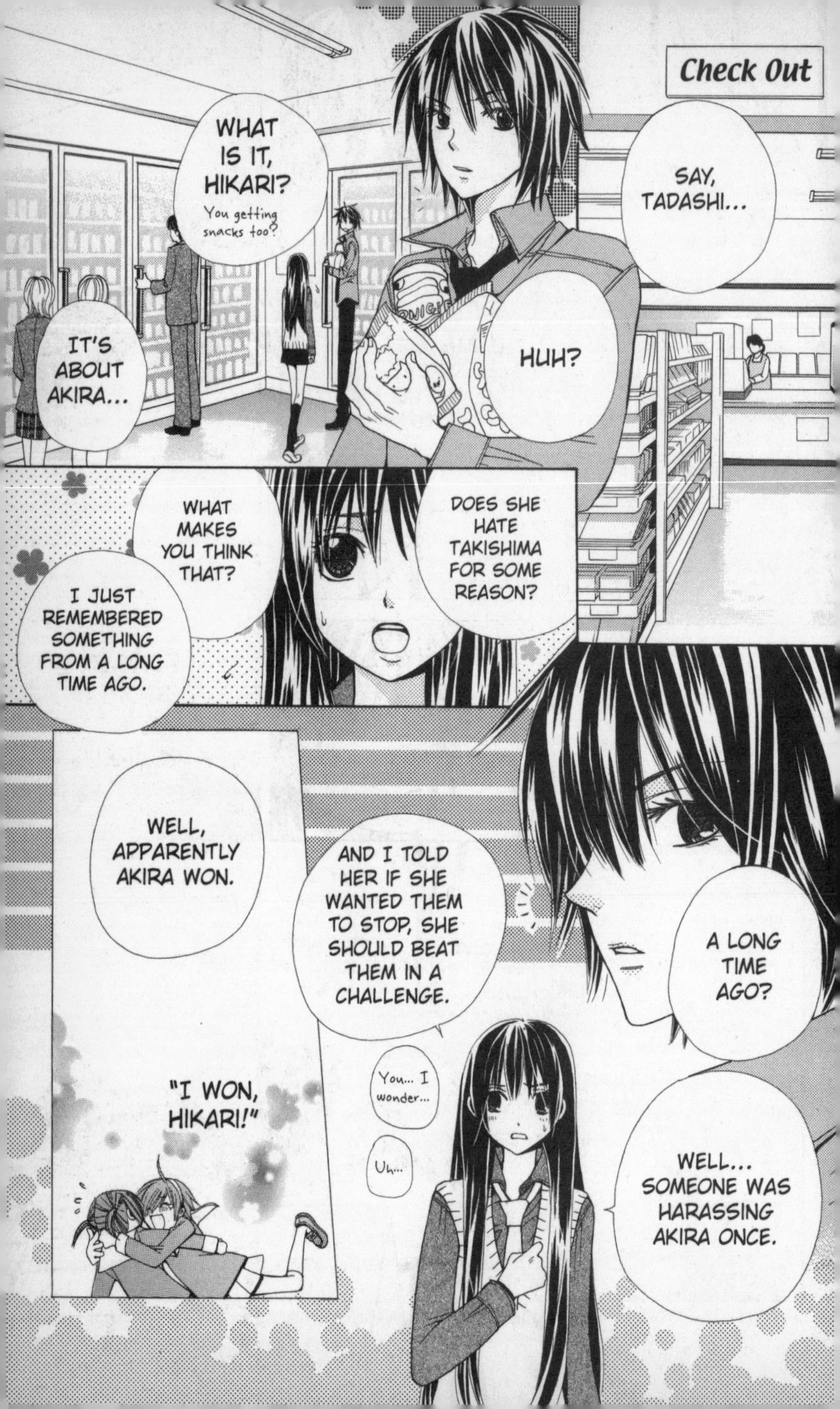

Check Out
SAY, TADASHI...
HUH?
WHAT IS IT, HIKARI?
You getting snacks too?
IT'S ABOUT AKIRA...
DOES SHE HATE TAKISHIMA FOR SOME REASON?
WHAT MAKES YOU THINK THAT?
I JUST REMEMBERED SOMETHING FROM A LONG TIME AGO.
A LONG TIME AGO?
WELL... SOMEONE WAS HARASSING AKIRA ONCE.
You... I wonder...
Uh...
AND I TOLD HER IF SHE WANTED THEM TO STOP, SHE SHOULD BEAT THEM IN A CHALLENGE.
WELL, APPARENTLY AKIRA WON.
"I WON, HIKARI!"

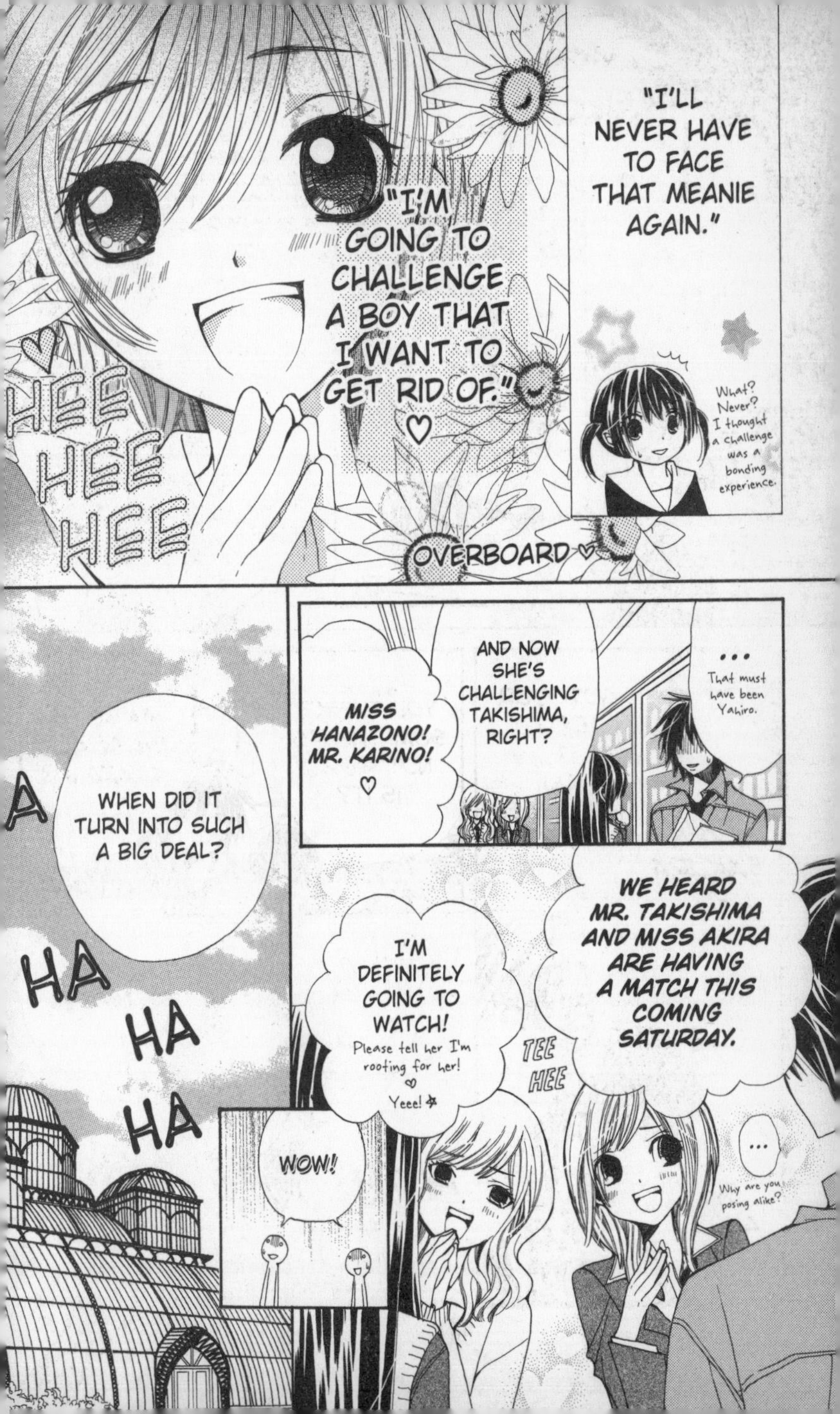
"I'LL NEVER HAVE TO FACE THAT MEANIE AGAIN."
What? Never? I thought a challenge was a bonding experience.
"I'M GOING TO CHALLENGE A BOY THAT I WANT TO GET RID OF." ♡
HEE HEE HEE
OVERBOARD ♡
...
That must have been Yahiro.
AND NOW SHE'S CHALLENGING TAKISHIMA, RIGHT?
MISS HANAZONO! MR. KARINO! ♡
WE HEARD MR. TAKISHIMA AND MISS AKIRA ARE HAVING A MATCH THIS COMING SATURDAY.
...
Why are you posing alike?
TEE HEE
I'M DEFINITELY GOING TO WATCH!
Please tell her I'm rooting for her! ♡ Yeee!
WOW!
WHEN DID IT TURN INTO SUCH A BIG DEAL?
A HA HA HA

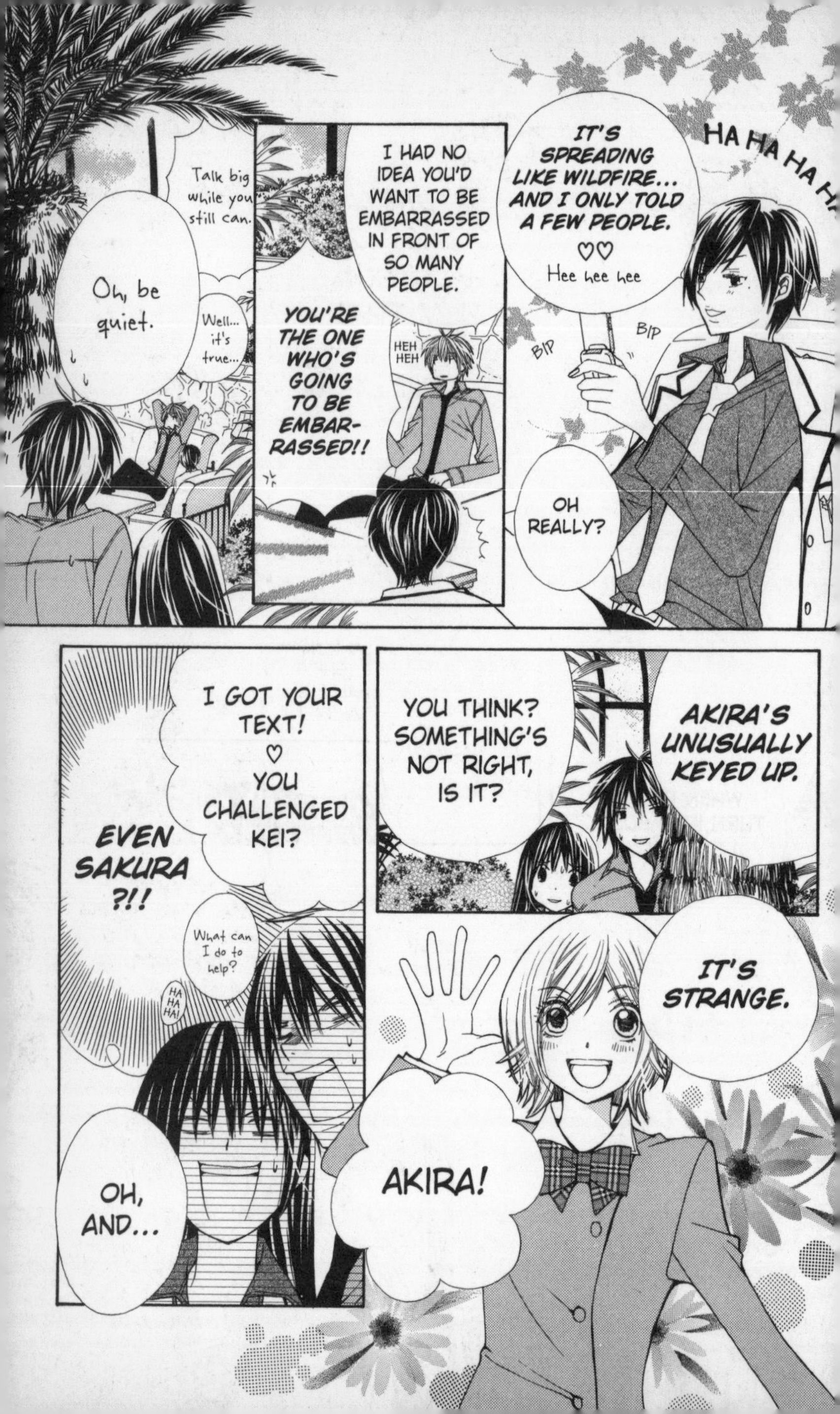
HA HA HA HA
IT'S SPREADING LIKE WILDFIRE... AND I ONLY TOLD A FEW PEOPLE. ♡♡
Hee hee hee
BIP
BIP
OH REALLY?
I HAD NO IDEA YOU'D WANT TO BE EMBARRASSED IN FRONT OF SO MANY PEOPLE.
HEH HEH
YOU'RE THE ONE WHO'S GOING TO BE EMBARRASSED!!
Talk big while you still can.
Well... it's true...
Oh, be quiet.
AKIRA'S UNUSUALLY KEYED UP.
YOU THINK? SOMETHING'S NOT RIGHT, IS IT?
IT'S STRANGE.
AKIRA!
I GOT YOUR TEXT! ♡ YOU CHALLENGED KEI?
EVEN SAKURA?!!
What can I do to help?
HA HA HA!
OH, AND...

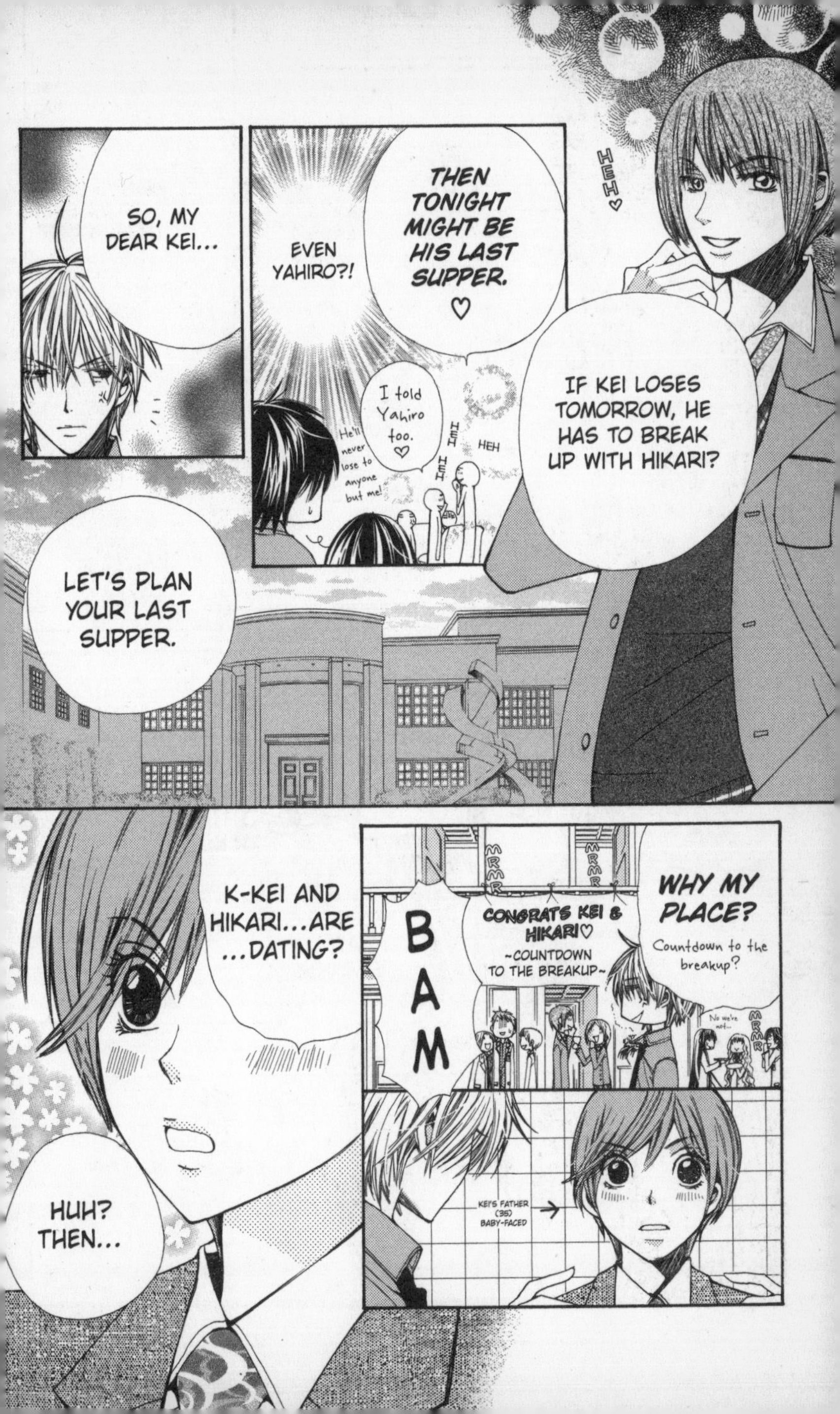

HEH ♡
IF KEI LOSES TOMORROW, HE HAS TO BREAK UP WITH HIKARI?
THEN TONIGHT MIGHT BE HIS LAST SUPPER. ♡
EVEN YAHIRO?!
I told Yahiro too. ♡
HEH HEH
HEH
He'll never lose to anyone but me!
SO, MY DEAR KEI...
LET'S PLAN YOUR LAST SUPPER.
WHY MY PLACE?
Countdown to the breakup?
MRMR
MRMR
CONGRATS KEI & HIKARI ♡
~COUNTDOWN TO THE BREAKUP~
No we're not...
MRMR
BAM
KEI'S FATHER (35) BABY-FACED
K-KEI AND HIKARI...ARE ...DATING?
HUH? THEN...

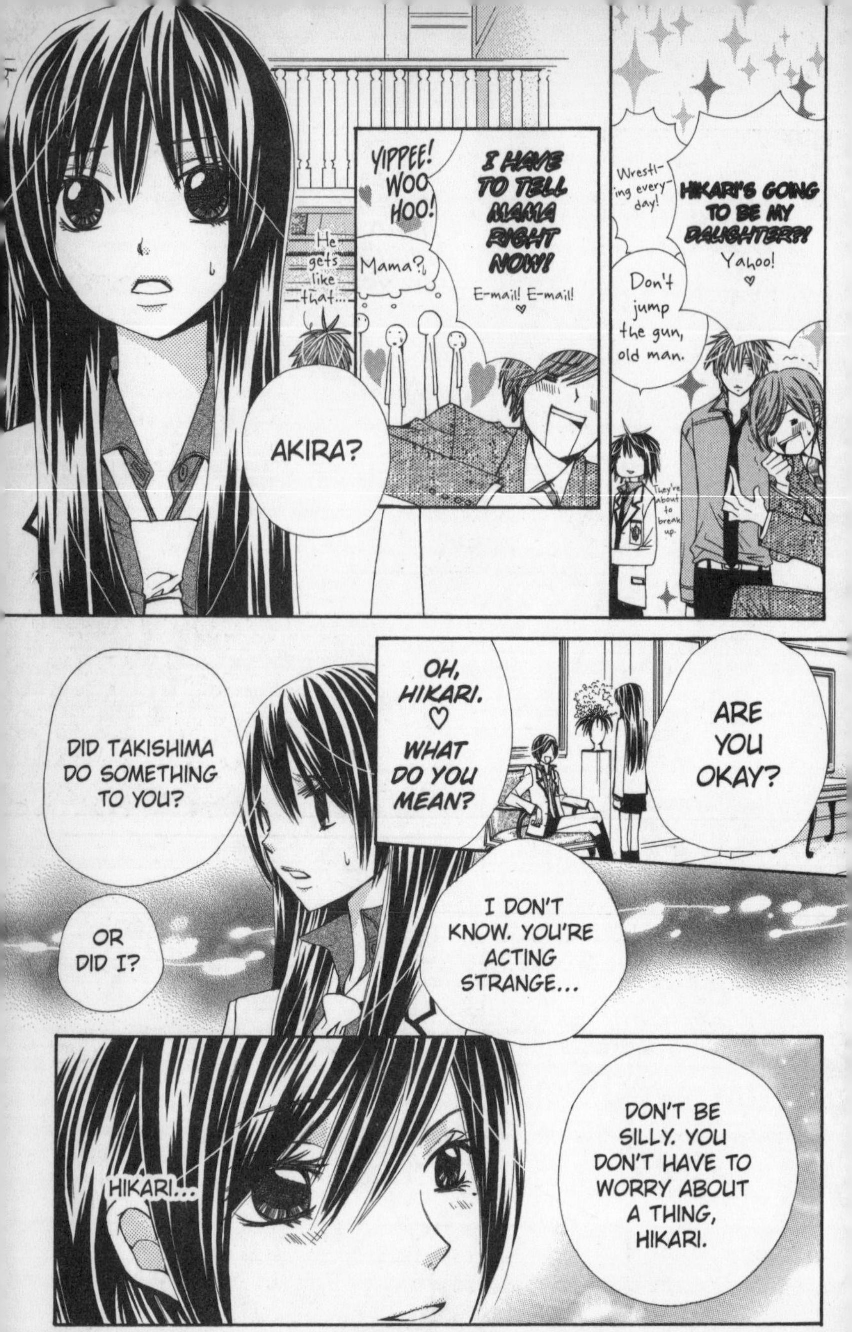
HIKARI'S GOING TO BE MY DAUGHTER?! Yahoo! ♡
Wrestling every day!
Don't jump the gun, old man.
They're about to break up.
I HAVE TO TELL MAMA RIGHT NOW!
E-mail! E-mail! ♡
YIPPEE! WOO HOO!
Mama?
He gets like that...
AKIRA?
ARE YOU OKAY?
OH, HIKARI. ♡ WHAT DO YOU MEAN?
I DON'T KNOW. YOU'RE ACTING STRANGE...
DID TAKISHIMA DO SOMETHING TO YOU?
OR DID I?
DON'T BE SILLY. YOU DON'T HAVE TO WORRY ABOUT A THING, HIKARI.
HIKARI...

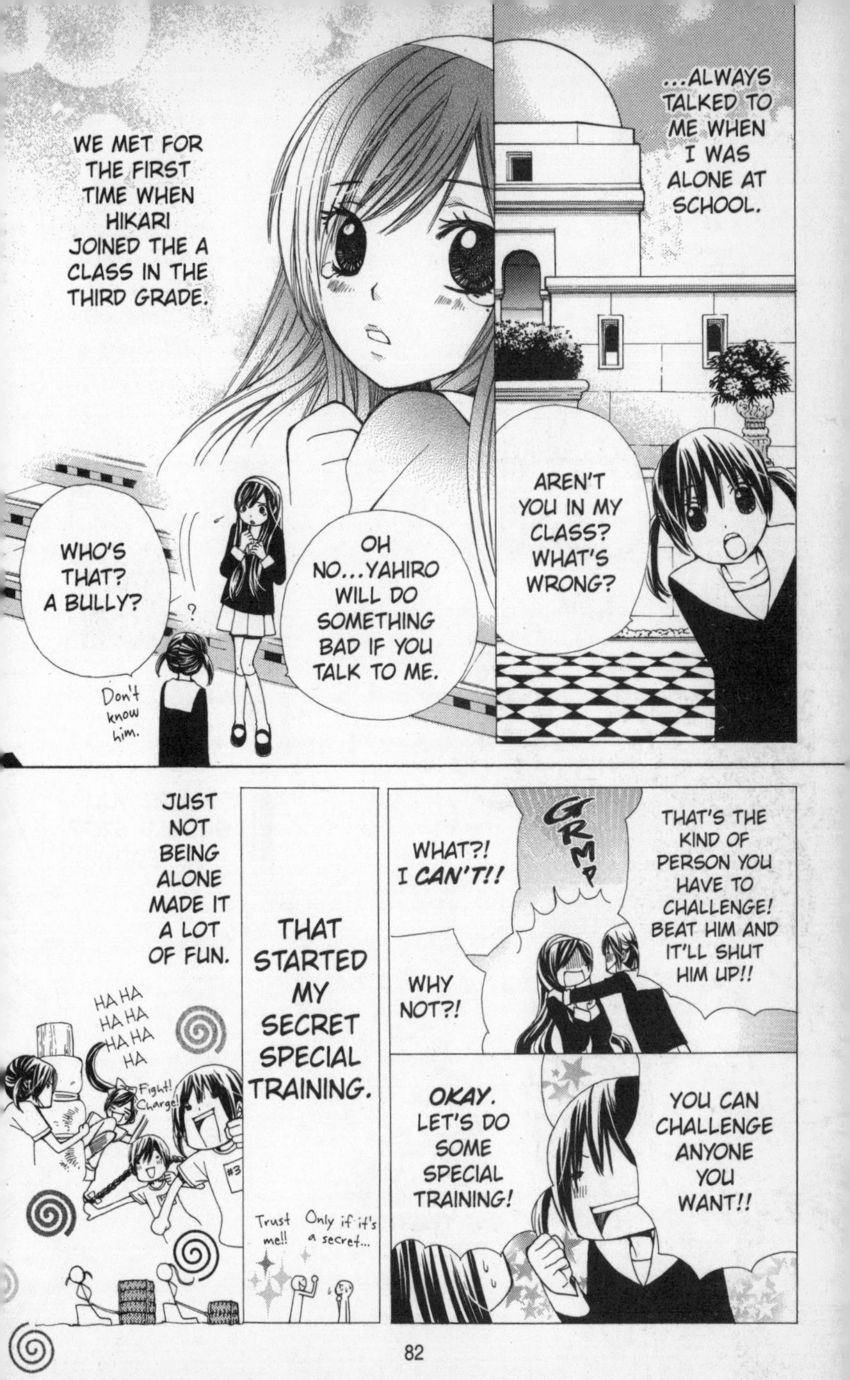
...ALWAYS TALKED TO ME WHEN I WAS ALONE AT SCHOOL.
AREN'T YOU IN MY CLASS? WHAT'S WRONG?
WE MET FOR THE FIRST TIME WHEN HIKARI JOINED THE A CLASS IN THE THIRD GRADE.
OH NO...YAHIRO WILL DO SOMETHING BAD IF YOU TALK TO ME.
WHO'S THAT? A BULLY?
?
Don't know him.
THAT'S THE KIND OF PERSON YOU HAVE TO CHALLENGE! BEAT HIM AND IT'LL SHUT HIM UP!!
GRMP
WHAT?! I CAN'T!!
WHY NOT?!
YOU CAN CHALLENGE ANYONE YOU WANT!!
OKAY. LET'S DO SOME SPECIAL TRAINING!
THAT STARTED MY SECRET SPECIAL TRAINING.
Only if it's a secret...
Trust me!!
JUST NOT BEING ALONE MADE IT A LOT OF FUN.
HA HA HA HA HA HA HA
Fight! Charge!

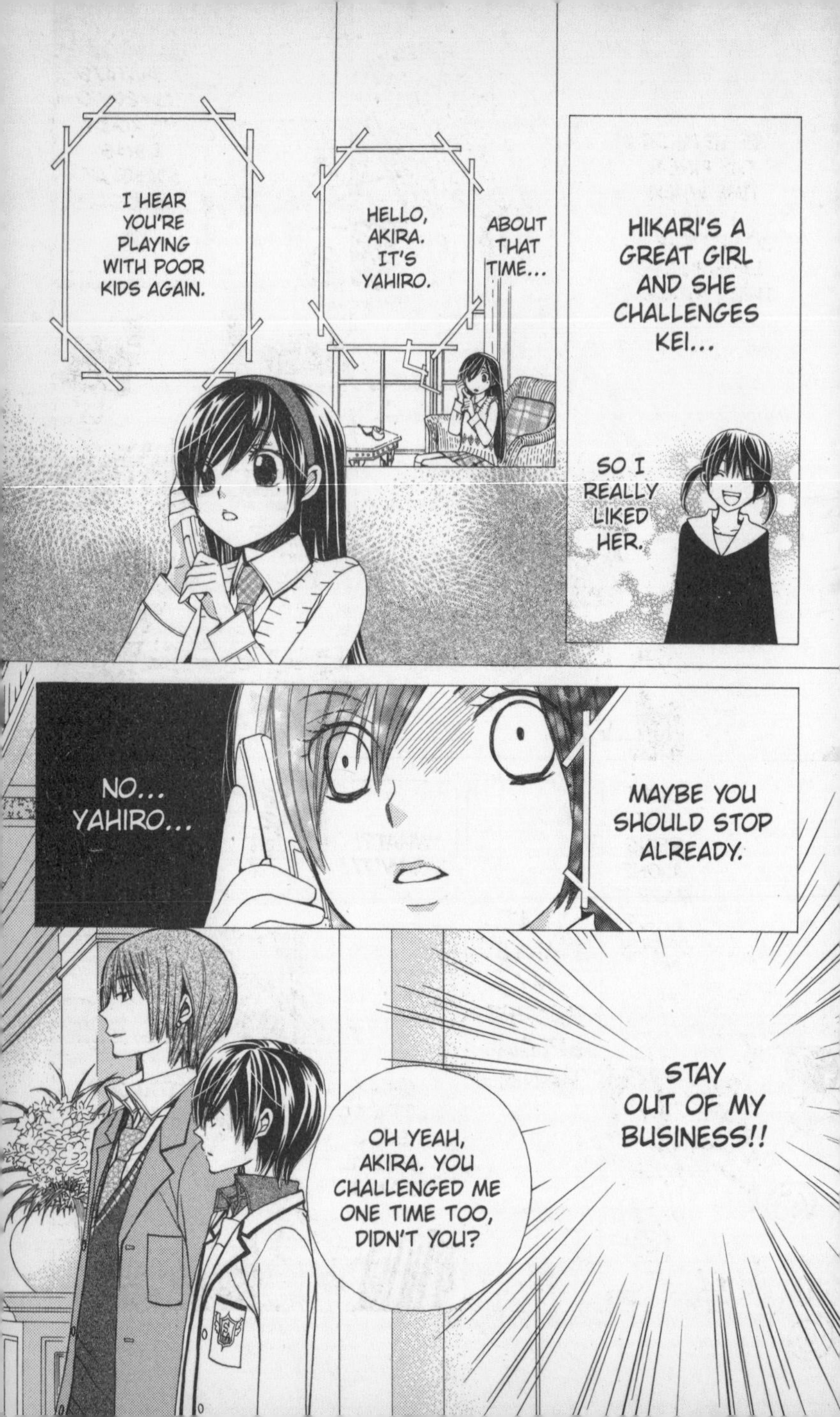
HIKARI'S A GREAT GIRL AND SHE CHALLENGES KEI...
SO I REALLY LIKED HER.
ABOUT THAT TIME...
HELLO, AKIRA. IT'S YAHIRO.
I HEAR YOU'RE PLAYING WITH POOR KIDS AGAIN.
MAYBE YOU SHOULD STOP ALREADY.
NO... YAHIRO...
STAY OUT OF MY BUSINESS!!
OH YEAH, AKIRA. YOU CHALLENGED ME ONE TIME TOO, DIDN'T YOU?

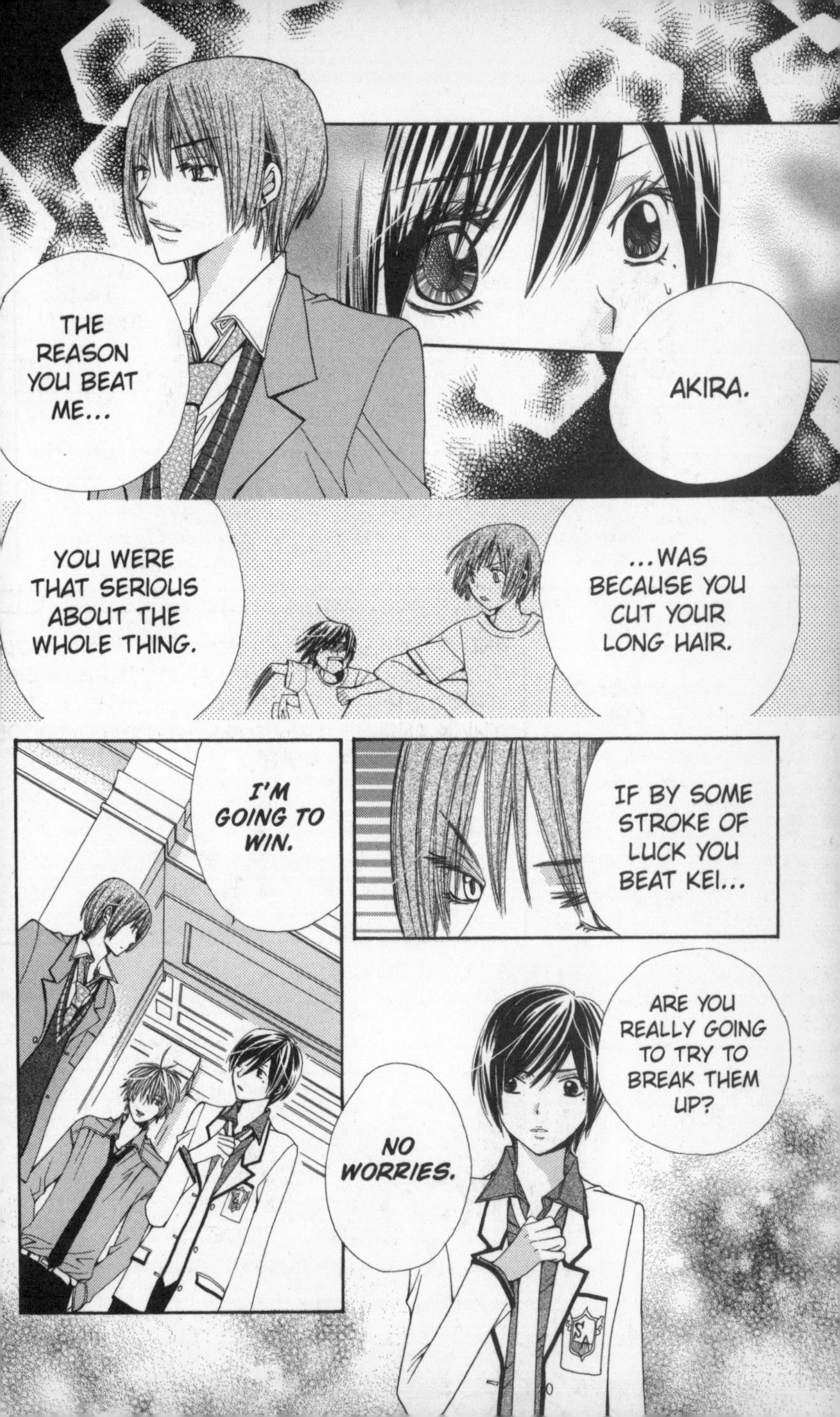
AKIRA.
THE REASON YOU BEAT ME...
...WAS BECAUSE YOU CUT YOUR LONG HAIR.
YOU WERE THAT SERIOUS ABOUT THE WHOLE THING.
IF BY SOME STROKE OF LUCK YOU BEAT KEI...
ARE YOU REALLY GOING TO TRY TO BREAK THEM UP?
NO WORRIES.
I'M GOING TO WIN.

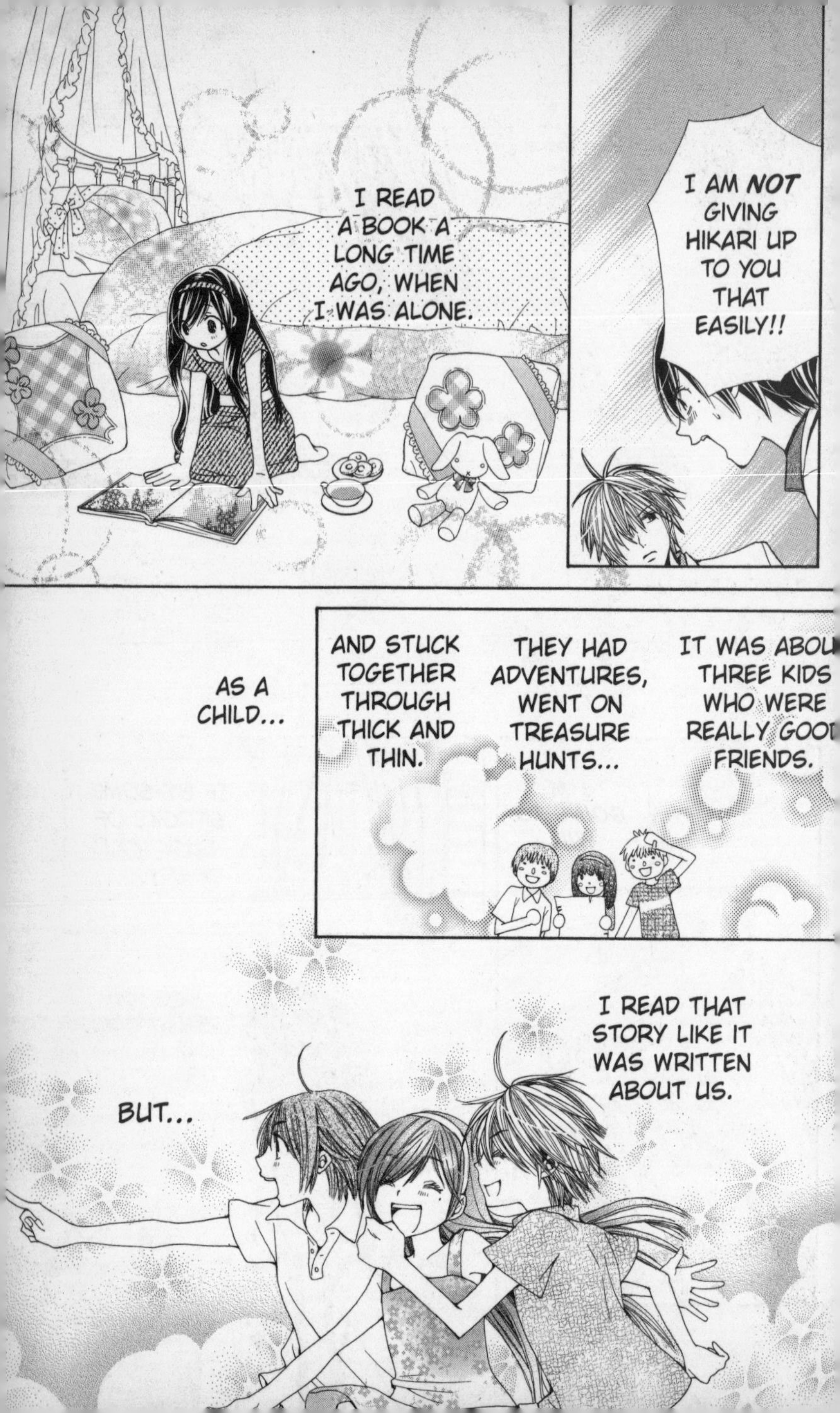
I AM NOT GIVING HIKARI UP TO YOU THAT EASILY!!
I READ A BOOK A LONG TIME AGO, WHEN I WAS ALONE.
IT WAS ABOU THREE KIDS WHO WERE REALLY GOO FRIENDS.
THEY HAD ADVENTURES, WENT ON TREASURE HUNTS...
AND STUCK TOGETHER THROUGH THICK AND THIN.
AS A CHILD...
I READ THAT STORY LIKE IT WAS WRITTEN ABOUT US.
BUT...

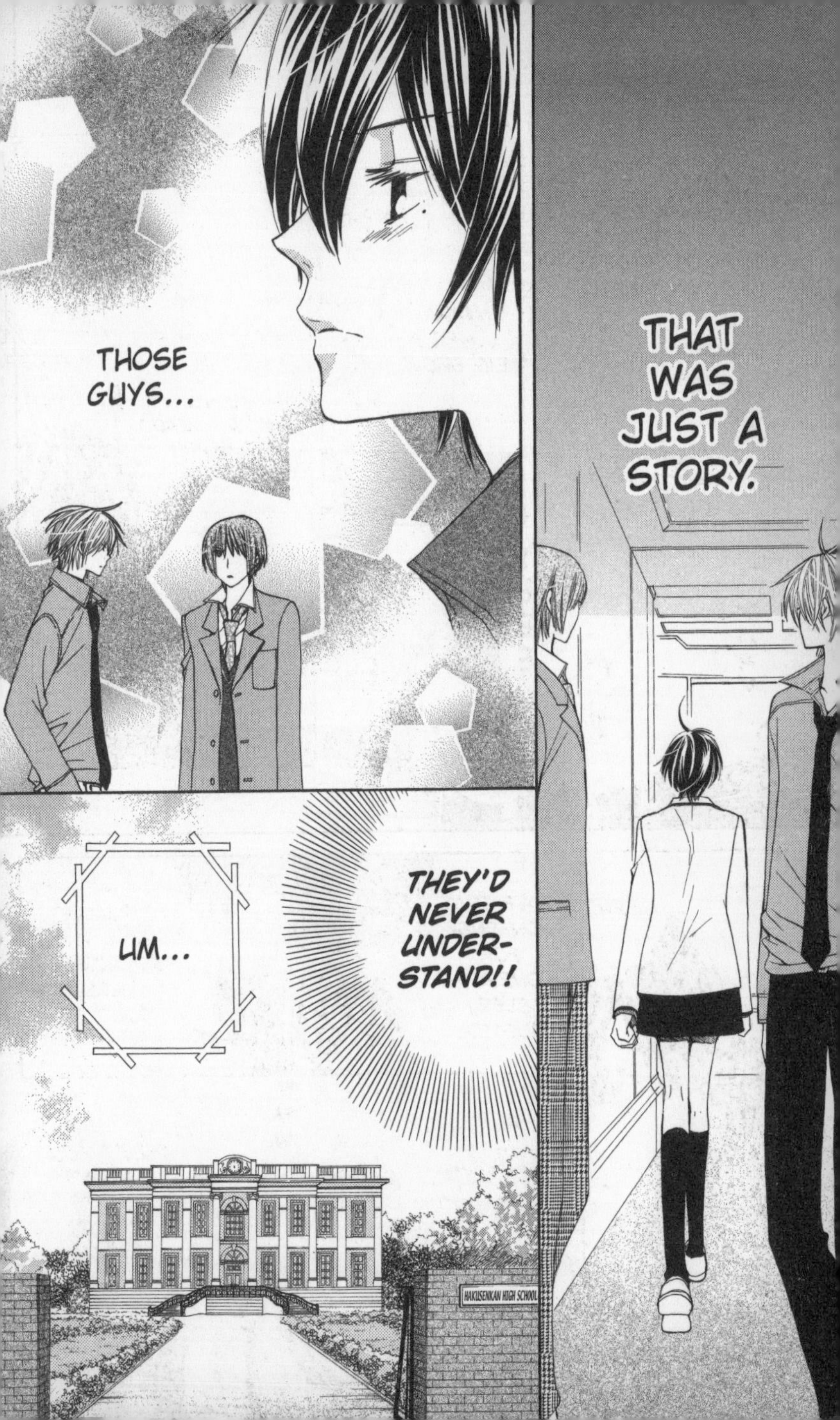
THAT WAS JUST A STORY.
THOSE GUYS...
THEY'D NEVER UNDER-STAND!!
UM...
HAKUSENKAN HIGH SCHOOL

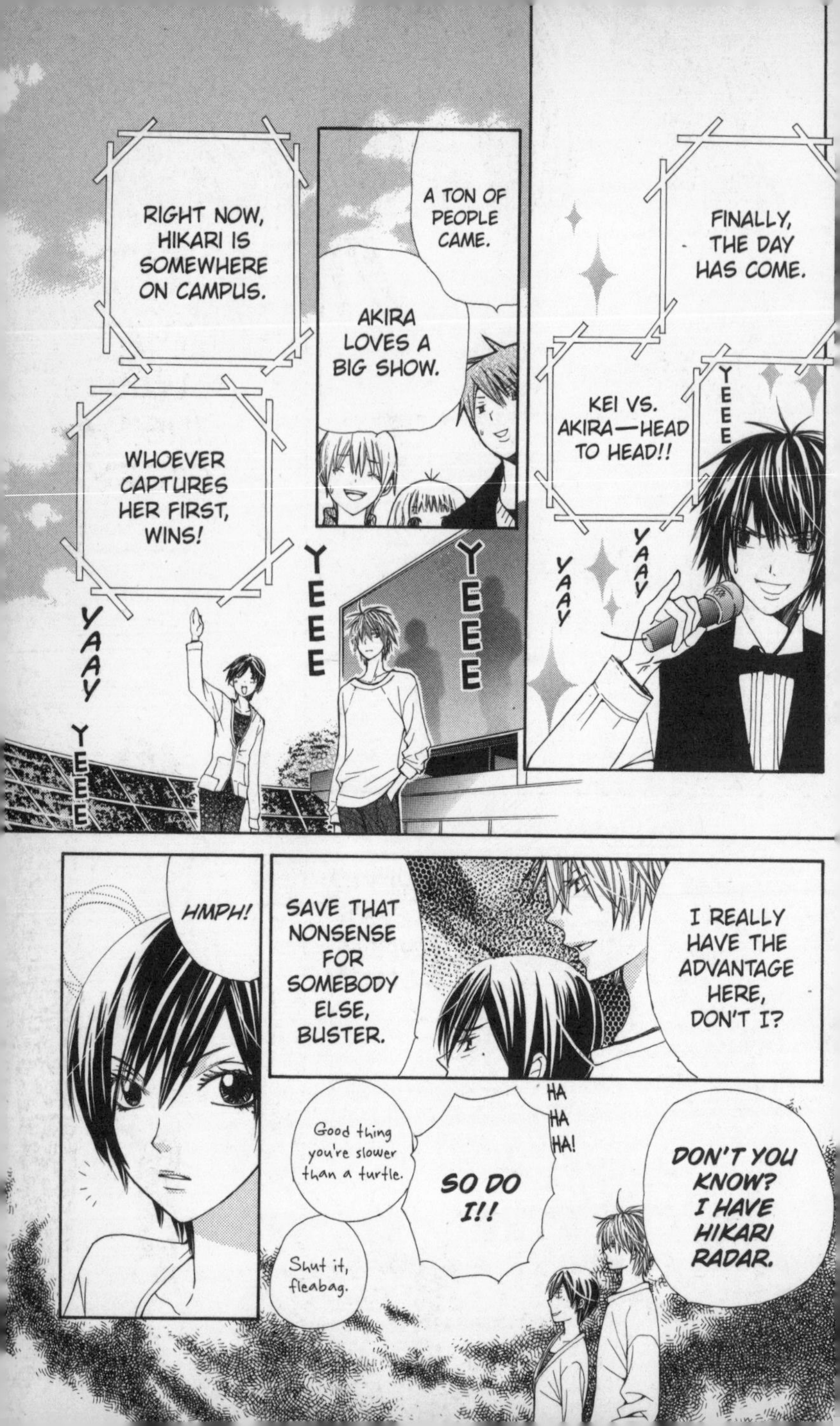
FINALLY, THE DAY HAS COME.
KEI VS. AKIRA—HEAD TO HEAD!!
YEEE
YAAY
YAAY
A TON OF PEOPLE CAME.
AKIRA LOVES A BIG SHOW.
RIGHT NOW, HIKARI IS SOMEWHERE ON CAMPUS.
WHOEVER CAPTURES HER FIRST, WINS!
YEEE
YEEE
YAAY
YEEE
I REALLY HAVE THE ADVANTAGE HERE, DON'T I?
SAVE THAT NONSENSE FOR SOMEBODY ELSE, BUSTER.
DON'T YOU KNOW? I HAVE HIKARI RADAR.
HA HA HA!
SO DO I!!
Good thing you're slower than a turtle.
Shut it, fleabag.
HMPH!

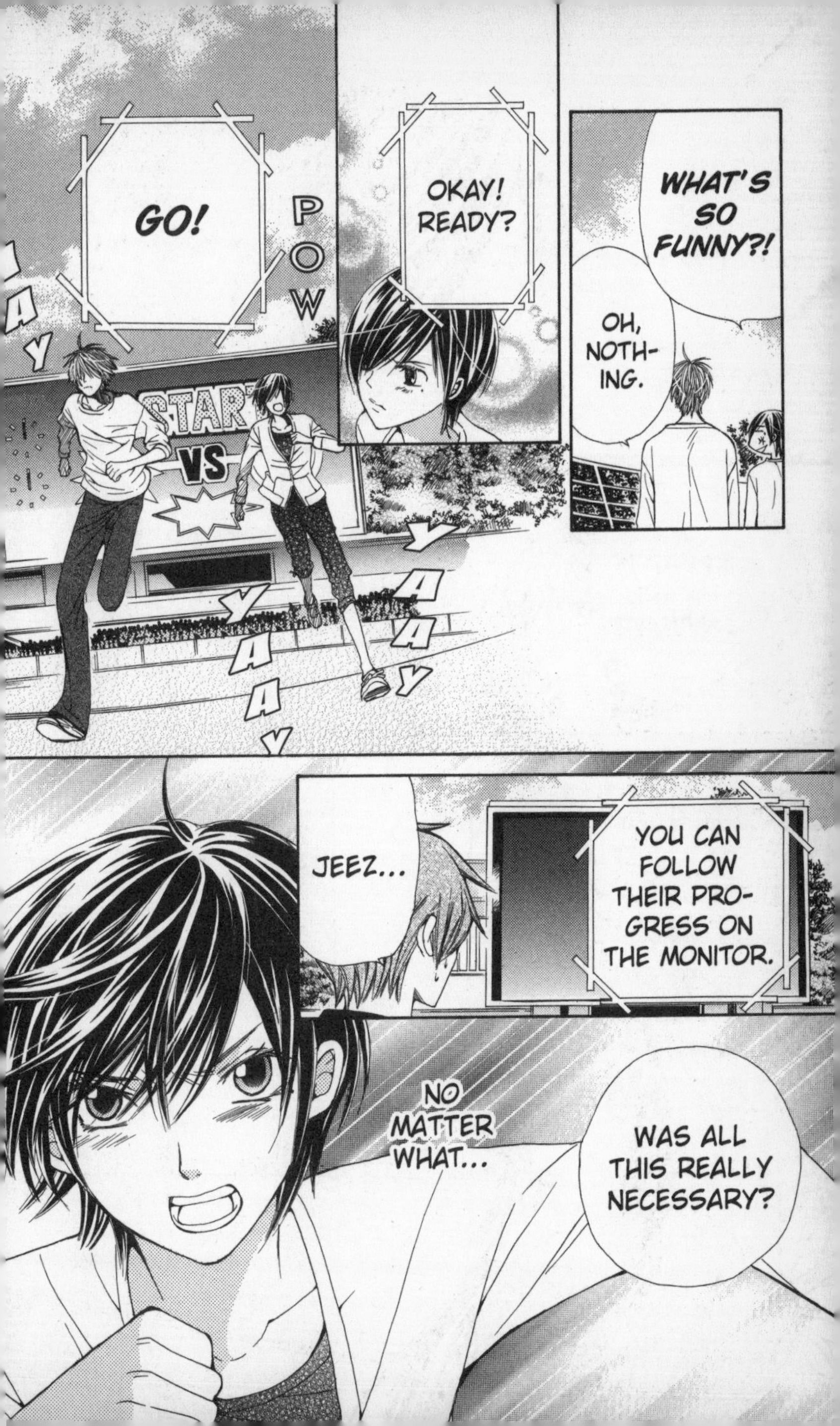
WHAT'S SO FUNNY?!
OH, NOTHING.
OKAY! READY?
GO!
POW
START
VS
YAAY
YAAY
YOU CAN FOLLOW THEIR PROGRESS ON THE MONITOR.
JEEZ...
WAS ALL THIS REALLY NECESSARY?
NO MATTER WHAT...

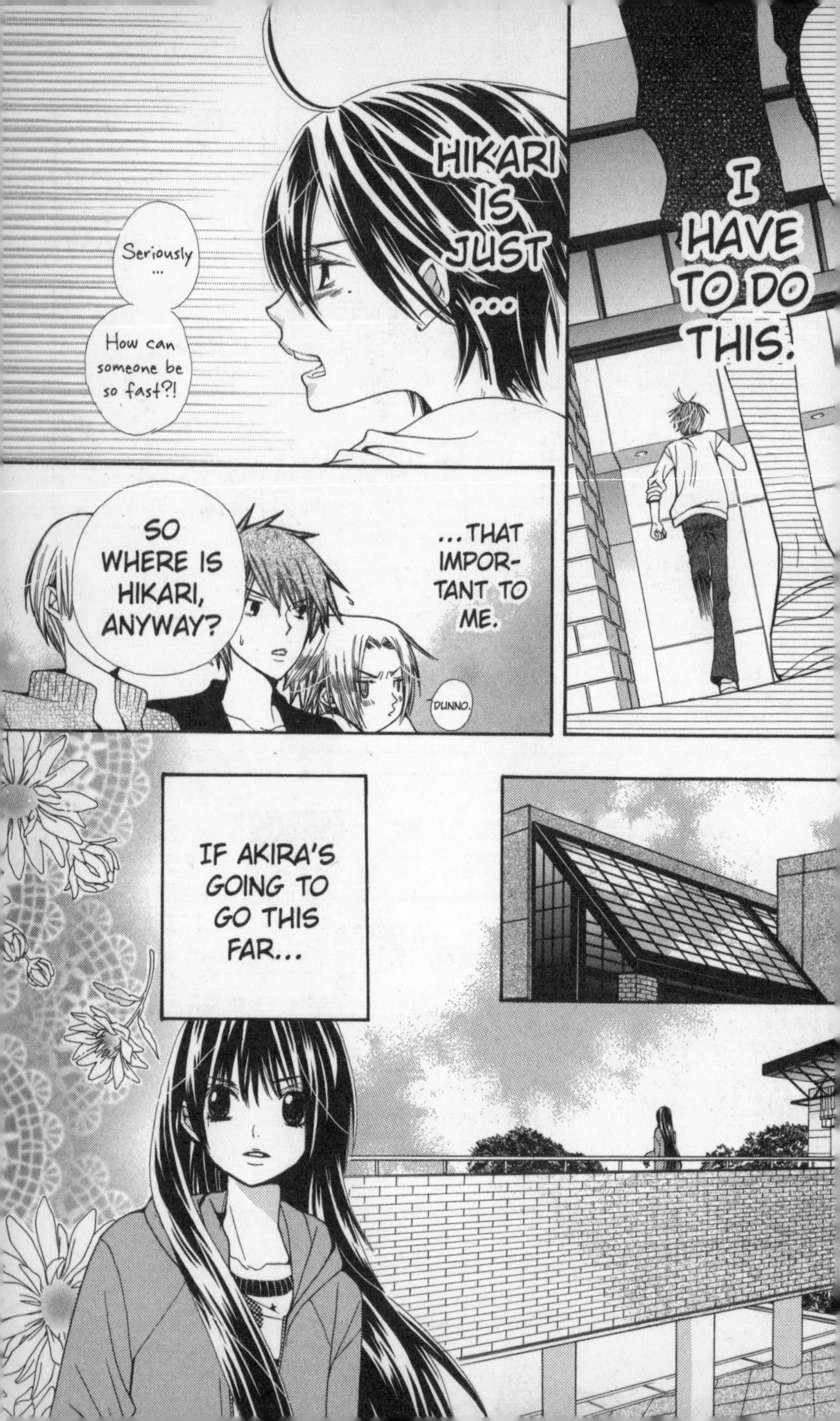
I HAVE TO DO THIS.
HIKARI IS JUST...
Seriously...
How can someone be so fast?!
...THAT IMPORTANT TO ME.
SO WHERE IS HIKARI, ANYWAY?
DUNNO.
IF AKIRA'S GOING TO GO THIS FAR...

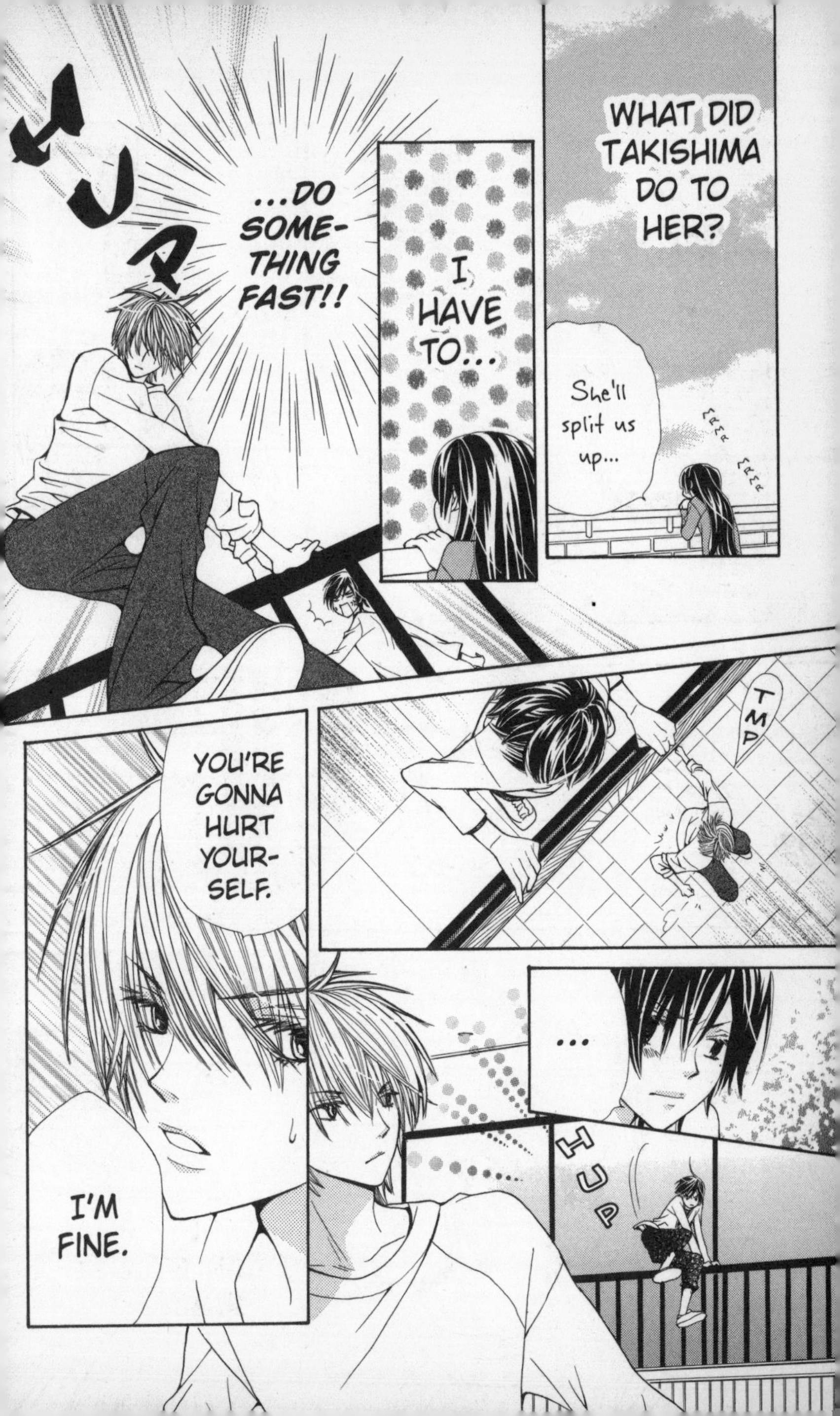
WHAT DID TAKISHIMA DO TO HER?
She'll split us up...
I HAVE TO...
...DO SOMETHING FAST!!
JUMP
TMP
...
HUP
YOU'RE GONNA HURT YOURSELF.
I'M FINE.

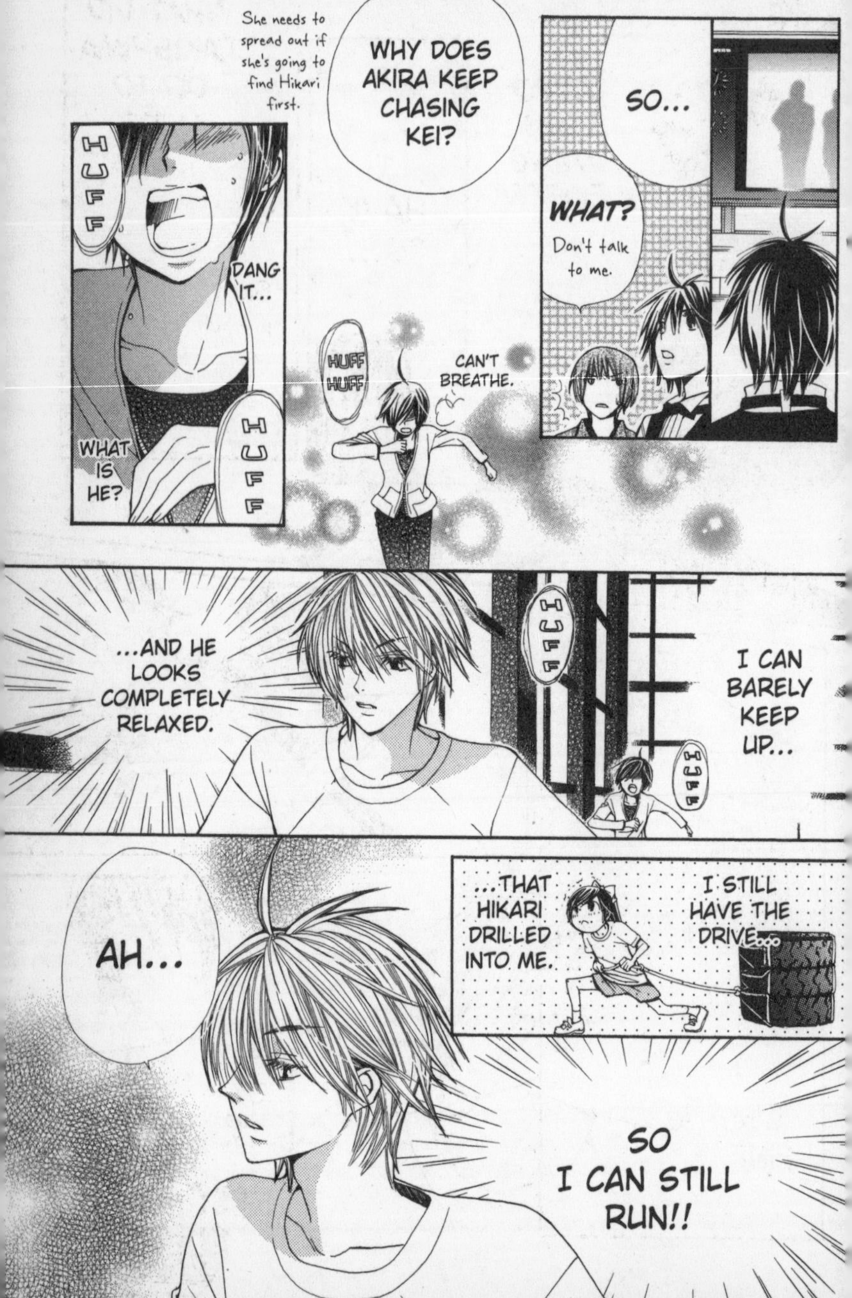

SO...
WHAT? Don't talk to me.
WHY DOES AKIRA KEEP CHASING KEI?
She needs to spread out if she's going to find Hikari first.
HUFF
DANG IT...
WHAT IS HE?
HUFF
CAN'T BREATHE.
HUFF HUFF
I CAN BARELY KEEP UP...
HUFF
HUFF
...AND HE LOOKS COMPLETELY RELAXED.
I STILL HAVE THE DRIVE...
...THAT HIKARI DRILLED INTO ME.
SO I CAN STILL RUN!!
AH...

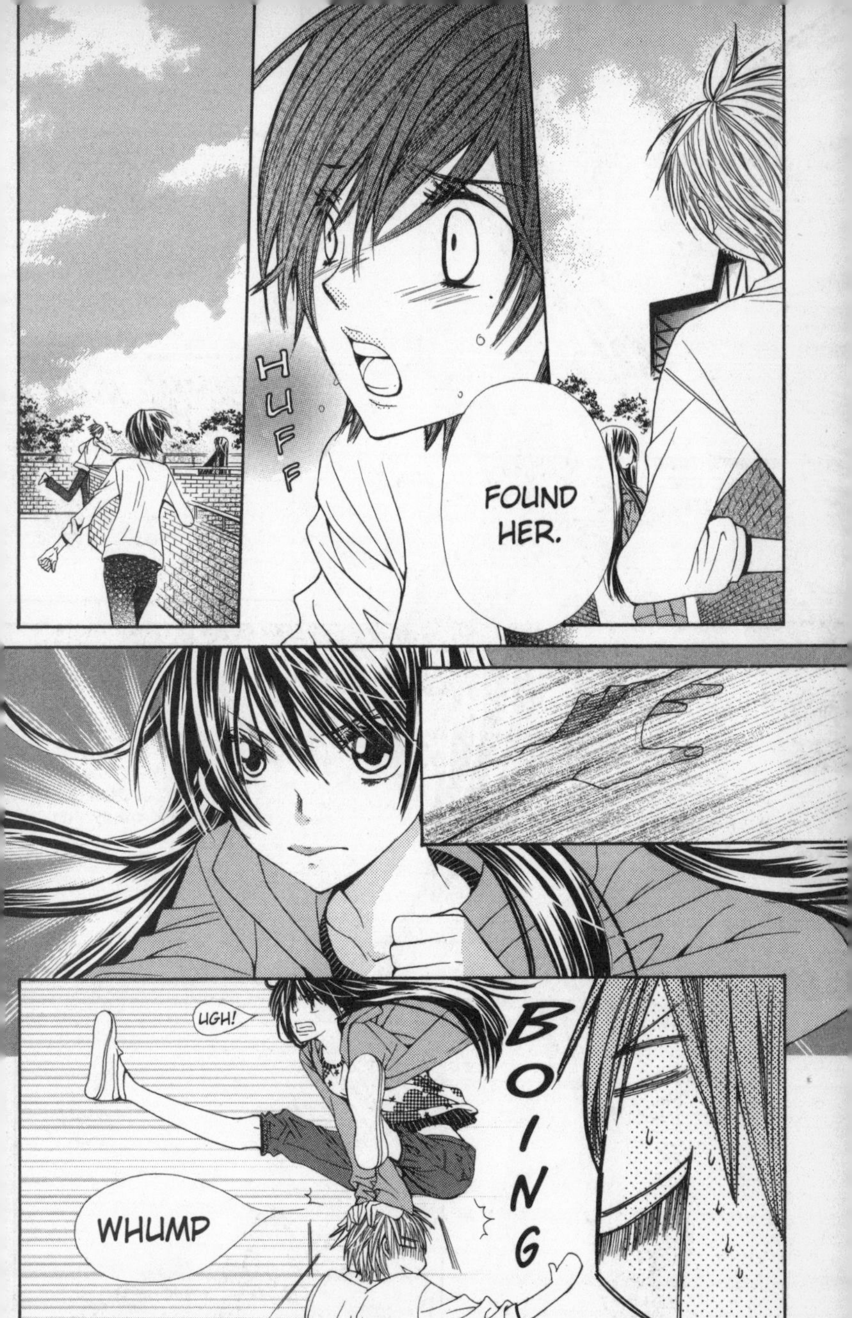
FOUND HER.
HUFF
BOING
UGH!
WHUMP

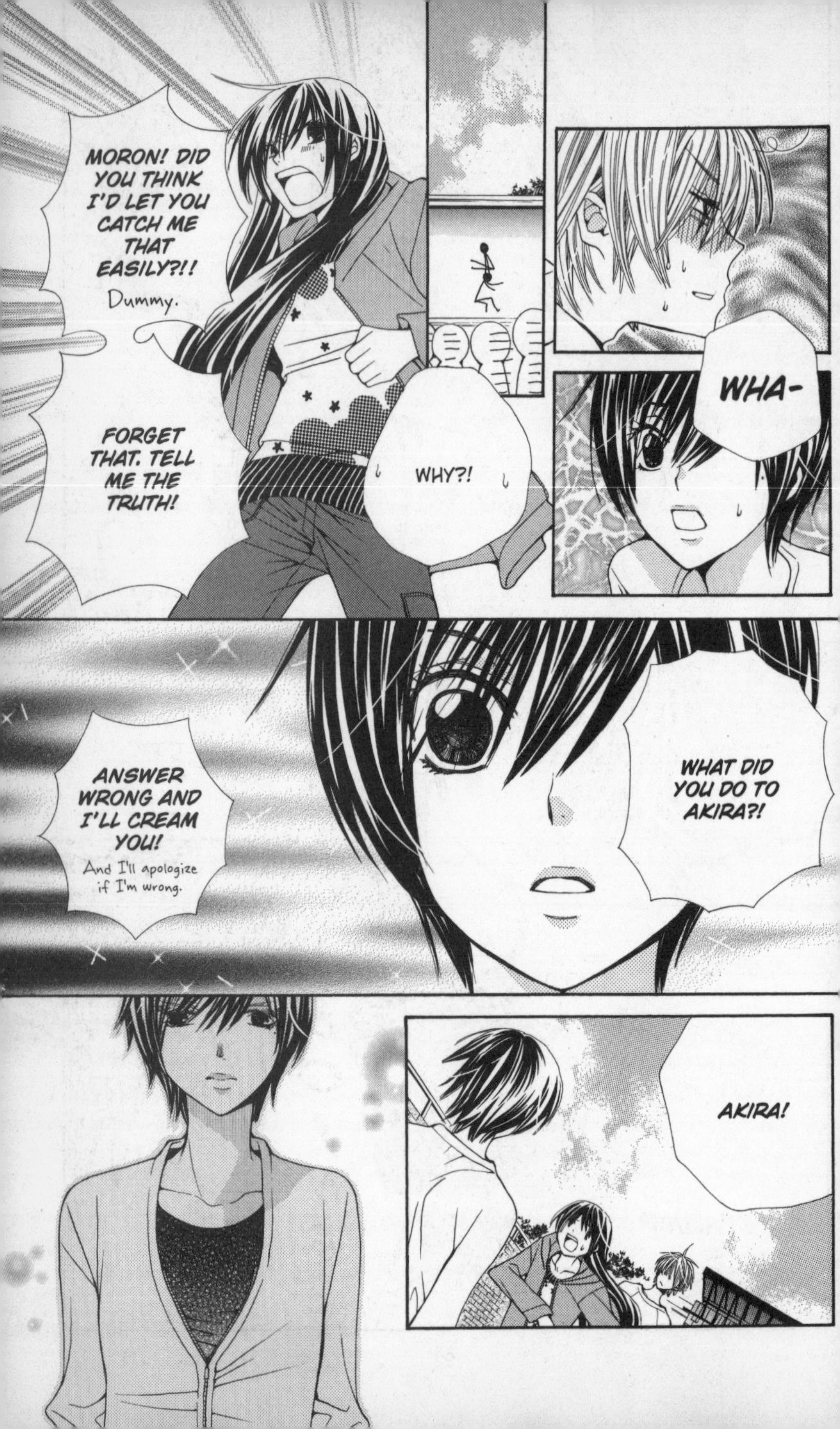
WHA-
WHY?!
MORON! DID YOU THINK I'D LET YOU CATCH ME THAT EASILY?!!
Dummy.
FORGET THAT. TELL ME THE TRUTH!
WHAT DID YOU DO TO AKIRA?!
ANSWER WRONG AND I'LL CREAM YOU!
And I'll apologize if I'm wrong.
AKIRA!

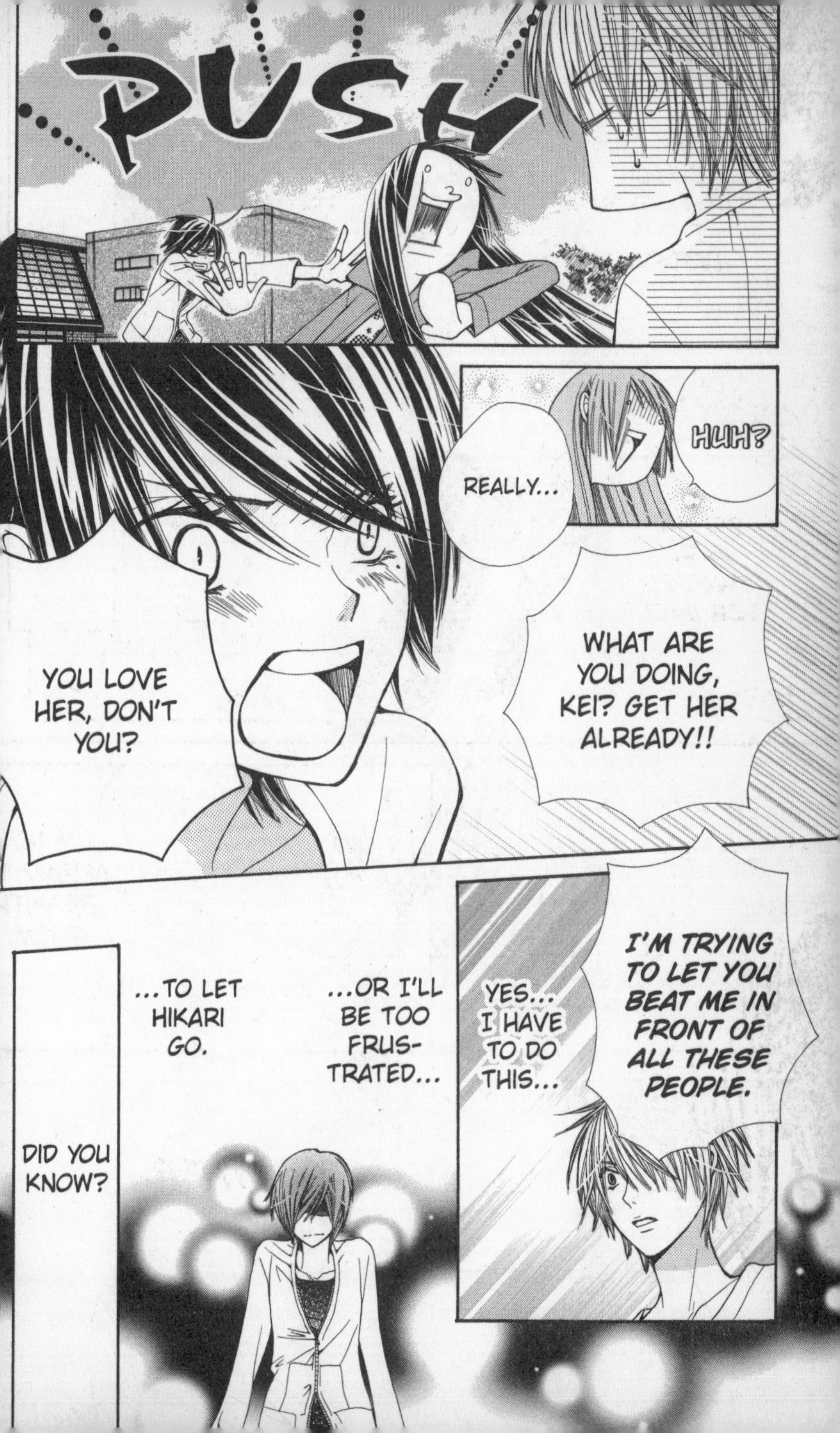
PUSH
HUH?
REALLY...
WHAT ARE YOU DOING, KEI? GET HER ALREADY!!
YOU LOVE HER, DON'T YOU?
I'M TRYING TO LET YOU BEAT ME IN FRONT OF ALL THESE PEOPLE.
YES... I HAVE TO DO THIS...
...OR I'LL BE TOO FRUS-TRATED...
...TO LET HIKARI GO.
DID YOU KNOW?

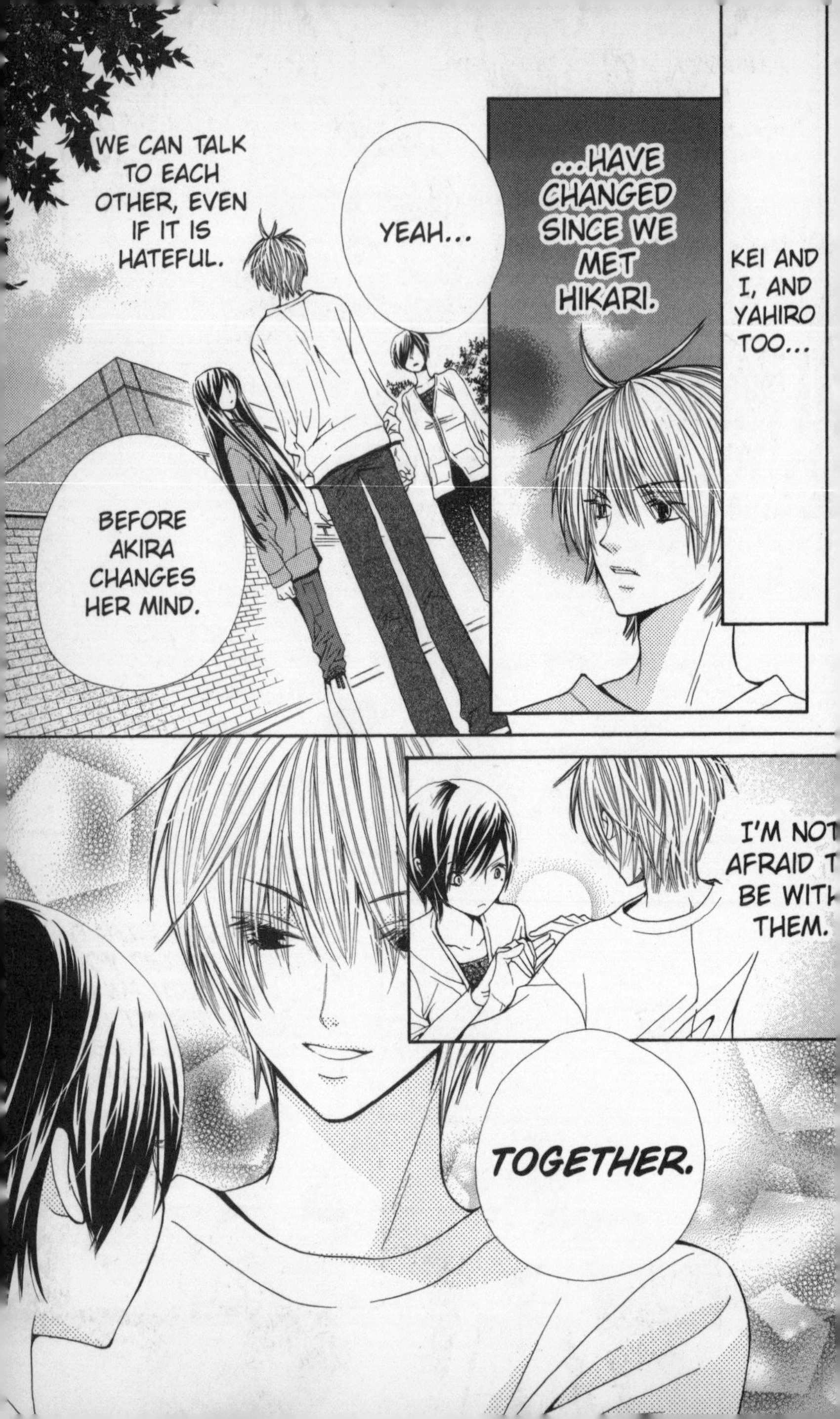
KEI AND I, AND YAHIRO TOO...
...HAVE CHANGED SINCE WE MET HIKARI.
WE CAN TALK TO EACH OTHER, EVEN IF IT IS HATEFUL.
YEAH...
BEFORE AKIRA CHANGES HER MIND.
I'M NOT AFRAID T BE WITH THEM.
TOGETHER.

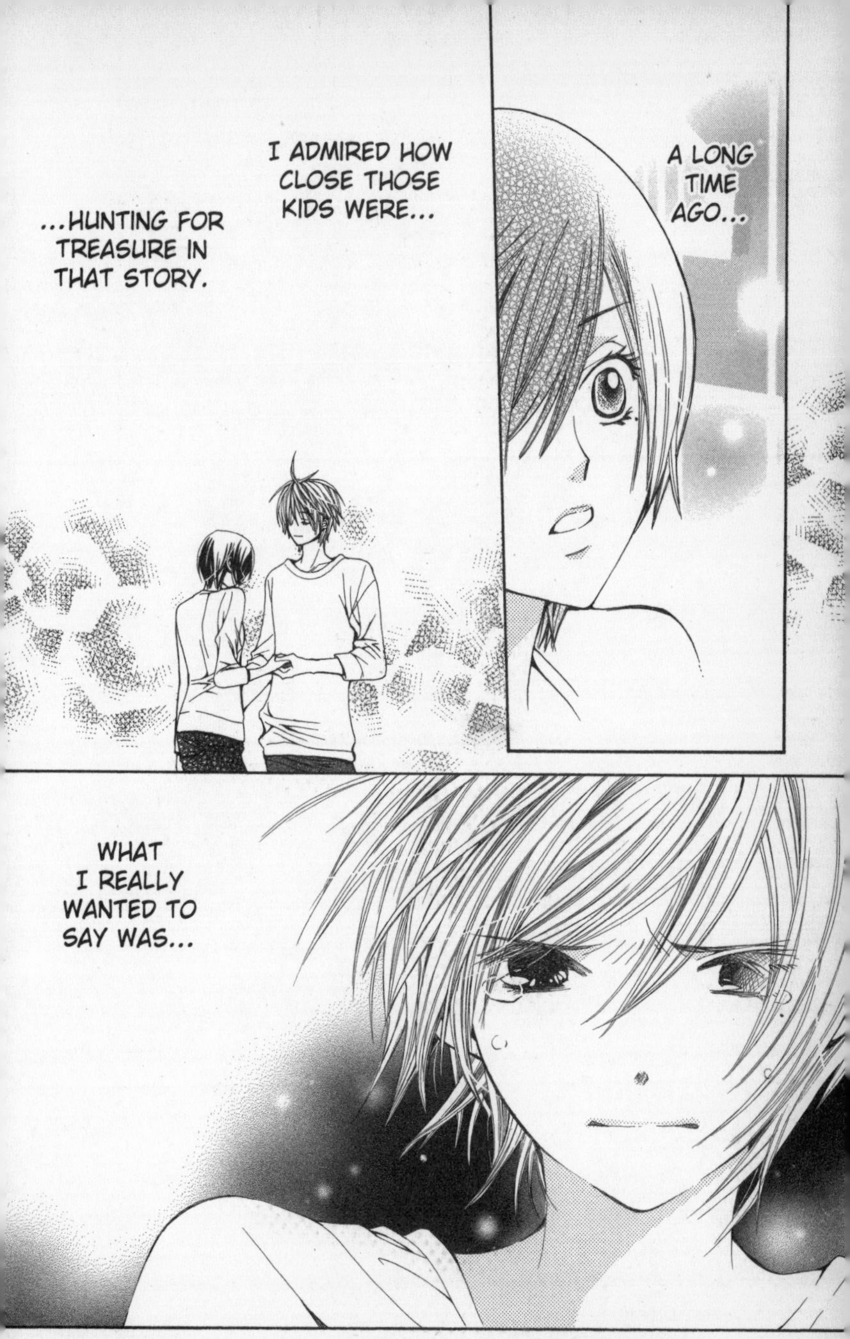
A LONG TIME AGO...
I ADMIRED HOW CLOSE THOSE KIDS WERE...
...HUNTING FOR TREASURE IN THAT STORY.
WHAT I REALLY WANTED TO SAY WAS...

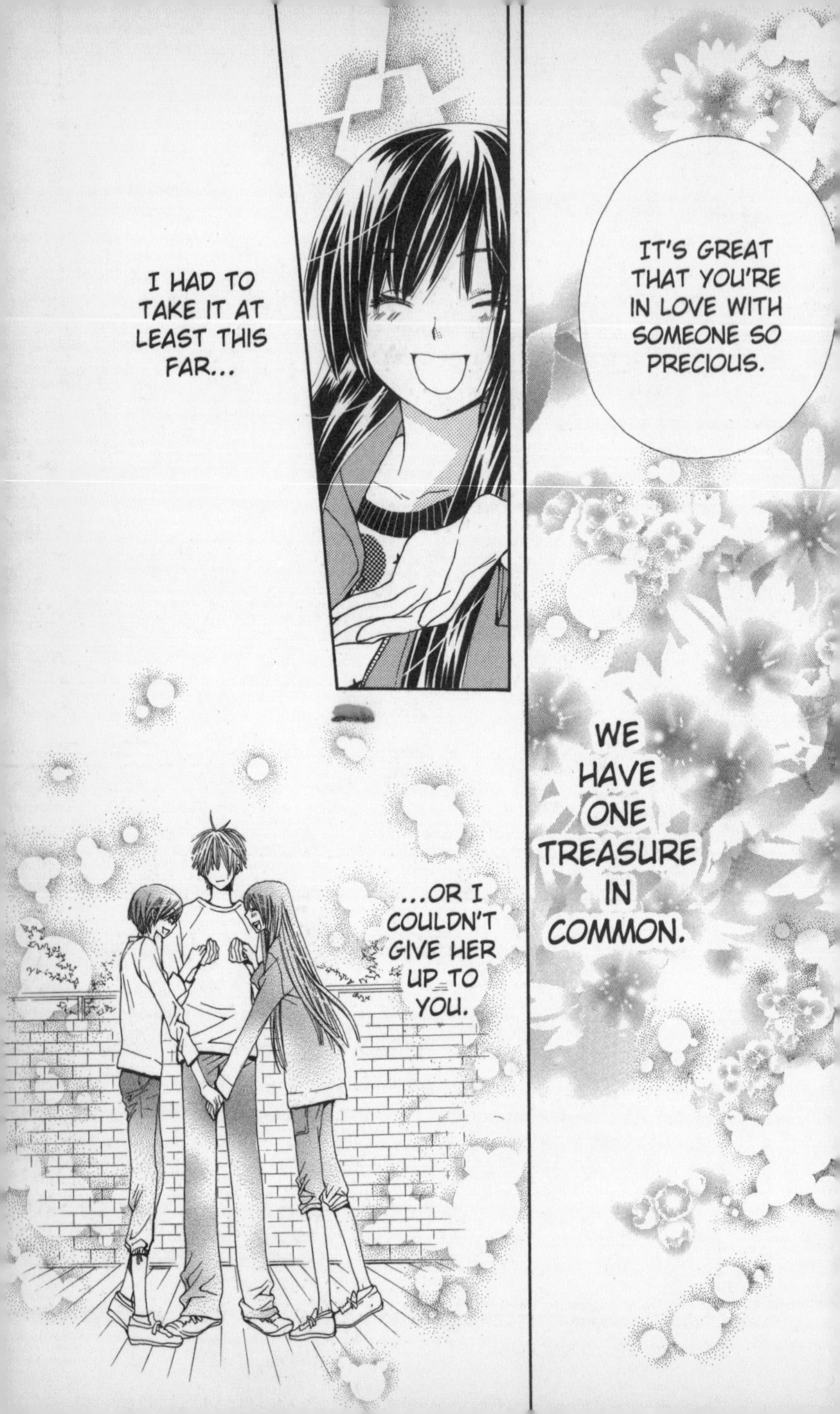
IT'S GREAT THAT YOU'RE IN LOVE WITH SOMEONE SO PRECIOUS.
WE HAVE ONE TREASURE IN COMMON.
I HAD TO TAKE IT AT LEAST THIS FAR...
...OR I COULDN'T GIVE HER UP TO YOU.

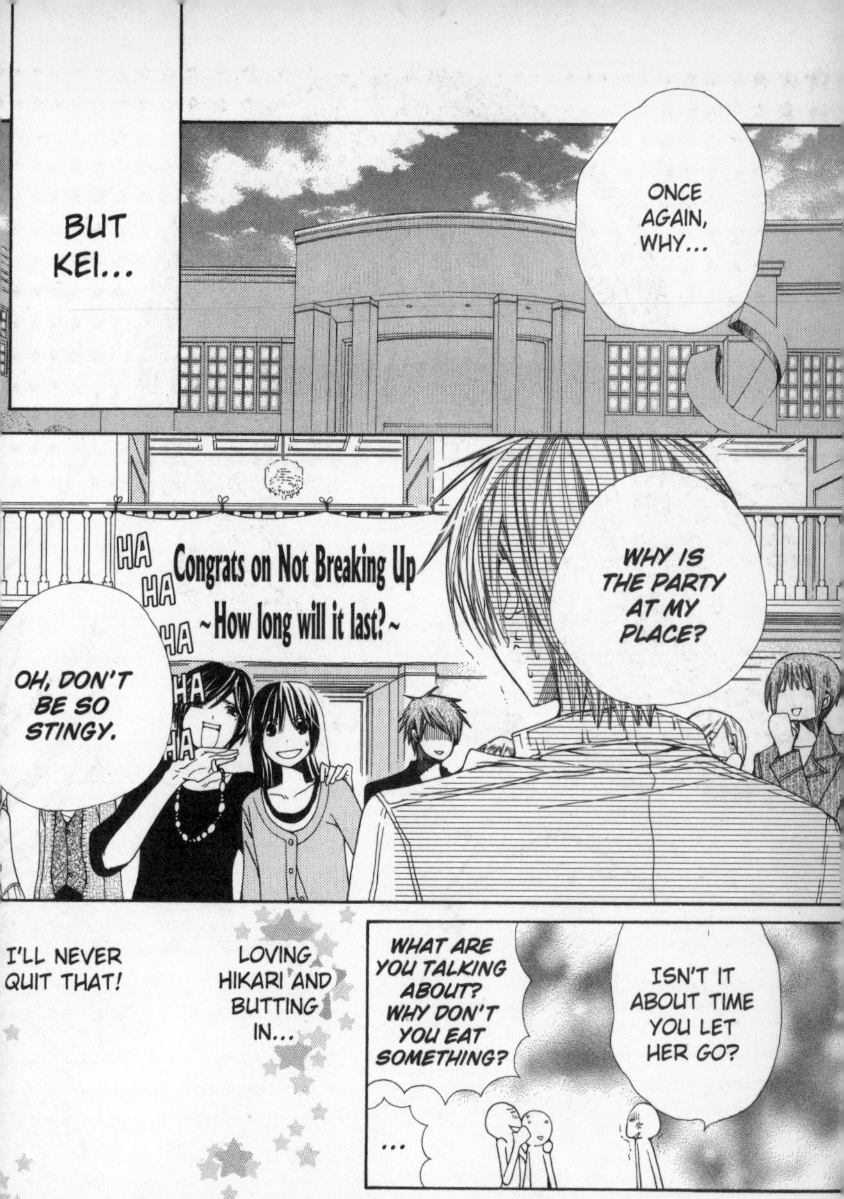
ONCE AGAIN, WHY...
BUT KEI...
WHY IS THE PARTY AT MY PLACE?
Congrats on Not Breaking Up ~How long will it last?~
HA HA HA HA HA
OH, DON'T BE SO STINGY.
ISN'T IT ABOUT TIME YOU LET HER GO?
WHAT ARE YOU TALKING ABOUT? WHY DON'T YOU EAT SOMETHING?
...
LOVING HIKARI AND BUTTING IN...
I'LL NEVER QUIT THAT!

PLUS, IT GIVES US A REASON TO COMMUNICATE.

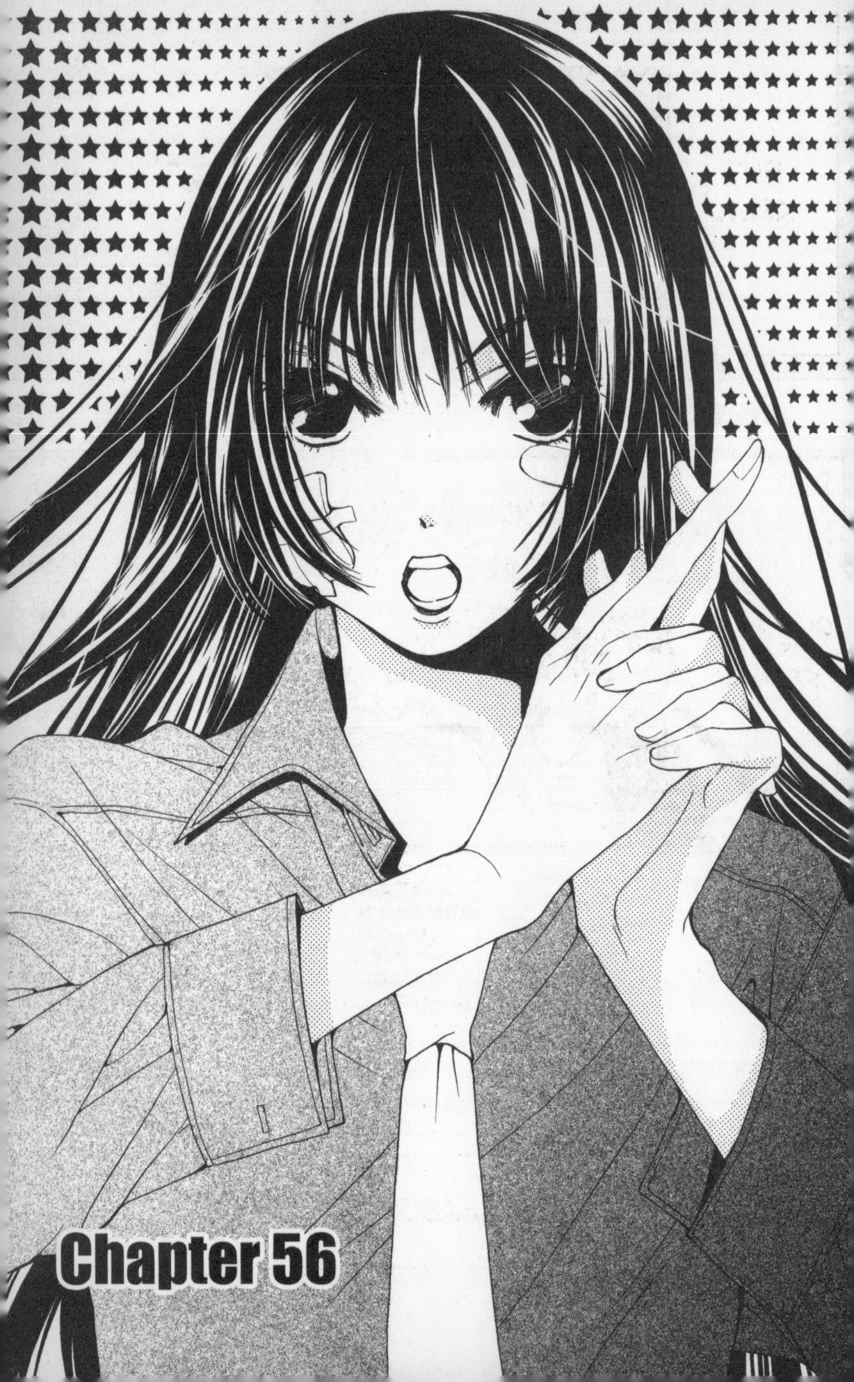
Chapter 56

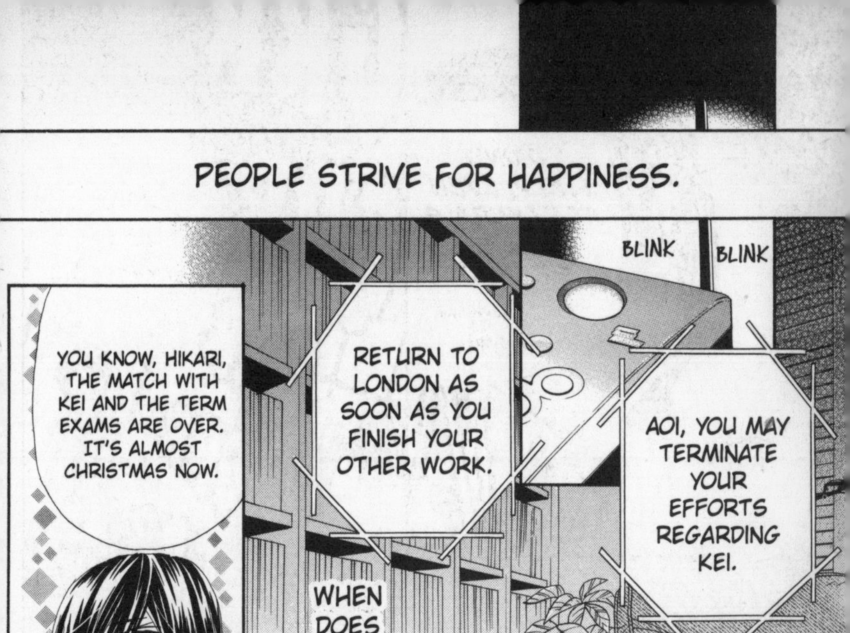
PEOPLE STRIVE FOR HAPPINESS.
BLINK
BLINK
AOI, YOU MAY TERMINATE YOUR EFFORTS REGARDING KEI.
RETURN TO LONDON AS SOON AS YOU FINISH YOUR OTHER WORK.
KEI IS FINALLY ACCEPTING MY INSTRUCTION.
WHEN DOES ONE FIND HAPPINESS?
BEEP
End of messages.
YOU KNOW, HIKARI, THE MATCH WITH KEI AND THE TERM EXAMS ARE OVER. IT'S ALMOST CHRISTMAS NOW.
RIGHT? SO...

•VOL. 10•

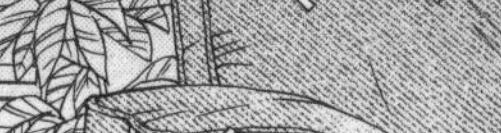
PLEASE GET MARRIED.
D

I'VE REACHED DOUBLE DIGITS...AND IT'S REALLY ALL BECAUSE OF YOU!
I NEVER THOUGHT THE ONE-TIME STORY I WROTE WOULD BECOME A SERIES AND THEN A CD AND CONTINUE FOR TEN VOLUMES!
IF SOMEONE TOLD ME THIS WOULD HAPPEN WHEN I FIRST WROTE S.A, I KNOW I WOULD HAVE BEEN SURPRISED.
I'M REALLY HAPPY! I'M STILL A BEGINNER, BUT I WILL GET BETTER. HONESTLY, THANK YOU VERY MUCH.

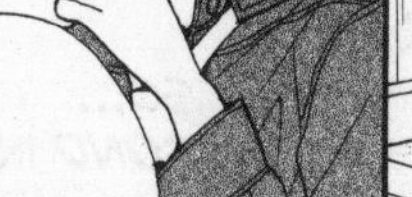
YOU'RE KIDDING, RIGHT?
HA HA HA! PLEASE! QUIT TEASING!

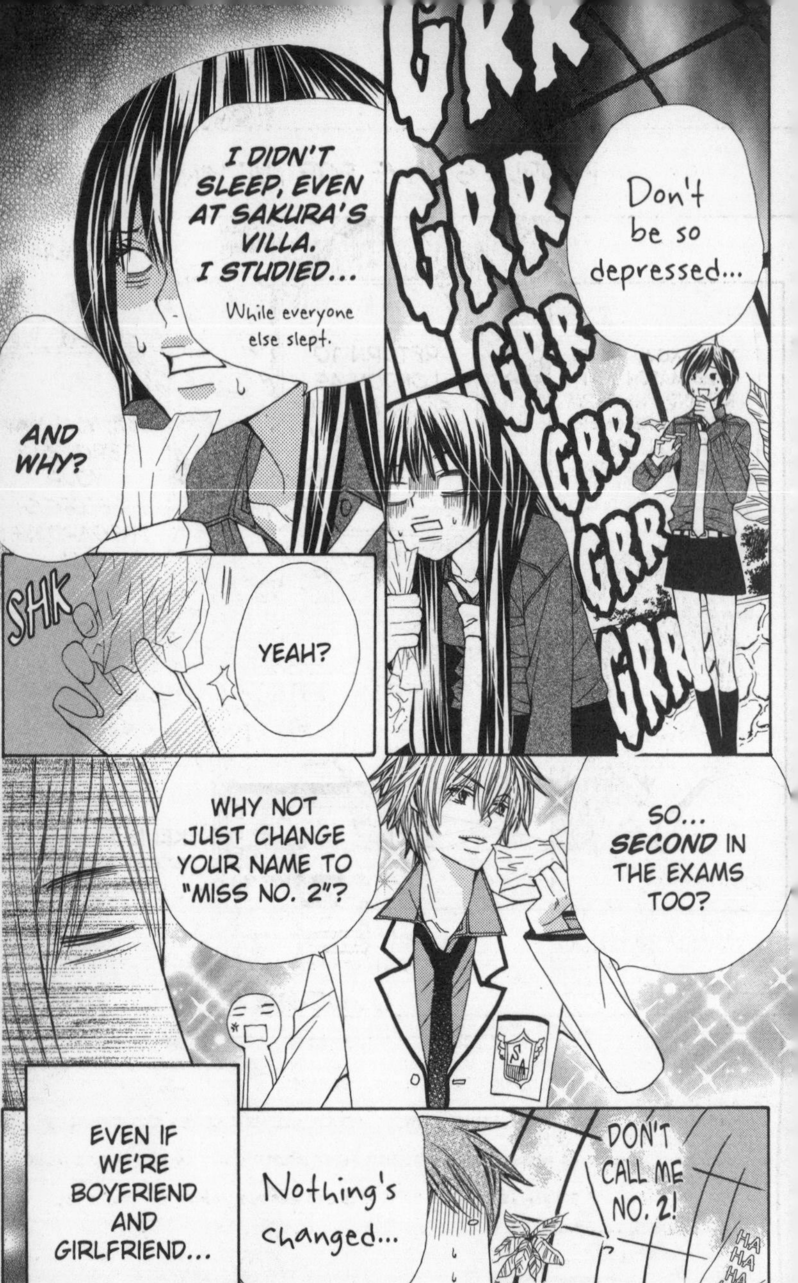

GKK
GRR
Don't be so depressed...
GRR GRR GRR GRR
I DIDN'T SLEEP, EVEN AT SAKURA'S VILLA. I STUDIED...
While everyone else slept.
AND WHY?
SHK
YEAH?
SO... SECOND IN THE EXAMS TOO?
WHY NOT JUST CHANGE YOUR NAME TO "MISS NO. 2"?
DON'T CALL ME NO. 2!
HA HA HA HA
Nothing's changed...
EVEN IF WE'RE BOYFRIEND AND GIRLFRIEND...

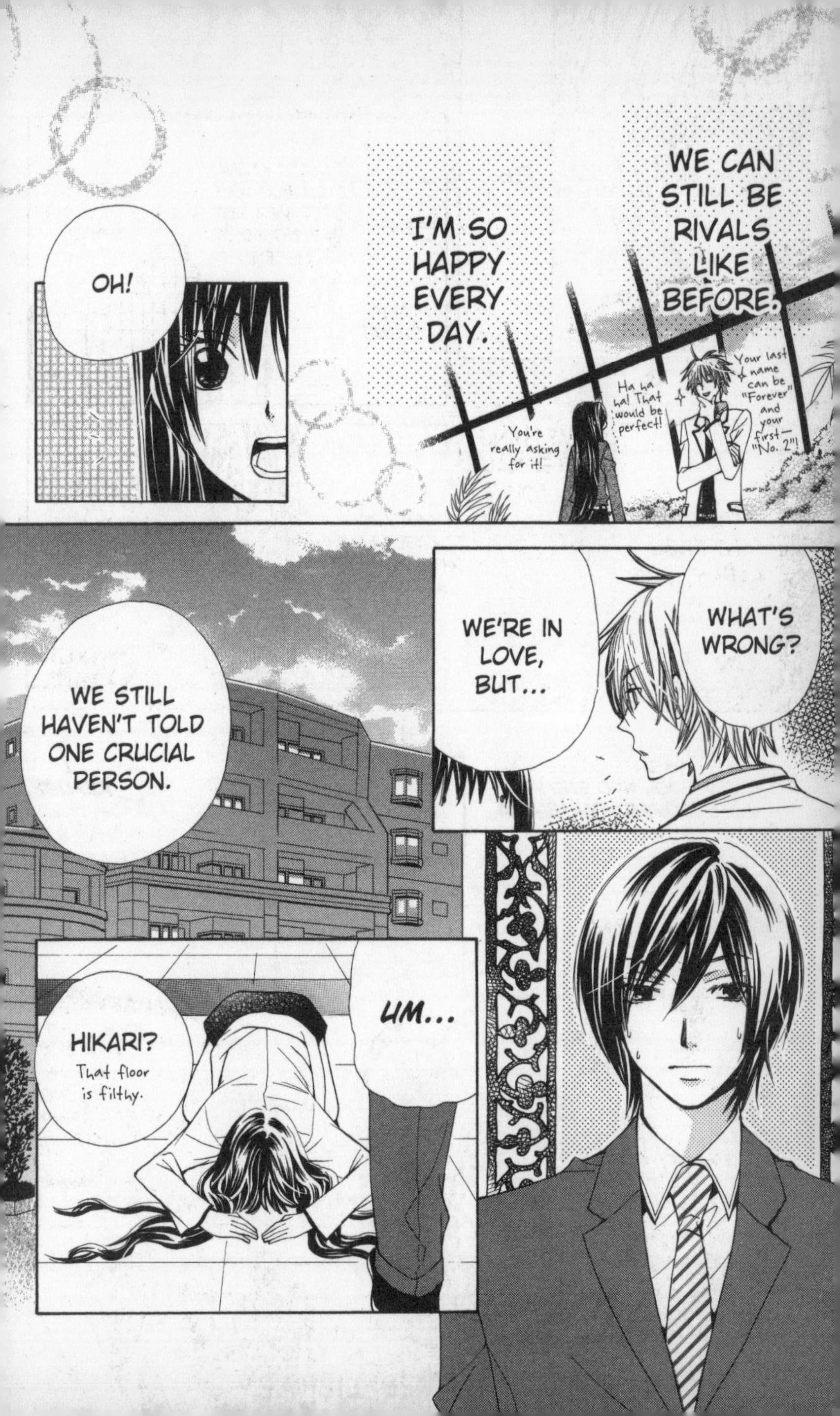
WE CAN STILL BE RIVALS LIKE BEFORE.
Your last name can be "Forever" and your first—"No. 2"!
Ha ha ha! That would be perfect!
You're really asking for it!
I'M SO HAPPY EVERY DAY.
OH!
WHAT'S WRONG?
WE'RE IN LOVE, BUT...
WE STILL HAVEN'T TOLD ONE CRUCIAL PERSON.
UM...
HIKARI?
That floor is filthy.

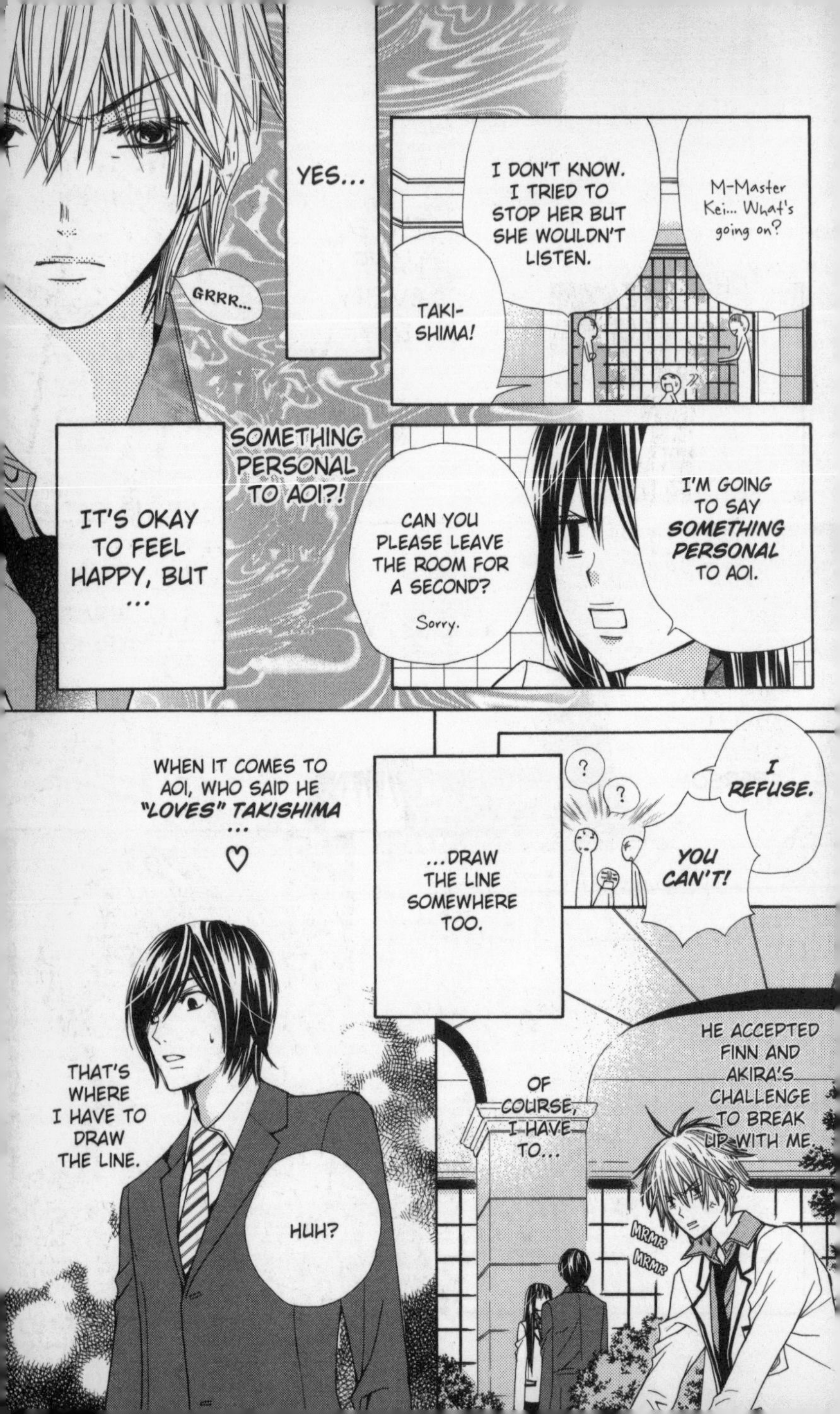
M-Master Kei... What's going on?
I DON'T KNOW. I TRIED TO STOP HER BUT SHE WOULDN'T LISTEN.
TAKI-SHIMA!
I'M GOING TO SAY ***SOMETHING PERSONAL*** TO AOI.
CAN YOU PLEASE LEAVE THE ROOM FOR A SECOND?
Sorry.
YES...
GRRR...
SOMETHING PERSONAL TO AOI?!
IT'S OKAY TO FEEL HAPPY, BUT ...
?
?
I REFUSE.
YOU CAN'T!
HE ACCEPTED FINN AND AKIRA'S CHALLENGE TO BREAK UP WITH ME.
OF COURSE, I HAVE TO...
MRMR
MRMR
...DRAW THE LINE SOMEWHERE TOO.
WHEN IT COMES TO AOI, WHO SAID HE ***"LOVES" TAKISHIMA*** ... ♡
THAT'S WHERE I HAVE TO DRAW THE LINE.
HUH?

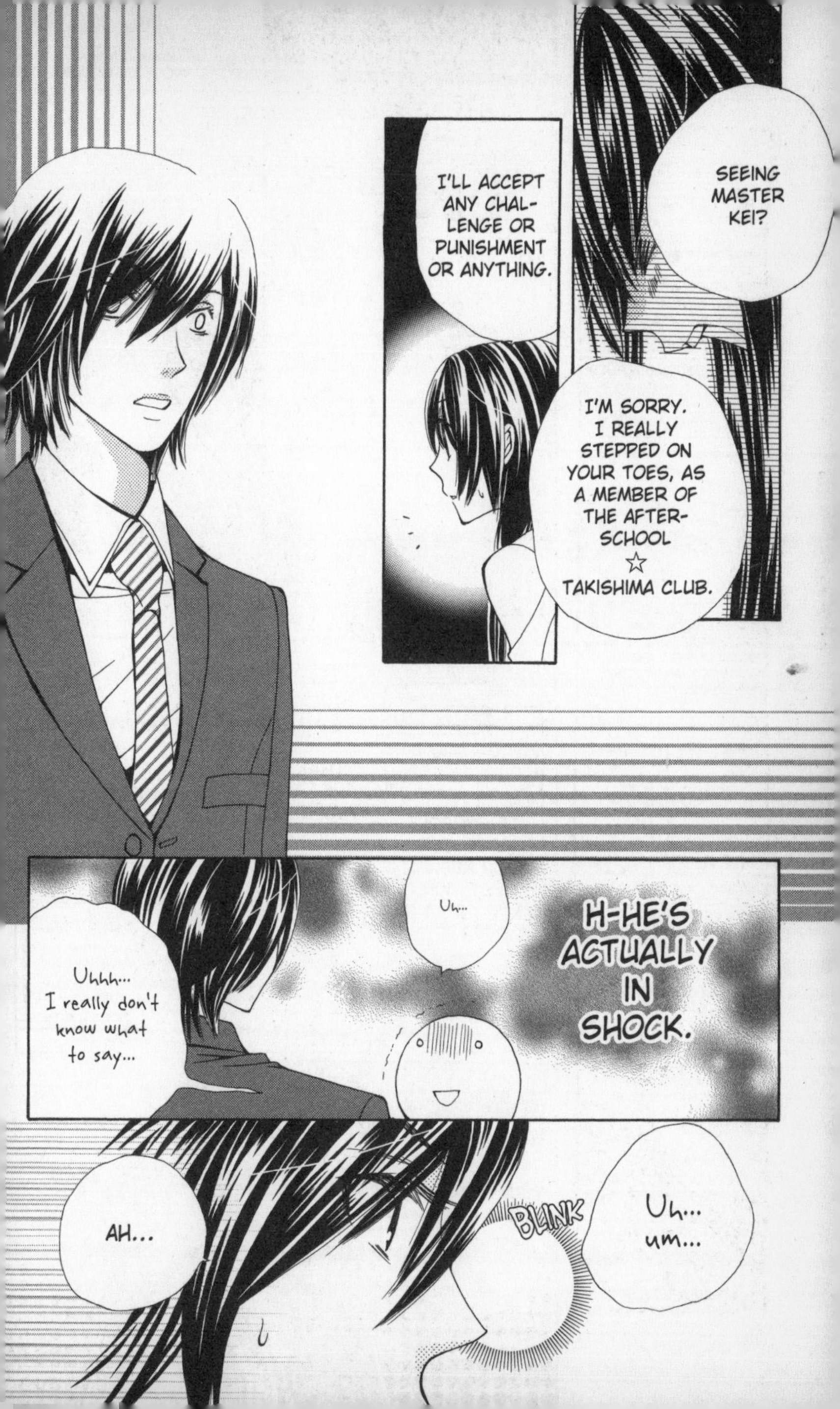
SEEING MASTER KEI?
I'M SORRY. I REALLY STEPPED ON YOUR TOES, AS A MEMBER OF THE AFTER-SCHOOL ☆ TAKISHIMA CLUB.
I'LL ACCEPT ANY CHAL-LENGE OR PUNISHMENT OR ANYTHING.
H-HE'S ACTUALLY IN SHOCK.
Uh...
Uhhh... I really don't know what to say...
Uh... um...
BLINK
AH...

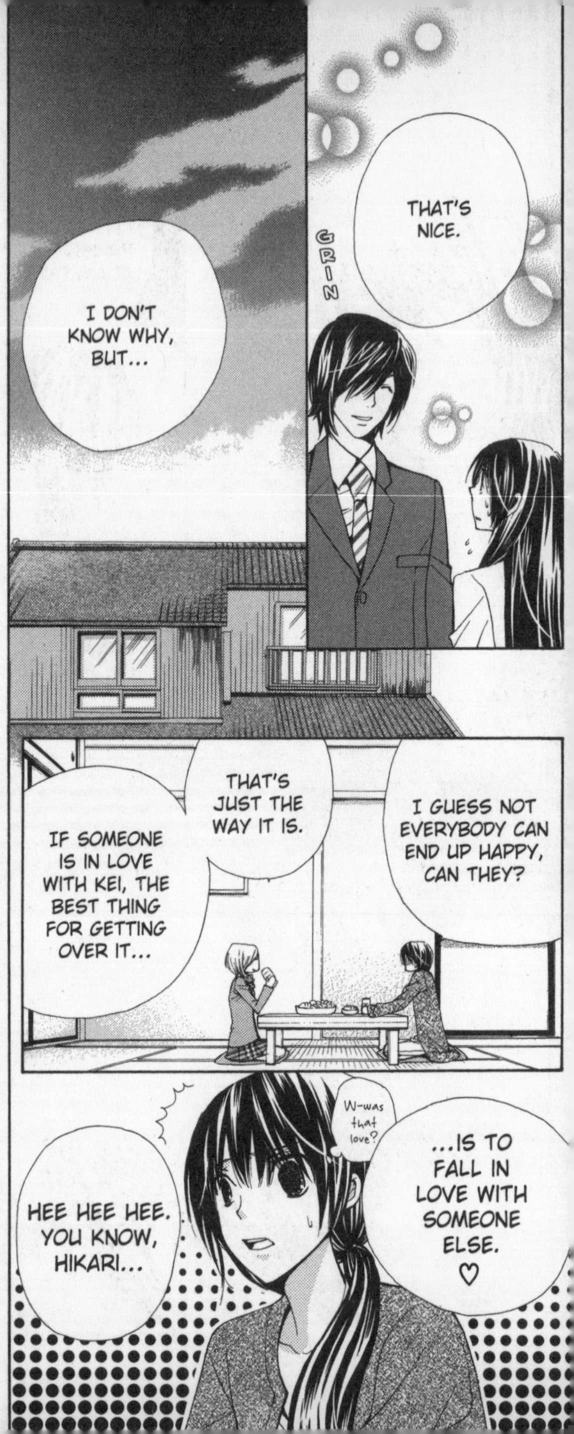
GRIN
THAT'S NICE.
I DON'T KNOW WHY, BUT...
I GUESS NOT EVERYBODY CAN END UP HAPPY, CAN THEY?
THAT'S JUST THE WAY IT IS.
IF SOMEONE IS IN LOVE WITH KEI, THE BEST THING FOR GETTING OVER IT...
W-was that love?
...IS TO FALL IN LOVE WITH SOMEONE ELSE. ♡
HEE HEE HEE. YOU KNOW, HIKARI...

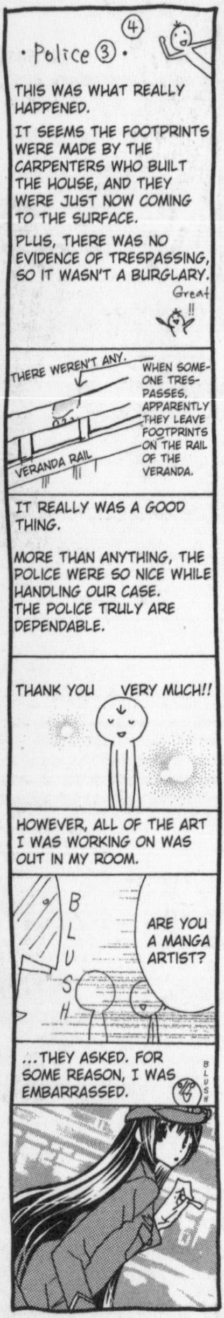
·Police ③·
④
THIS WAS WHAT REALLY HAPPENED.
IT SEEMS THE FOOTPRINTS WERE MADE BY THE CARPENTERS WHO BUILT THE HOUSE, AND THEY WERE JUST NOW COMING TO THE SURFACE.
PLUS, THERE WAS NO EVIDENCE OF TRESPASSING, SO IT WASN'T A BURGLARY.
Great!!
THERE WEREN'T ANY.
WHEN SOMEONE TRESPASSES, APPARENTLY THEY LEAVE FOOTPRINTS ON THE RAIL OF THE VERANDA.
VERANDA RAIL
IT REALLY WAS A GOOD THING.
MORE THAN ANYTHING, THE POLICE WERE SO NICE WHILE HANDLING OUR CASE.
THE POLICE TRULY ARE DEPENDABLE.
THANK YOU VERY MUCH!!
HOWEVER, ALL OF THE ART I WAS WORKING ON WAS OUT IN MY ROOM.
BLUSH
ARE YOU A MANGA ARTIST?
...THEY ASKED. FOR SOME REASON, I WAS EMBARRASSED.
BLUSH

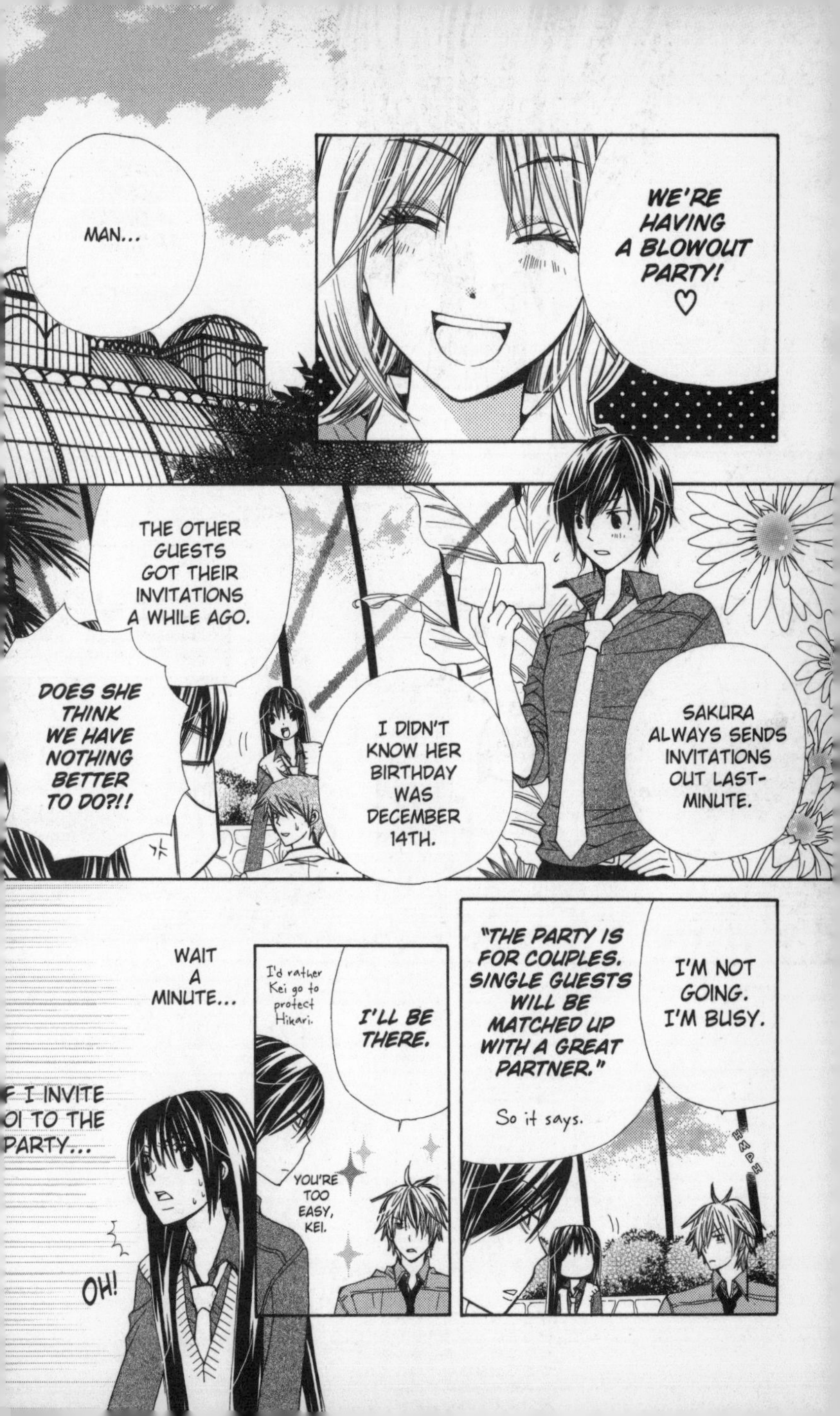
WE'RE HAVING A BLOWOUT PARTY! ♡
MAN...
SAKURA ALWAYS SENDS INVITATIONS OUT LAST-MINUTE.
I DIDN'T KNOW HER BIRTHDAY WAS DECEMBER 14TH.
THE OTHER GUESTS GOT THEIR INVITATIONS A WHILE AGO.
DOES SHE THINK WE HAVE NOTHING BETTER TO DO?!!
I'M NOT GOING. I'M BUSY.
HMPH
"THE PARTY IS FOR COUPLES. SINGLE GUESTS WILL BE MATCHED UP WITH A GREAT PARTNER."
So it says.
I'LL BE THERE.
I'd rather Kei go to protect Hikari.
YOU'RE TOO EASY, KEI.
WAIT A MINUTE...
F I INVITE OI TO THE PARTY...
OH!

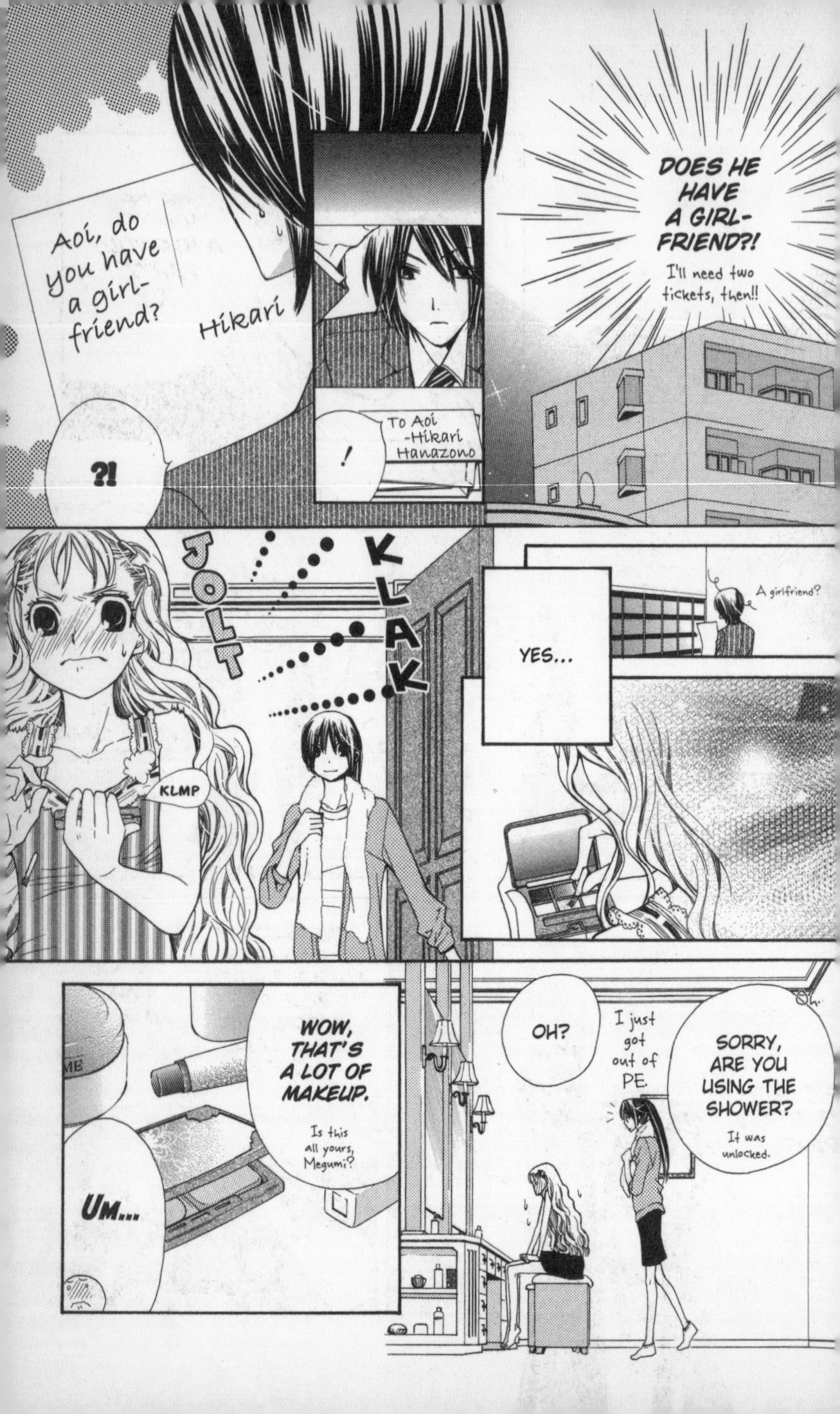

DOES HE HAVE A GIRL-FRIEND?!
I'll need two tickets, then!!
To Aoi -Hikari Hanazono
!
Aoi, do you have a girl-friend?
Hikari
?!
A girlfriend?
YES...
KLAK
JOLT
KLMP
Oh.
OH?
I just got out of PE.
SORRY, ARE YOU USING THE SHOWER?
It was unlocked.
WOW, THAT'S A LOT OF MAKEUP.
Is this all yours, Megumi?
UM...

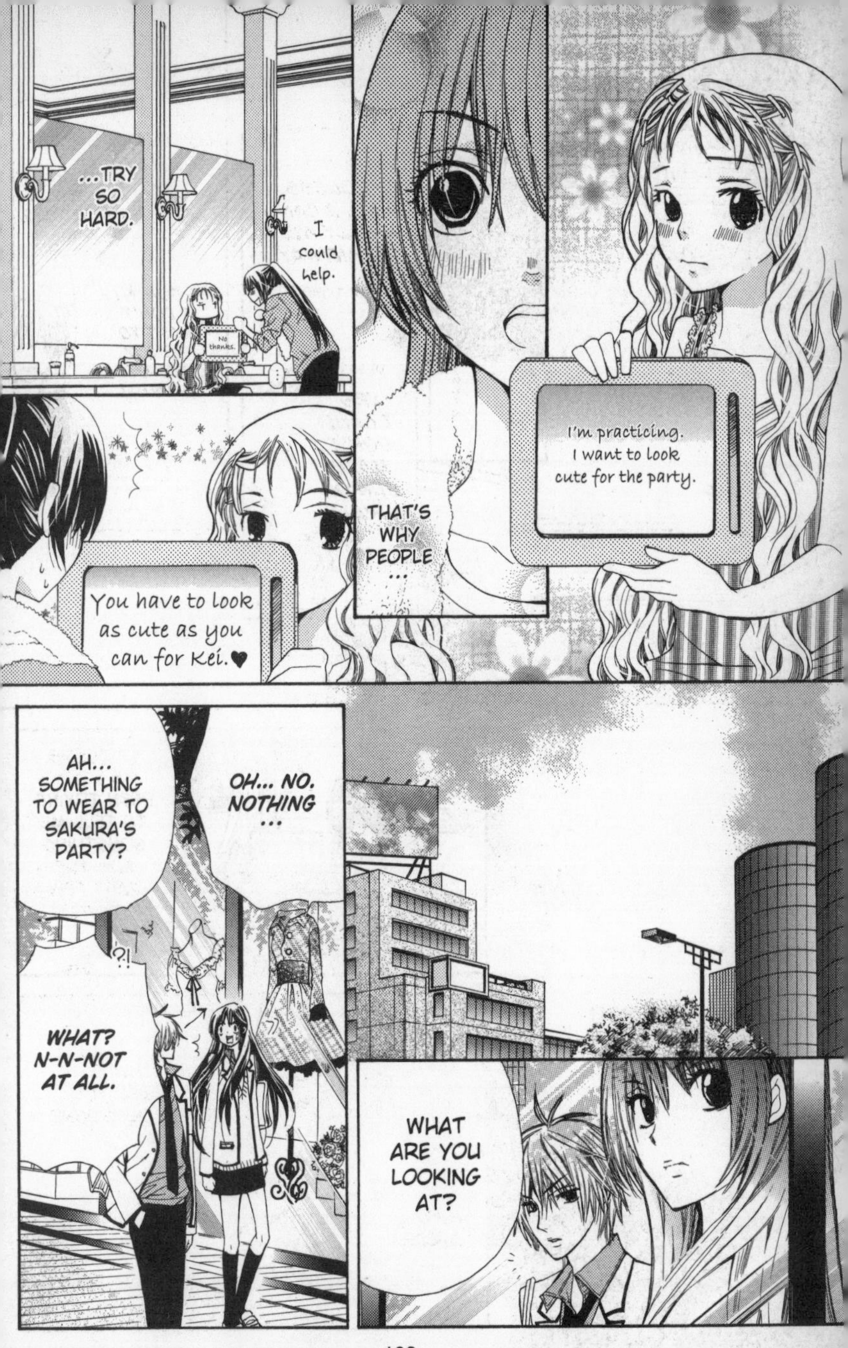
I'm practicing. I want to look cute for the party.
THAT'S WHY PEOPLE ...
...TRY SO HARD.
I could help.
No thanks.
You have to look as cute as you can for Kei.♥
WHAT ARE YOU LOOKING AT?
OH... NO. NOTHING ...
AH... SOMETHING TO WEAR TO SAKURA'S PARTY?
?!
WHAT? N-N-NOT AT ALL.

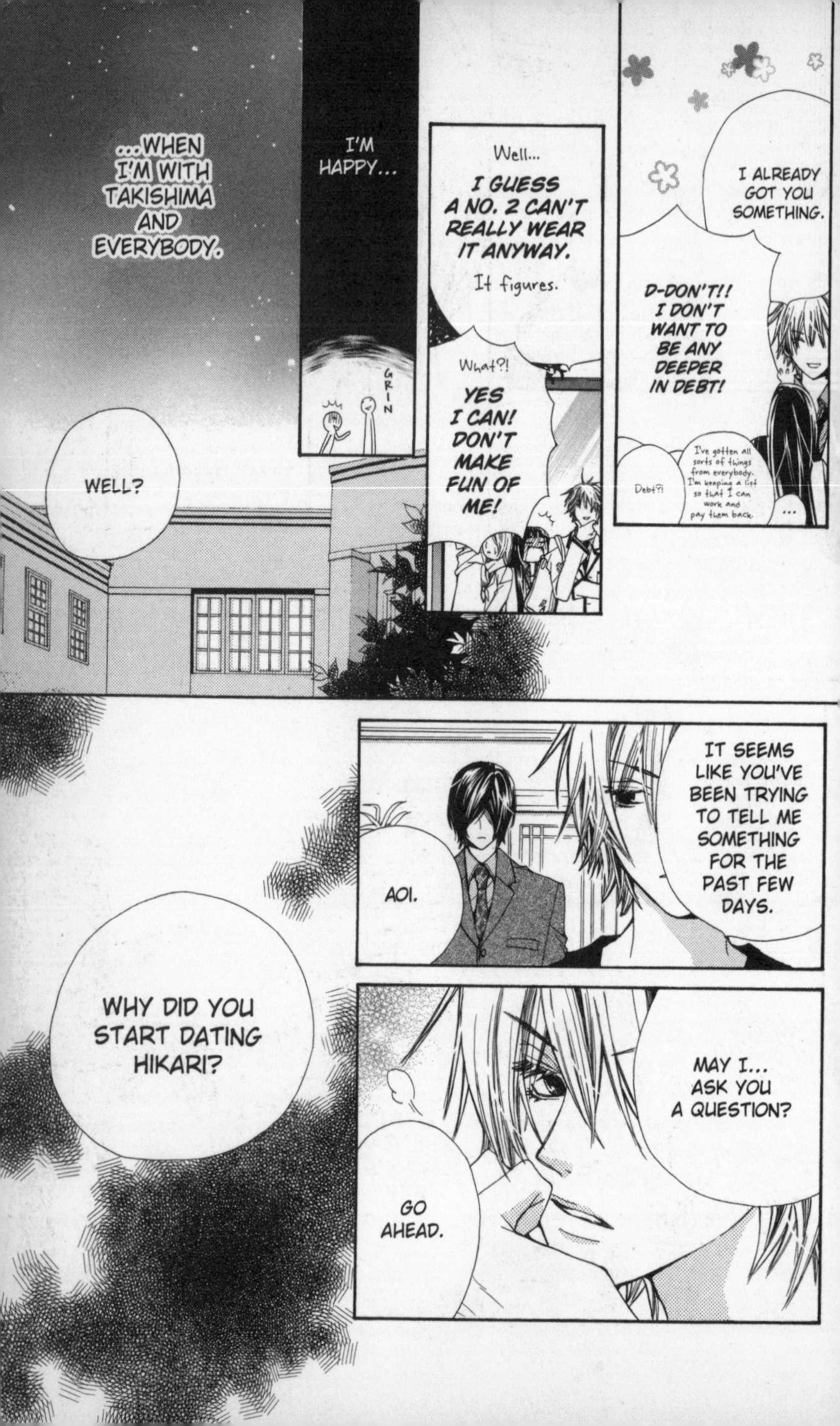

I ALREADY GOT YOU SOMETHING.
D-DON'T!! I DON'T WANT TO BE ANY DEEPER IN DEBT!
...
I've gotten all sorts of things from everybody. I'm keeping a list so that I can work and pay them back.
Debt?!
Well...
I GUESS A NO. 2 CAN'T REALLY WEAR IT ANYWAY.
It figures.
What?!
YES I CAN! DON'T MAKE FUN OF ME!
I'M HAPPY...
GRIN
...WHEN I'M WITH TAKISHIMA AND EVERYBODY.
WELL?
IT SEEMS LIKE YOU'VE BEEN TRYING TO TELL ME SOMETHING FOR THE PAST FEW DAYS.
AOI.
MAY I... ASK YOU A QUESTION?
GO AHEAD.
WHY DID YOU START DATING HIKARI?

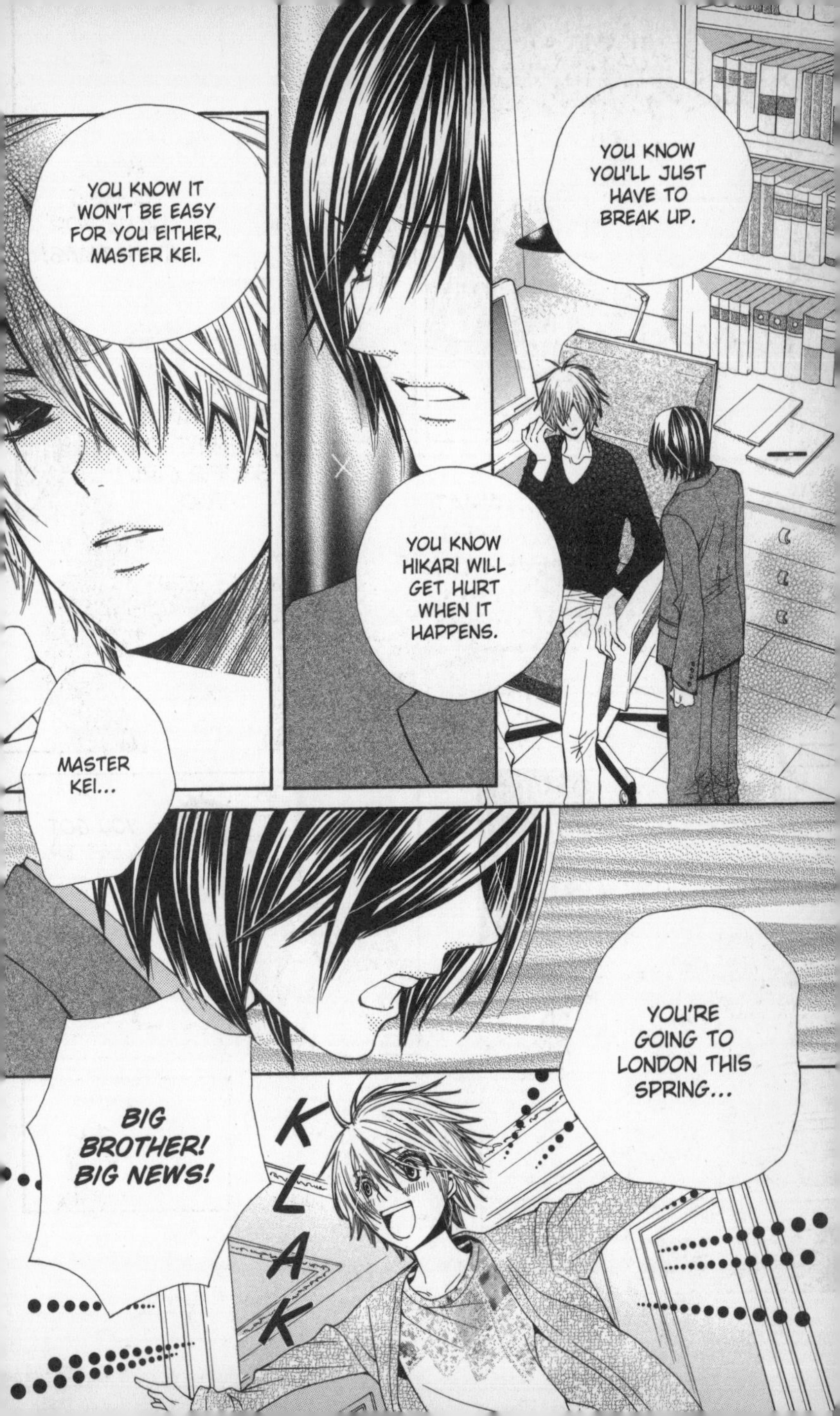
YOU KNOW YOU'LL JUST HAVE TO BREAK UP.
YOU KNOW HIKARI WILL GET HURT WHEN IT HAPPENS.
YOU KNOW IT WON'T BE EASY FOR YOU EITHER, MASTER KEI.
MASTER KEI...
YOU'RE GOING TO LONDON THIS SPRING...
KLAK
BIG BROTHER! BIG NEWS!

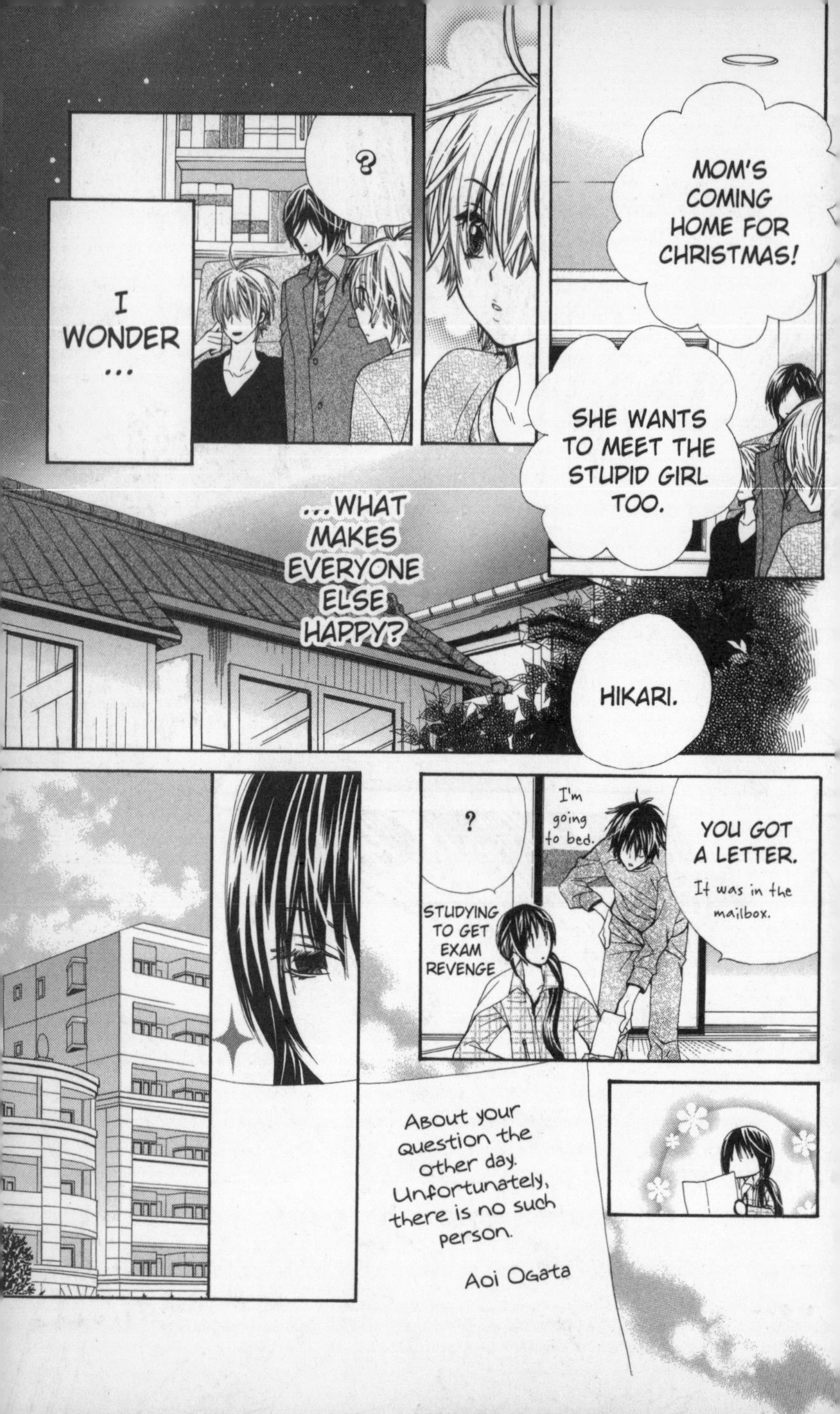
MOM'S COMING HOME FOR CHRISTMAS!
SHE WANTS TO MEET THE STUPID GIRL TOO.
?
I WONDER ...
...WHAT MAKES EVERYONE ELSE HAPPY?
HIKARI.
YOU GOT A LETTER.
It was in the mailbox.
I'm going to bed.
?
STUDYING TO GET EXAM REVENGE
About your question the other day. Unfortunately, there is no such person.
Aoi Ogata

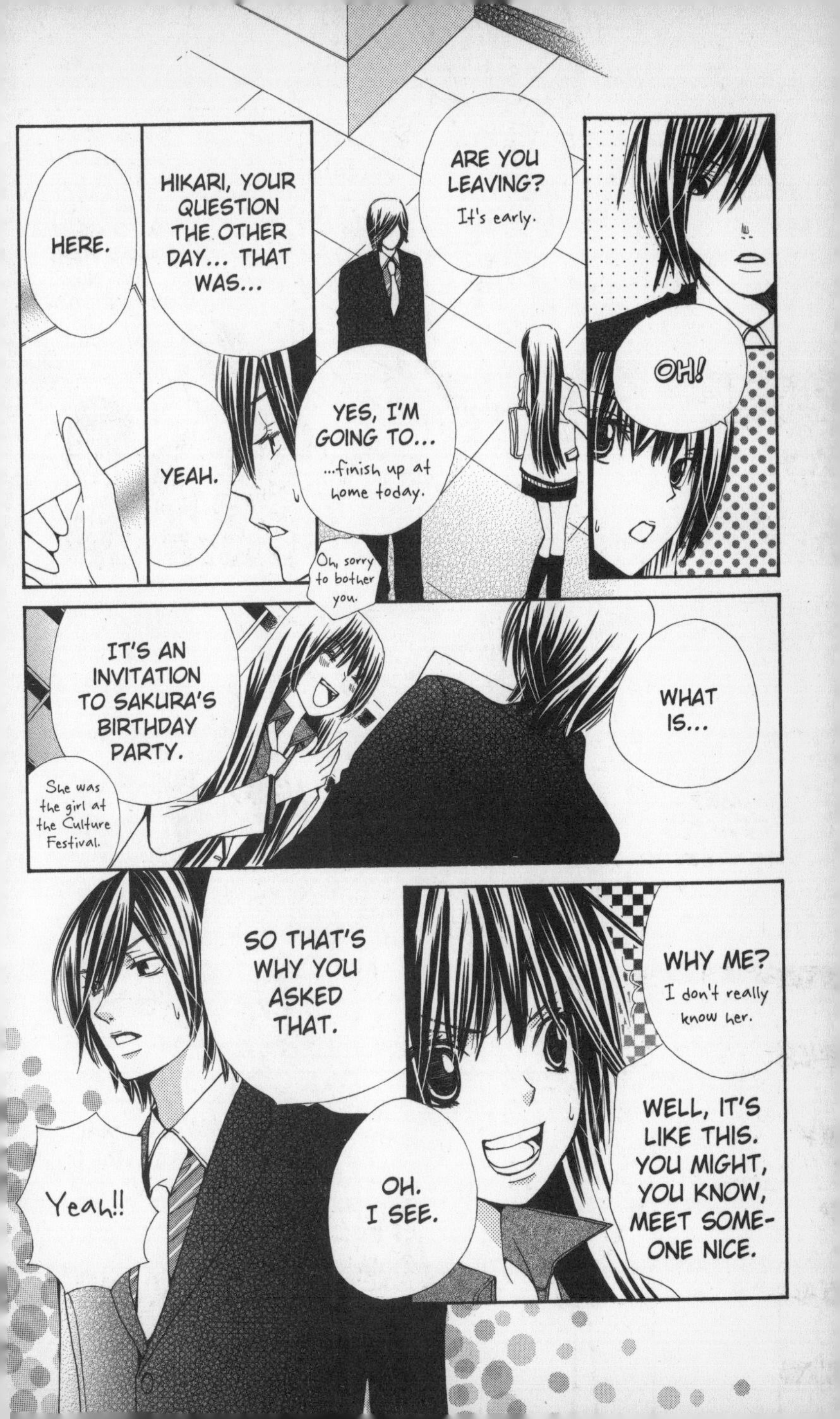
ARE YOU LEAVING?
It's early.
OH!
YES, I'M GOING TO...
...finish up at home today.
Oh, sorry to bother you.
HIKARI, YOUR QUESTION THE OTHER DAY... THAT WAS...
YEAH.
HERE.
WHAT IS...
IT'S AN INVITATION TO SAKURA'S BIRTHDAY PARTY.
She was the girl at the Culture Festival.
WHY ME?
I don't really know her.
WELL, IT'S LIKE THIS. YOU MIGHT, YOU KNOW, MEET SOME-ONE NICE.
OH. I SEE.
SO THAT'S WHY YOU ASKED THAT.
Yeah!!

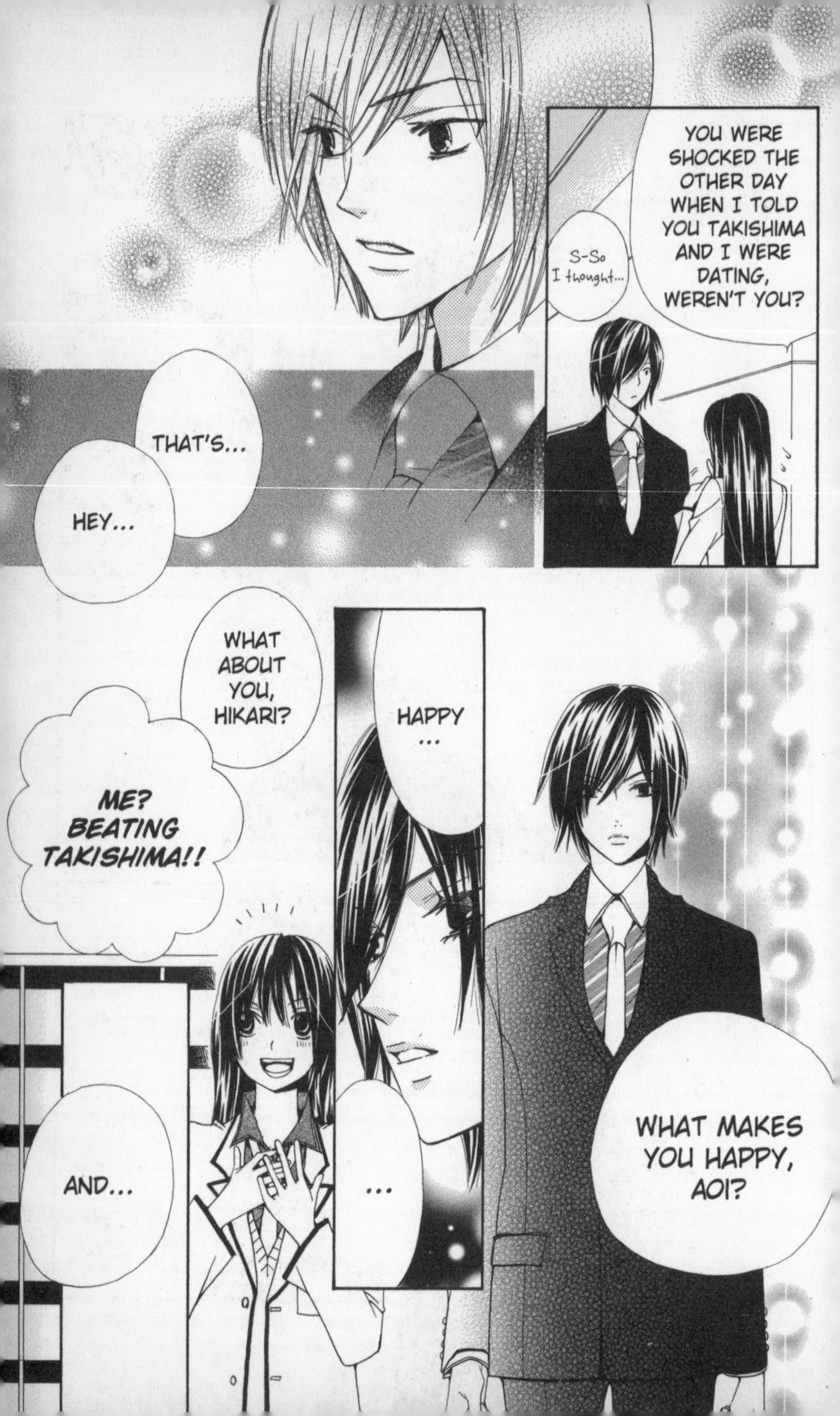
YOU WERE SHOCKED THE OTHER DAY WHEN I TOLD YOU TAKISHIMA AND I WERE DATING, WEREN'T YOU?
S-So I thought...
THAT'S...
HEY...
WHAT MAKES YOU HAPPY, AOI?
HAPPY ...
...
WHAT ABOUT YOU, HIKARI?
ME? BEATING TAKISHIMA!!
AND...

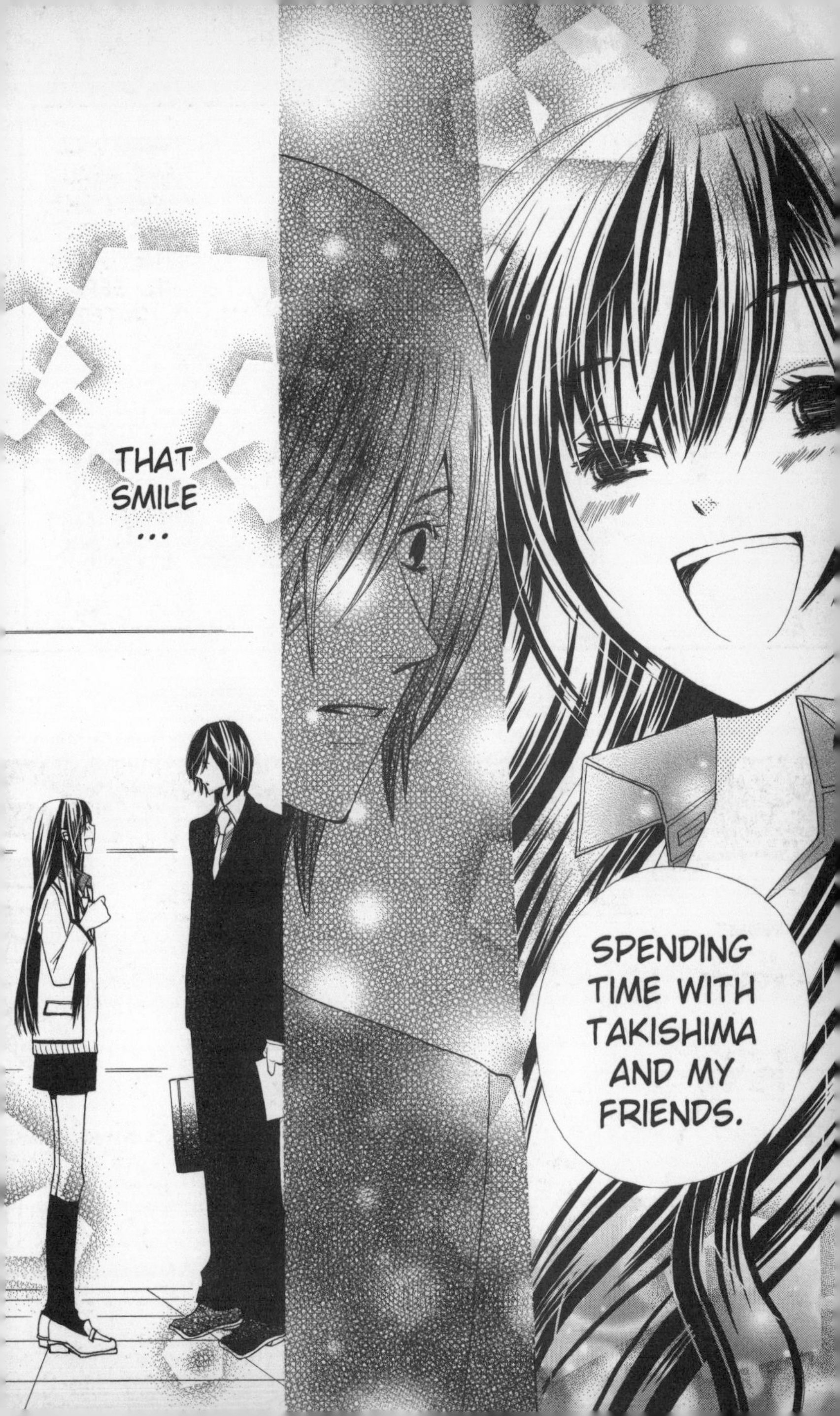
SPENDING TIME WITH TAKISHIMA AND MY FRIENDS.
THAT SMILE ...

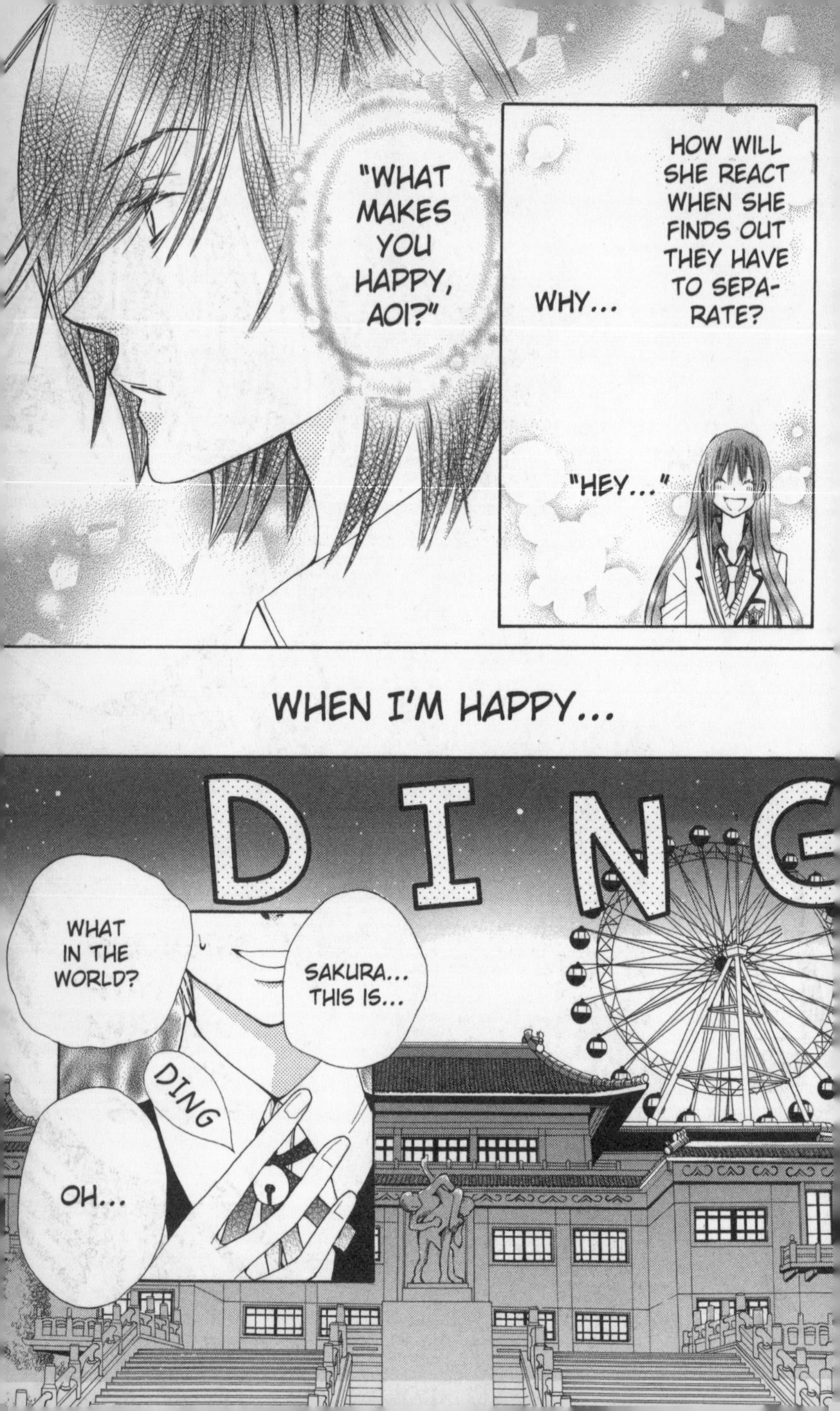
HOW WILL SHE REACT WHEN SHE FINDS OUT THEY HAVE TO SEPARATE?
WHY...
"HEY..."
"WHAT MAKES YOU HAPPY, AOI?"
WHEN I'M HAPPY...
DING
SAKURA... THIS IS...
WHAT IN THE WORLD?
DING
OH...

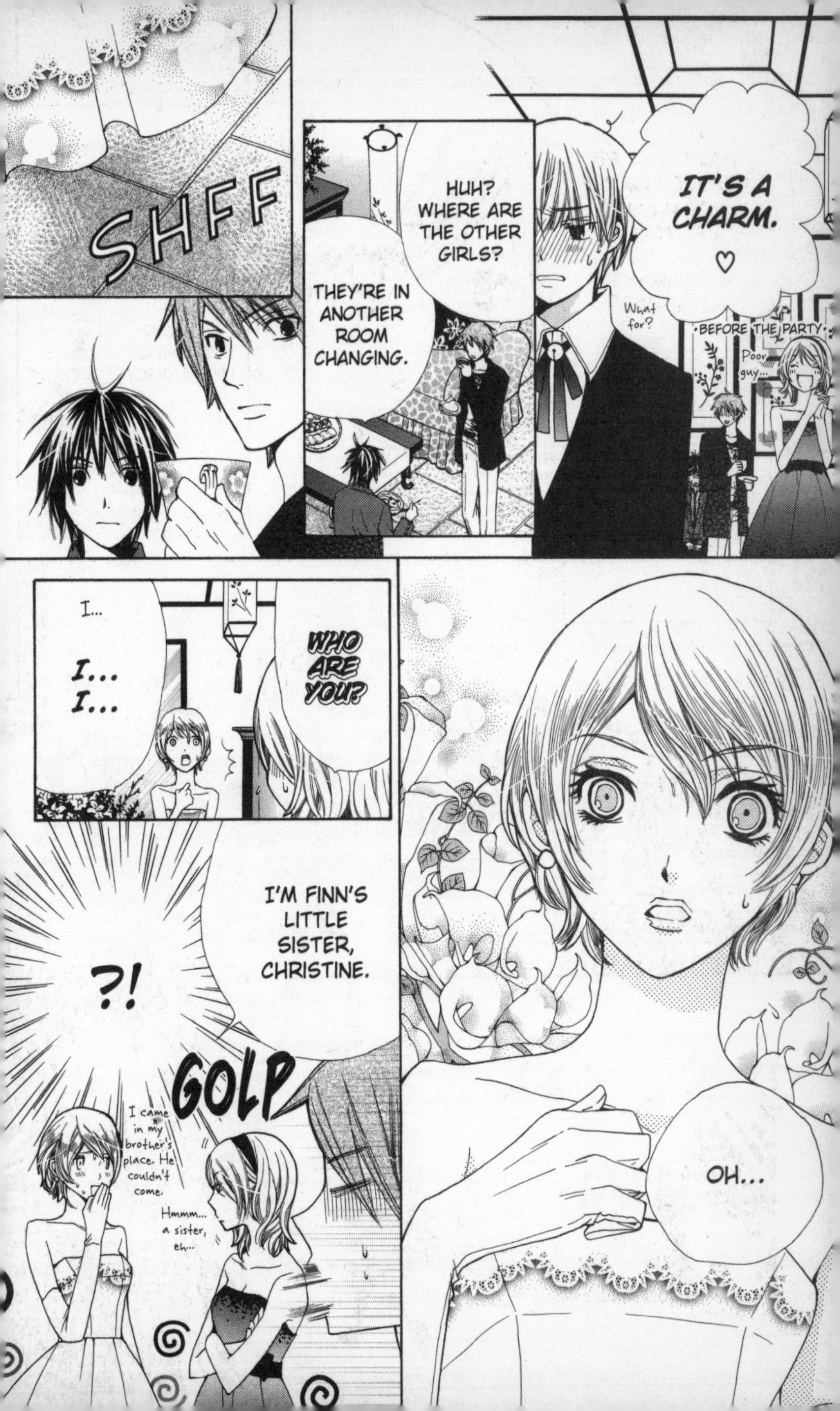
IT'S A CHARM.
♥
What for?
BEFORE THE PARTY
Poor guy...
HUH? WHERE ARE THE OTHER GIRLS?
THEY'RE IN ANOTHER ROOM CHANGING.
SHFF
OH...
WHO ARE YOU?
I...
I... I...
I'M FINN'S LITTLE SISTER, CHRISTINE.
?!
GOLP
I came in my brother's place. He couldn't come.
Hmmm... a sister, eh...

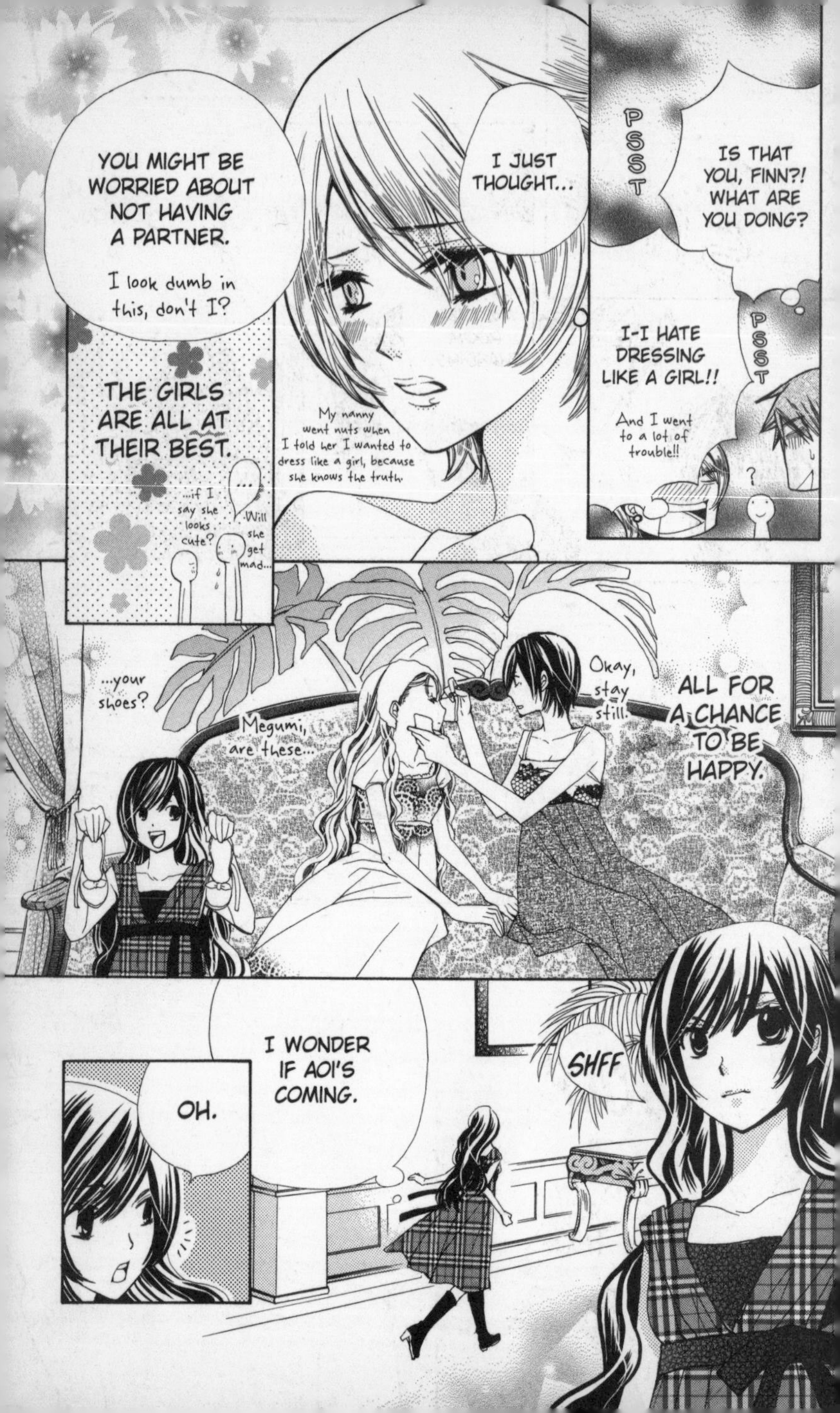
IS THAT YOU, FINN?! WHAT ARE YOU DOING?
PSST
PSST
I-I HATE DRESSING LIKE A GIRL!!
And I went to a lot of trouble!!
?
I JUST THOUGHT...
YOU MIGHT BE WORRIED ABOUT NOT HAVING A PARTNER.
I look dumb in this, don't I?
My nanny went nuts when I told her I wanted to dress like a girl, because she knows the truth.
THE GIRLS ARE ALL AT THEIR BEST.
...
Will she get mad...
...if I say she looks cute?
ALL FOR A CHANCE TO BE HAPPY.
Okay, stay still.
Megumi, are these...
...your shoes?
SHFF
I WONDER IF AOI'S COMING.
OH.

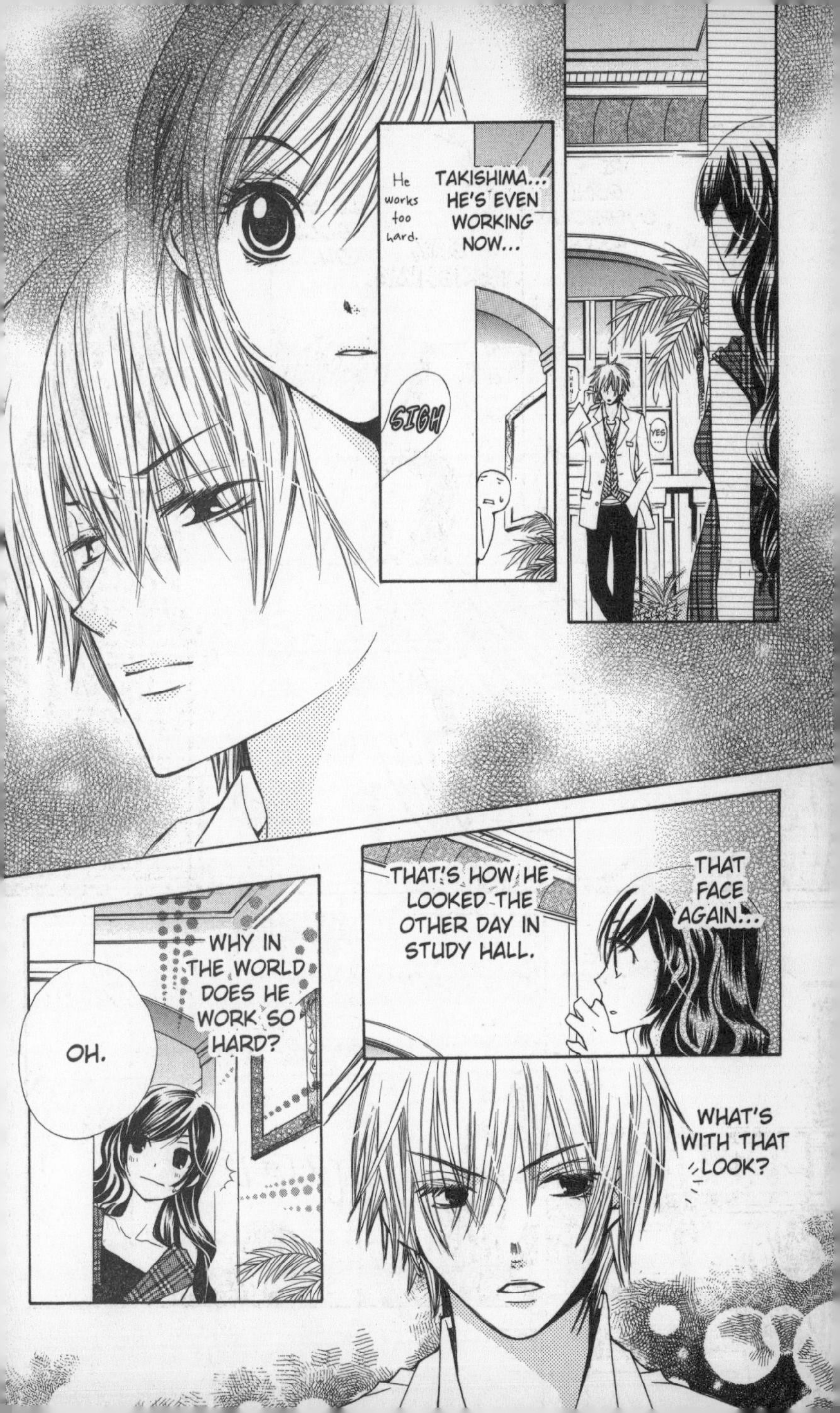
TAKISHIMA... HE'S EVEN WORKING NOW...
He works too hard.
SIGH
THAT FACE AGAIN...
THAT'S HOW HE LOOKED THE OTHER DAY IN STUDY HALL.
WHAT'S WITH THAT LOOK?
WHY IN THE WORLD DOES HE WORK SO HARD?
OH.

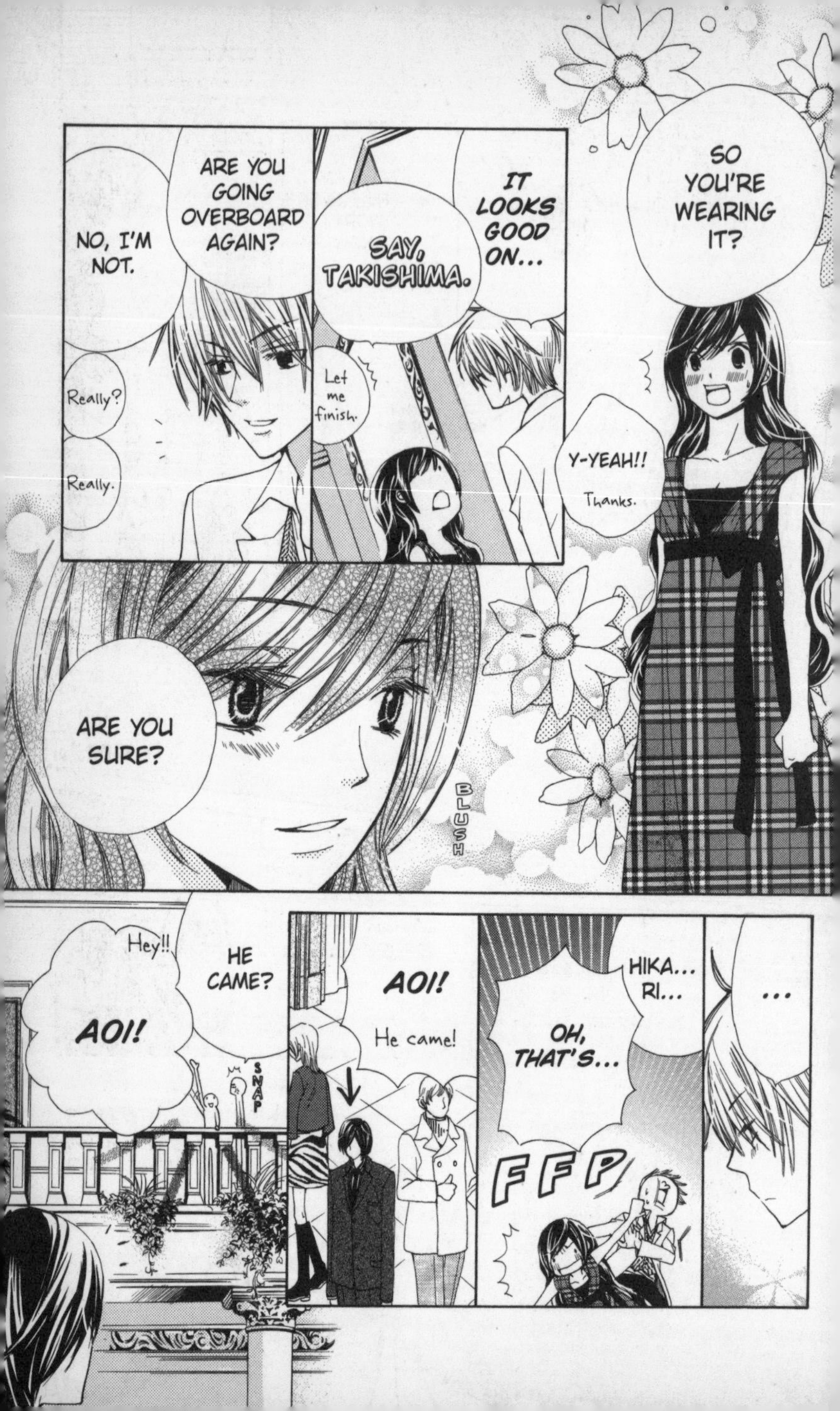
SO YOU'RE WEARING IT?
Y-YEAH!!
Thanks.
IT LOOKS GOOD ON...
SAY, TAKISHIMA.
Let me finish.
ARE YOU GOING OVERBOARD AGAIN?
NO, I'M NOT.
Really?
Really.
ARE YOU SURE?
BLUSH
...
HIKA... RI...
OH, THAT'S...
FFP
AOI!
He came!
HE CAME?
Hey!!
AOI!
SNAP

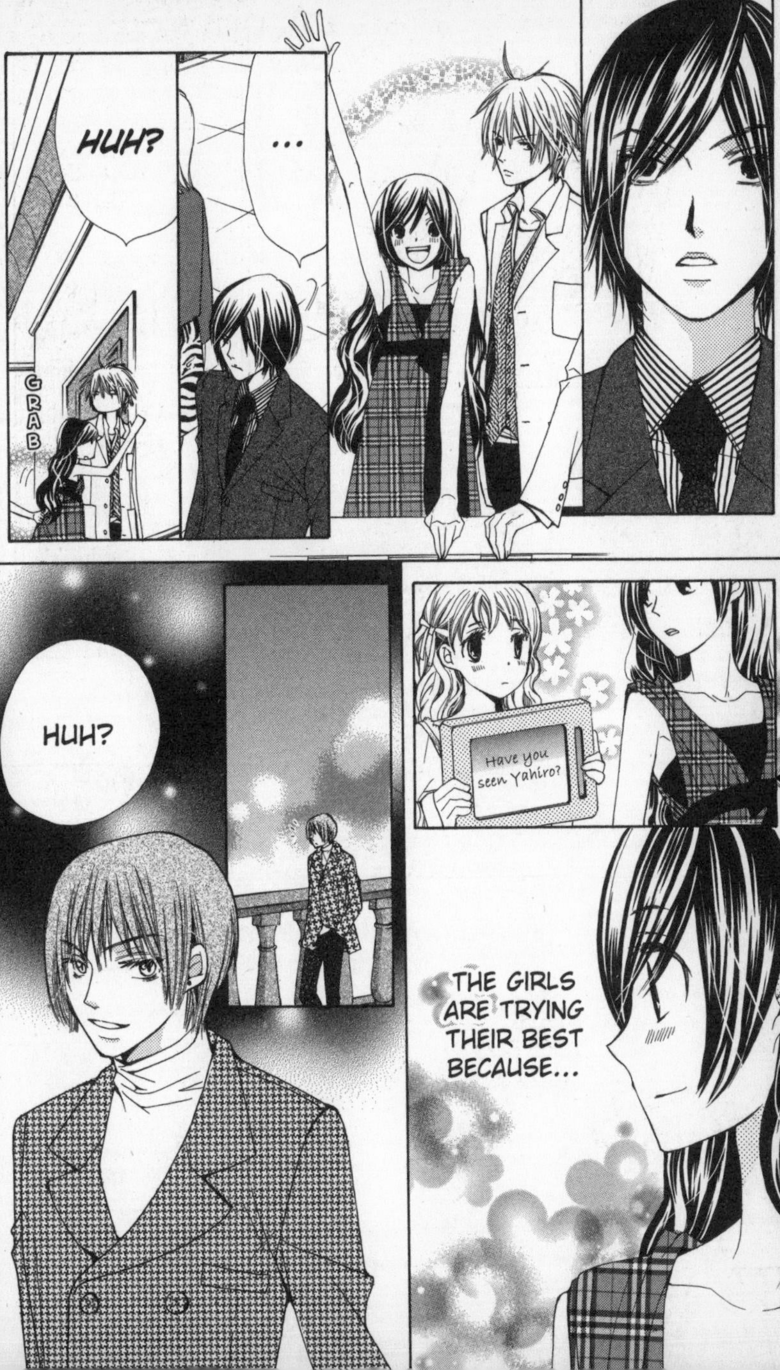
...
HUH?
GRAB
Have you seen Yahiro?
THE GIRLS ARE TRYING THEIR BEST BECAUSE...
HUH?

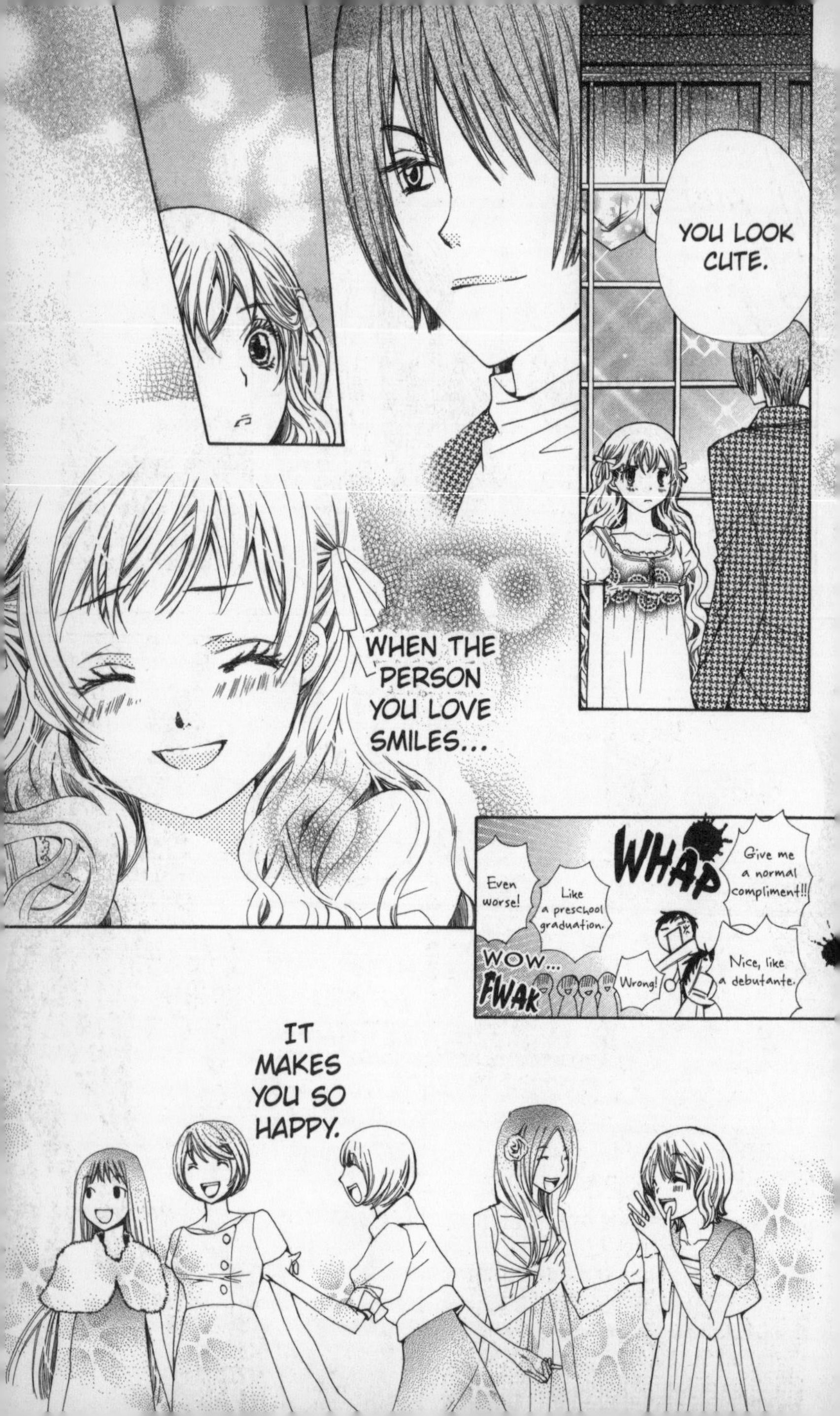
YOU LOOK CUTE.
WHEN THE PERSON YOU LOVE SMILES...
Give me a normal compliment!!
WHAP
Nice, like a debutante.
Wrong!
Like a preschool graduation.
Even worse!
WOW...
FWAK
IT MAKES YOU SO HAPPY.

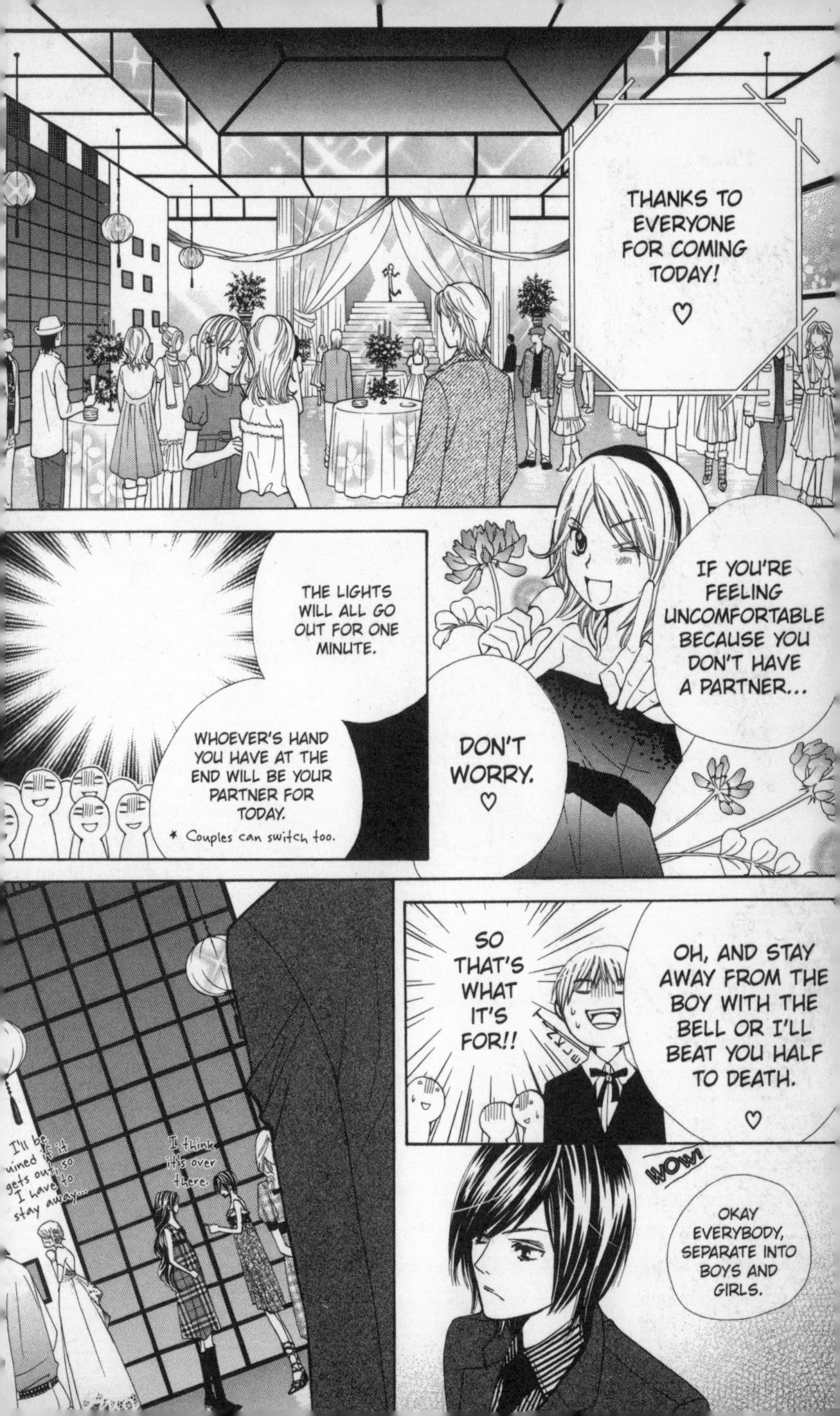
THANKS TO EVERYONE FOR COMING TODAY! ♡
IF YOU'RE FEELING UNCOMFORTABLE BECAUSE YOU DON'T HAVE A PARTNER...
DON'T WORRY. ♡
THE LIGHTS WILL ALL GO OUT FOR ONE MINUTE.
WHOEVER'S HAND YOU HAVE AT THE END WILL BE YOUR PARTNER FOR TODAY.
* Couples can switch too.
OH, AND STAY AWAY FROM THE BOY WITH THE BELL OR I'LL BEAT YOU HALF TO DEATH. ♡
SO THAT'S WHAT IT'S FOR!!
WOW!
OKAY EVERYBODY, SEPARATE INTO BOYS AND GIRLS.
I think it's over there.
I'll be uined if it gets out, so I have to stay away...

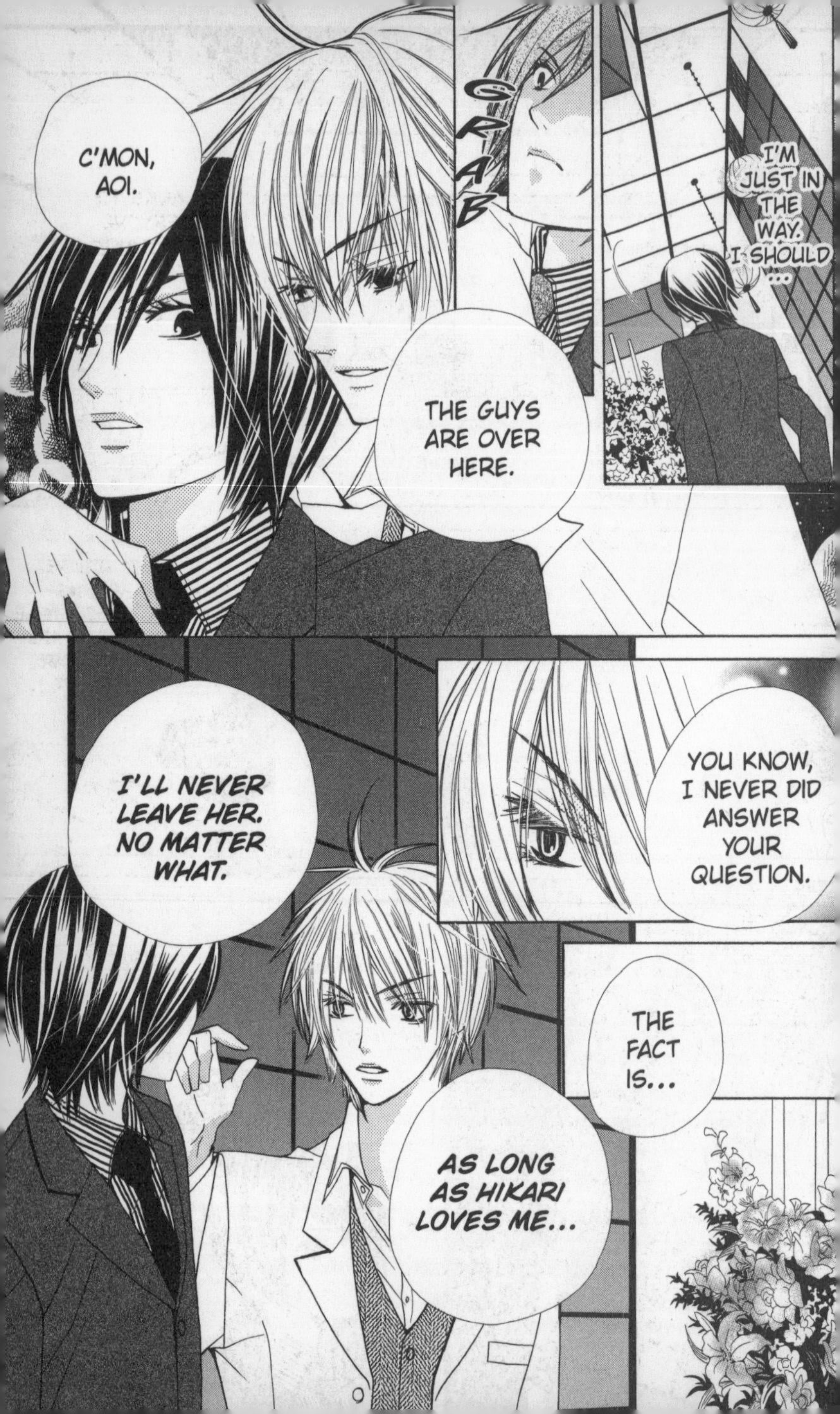
I'M JUST IN THE WAY. I SHOULD...
GRAB
C'MON, AOI.
THE GUYS ARE OVER HERE.
YOU KNOW, I NEVER DID ANSWER YOUR QUESTION.
THE FACT IS...
AS LONG AS HIKARI LOVES ME...
I'LL NEVER LEAVE HER. NO MATTER WHAT.

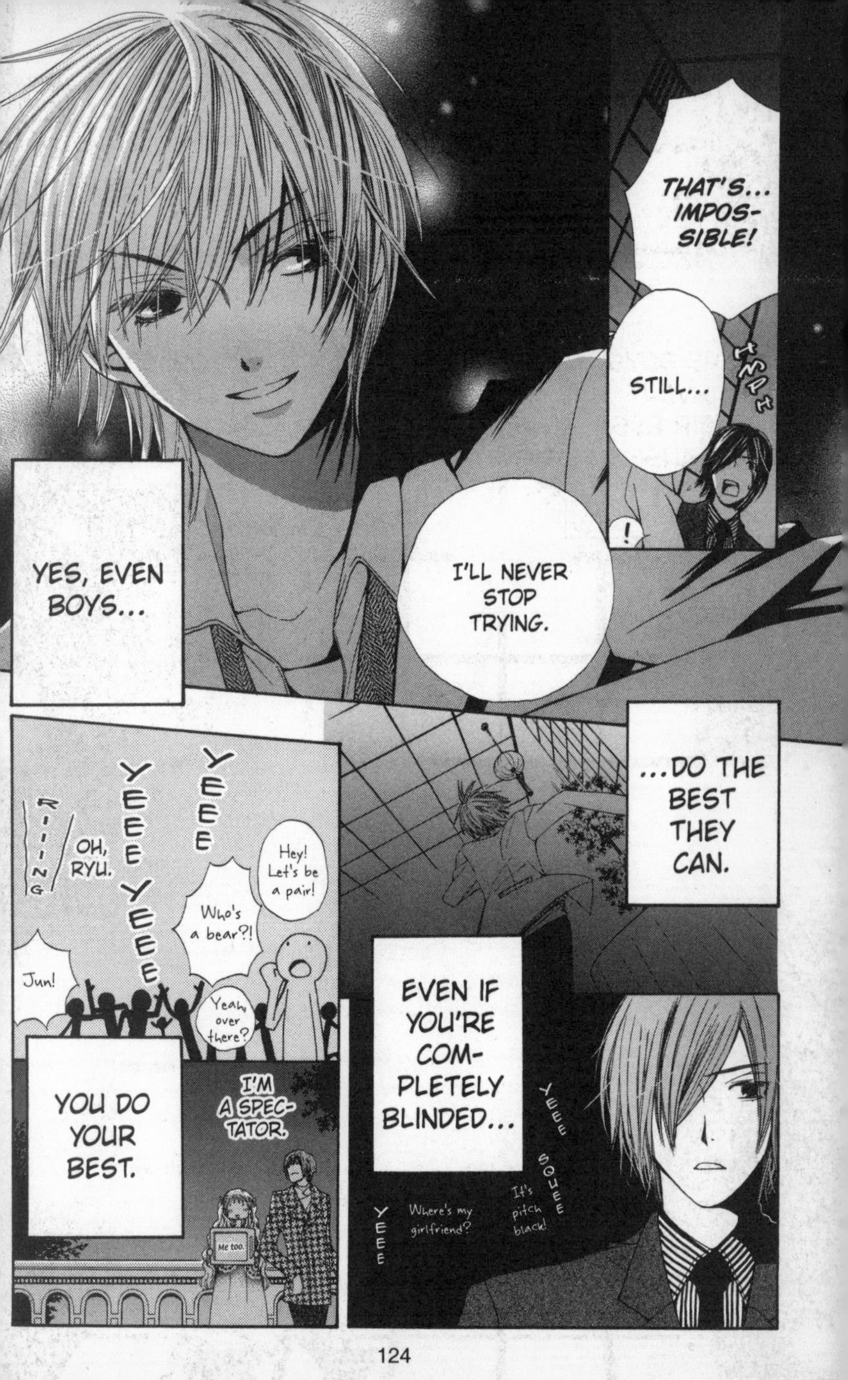
THAT'S... IMPOSSIBLE!
STILL...
!
I'LL NEVER STOP TRYING.
YES, EVEN BOYS...
...DO THE BEST THEY CAN.
YEEE
YEEE YEEE
RIIING
OH, RYU.
Hey! Let's be a pair!
Who's a bear?!
Jun!
Yeah over there?
EVEN IF YOU'RE COMPLETELY BLINDED...
YEEE
SQUEE
It's pitch black!
Where's my girlfriend?
YEEE
YOU DO YOUR BEST.
I'M A SPECTATOR.
Me too.

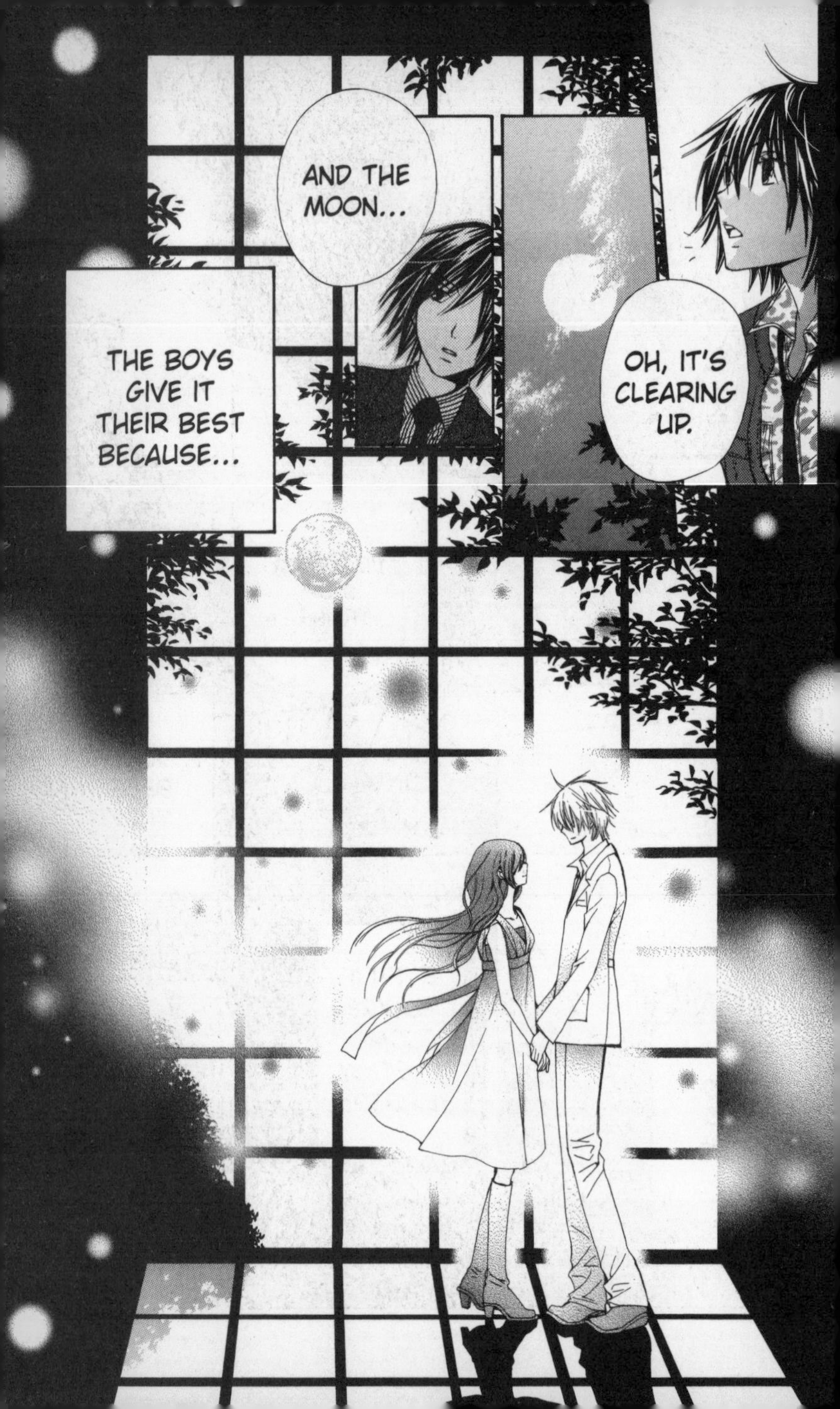
OH, IT'S CLEARING UP.
AND THE MOON...
THE BOYS GIVE IT THEIR BEST BECAUSE...

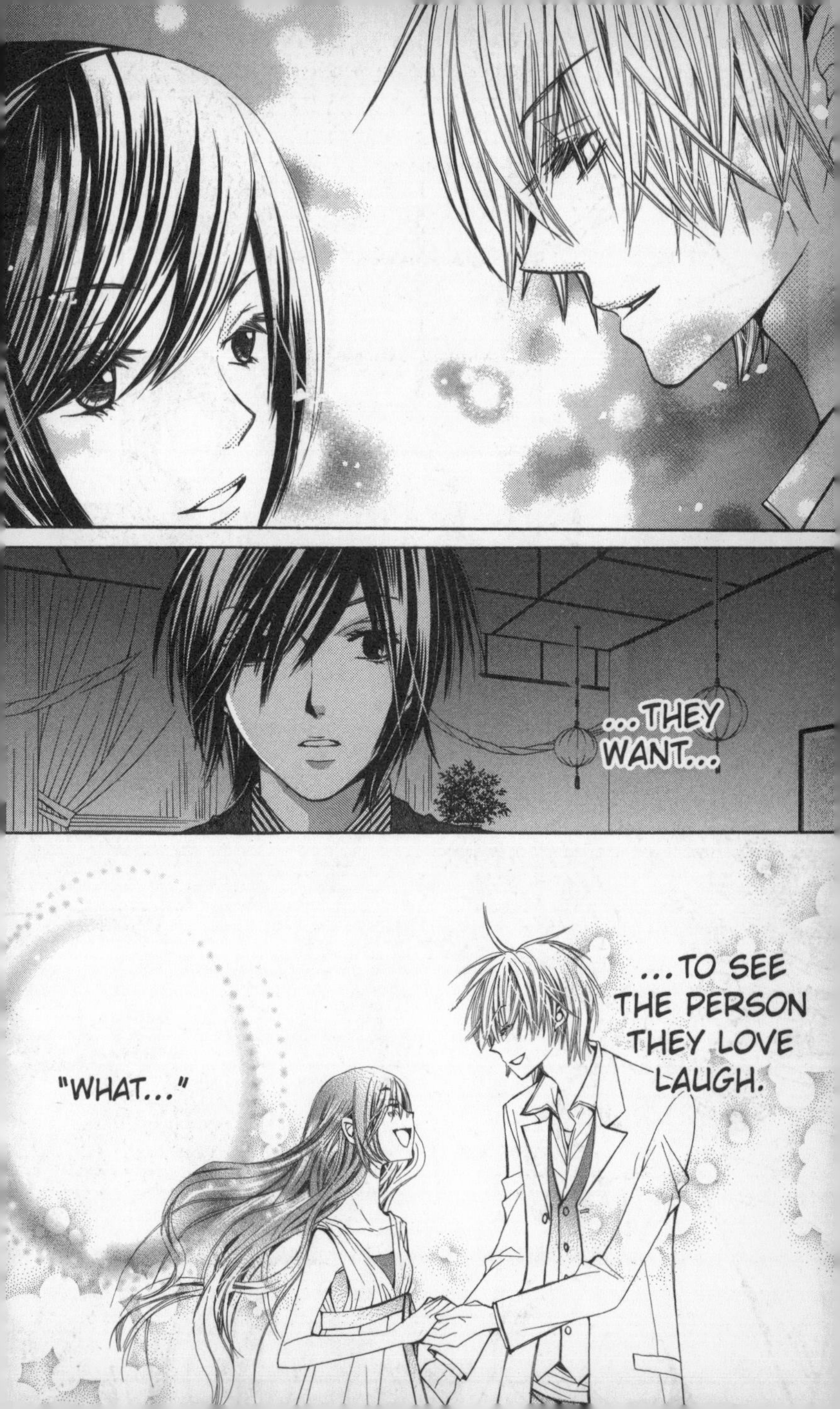
...THEY WANT...
...TO SEE THE PERSON THEY LOVE LAUGH.
"WHAT..."

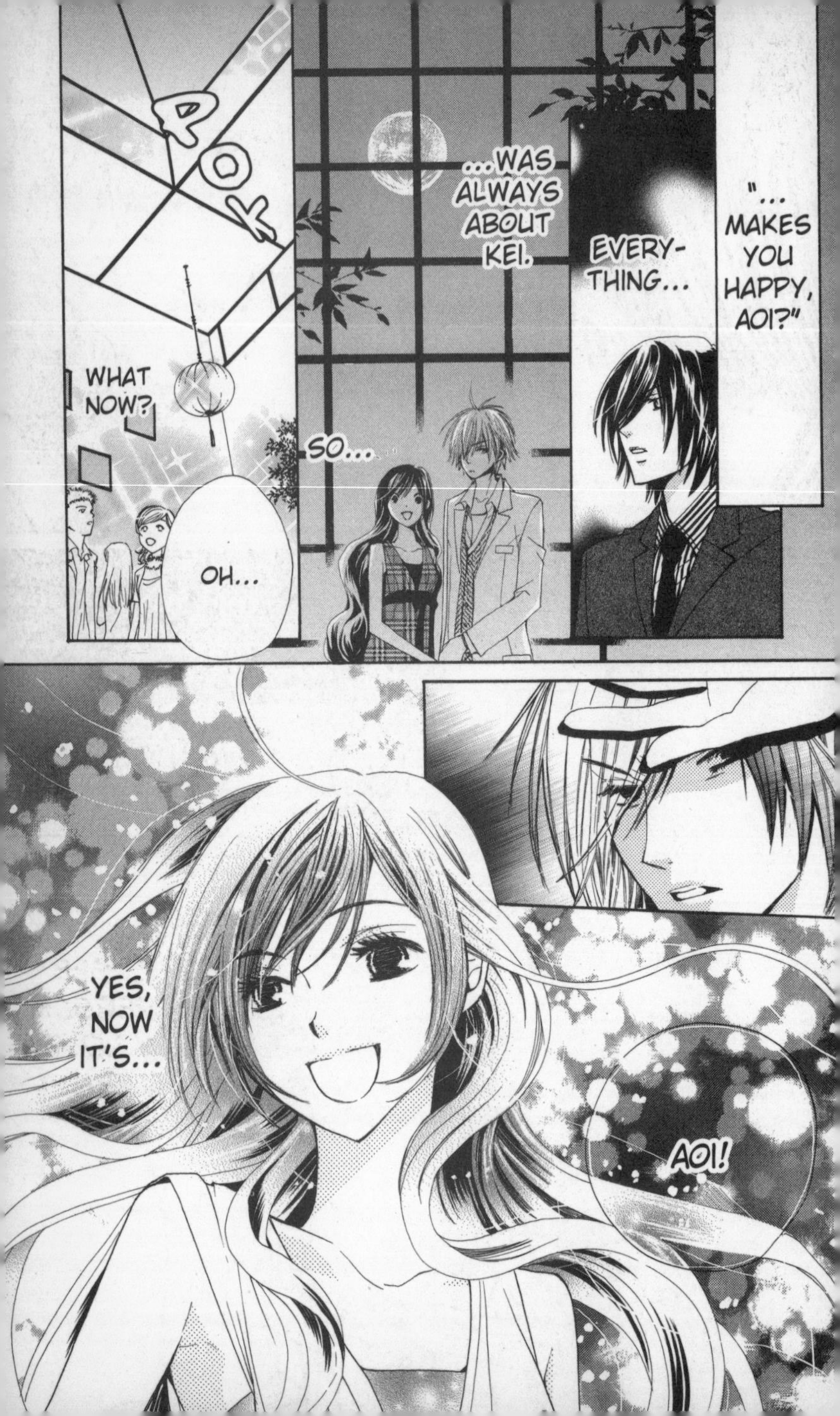
"... MAKES YOU HAPPY, AOI?"
EVERY-THING...
...WAS ALWAYS ABOUT KEI.
SO...
POK
WHAT NOW?
OH...
AOI!
YES, NOW IT'S...

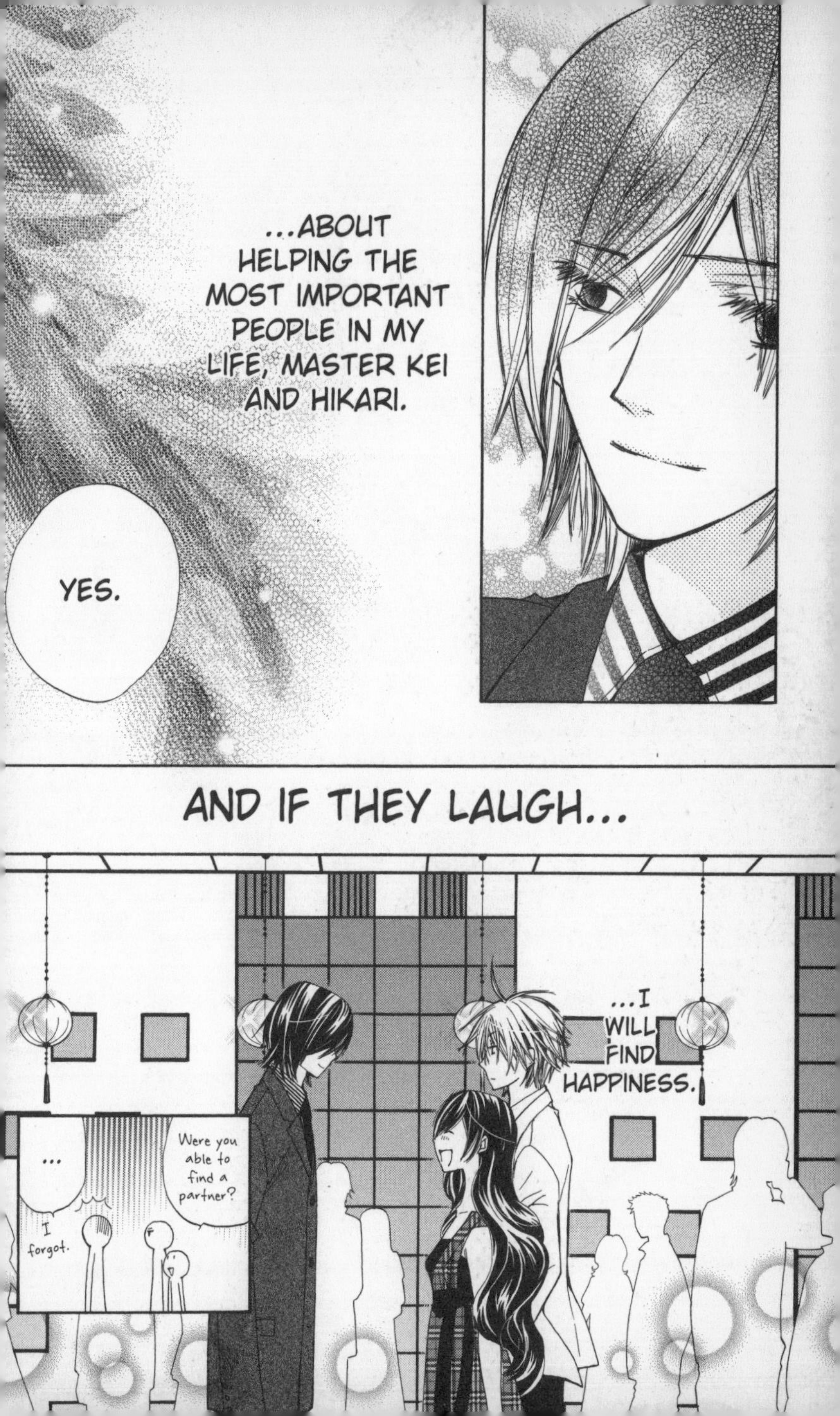
...ABOUT HELPING THE MOST IMPORTANT PEOPLE IN MY LIFE, MASTER KEI AND HIKARI.
YES.
AND IF THEY LAUGH...
...I WILL FIND HAPPINESS.
Were you able to find a partner?
...
I forgot.

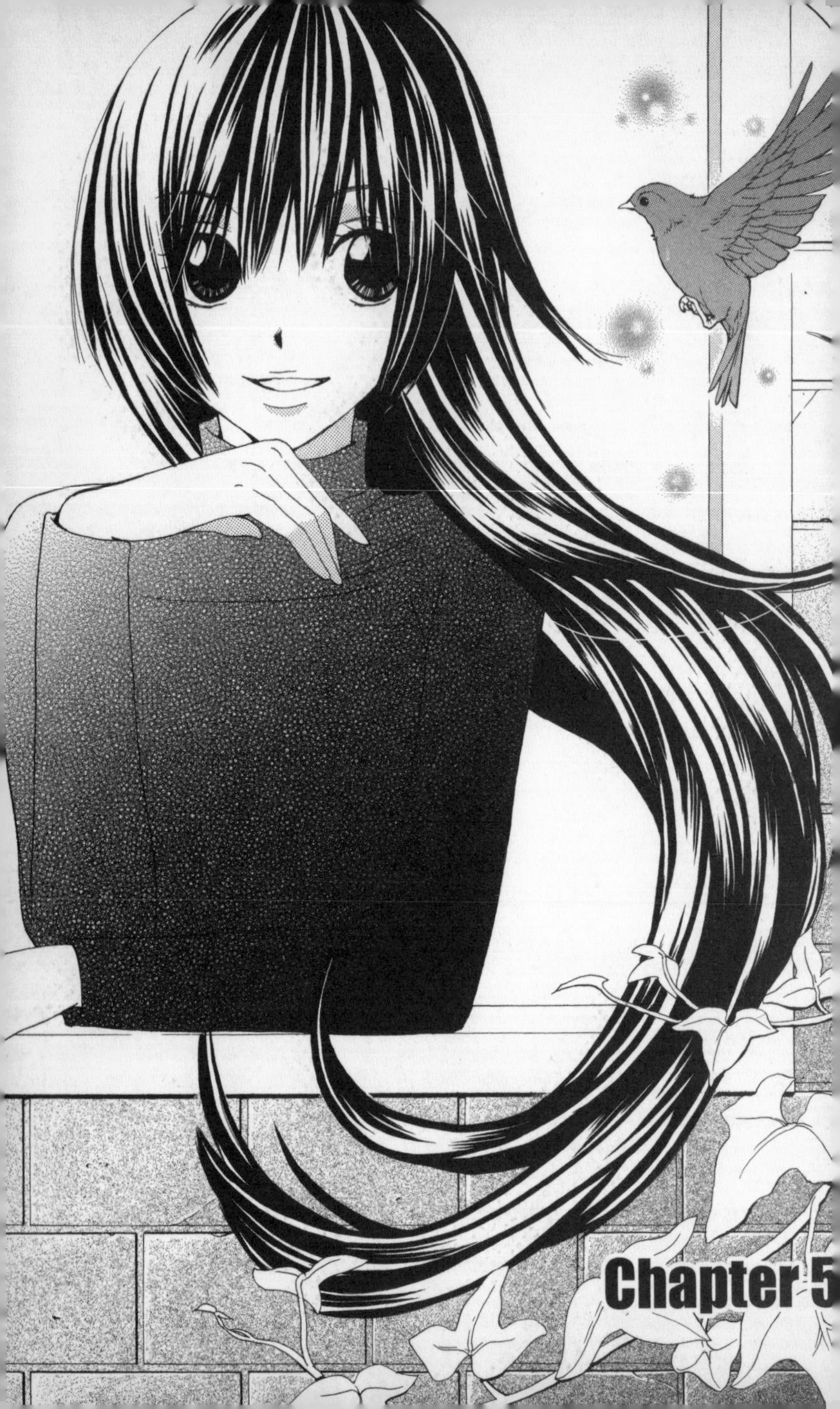
Chapter 5

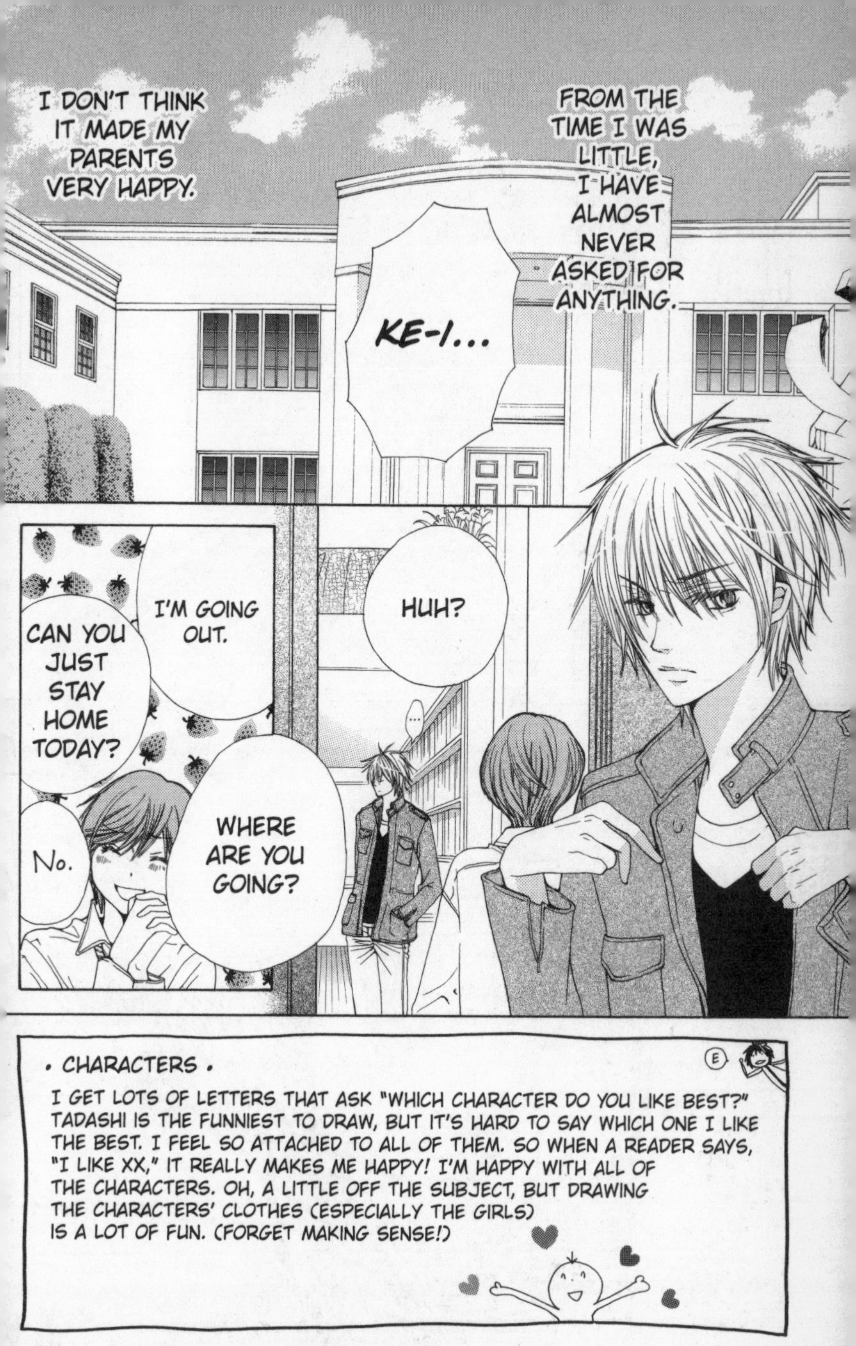
FROM THE TIME I WAS LITTLE, I HAVE ALMOST NEVER ASKED FOR ANYTHING.
KE-I...
I DON'T THINK IT MADE MY PARENTS VERY HAPPY.
HUH?
...
I'M GOING OUT.
CAN YOU JUST STAY HOME TODAY?
WHERE ARE YOU GOING?
No.

• CHARACTERS •

I GET LOTS OF LETTERS THAT ASK "WHICH CHARACTER DO YOU LIKE BEST?" TADASHI IS THE FUNNIEST TO DRAW, BUT IT'S HARD TO SAY WHICH ONE I LIKE THE BEST. I FEEL SO ATTACHED TO ALL OF THEM. SO WHEN A READER SAYS, "I LIKE XX," IT REALLY MAKES ME HAPPY! I'M HAPPY WITH ALL OF THE CHARACTERS. OH, A LITTLE OFF THE SUBJECT, BUT DRAWING THE CHARACTERS' CLOTHES (ESPECIALLY THE GIRLS) IS A LOT OF FUN. (FORGET MAKING SENSE!)

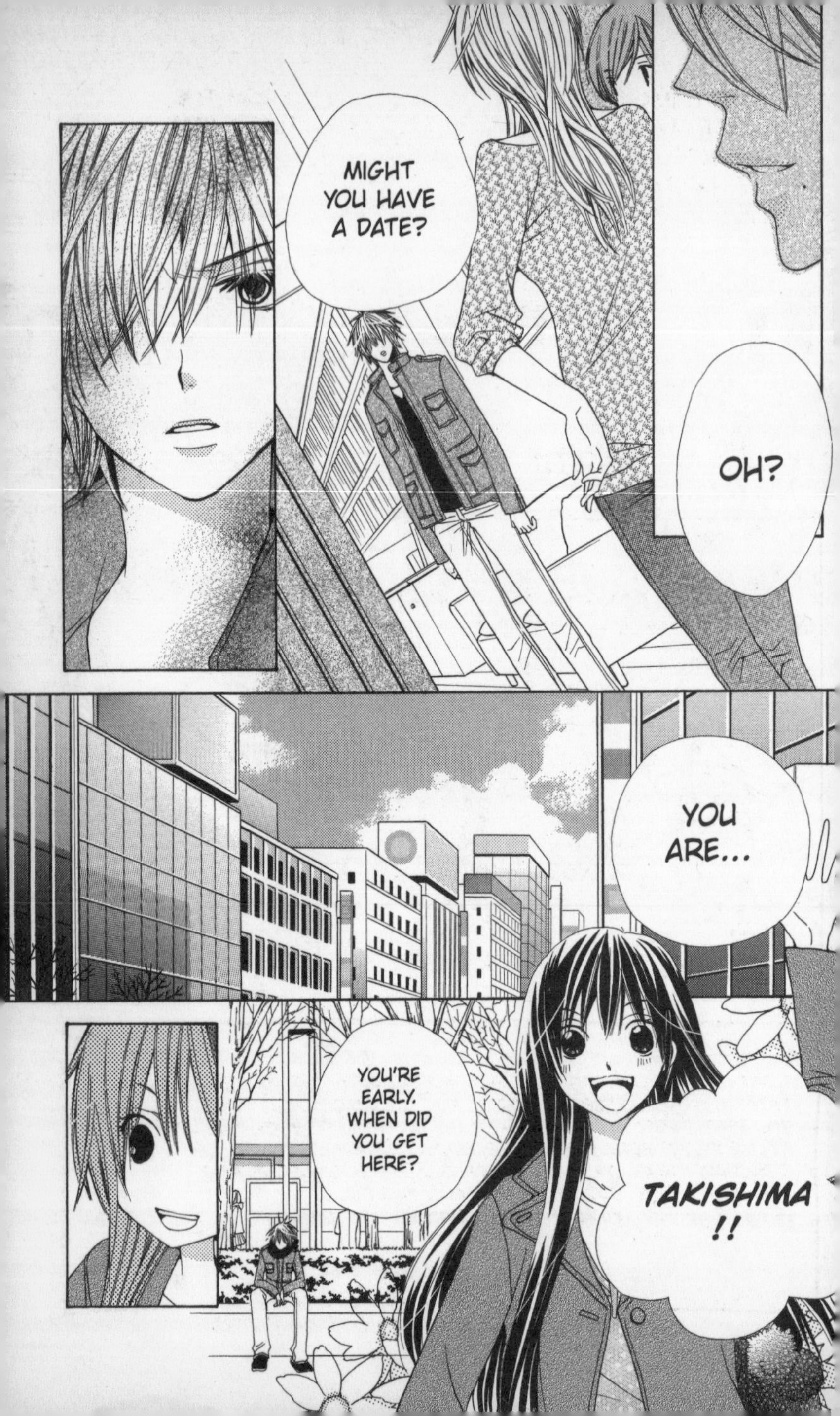
OH?
MIGHT YOU HAVE A DATE?
YOU ARE...
TAKISHIMA !!
YOU'RE EARLY. WHEN DID YOU GET HERE?

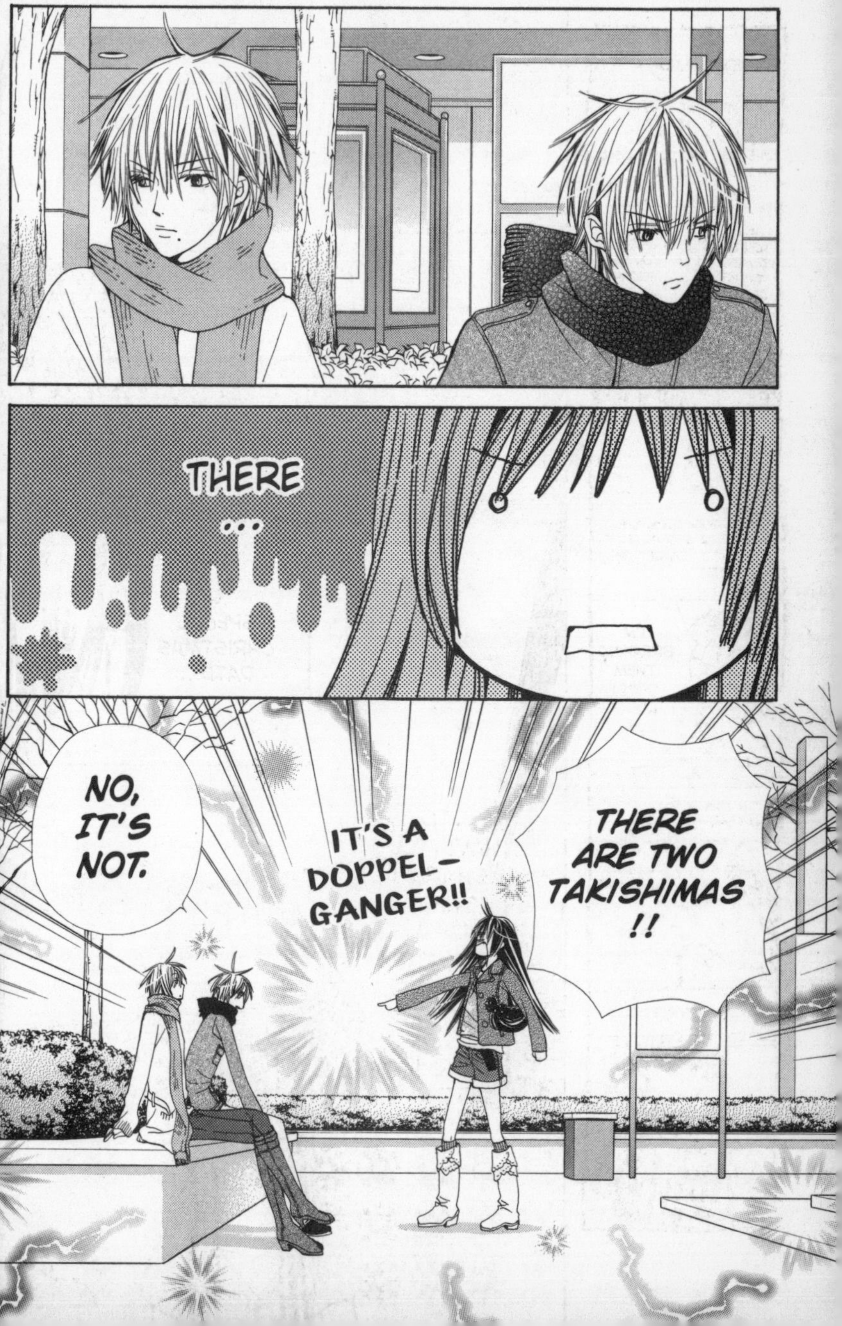
THERE ...
THERE ARE TWO TAKISHIMAS !!
IT'S A DOPPEL-GANGER!!
NO, IT'S NOT.

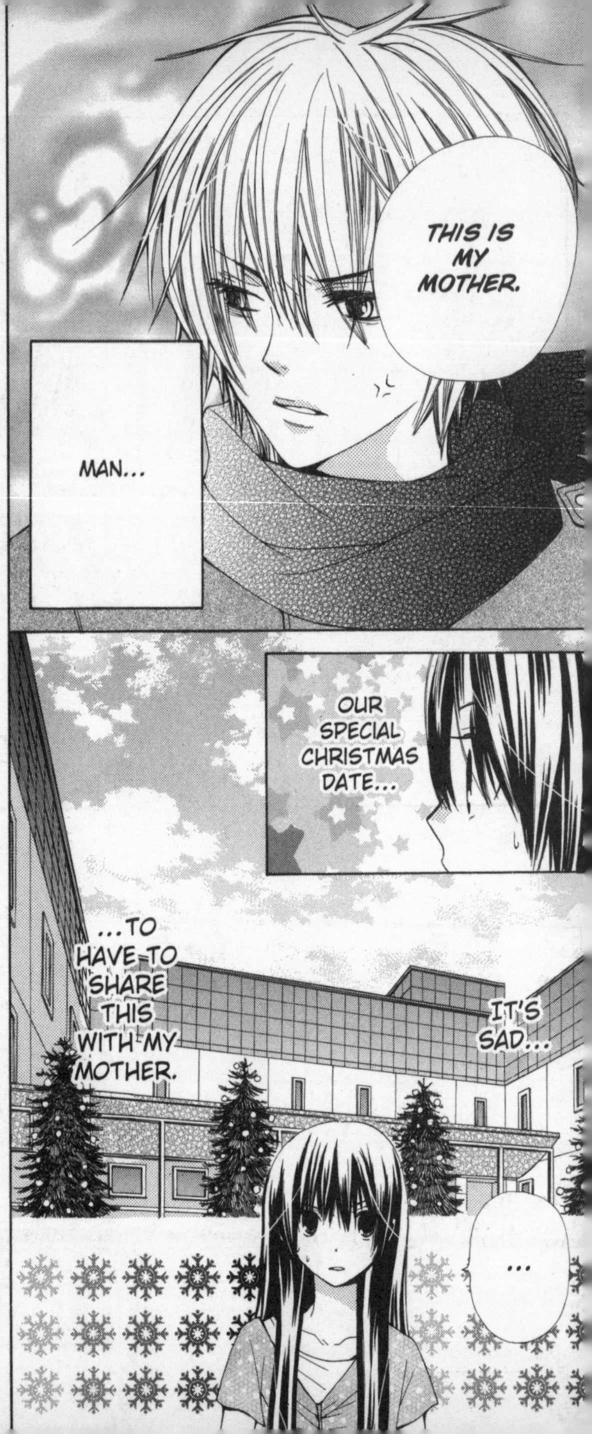
THIS IS MY MOTHER.
MAN...
OUR SPECIAL CHRISTMAS DATE...
IT'S SAD...
...TO HAVE TO SHARE THIS WITH MY MOTHER.
...

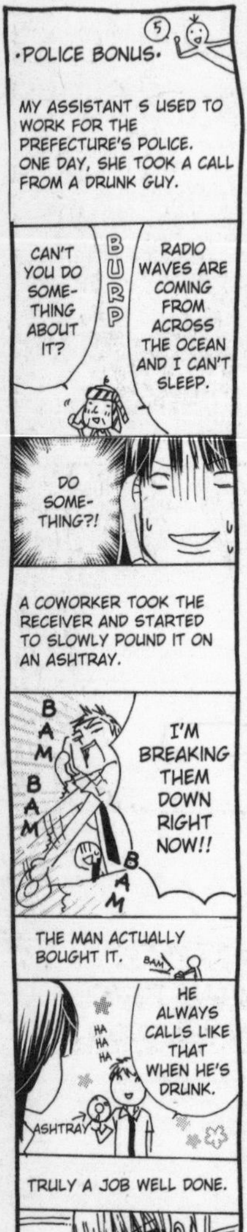
5
•POLICE BONUS•
MY ASSISTANT S USED TO WORK FOR THE PREFECTURE'S POLICE. ONE DAY, SHE TOOK A CALL FROM A DRUNK GUY.
RADIO WAVES ARE COMING FROM ACROSS THE OCEAN AND I CAN'T SLEEP.
BURP
CAN'T YOU DO SOMETHING ABOUT IT?
DO SOMETHING?!
A COWORKER TOOK THE RECEIVER AND STARTED TO SLOWLY POUND IT ON AN ASHTRAY.
I'M BREAKING THEM DOWN RIGHT NOW!!
BAM BAM
BAM
THE MAN ACTUALLY BOUGHT IT.
BAM
HE ALWAYS CALLS LIKE THAT WHEN HE'S DRUNK.
HA HA HA
ASHTRAY
TRULY A JOB WELL DONE.
SA

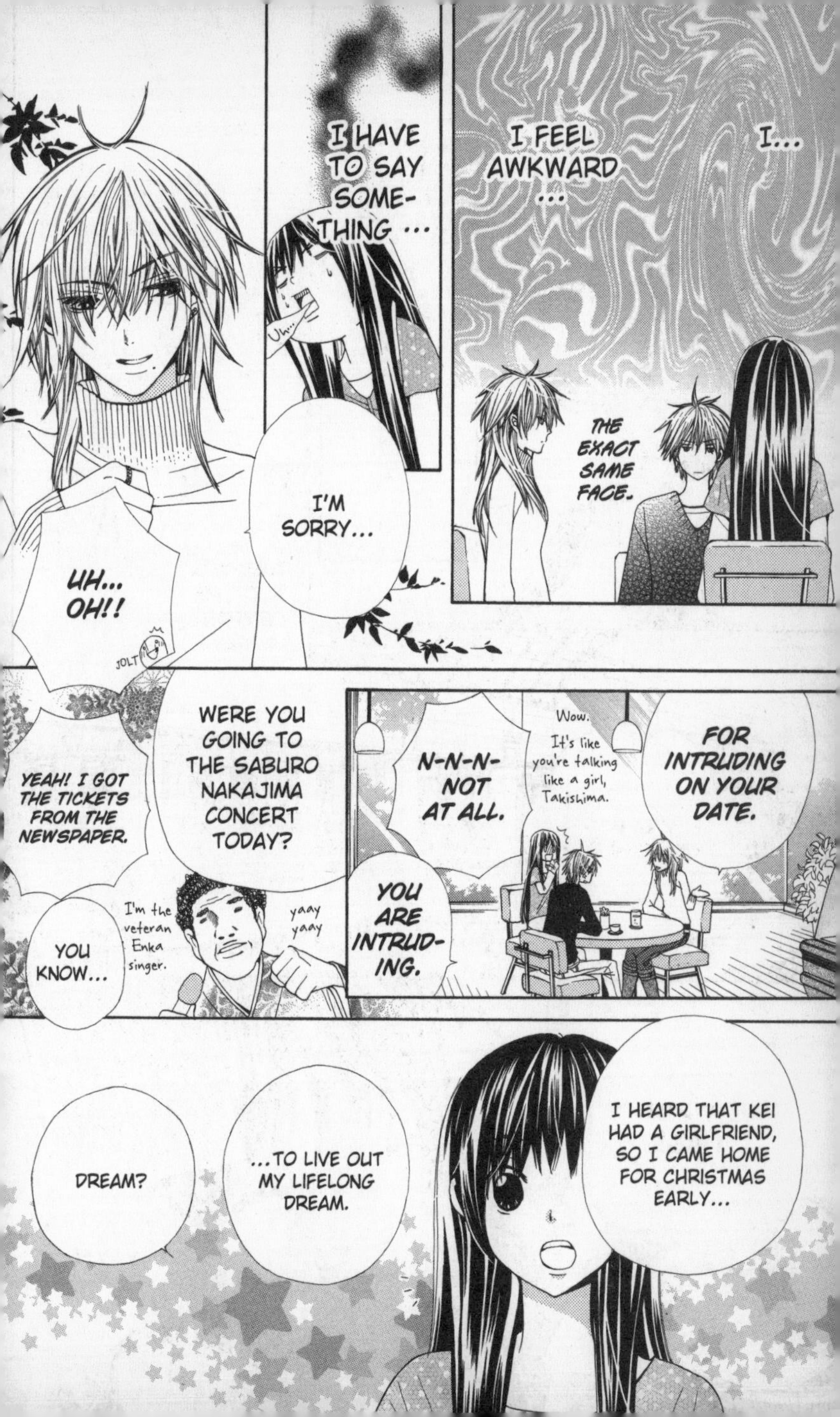
I...
I FEEL AWKWARD ...
THE EXACT SAME FACE.
I HAVE TO SAY SOME-THING ...
Uh...
I'M SORRY...
UH... OH!!
JOLT
FOR INTRUDING ON YOUR DATE.
Wow. It's like you're talking like a girl, Takishima.
N-N-N-NOT AT ALL.
YOU ARE INTRUD-ING.
WERE YOU GOING TO THE SABURO NAKAJIMA CONCERT TODAY?
YEAH! I GOT THE TICKETS FROM THE NEWSPAPER.
yaay yaay
I'm the veteran Enka singer.
YOU KNOW...
I HEARD THAT KEI HAD A GIRLFRIEND, SO I CAME HOME FOR CHRISTMAS EARLY...
...TO LIVE OUT MY LIFELONG DREAM.
DREAM?

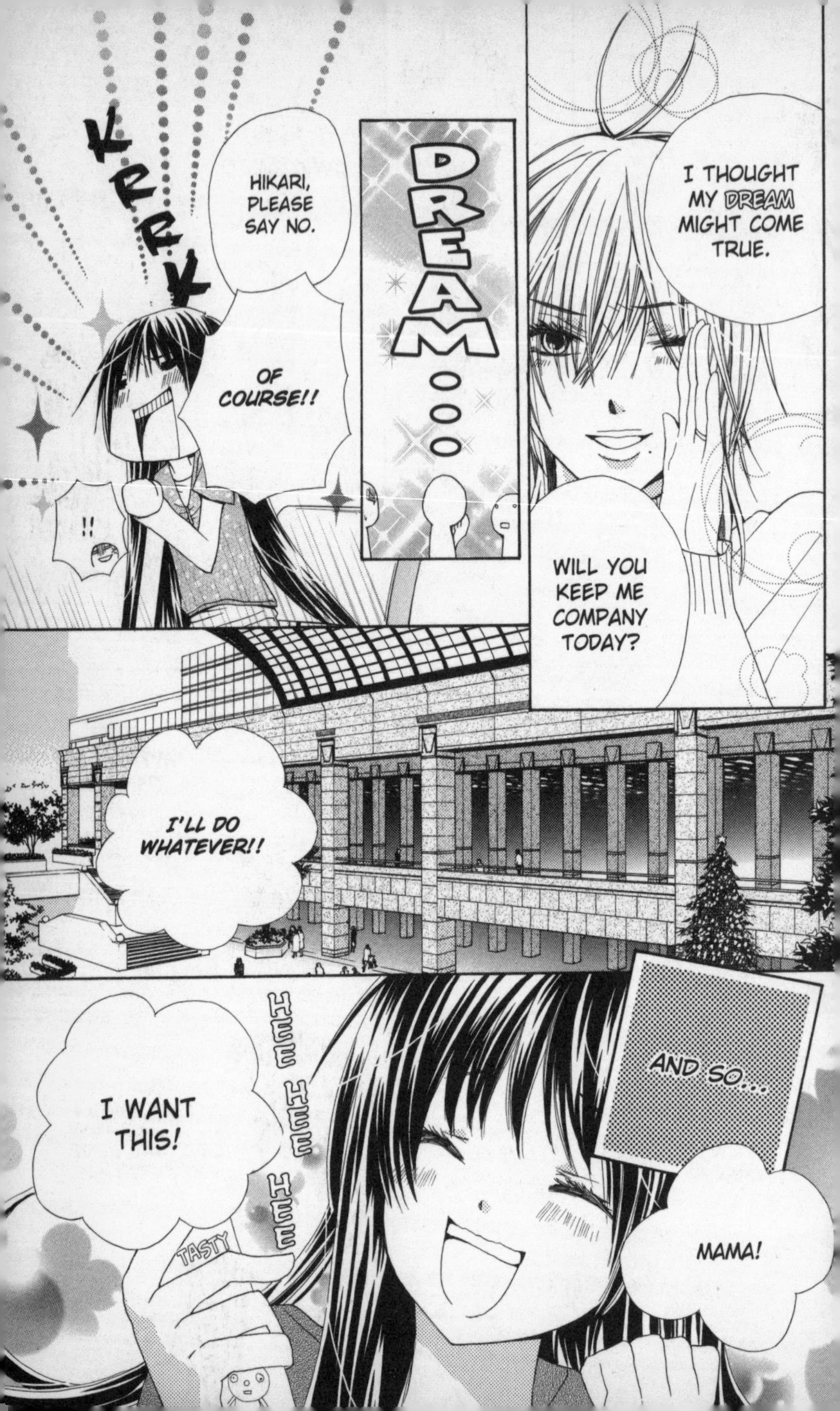
I THOUGHT MY DREAM MIGHT COME TRUE.
WILL YOU KEEP ME COMPANY TODAY?
DREAM...
HIKARI, PLEASE SAY NO.
KRRK
OF COURSE!!
!!
I'LL DO WHATEVER!!
AND SO...
MAMA!
HEE HEE HEE
TASTY
I WANT THIS!

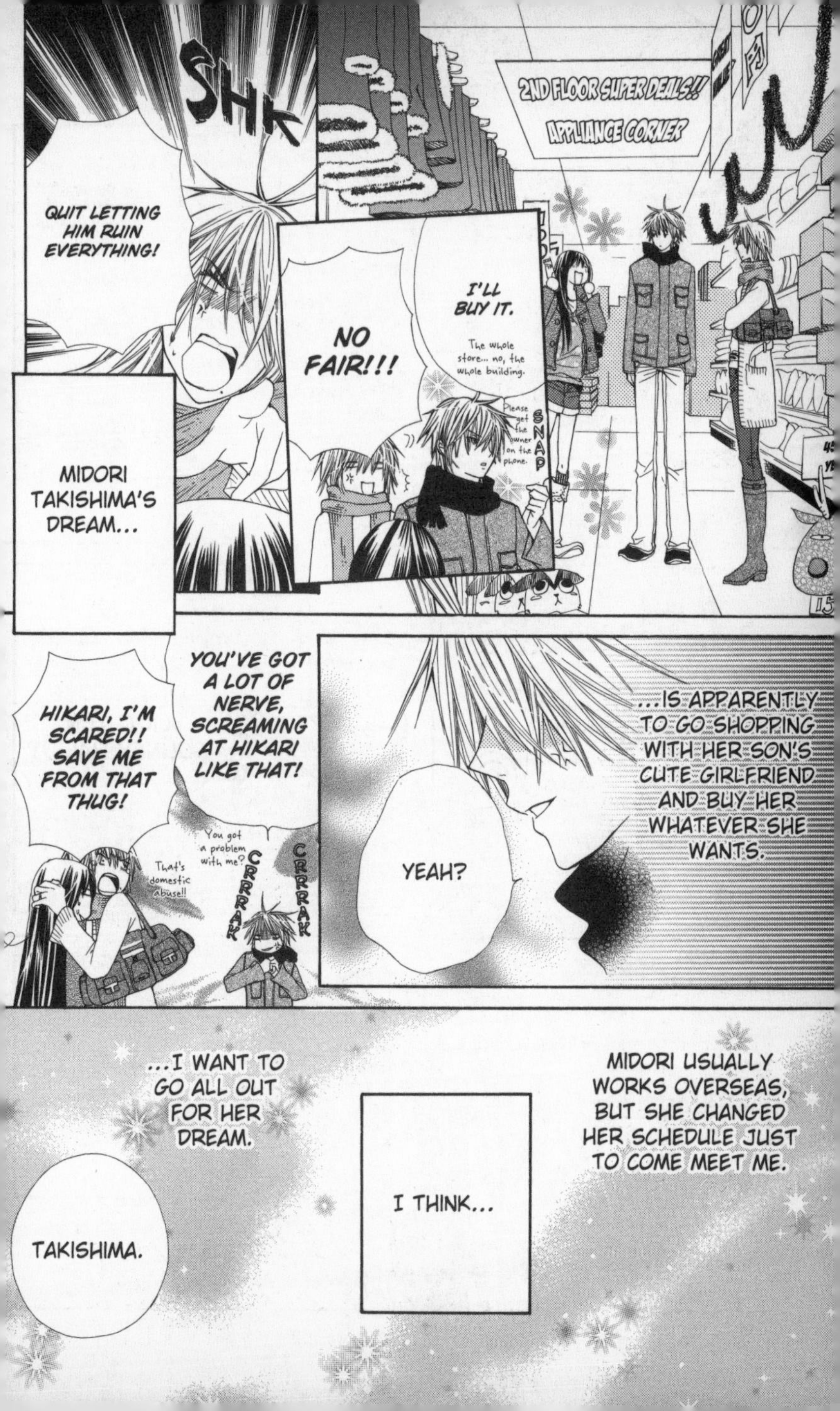

2ND FLOOR SUPER DEALS!!
APPLIANCE CORNER
I'LL BUY IT.
The whole store... no, the whole building.
Please get the owner on the phone.
SNAP
NO FAIR!!!
SHK
QUIT LETTING HIM RUIN EVERYTHING!
MIDORI TAKISHIMA'S DREAM...
...IS APPARENTLY TO GO SHOPPING WITH HER SON'S CUTE GIRLFRIEND AND BUY HER WHATEVER SHE WANTS.
YEAH?
YOU'VE GOT A LOT OF NERVE, SCREAMING AT HIKARI LIKE THAT!
HIKARI, I'M SCARED!! SAVE ME FROM THAT THUG!
CRRRAK
You got a problem with me?
CRRRAK
That's domestic abuse!!
MIDORI USUALLY WORKS OVERSEAS, BUT SHE CHANGED HER SCHEDULE JUST TO COME MEET ME.
I THINK...
...I WANT TO GO ALL OUT FOR HER DREAM.
TAKISHIMA.

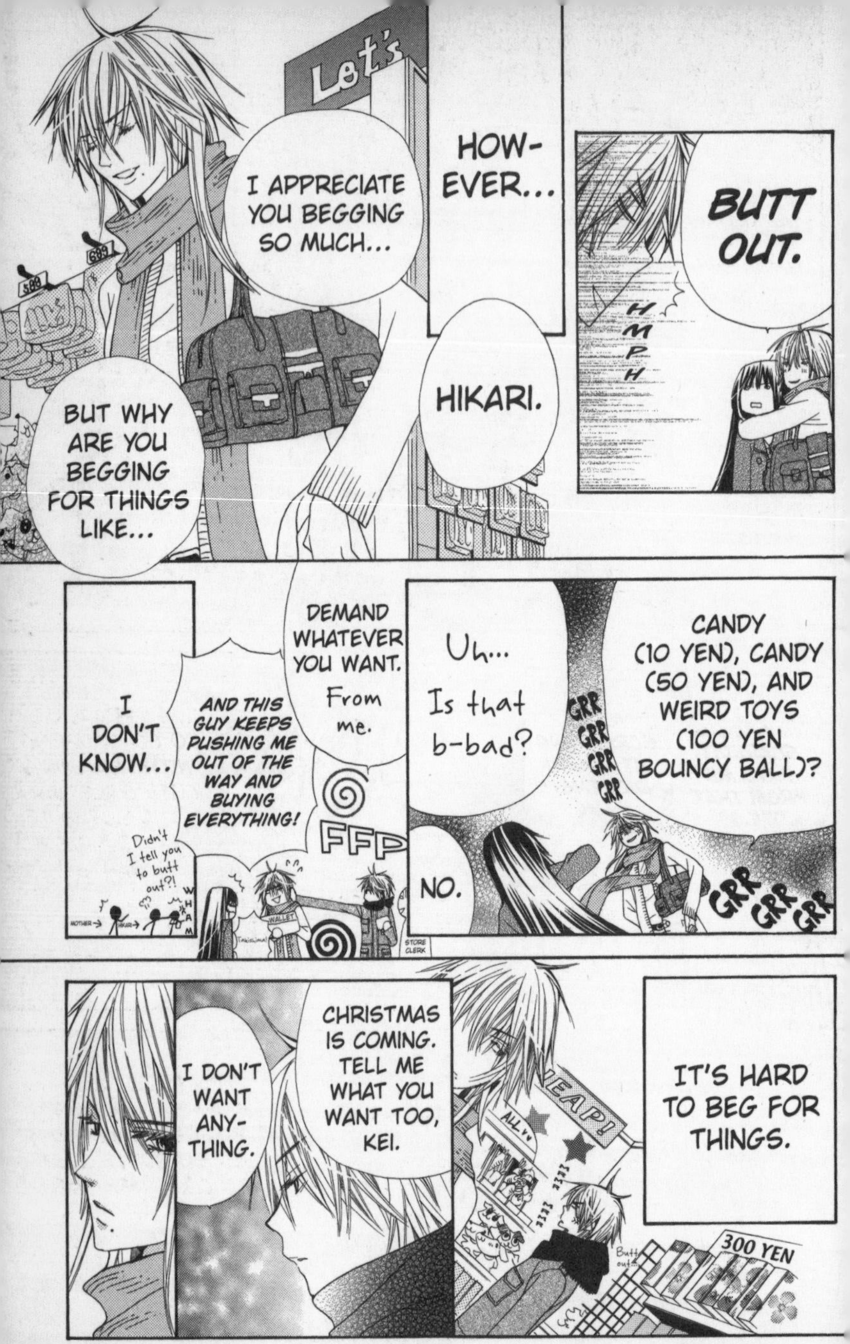
BUTT OUT.
HMPH
HOW-EVER...
I APPRECIATE YOU BEGGING SO MUCH...
Let's
HIKARI.
BUT WHY ARE YOU BEGGING FOR THINGS LIKE...
CANDY (10 YEN), CANDY (50 YEN), AND WEIRD TOYS (100 YEN BOUNCY BALL)?
GRR GRR GRR GRR
GRR GRR GRR
Uh... Is that b-bad?
NO.
DEMAND WHATEVER YOU WANT.
From me.
FFP
AND THIS GUY KEEPS PUSHING ME OUT OF THE WAY AND BUYING EVERYTHING!
I DON'T KNOW...
Didn't I tell you to butt out?!
WHAM
MOTHER
WALLET
STORE CLERK
IT'S HARD TO BEG FOR THINGS.
HEAP!
300 YEN
Butt out...
CHRISTMAS IS COMING. TELL ME WHAT YOU WANT TOO, KEI.
I DON'T WANT ANY-THING.

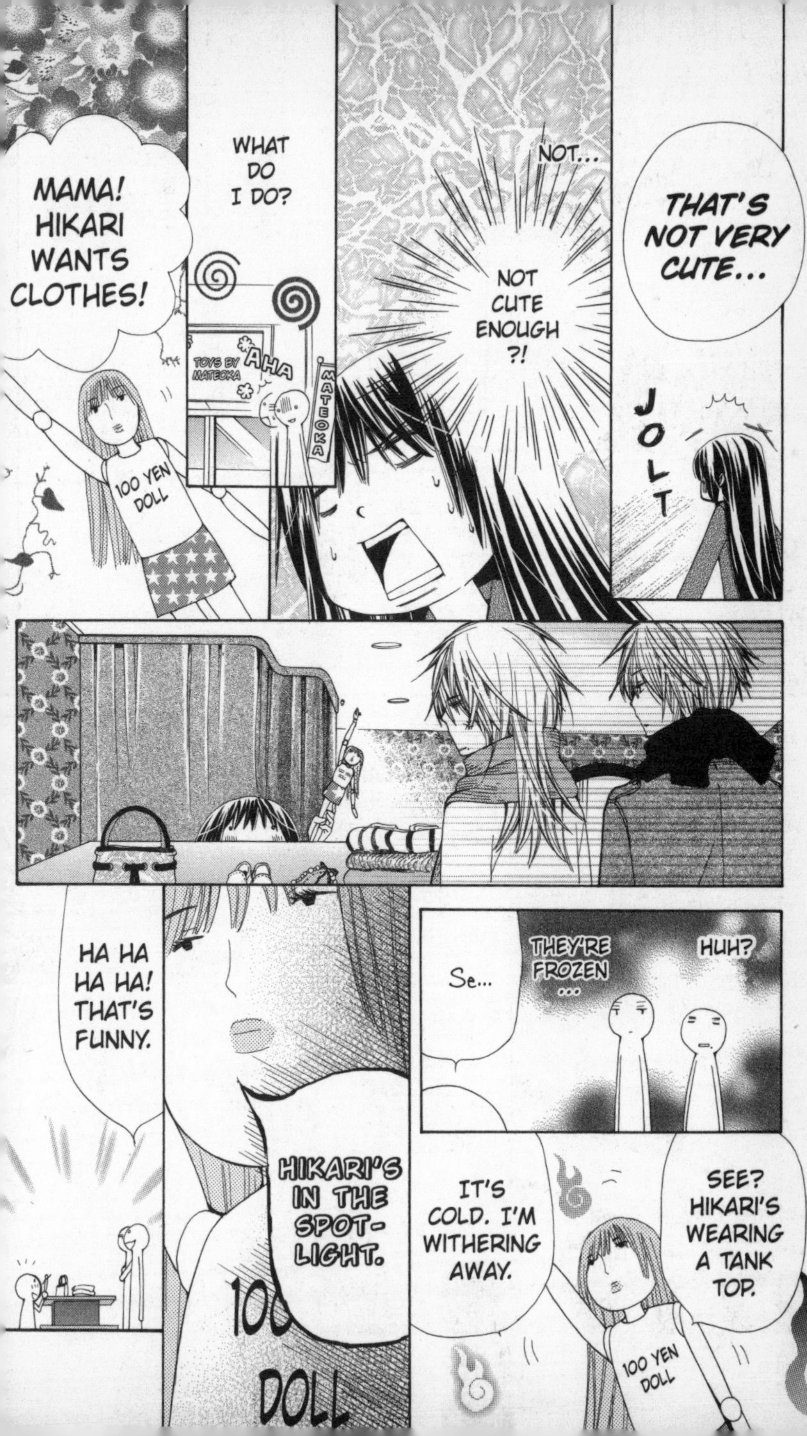
THAT'S NOT VERY CUTE...
JOLT
NOT...
NOT CUTE ENOUGH ?!
WHAT DO I DO?
TOYS BY MATEOKA
AHA
MATEOKA
MAMA! HIKARI WANTS CLOTHES!
100 YEN DOLL
HUH?
THEY'RE FROZEN ...
Se...
SEE? HIKARI'S WEARING A TANK TOP.
IT'S COLD. I'M WITHERING AWAY.
100 YEN DOLL
HIKARI'S IN THE SPOT-LIGHT.
HA HA HA HA! THAT'S FUNNY.

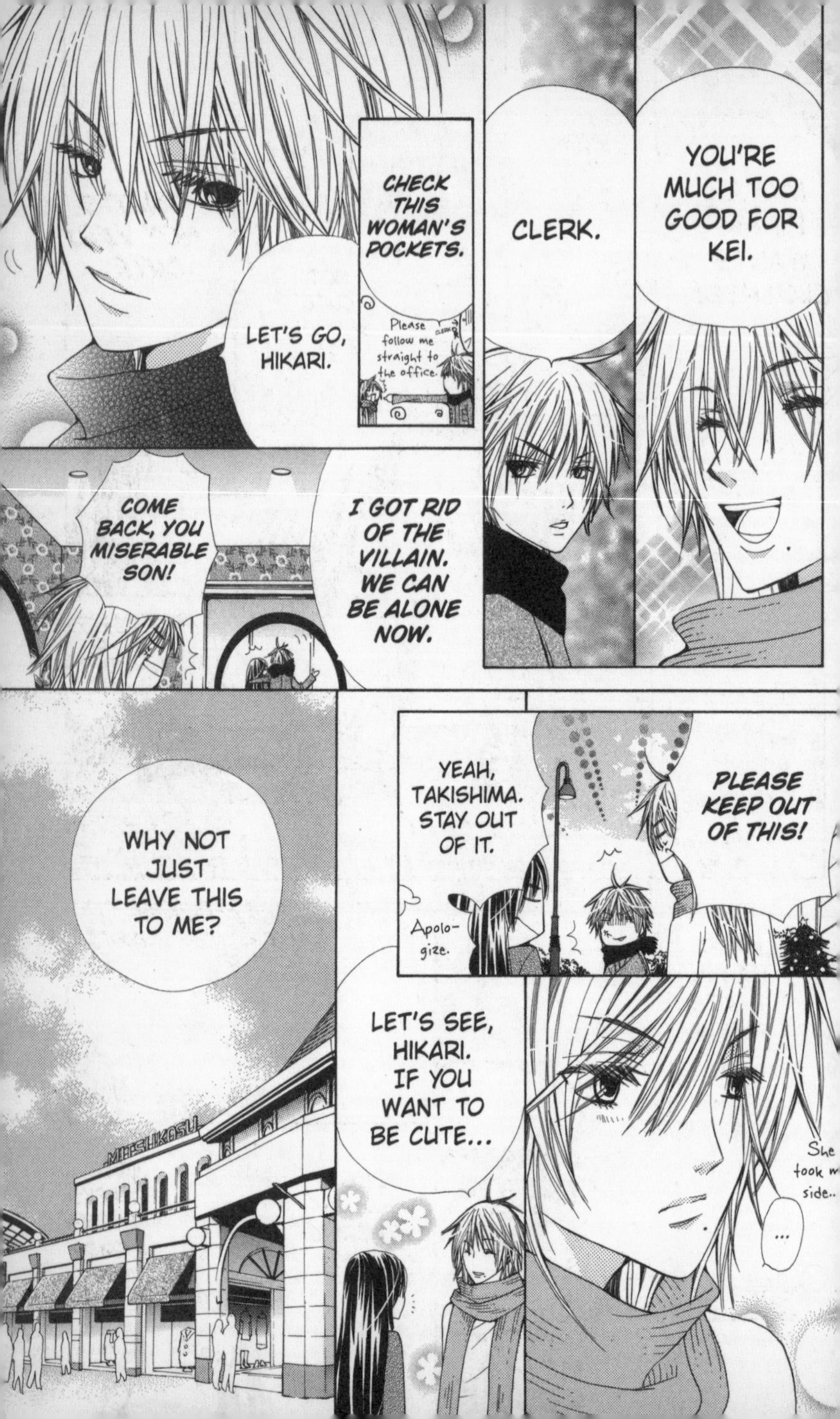
YOU'RE MUCH TOO GOOD FOR KEI.
CLERK.
CHECK THIS WOMAN'S POCKETS.
CLERK
Please follow me straight to the office.
LET'S GO, HIKARI.
I GOT RID OF THE VILLAIN. WE CAN BE ALONE NOW.
COME BACK, YOU MISERABLE SON!
PLEASE KEEP OUT OF THIS!
YEAH, TAKISHIMA. STAY OUT OF IT.
Apolo-gize.
She took m side..
...
LET'S SEE, HIKARI. IF YOU WANT TO BE CUTE...
WHY NOT JUST LEAVE THIS TO ME?

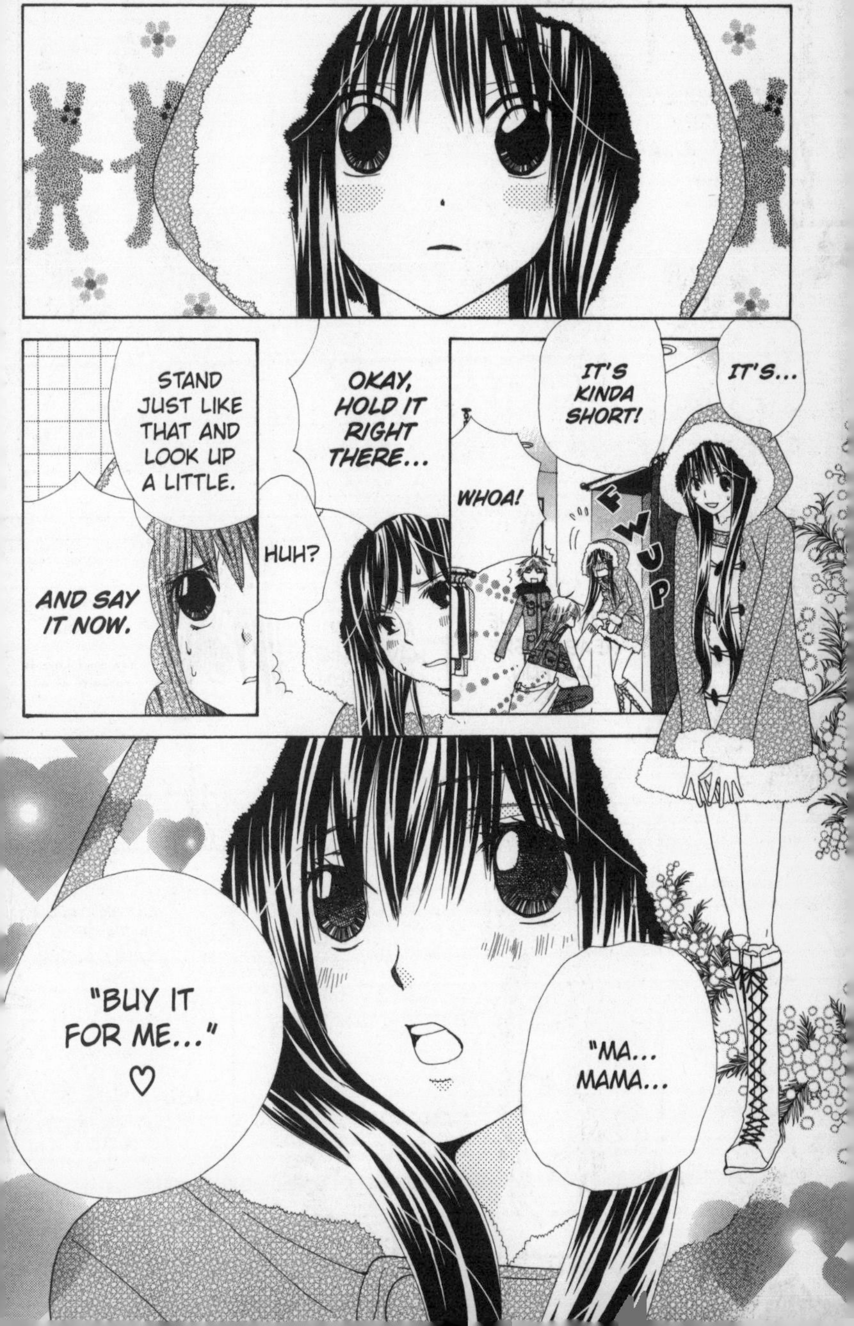
IT'S...
IT'S KINDA SHORT!
WHOA!
FWUP
OKAY, HOLD IT RIGHT THERE...
HUH?
STAND JUST LIKE THAT AND LOOK UP A LITTLE.
AND SAY IT NOW.
"MA... MAMA...
"BUY IT FOR ME..." ♡

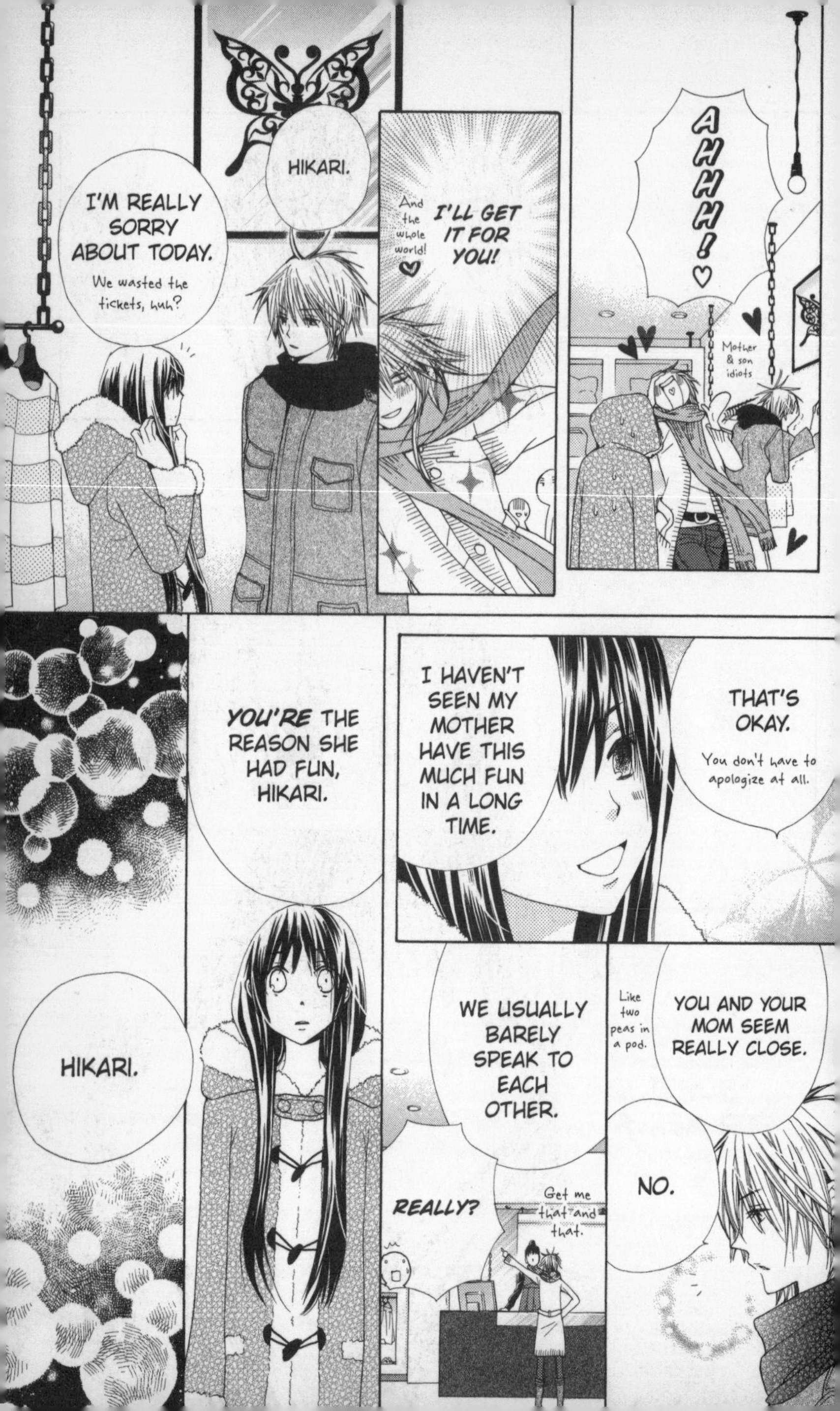
AHHHH! ♥
Mother & son idiots
I'LL GET IT FOR YOU!
And the whole world! ♥
HIKARI.
I'M REALLY SORRY ABOUT TODAY.
We wasted the tickets, huh?
THAT'S OKAY.
You don't have to apologize at all.
I HAVEN'T SEEN MY MOTHER HAVE THIS MUCH FUN IN A LONG TIME.
YOU AND YOUR MOM SEEM REALLY CLOSE.
Like two peas in a pod.
NO.
WE USUALLY BARELY SPEAK TO EACH OTHER.
REALLY?
Get me that and that.
YOU'RE THE REASON SHE HAD FUN, HIKARI.
HIKARI.

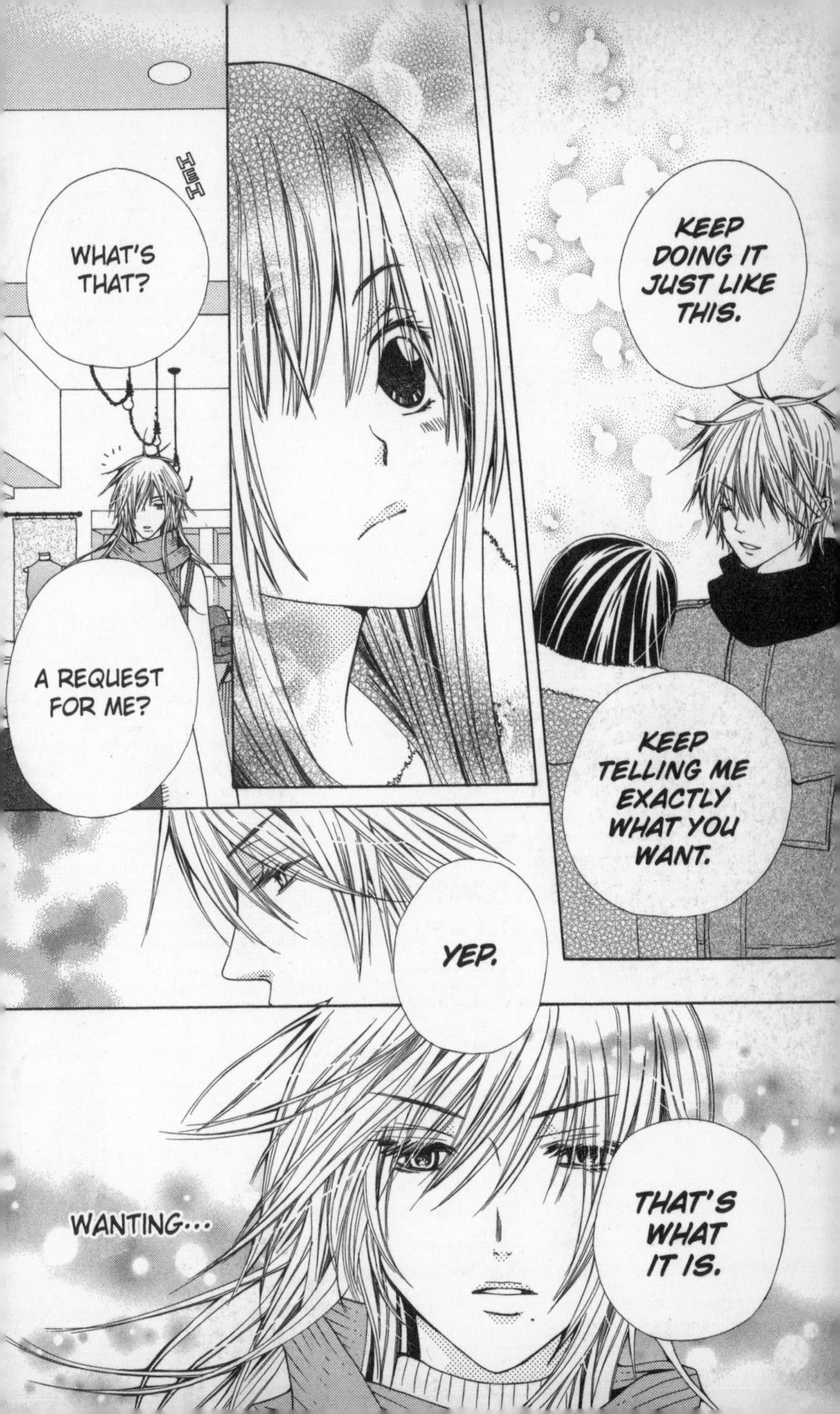
KEEP DOING IT JUST LIKE THIS.
KEEP TELLING ME EXACTLY WHAT YOU WANT.
HEH
WHAT'S THAT?
A REQUEST FOR ME?
YEP.
THAT'S WHAT IT IS.
WANTING...

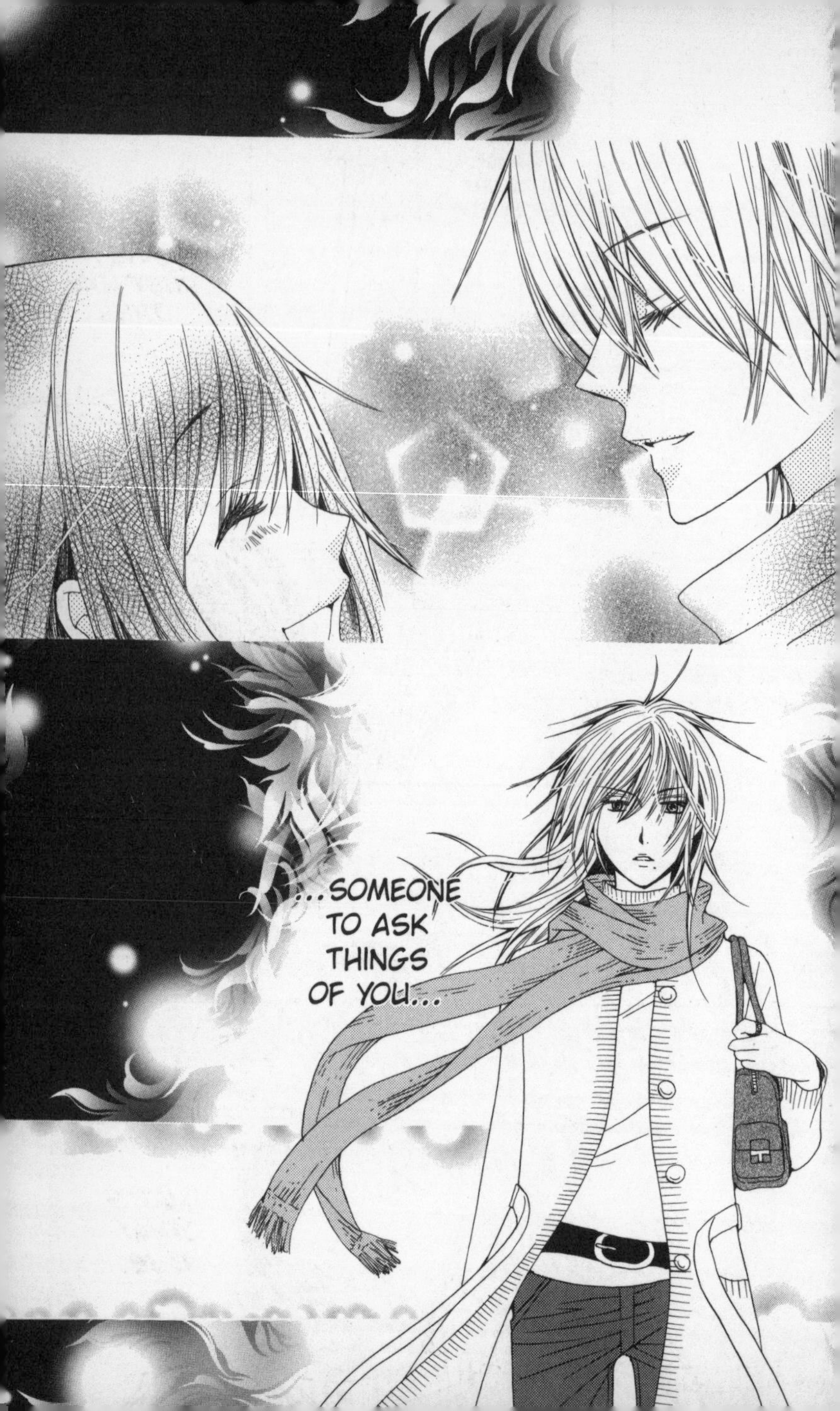
...SOMEONE TO ASK THINGS OF YOU...

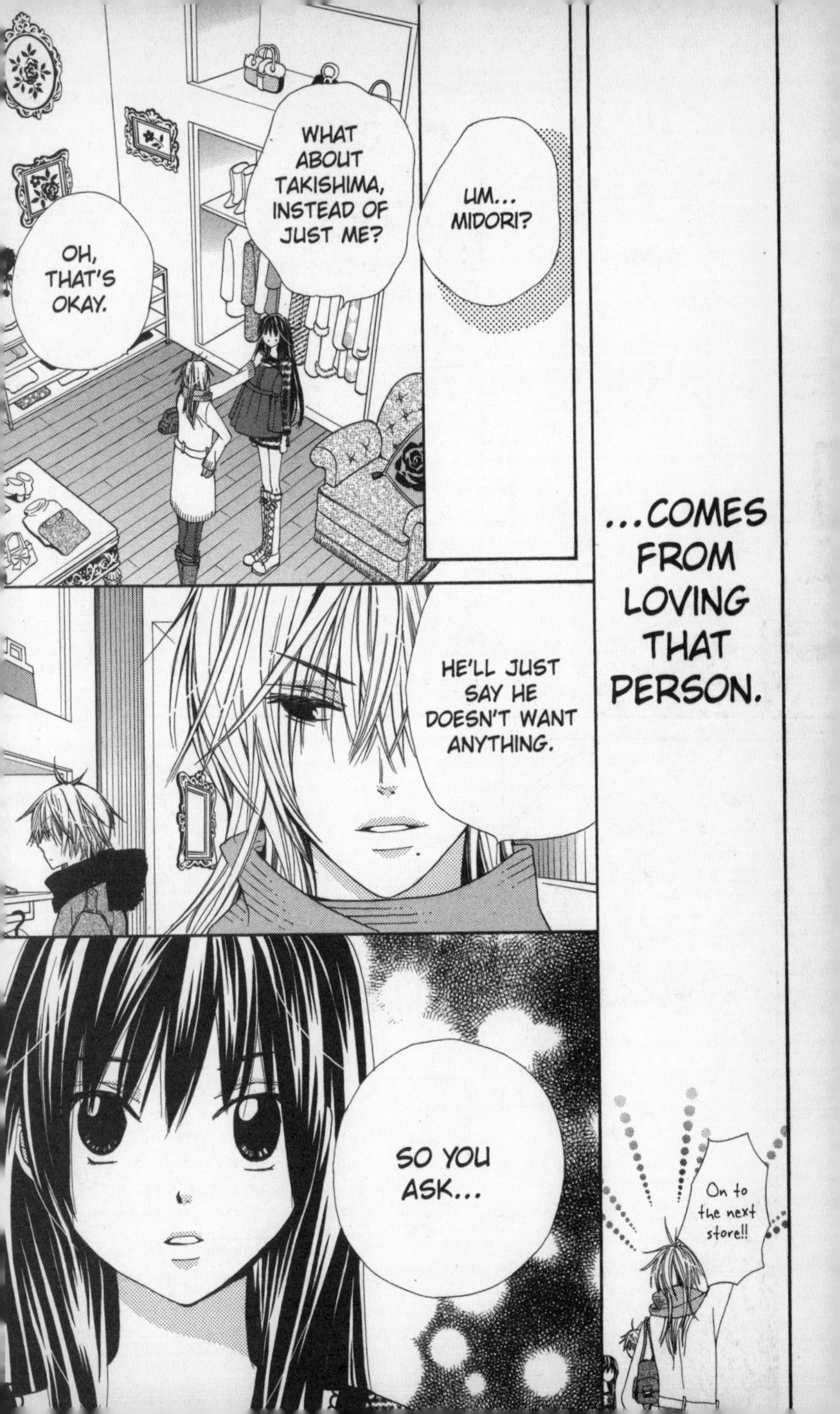
...COMES FROM LOVING THAT PERSON.
On to the next store!!
UM... MIDORI?
WHAT ABOUT TAKISHIMA, INSTEAD OF JUST ME?
OH, THAT'S OKAY.
HE'LL JUST SAY HE DOESN'T WANT ANYTHING.
SO YOU ASK...

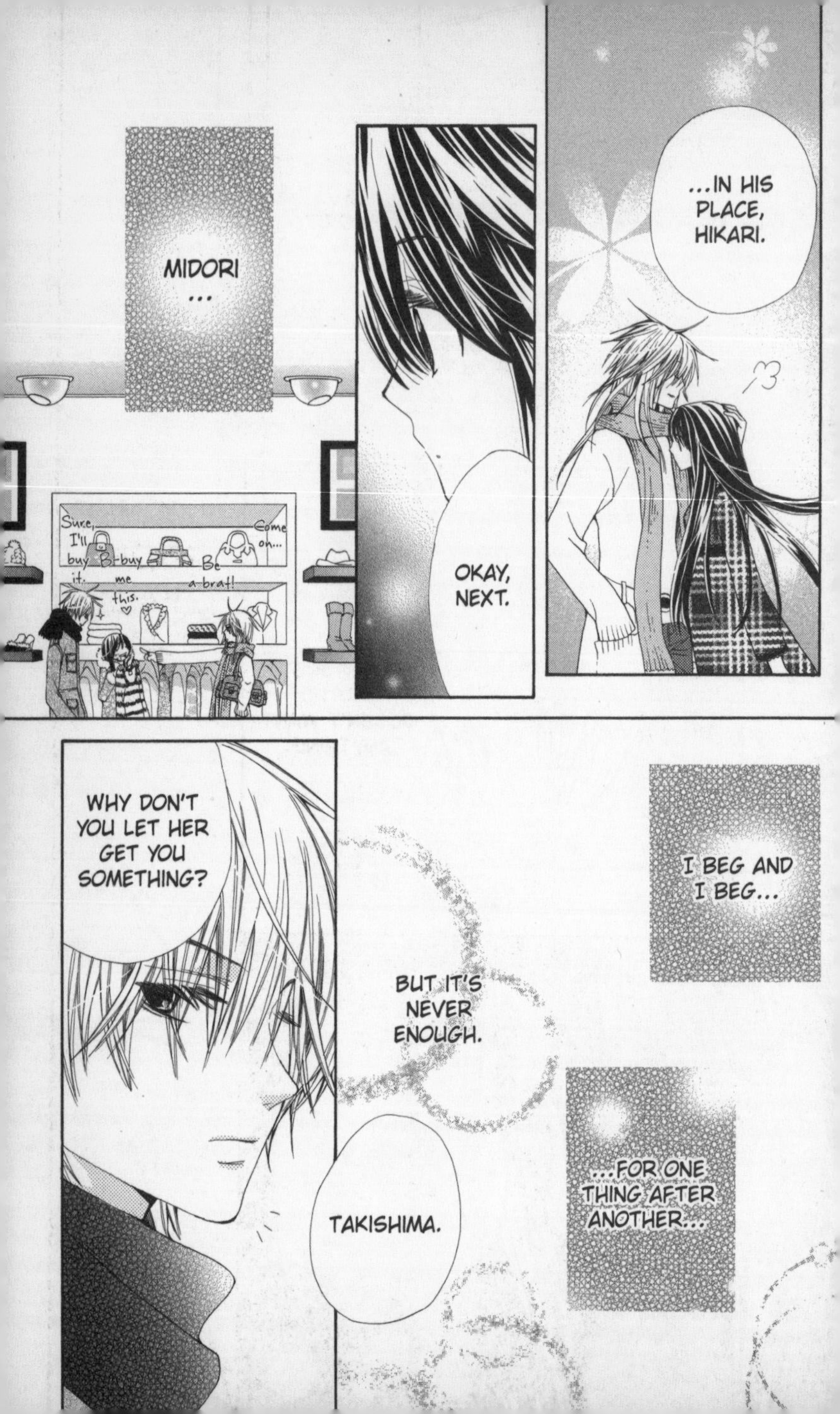
...IN HIS PLACE, HIKARI.
OKAY, NEXT.
MIDORI ...
Come on...
Be a brat!
Sure, I'll buy it.
B-buy me this. ♡
I BEG AND I BEG...
...FOR ONE THING AFTER ANOTHER...
BUT IT'S NEVER ENOUGH.
TAKISHIMA.
WHY DON'T YOU LET HER GET YOU SOMETHING?

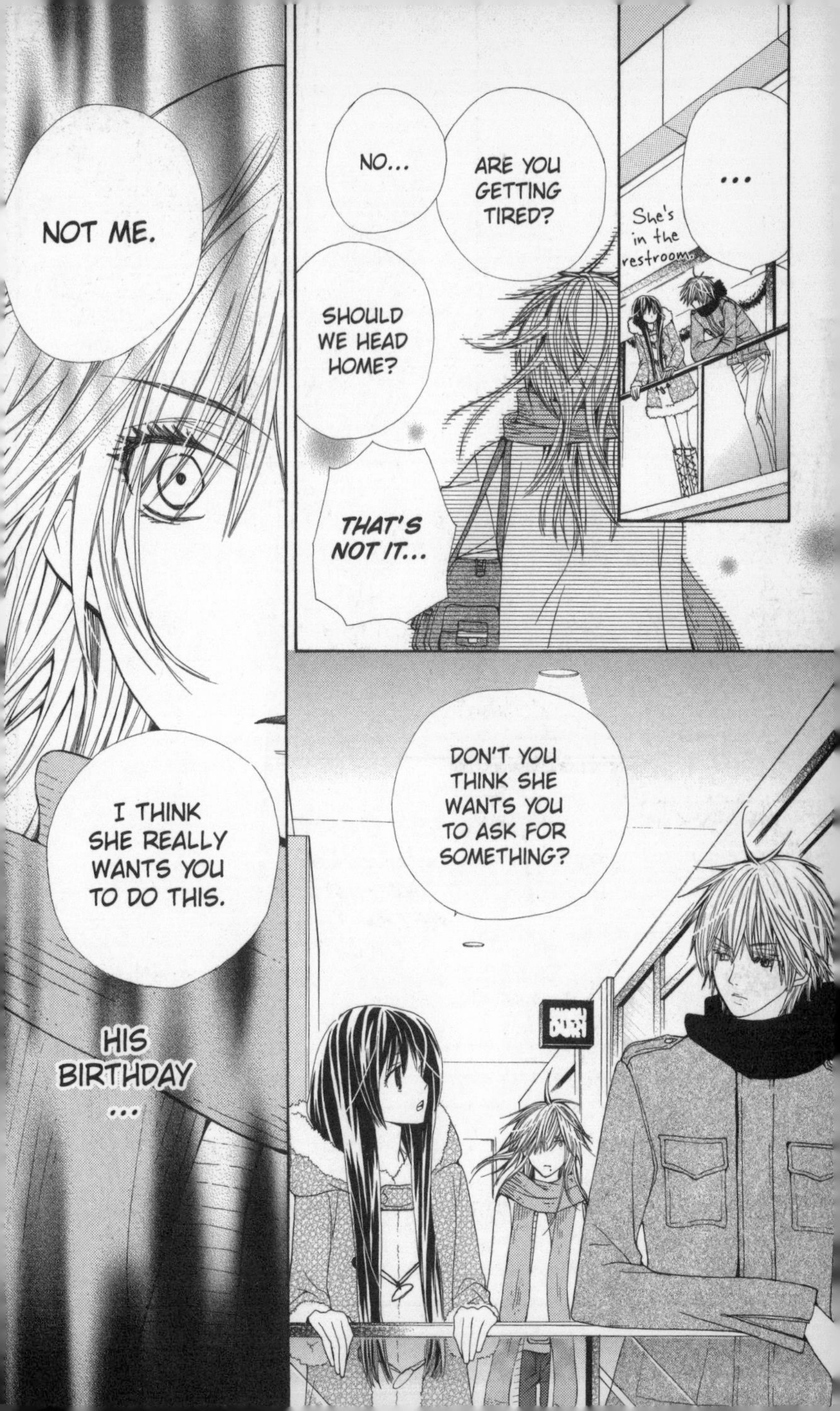
...
She's in the restroom.
ARE YOU GETTING TIRED?
NO...
SHOULD WE HEAD HOME?
THAT'S NOT IT...
DON'T YOU THINK SHE WANTS YOU TO ASK FOR SOMETHING?
NOT ME.
I THINK SHE REALLY WANTS YOU TO DO THIS.
HIS BIRTHDAY...

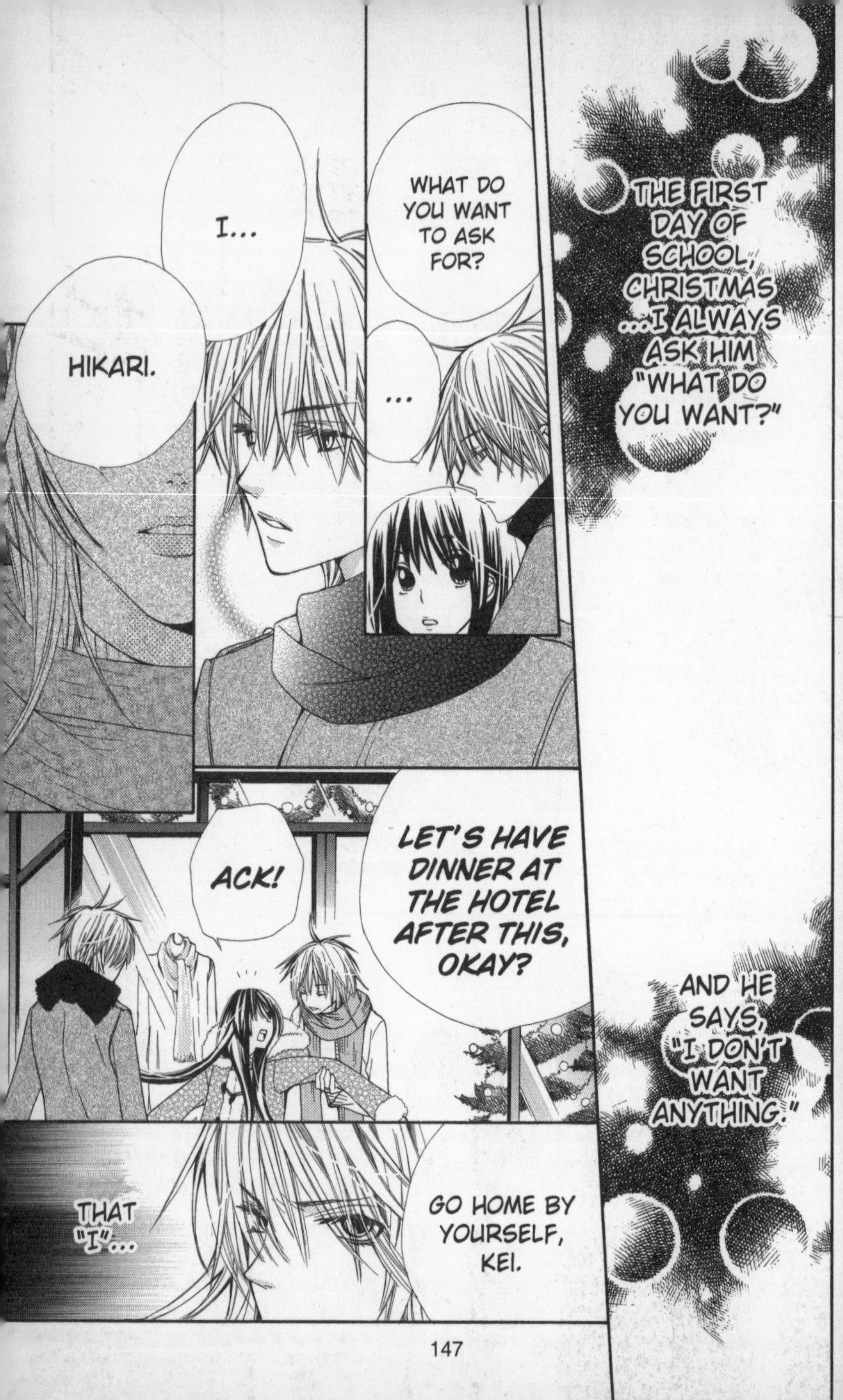
THE FIRST DAY OF SCHOOL, CHRISTMAS ...I ALWAYS ASK HIM "WHAT DO YOU WANT?"
AND HE SAYS, "I DON'T WANT ANYTHING."
WHAT DO YOU WANT TO ASK FOR?
...
I...
HIKARI.
LET'S HAVE DINNER AT THE HOTEL AFTER THIS, OKAY?
ACK!
GO HOME BY YOURSELF, KEI.
THAT "I"...

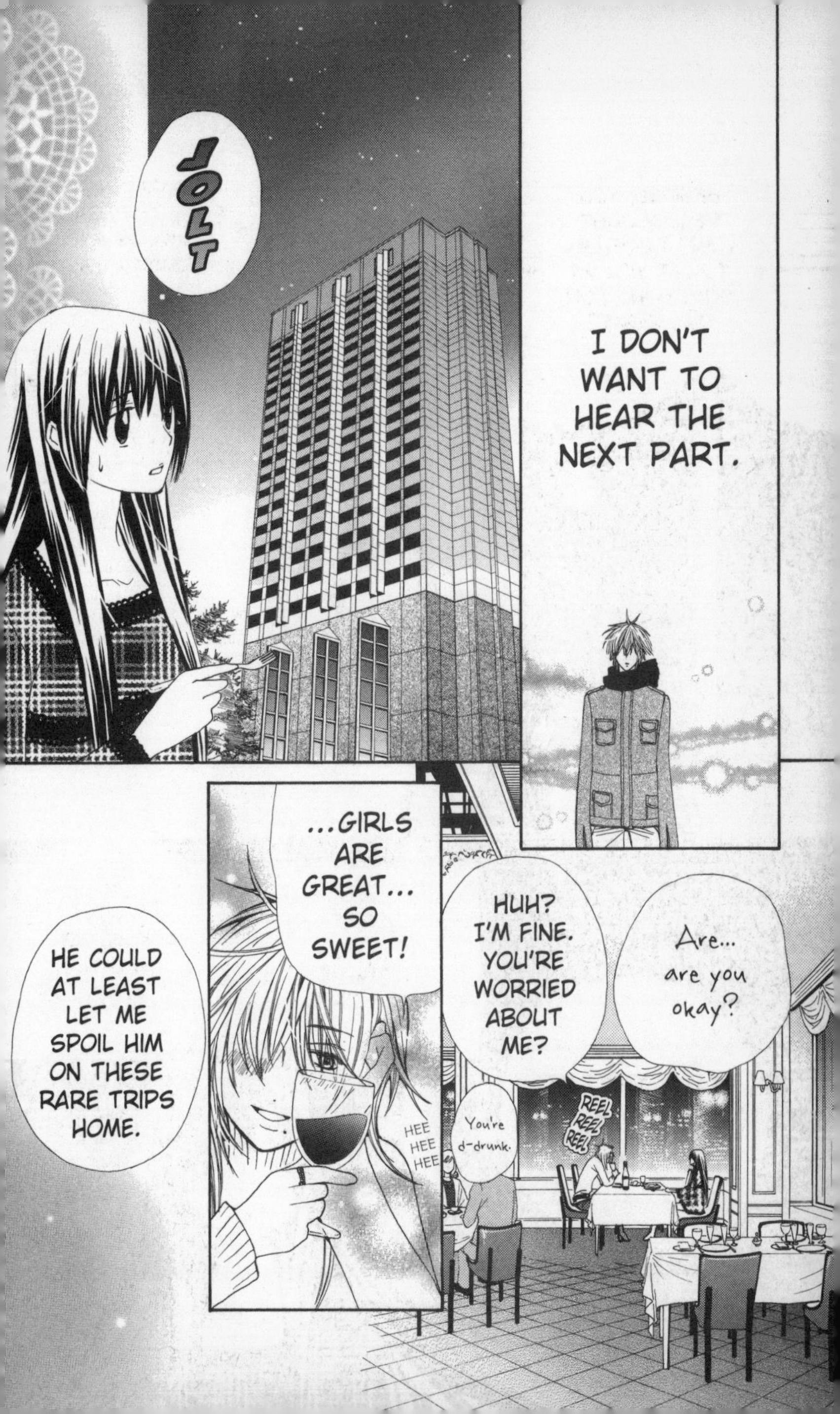
I DON'T WANT TO HEAR THE NEXT PART.
JOLT
Are... are you okay?
HUH? I'M FINE. YOU'RE WORRIED ABOUT ME?
REEL REEL REEL
You're d-drunk.
...GIRLS ARE GREAT... SO SWEET!
HEE HEE HEE
HE COULD AT LEAST LET ME SPOIL HIM ON THESE RARE TRIPS HOME.

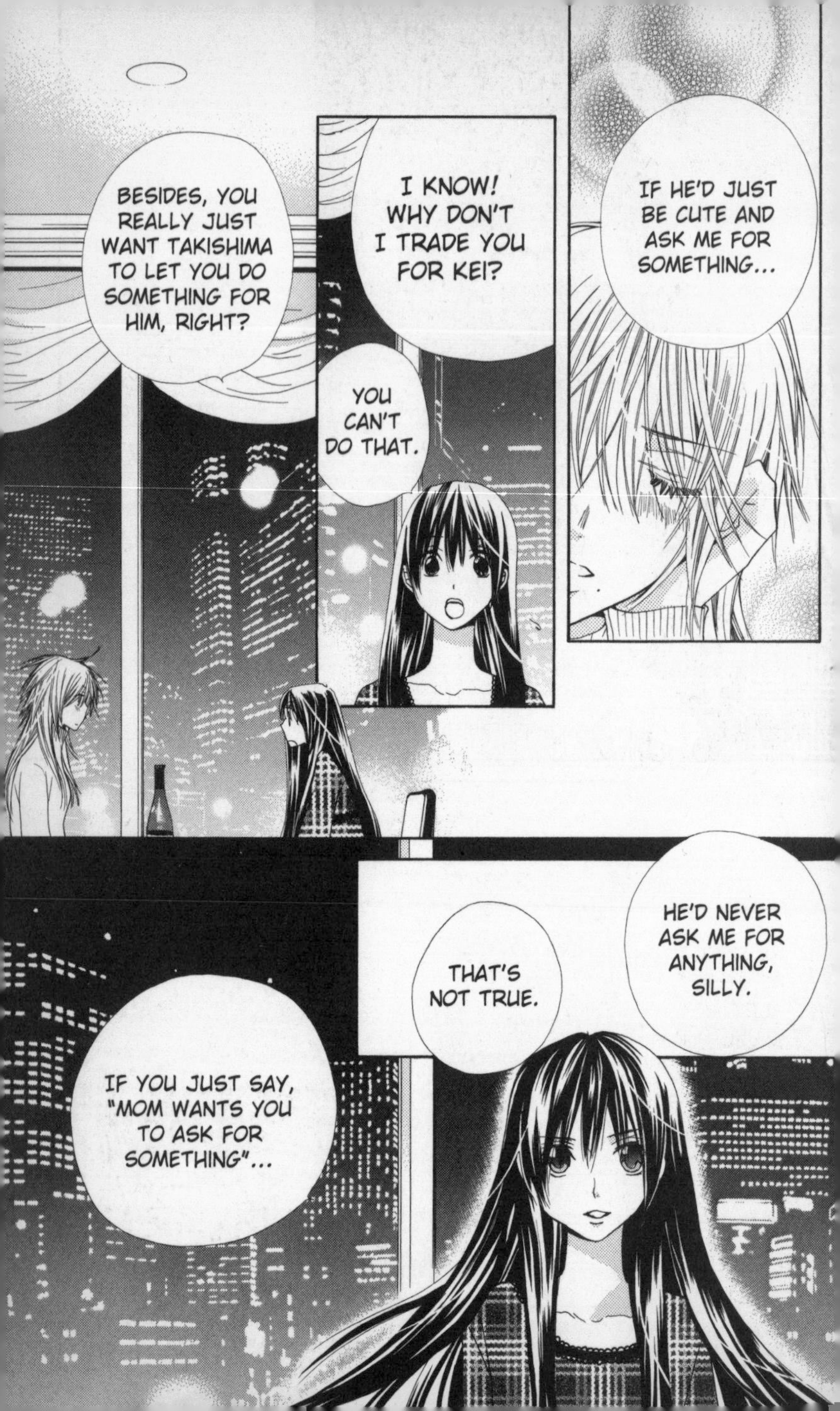
IF HE'D JUST BE CUTE AND ASK ME FOR SOMETHING...
I KNOW! WHY DON'T I TRADE YOU FOR KEI?
YOU CAN'T DO THAT.
BESIDES, YOU REALLY JUST WANT TAKISHIMA TO LET YOU DO SOMETHING FOR HIM, RIGHT?
HE'D NEVER ASK ME FOR ANYTHING, SILLY.
THAT'S NOT TRUE.
IF YOU JUST SAY, "MOM WANTS YOU TO ASK FOR SOMETHING"...

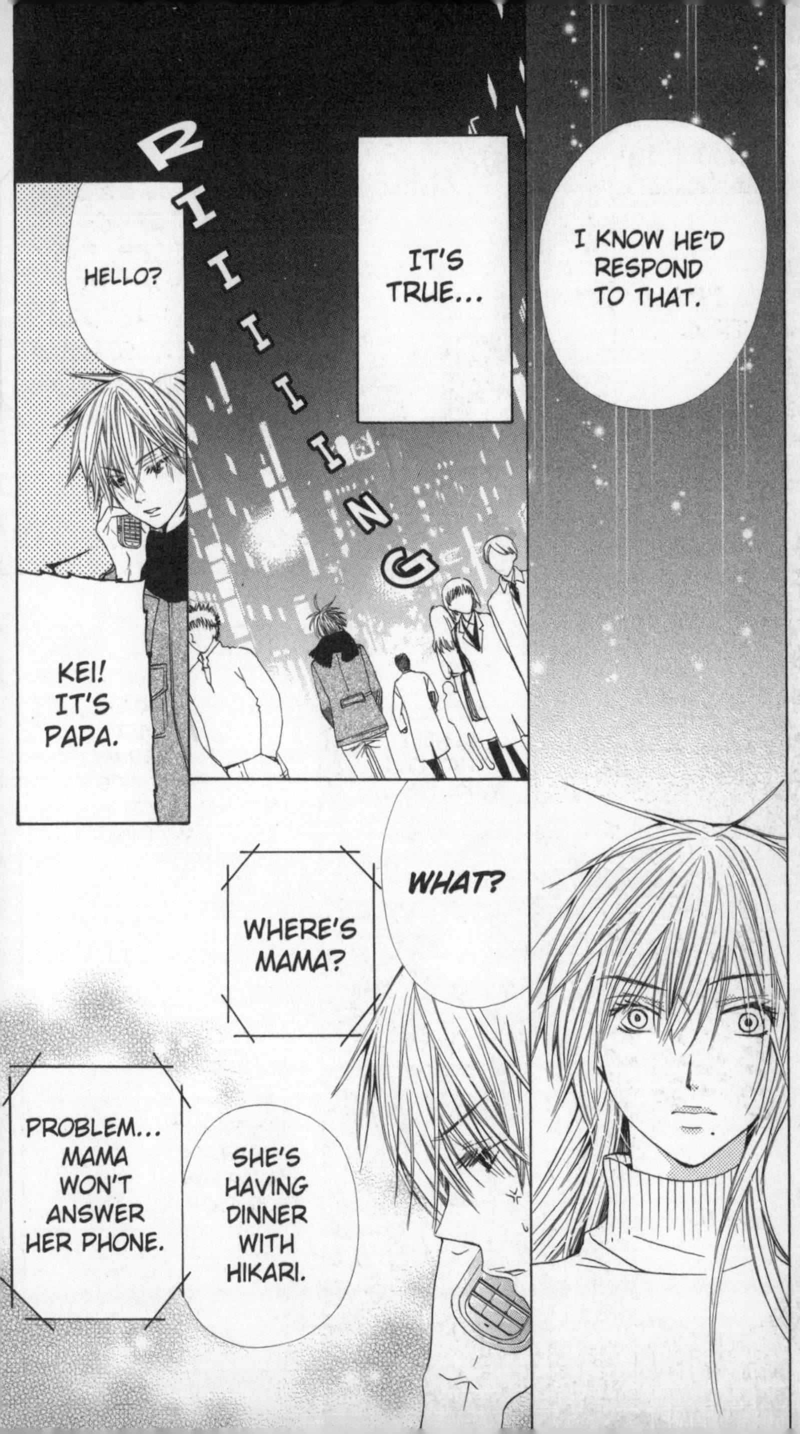
I KNOW HE'D RESPOND TO THAT.
IT'S TRUE...
RIIIIING
HELLO?
KEI! IT'S PAPA.
WHAT?
WHERE'S MAMA?
SHE'S HAVING DINNER WITH HIKARI.
PROBLEM... MAMA WON'T ANSWER HER PHONE.

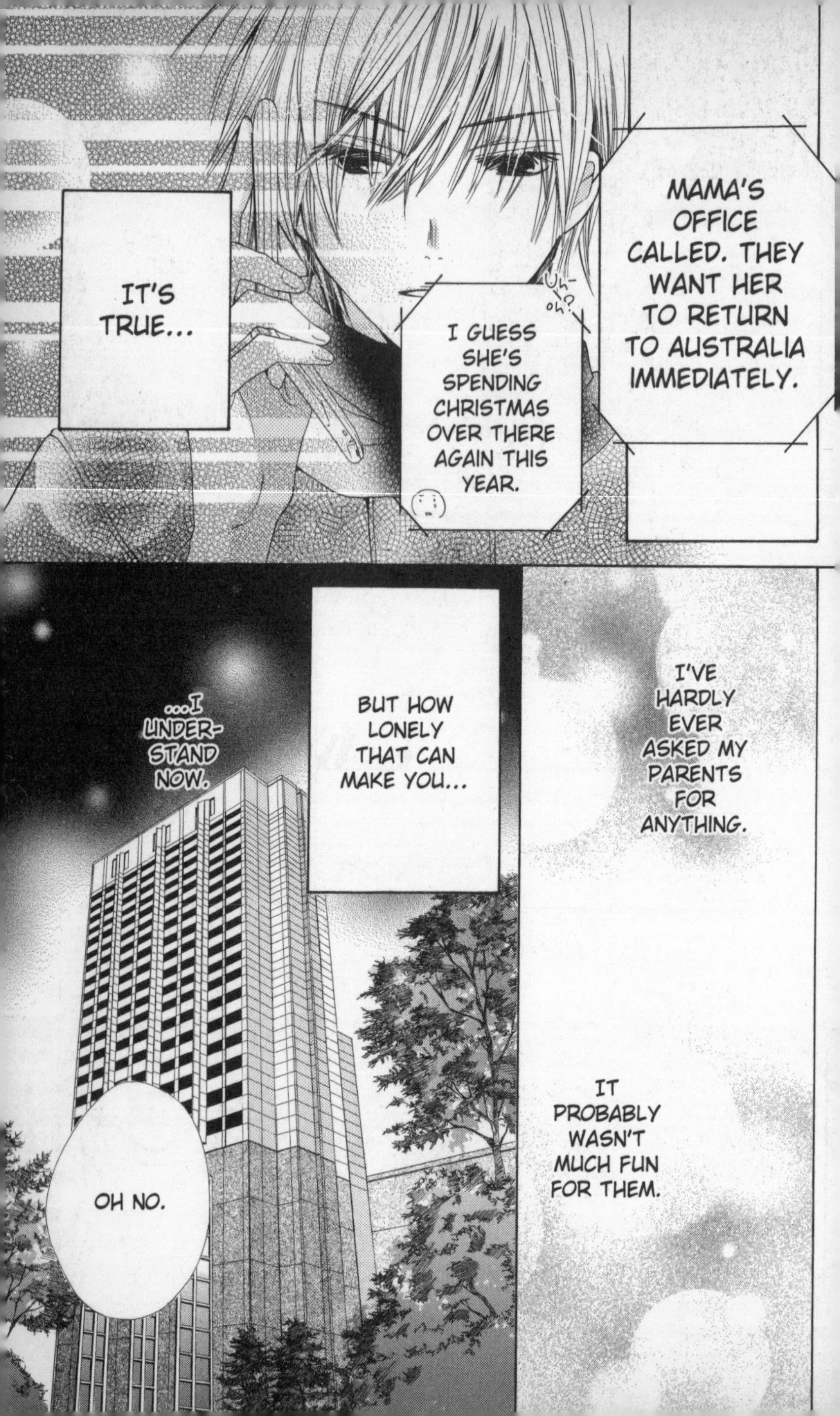
MAMA'S OFFICE CALLED. THEY WANT HER TO RETURN TO AUSTRALIA IMMEDIATELY.
Uh-oh?
I GUESS SHE'S SPENDING CHRISTMAS OVER THERE AGAIN THIS YEAR.
IT'S TRUE...
I'VE HARDLY EVER ASKED MY PARENTS FOR ANYTHING.
IT PROBABLY WASN'T MUCH FUN FOR THEM.
BUT HOW LONELY THAT CAN MAKE YOU...
...I UNDER-STAND NOW.
OH NO.

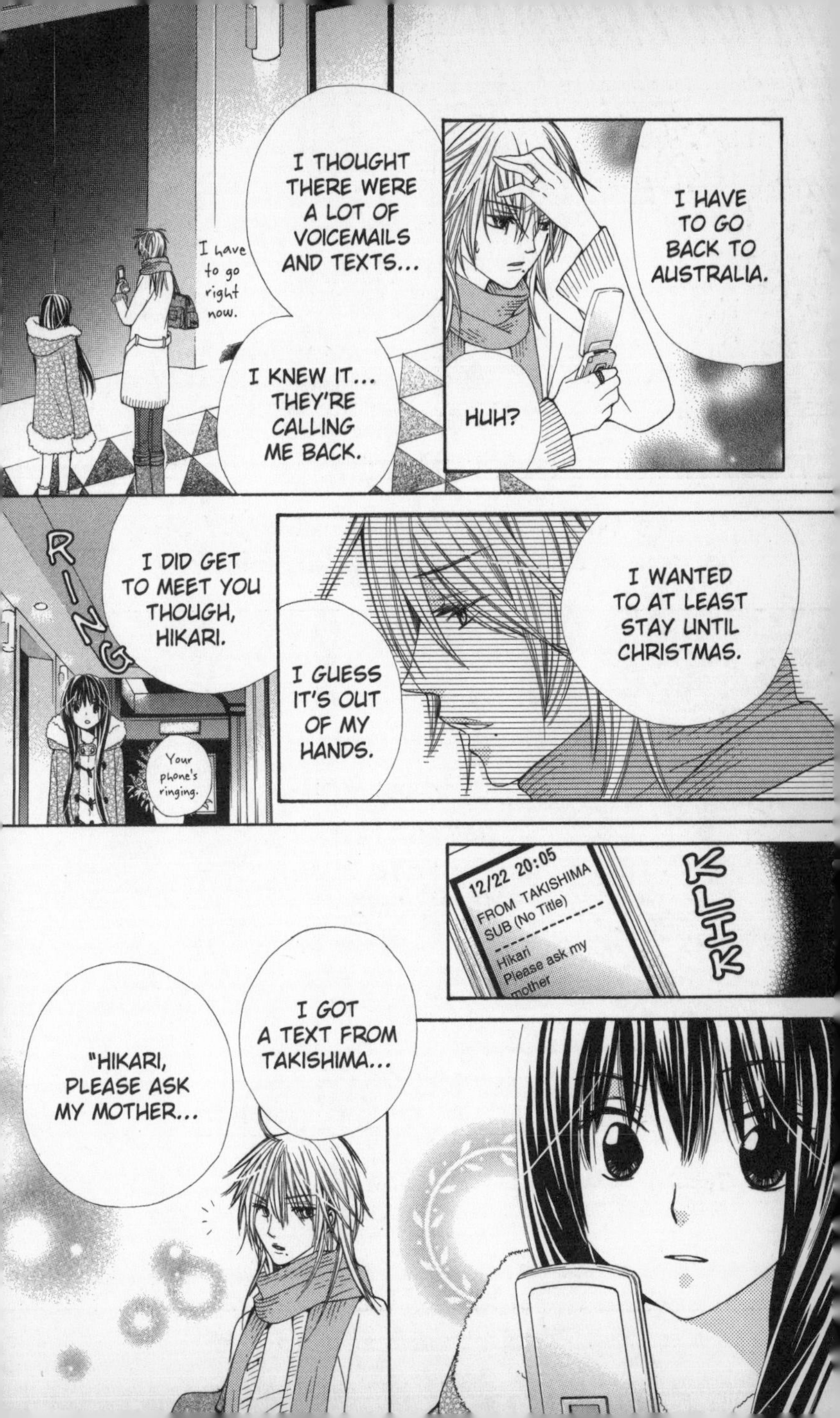
I HAVE TO GO BACK TO AUSTRALIA.
HUH?
I THOUGHT THERE WERE A LOT OF VOICEMAILS AND TEXTS...
I KNEW IT... THEY'RE CALLING ME BACK.
I have to go right now.
I WANTED TO AT LEAST STAY UNTIL CHRISTMAS.
I GUESS IT'S OUT OF MY HANDS.
I DID GET TO MEET YOU THOUGH, HIKARI.
RING
Your phone's ringing.
KLIK
12/22 20:05
FROM TAKISHIMA
SUB (No Title)
Hikari
Please ask my mother
I GOT A TEXT FROM TAKISHIMA...
"HIKARI, PLEASE ASK MY MOTHER...

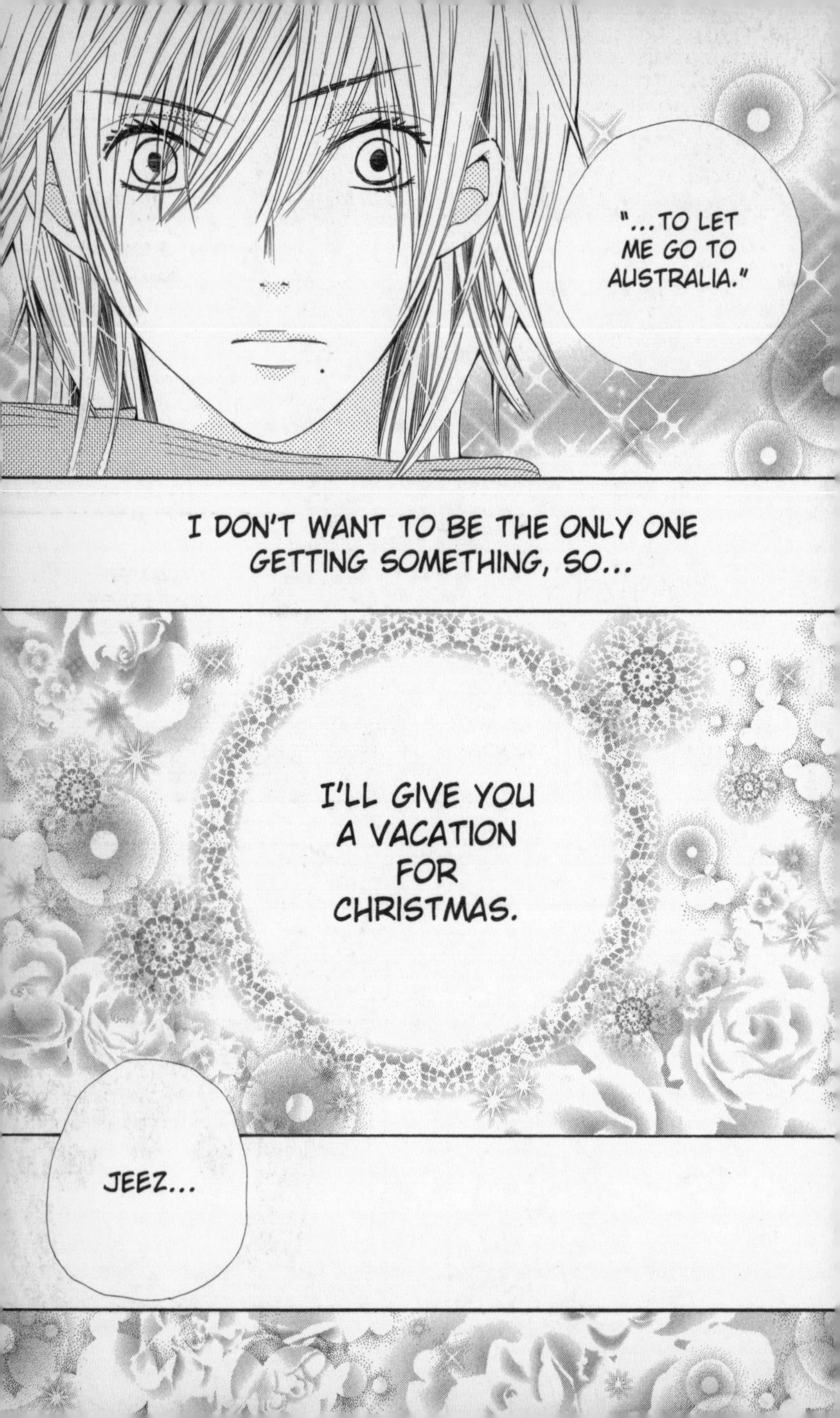
"...TO LET ME GO TO AUSTRALIA."
I DON'T WANT TO BE THE ONLY ONE GETTING SOMETHING, SO...
I'LL GIVE YOU A VACATION FOR CHRISTMAS.
JEEZ...

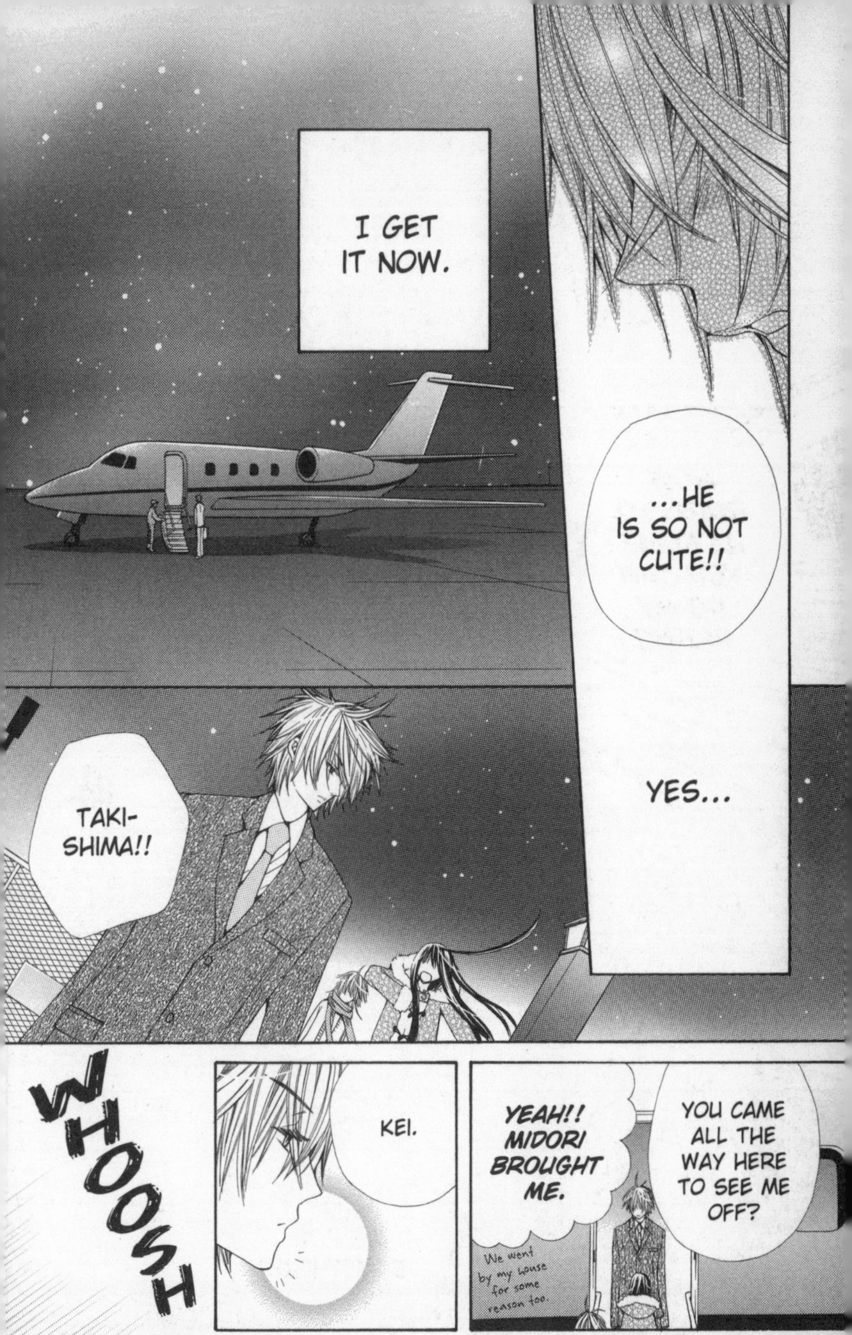
...HE IS SO NOT CUTE!!
YES...
I GET IT NOW.
TAKI-SHIMA!!
YOU CAME ALL THE WAY HERE TO SEE ME OFF?
YEAH!! MIDORI BROUGHT ME.
We went by my house for some reason too.
KEI.
WHOOSH

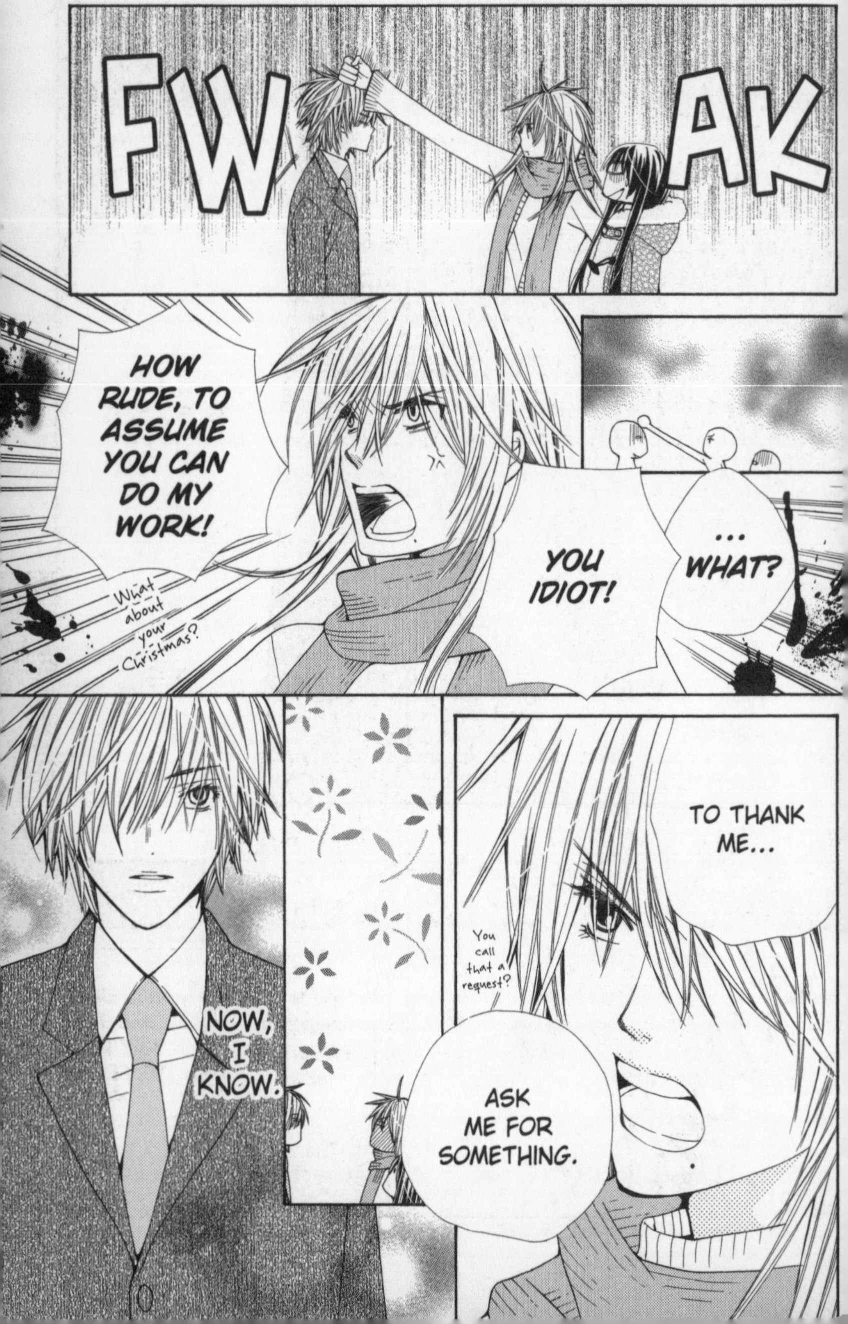
FWAK
... WHAT?
YOU IDIOT!
HOW RUDE, TO ASSUME YOU CAN DO MY WORK!
What about your Christmas?
TO THANK ME...
You call that a request?
ASK ME FOR SOMETHING.
NOW, I KNOW.

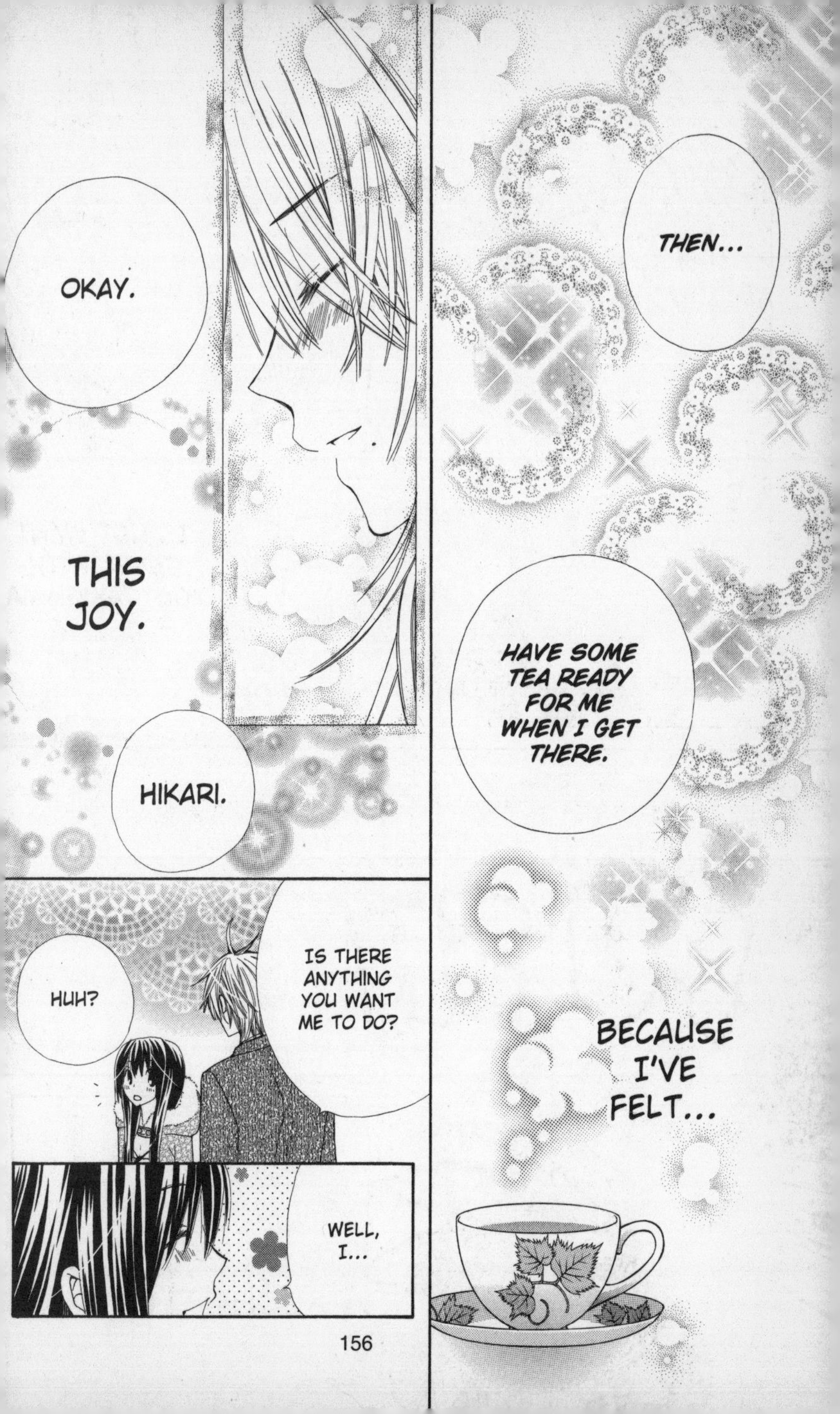
THEN...
HAVE SOME TEA READY FOR ME WHEN I GET THERE.
BECAUSE I'VE FELT...
THIS JOY.
OKAY.
HIKARI.
IS THERE ANYTHING YOU WANT ME TO DO?
HUH?
WELL, I...

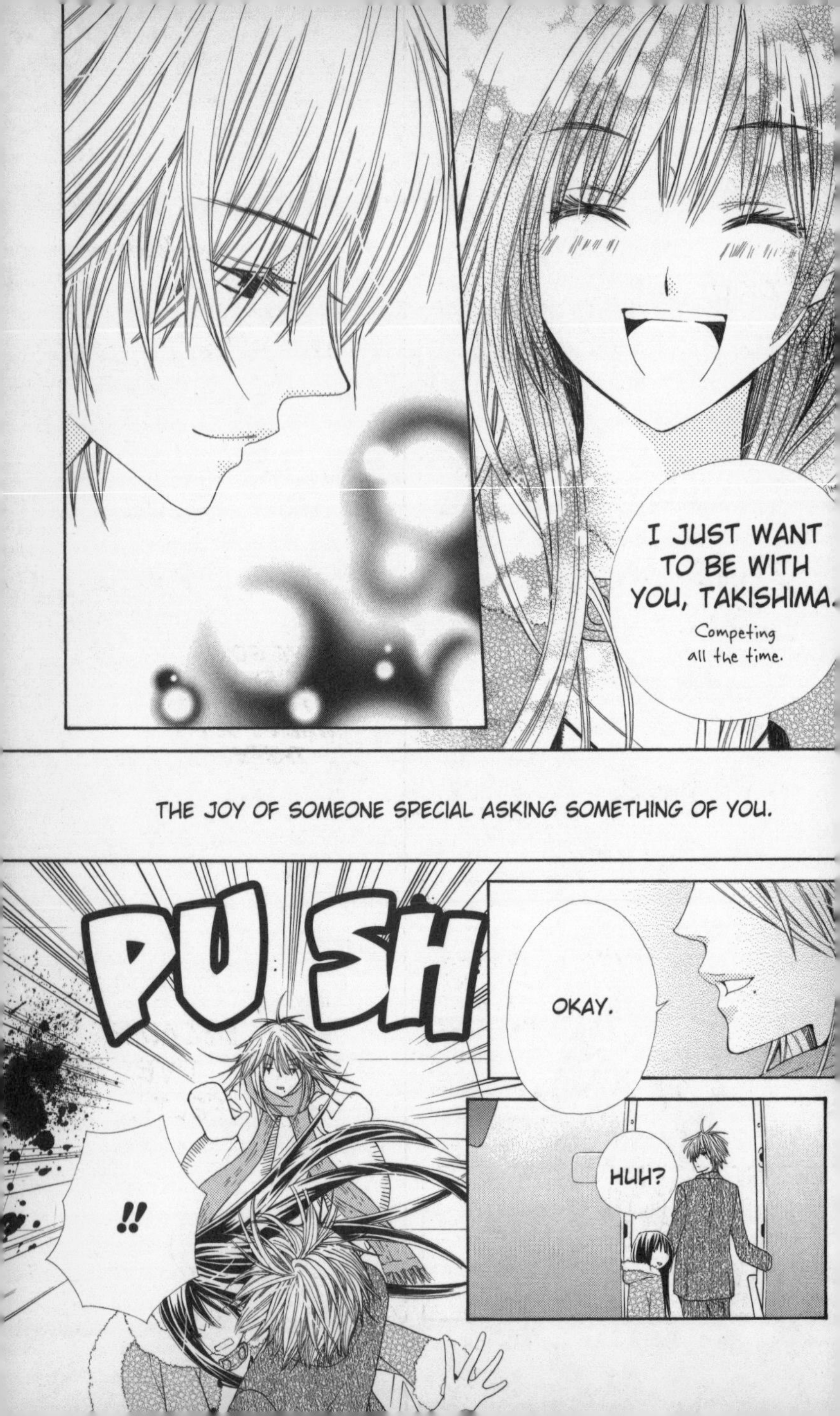
I JUST WANT TO BE WITH YOU, TAKISHIMA.
Competing all the time.
THE JOY OF SOMEONE SPECIAL ASKING SOMETHING OF YOU.
OKAY.
HUH?
PUSH
!!

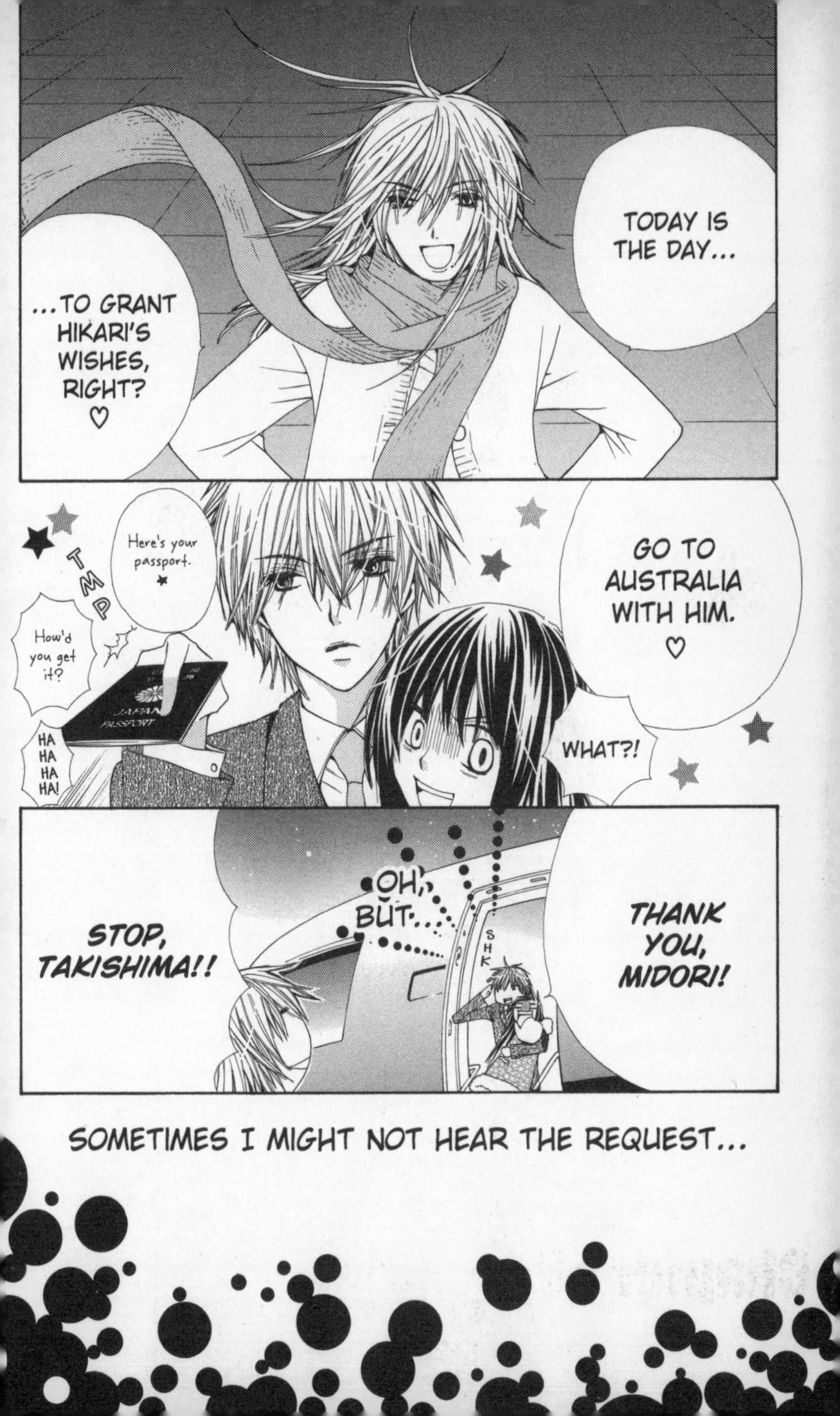
TODAY IS THE DAY...
...TO GRANT HIKARI'S WISHES, RIGHT? ♡
GO TO AUSTRALIA WITH HIM. ♡
WHAT?!
Here's your passport.
TMP
How'd you get it?
HA HA HA HA!
THANK YOU, MIDORI!
SHK
OH, BUT...
STOP, TAKISHIMA!!

SOMETIMES I MIGHT NOT HEAR THE REQUEST...

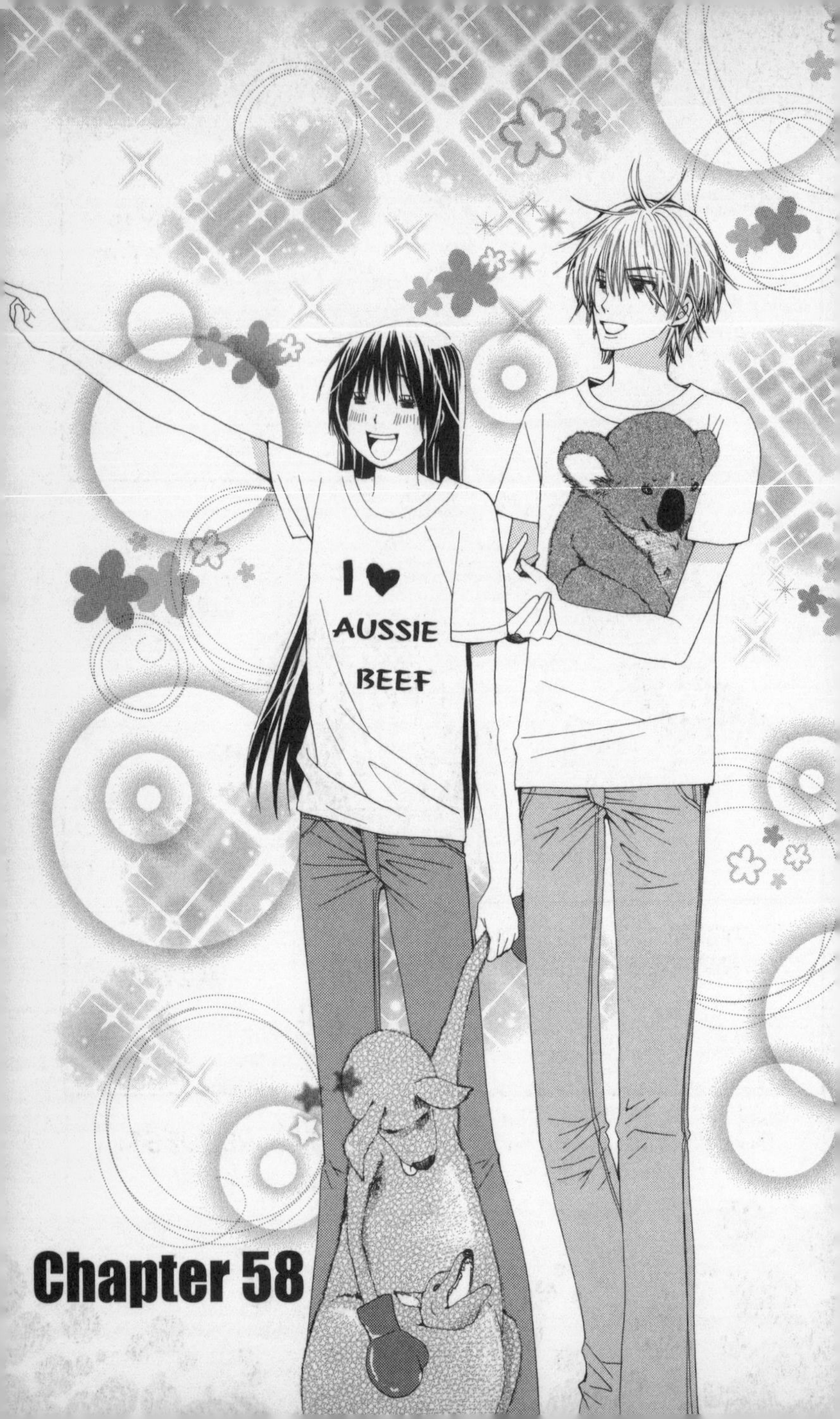
I ♥ AUSSIE BEEF

Chapter 58

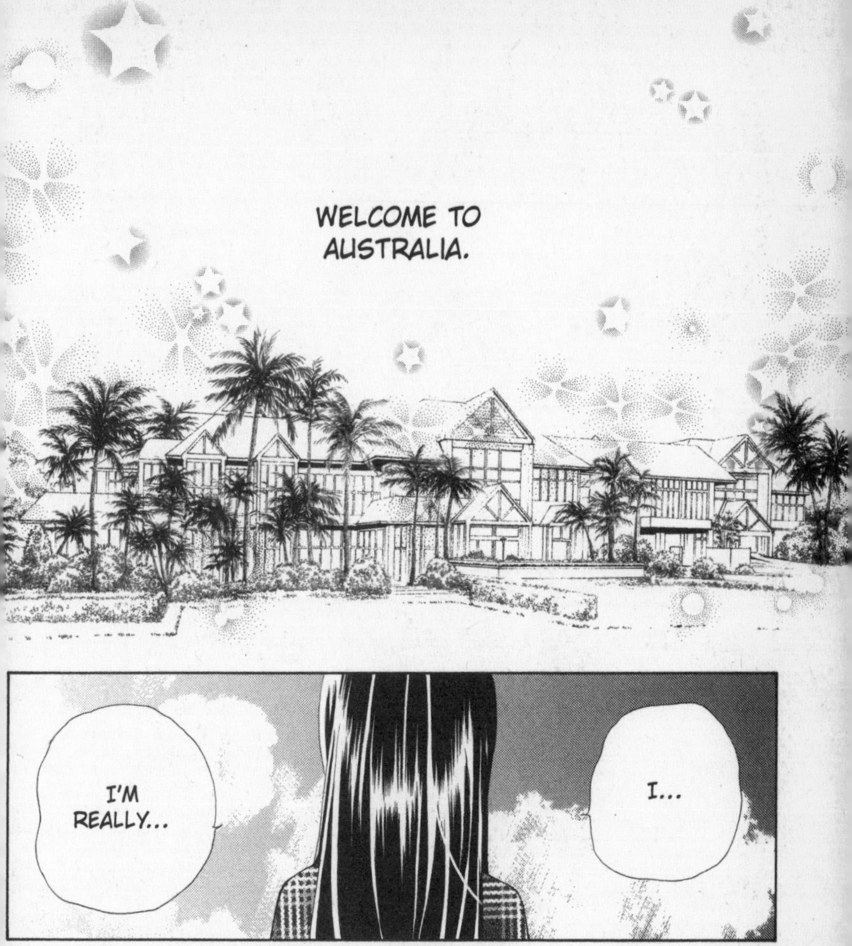
WELCOME TO AUSTRALIA.
I...
I'M REALLY...

• THIS AND THAT •

- KEI AND HIKARI ARE FINALLY TOGETHER. WHAT WILL HAPPEN NOW? I'M GOING TO ENJOY DRAWING THE NEXT PART. PLEASE STICK WITH US, IF YOU WANT TO!
- THANK YOU FOR ALL THE LETTERS! THEY REALLY ENCOURAGE ME. CONGRATULATIONS TO EVERYONE WHO FOUND JOBS OR MADE IT INTO THE NEXT LEVEL OF SCHOOL! READING THE PERSONAL NEWS IN YOUR LETTERS MAKES ME HAPPY TOO! YOU DID IT!
- TO THE PERSON WHO SENT THE LUMA COLOR INKS... THANK YOU VERY MUCH!! I'M USING THEM FOR THE COVERS. ALL THE PRETTY COLORS ARE IMPRESSIVE!!

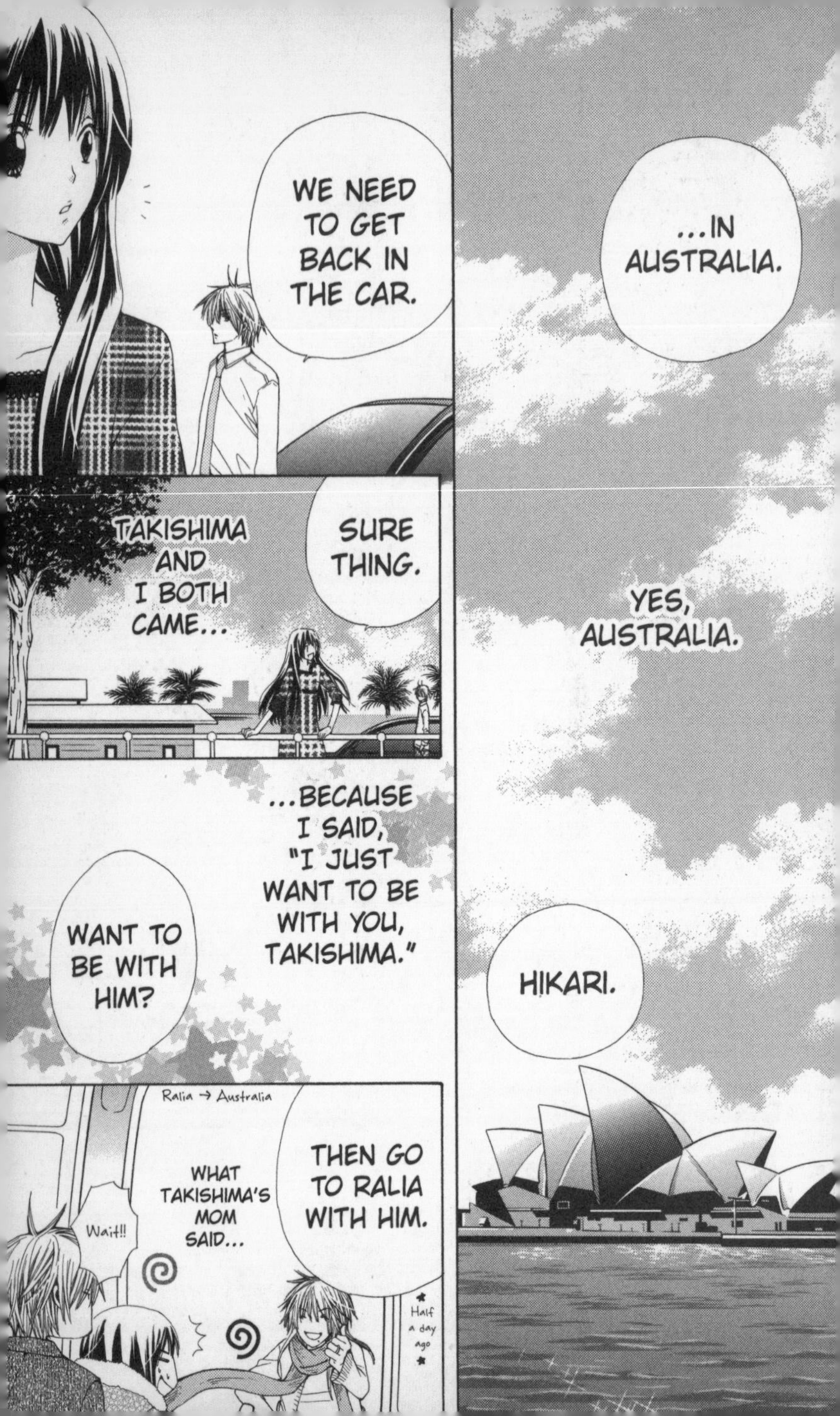
...IN AUSTRALIA.
YES, AUSTRALIA.
HIKARI.
WE NEED TO GET BACK IN THE CAR.
SURE THING.
TAKISHIMA AND I BOTH CAME...
...BECAUSE I SAID, "I JUST WANT TO BE WITH YOU, TAKISHIMA."
WANT TO BE WITH HIM?
Ralia → Australia
THEN GO TO RALIA WITH HIM.
WHAT TAKISHIMA'S MOM SAID...
Wait!!
Half a day ago

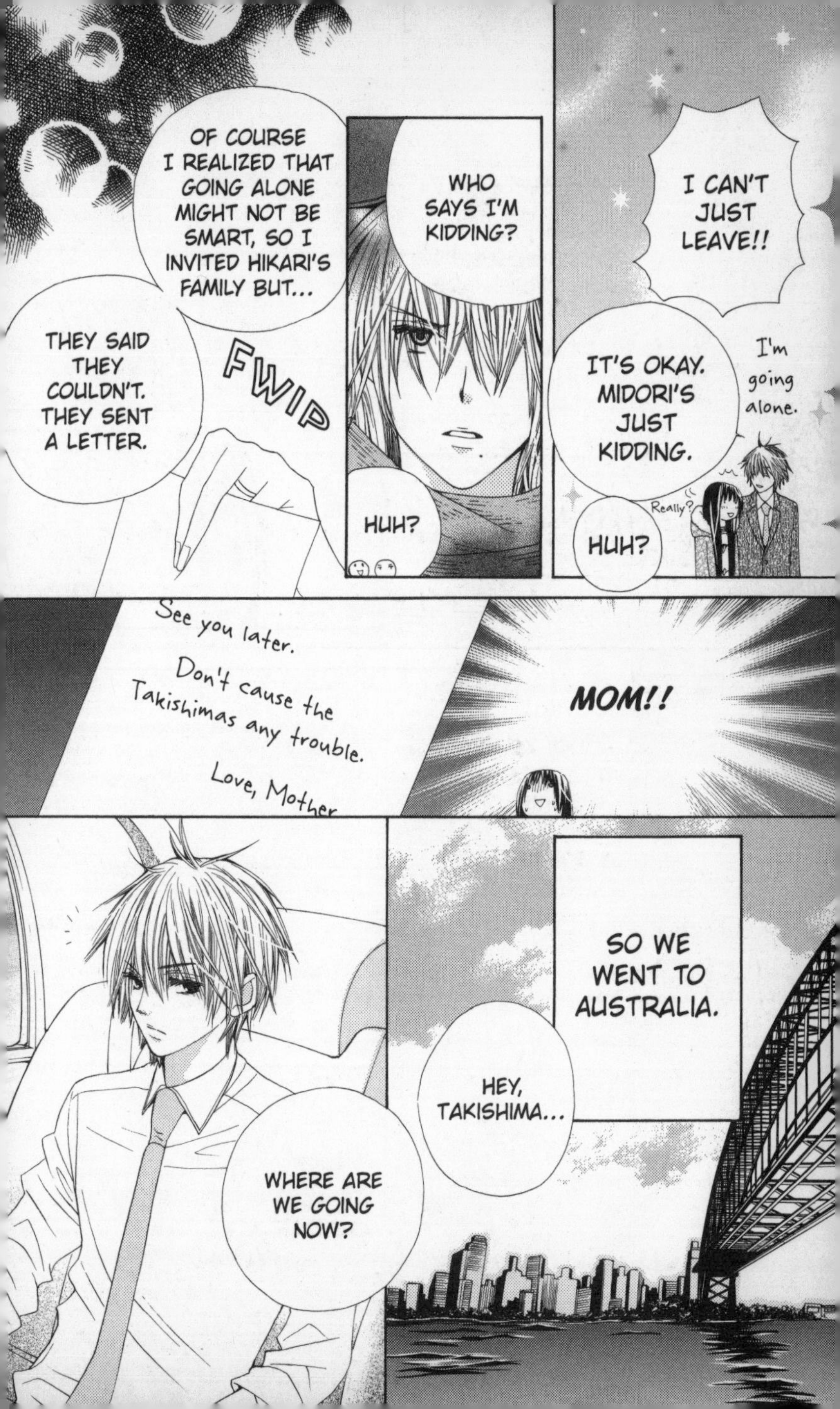
I CAN'T JUST LEAVE!!
I'm going alone.
IT'S OKAY. MIDORI'S JUST KIDDING.
Really?
HUH?
WHO SAYS I'M KIDDING?
HUH?
OF COURSE I REALIZED THAT GOING ALONE MIGHT NOT BE SMART, SO I INVITED HIKARI'S FAMILY BUT...
FWIP
THEY SAID THEY COULDN'T. THEY SENT A LETTER.
MOM!!
See you later.
Don't cause the Takishimas any trouble.
Love, Mother
SO WE WENT TO AUSTRALIA.
HEY, TAKISHIMA...
WHERE ARE WE GOING NOW?

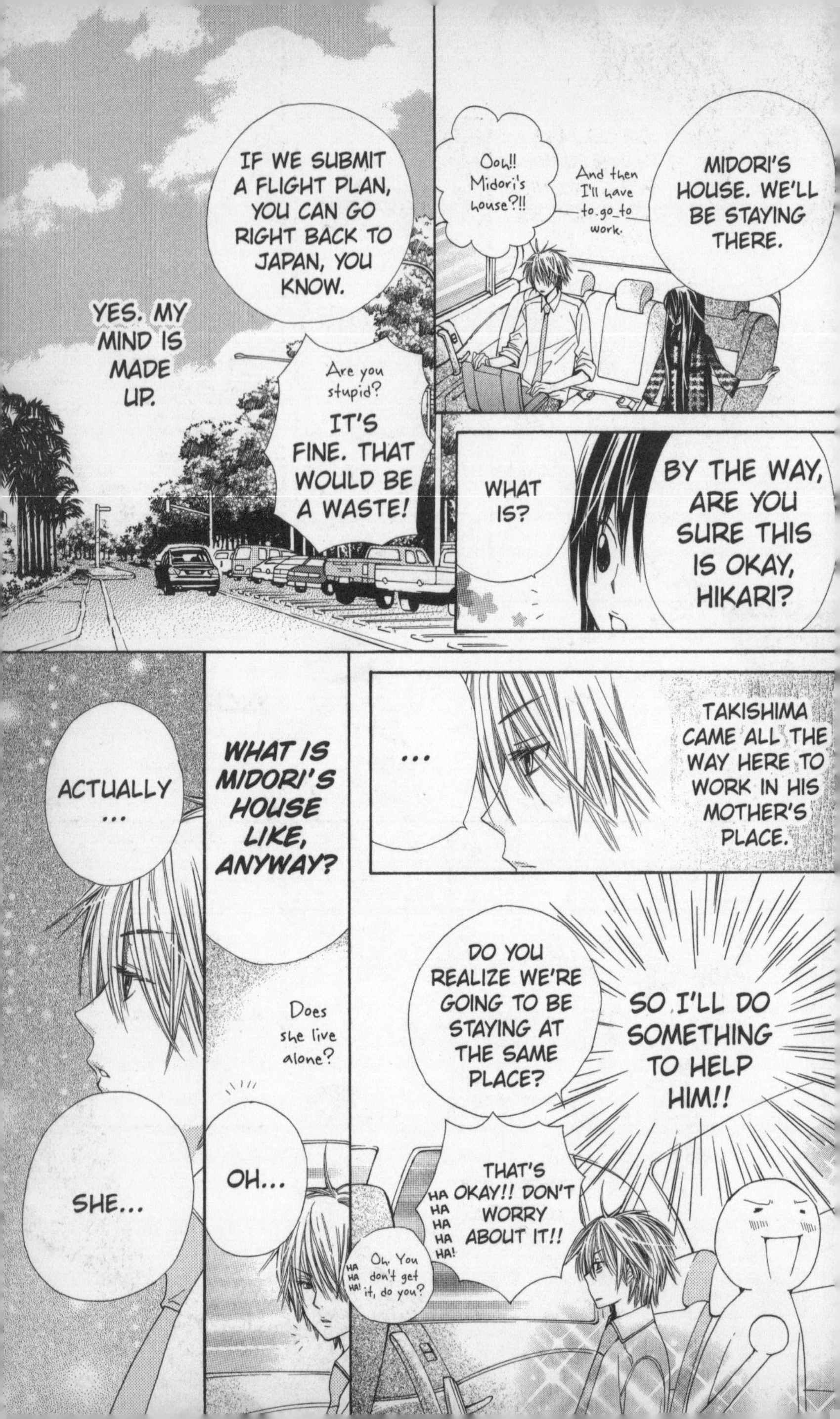
MIDORI'S HOUSE. WE'LL BE STAYING THERE.
And then I'll have to go to work.
Ooh!! Midori's house?!!
BY THE WAY, ARE YOU SURE THIS IS OKAY, HIKARI?
WHAT IS?
IF WE SUBMIT A FLIGHT PLAN, YOU CAN GO RIGHT BACK TO JAPAN, YOU KNOW.
Are you stupid?
IT'S FINE. THAT WOULD BE A WASTE!
YES. MY MIND IS MADE UP.
TAKISHIMA CAME ALL THE WAY HERE TO WORK IN HIS MOTHER'S PLACE.
...
SO I'LL DO SOMETHING TO HELP HIM!!
DO YOU REALIZE WE'RE GOING TO BE STAYING AT THE SAME PLACE?
THAT'S OKAY!! DON'T WORRY ABOUT IT!!
HA HA HA HA HA!
Oh. You don't get it, do you?
HA HA HA!
WHAT IS MIDORI'S HOUSE LIKE, ANYWAY?
Does she live alone?
OH...
ACTUALLY...
SHE...

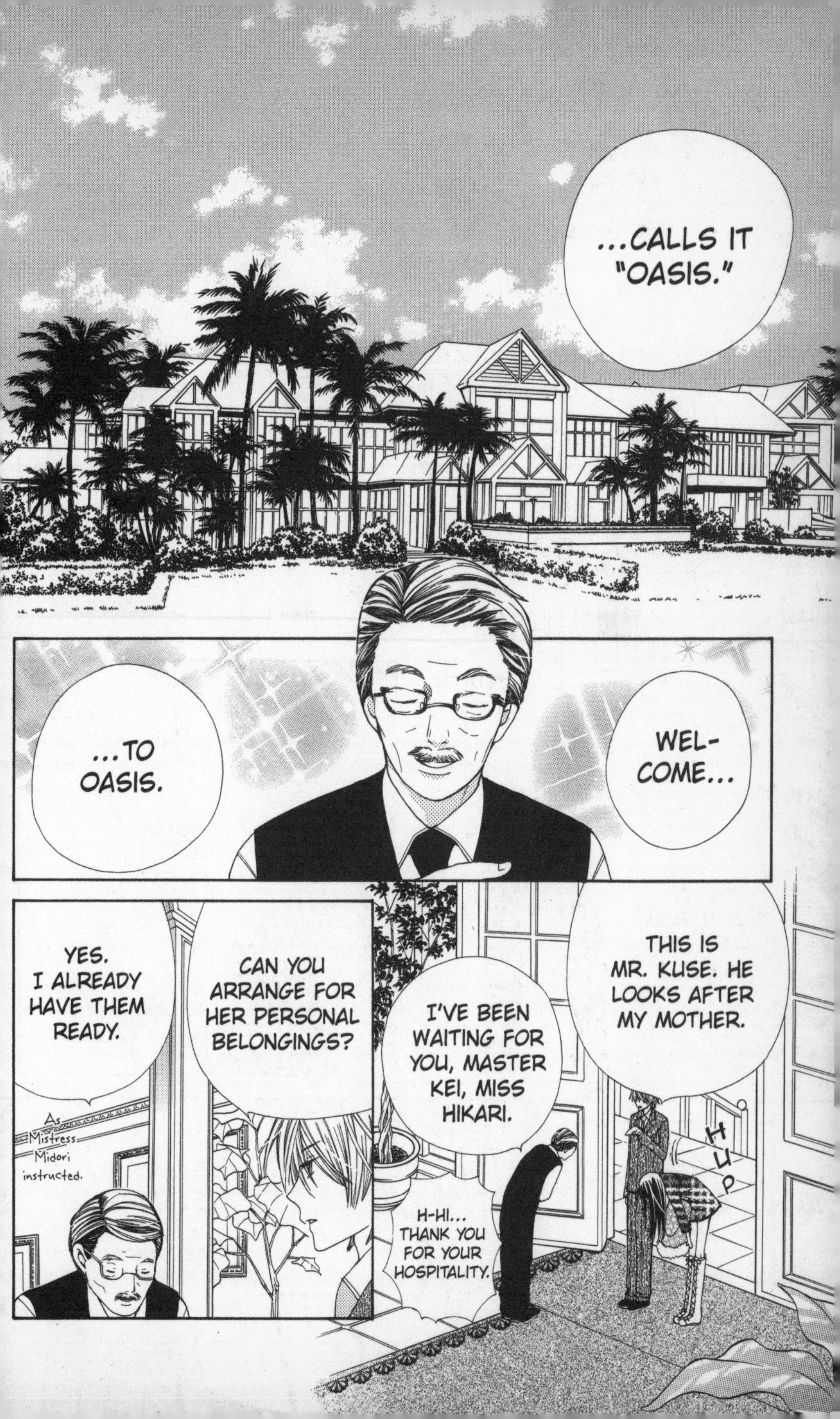
...CALLS IT "OASIS."
WEL-COME...
...TO OASIS.
THIS IS MR. KUSE. HE LOOKS AFTER MY MOTHER.
I'VE BEEN WAITING FOR YOU, MASTER KEI, MISS HIKARI.
HUP
H-HI... THANK YOU FOR YOUR HOSPITALITY.
CAN YOU ARRANGE FOR HER PERSONAL BELONGINGS?
YES. I ALREADY HAVE THEM READY.
As Mistress Midori instructed.

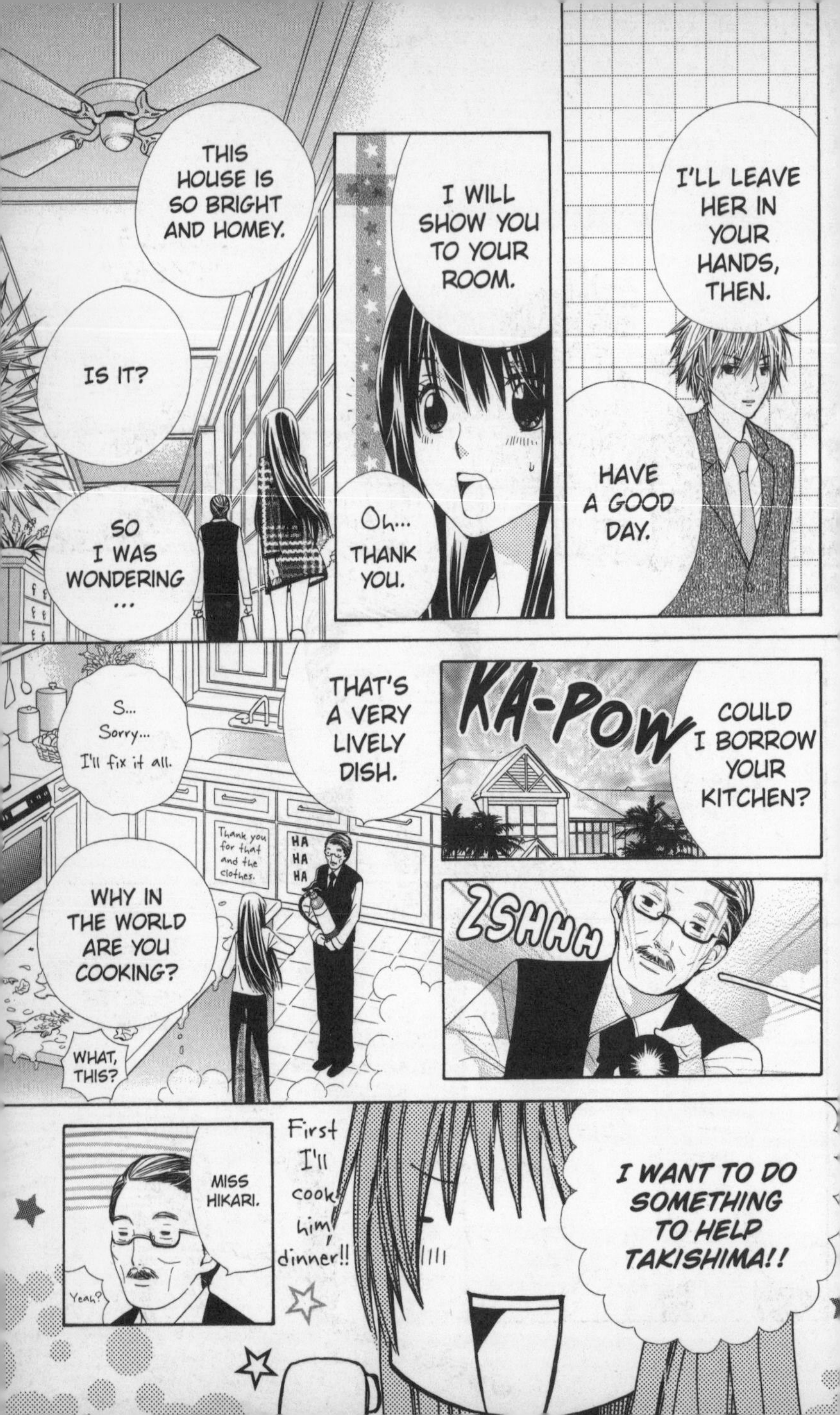

I'LL LEAVE HER IN YOUR HANDS, THEN.
HAVE A GOOD DAY.
I WILL SHOW YOU TO YOUR ROOM.
Oh... THANK YOU.
THIS HOUSE IS SO BRIGHT AND HOMEY.
IS IT?
SO I WAS WONDERING...
COULD I BORROW YOUR KITCHEN?
KA-POW
ZSHHH
THAT'S A VERY LIVELY DISH.
HA HA HA
Thank you for that and the clothes.
S... Sorry... I'll fix it all.
WHY IN THE WORLD ARE YOU COOKING?
WHAT, THIS?
I WANT TO DO SOMETHING TO HELP TAKISHIMA!!
First I'll cook him dinner!!
MISS HIKARI.
Yeah?

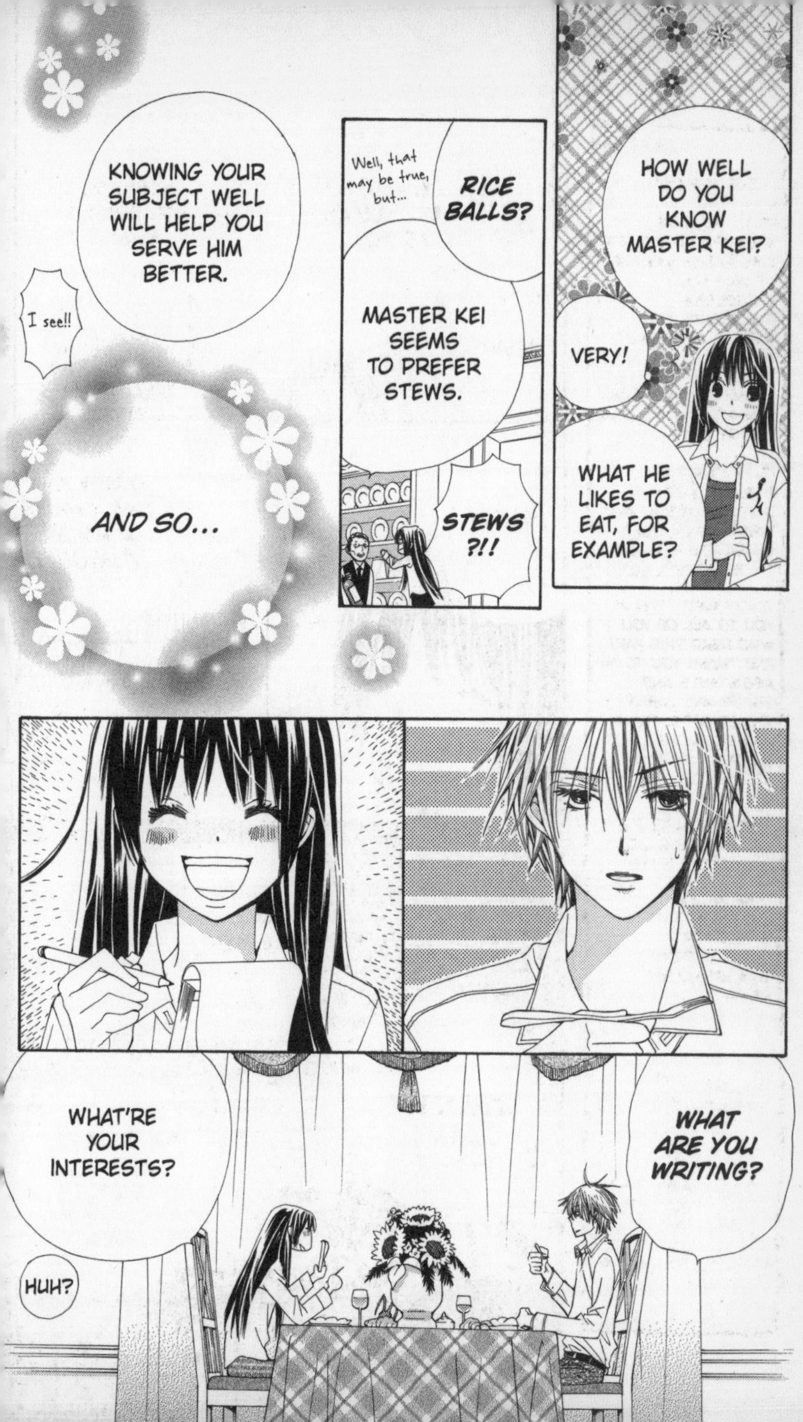
HOW WELL DO YOU KNOW MASTER KEI?
VERY!
WHAT HE LIKES TO EAT, FOR EXAMPLE?
RICE BALLS?
Well, that may be true, but...
MASTER KEI SEEMS TO PREFER STEWS.
STEWS ?!!
KNOWING YOUR SUBJECT WELL WILL HELP YOU SERVE HIM BETTER.
I see!!
AND SO...
WHAT ARE YOU WRITING?
WHAT'RE YOUR INTERESTS?
HUH?

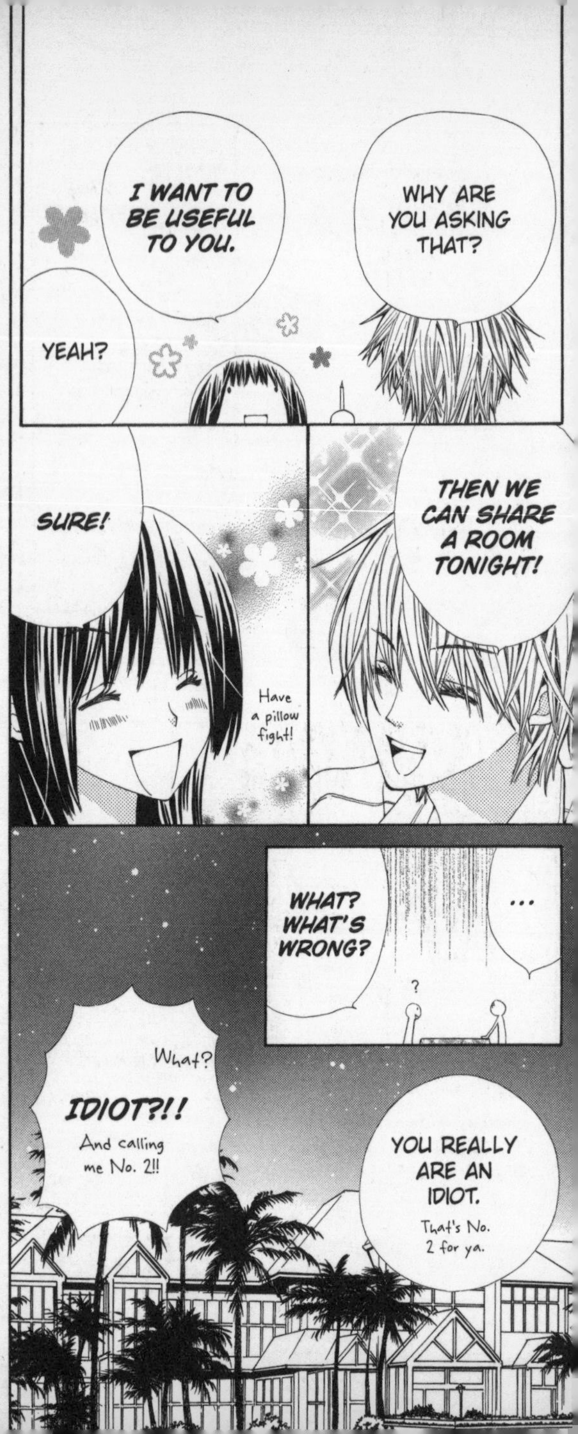
WHY ARE YOU ASKING THAT?
I WANT TO BE USEFUL TO YOU.
YEAH?
THEN WE CAN SHARE A ROOM TONIGHT!
SURE!
Have a pillow fight!
...
WHAT? WHAT'S WRONG?
?
YOU REALLY ARE AN IDIOT.
That's No. 2 for ya.
What?
IDIOT?!!
And calling me No. 2!!

6

·THIS AND THAT·

·THIS TIME THE QUARTER PAGE THEME WAS POLICE ☆ FEVER... IT WAS SUCH A SHOCKING EXPERIENCE, MY NERVES WERE SHOT! HA HA!

THANK YOU SO MUCH FOR STICKING WITH ME TO THE END!!

·THIS TIME THE REQUEST FOR THE QUARTER-PAGES WAS "WORKING ON S.A." THANK YOU FOR ALL THE SUGGESTIONS!!

·OKAY, WELL, THANK YOU TO ALL OF YOU WHO READ THIS FAR! AND THANK YOU TO MY ASSISTANTS AND EDITOR AND FAMILY AND FRIENDS. THANK YOU SO MUCH! I HOPE WE MEET AGAIN IN VOLUME 11!!

IF YOU'D LIKE TO, PLEASE SEND US YOUR THOUGHTS.

MAKI MINAMI
C/O VIZ MEDIA
S.A EDITOR
P.O. BOX 77010
SAN FRANCISCO,
CA 94107

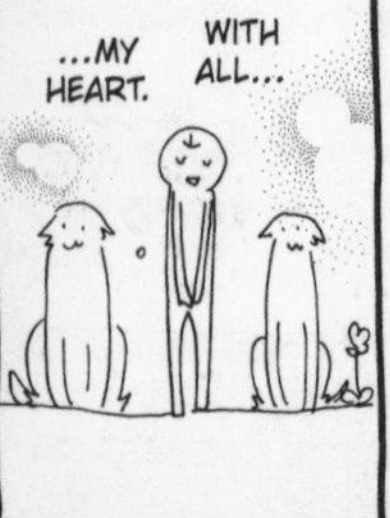
WITH ALL...
...MY HEART.

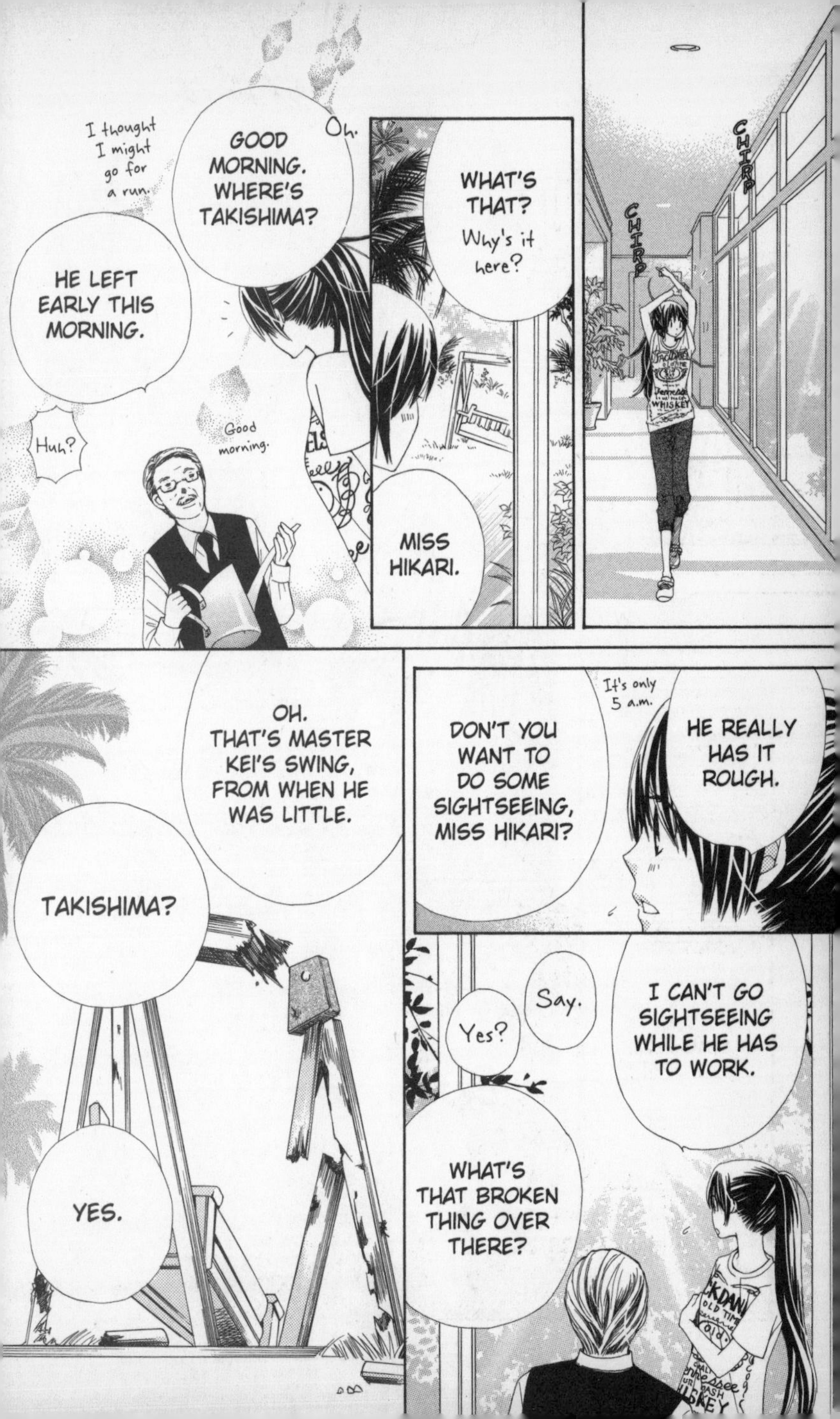
CHIRP
CHIRP
WHAT'S THAT?
Why's it here?
MISS HIKARI.
Oh.
GOOD MORNING. WHERE'S TAKISHIMA?
I thought I might go for a run.
HE LEFT EARLY THIS MORNING.
Good morning.
Huh?
HE REALLY HAS IT ROUGH.
It's only 5 a.m.
DON'T YOU WANT TO DO SOME SIGHTSEEING, MISS HIKARI?
I CAN'T GO SIGHTSEEING WHILE HE HAS TO WORK.
Say.
Yes?
WHAT'S THAT BROKEN THING OVER THERE?
OH. THAT'S MASTER KEI'S SWING, FROM WHEN HE WAS LITTLE.
TAKISHIMA?
YES.

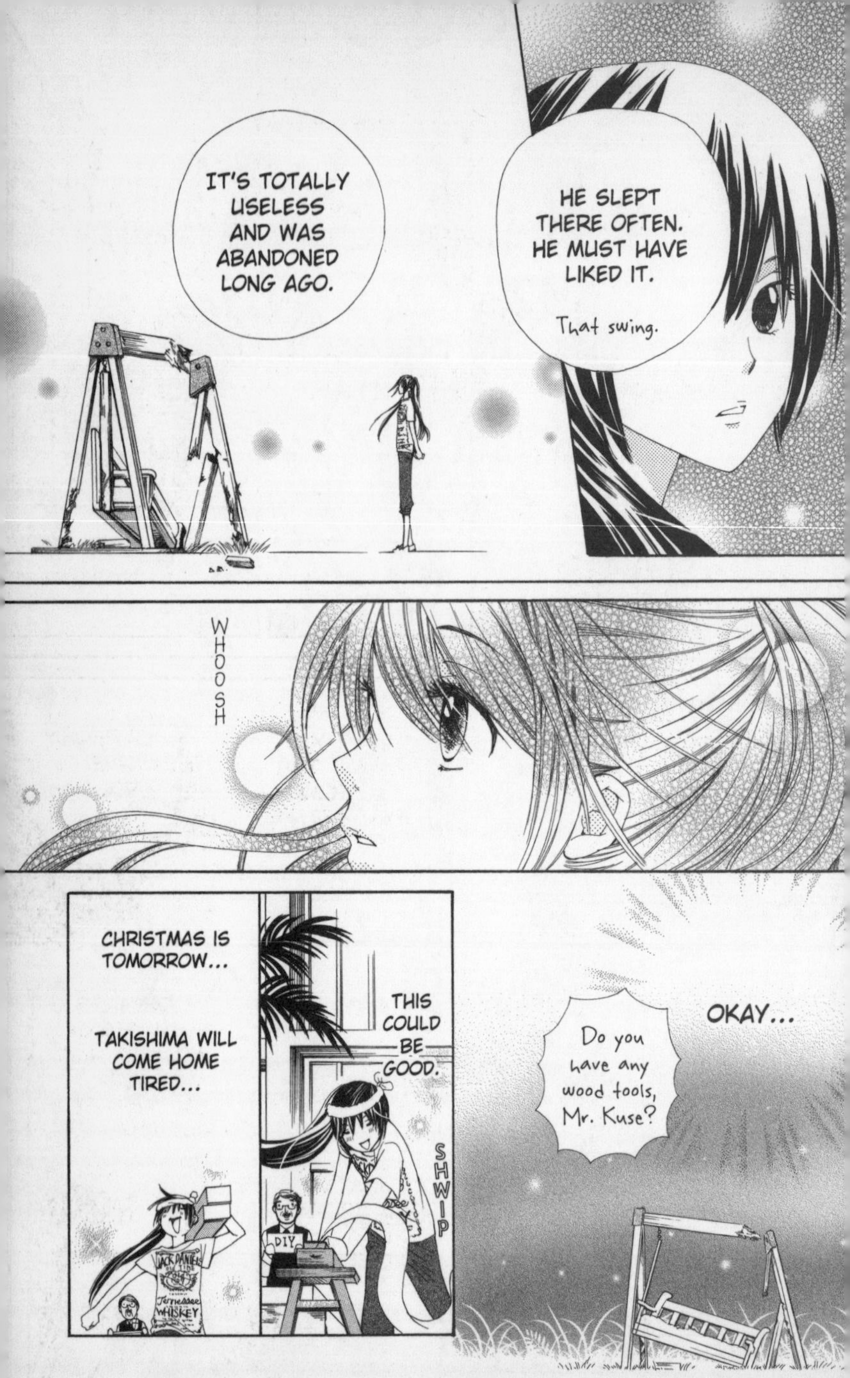
HE SLEPT THERE OFTEN. HE MUST HAVE LIKED IT.
That swing.
IT'S TOTALLY USELESS AND WAS ABANDONED LONG AGO.
WHOOSH
OKAY...
Do you have any wood tools, Mr. Kuse?
THIS COULD BE GOOD.
SHWIP
DIY
CHRISTMAS IS TOMORROW...
TAKISHIMA WILL COME HOME TIRED...

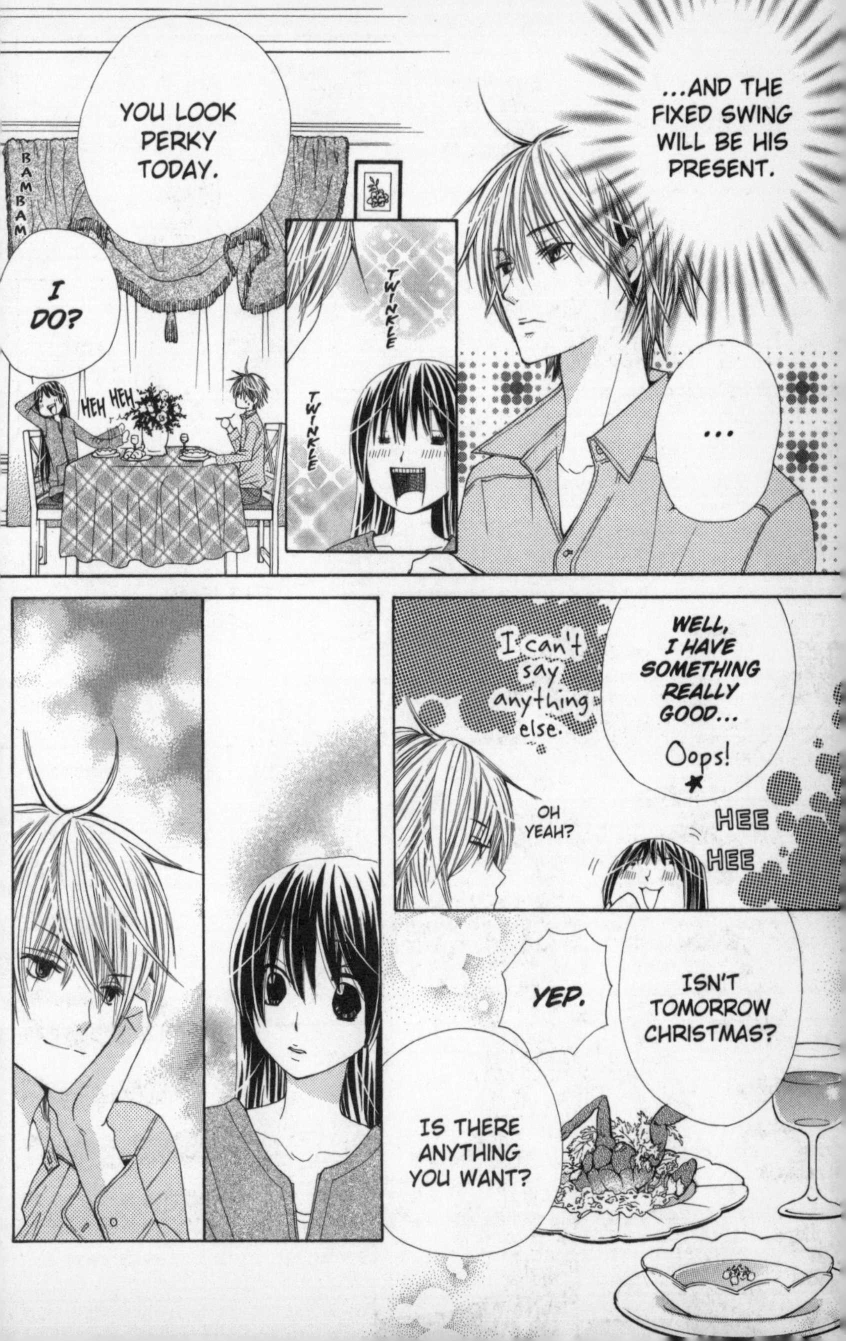
...AND THE FIXED SWING WILL BE HIS PRESENT.
...
TWINKLE
TWINKLE
YOU LOOK PERKY TODAY.
BAMBAM
I DO?
HEH HEH
WELL, I HAVE SOMETHING REALLY GOOD...
Oops!
I can't say anything else.
OH YEAH?
HEE HEE
ISN'T TOMORROW CHRISTMAS?
YEP.
IS THERE ANYTHING YOU WANT?

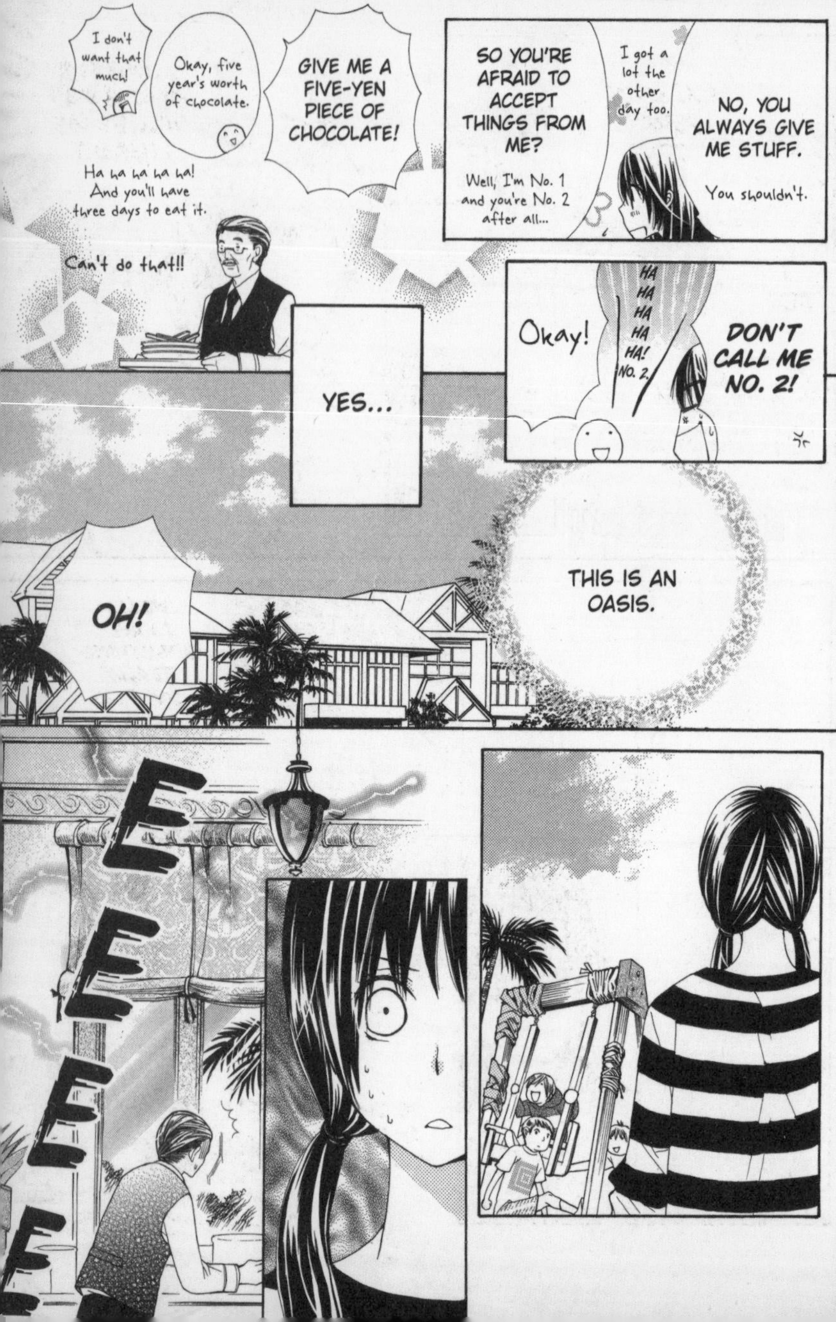
NO, YOU ALWAYS GIVE ME STUFF.
You shouldn't.
I got a lot the other day too.
SO YOU'RE AFRAID TO ACCEPT THINGS FROM ME?
Well, I'm No. 1 and you're No. 2 after all...
GIVE ME A FIVE-YEN PIECE OF CHOCOLATE!
Okay, five year's worth of chocolate.
I don't want that much!
Ha ha ha ha ha! And you'll have three days to eat it.
Can't do that!!
DON'T CALL ME NO. 2!
HA HA HA HA HA! NO. 2.
Okay!
YES...
THIS IS AN OASIS.
OH!
EEEEE

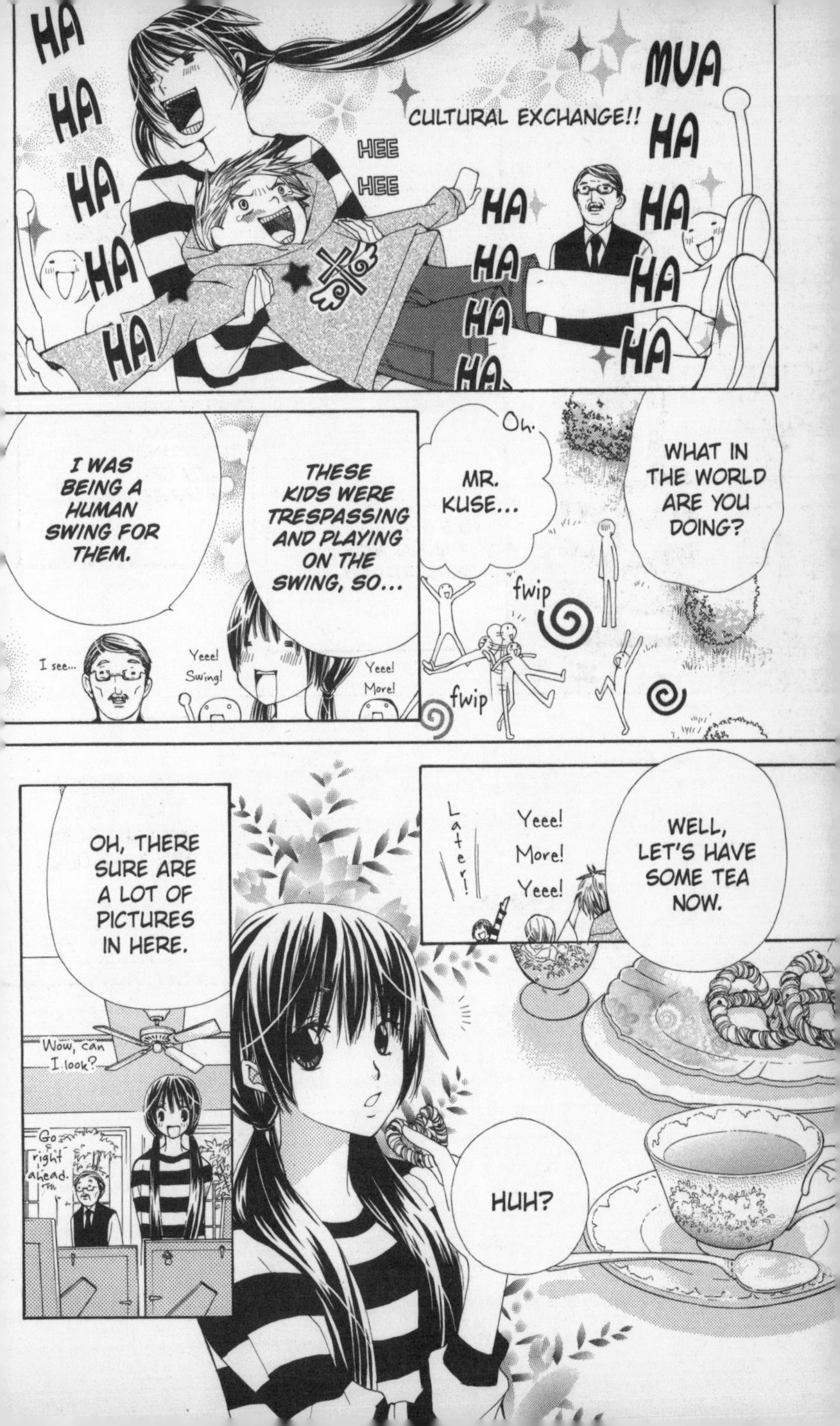
MUA HA HA HA HA
CULTURAL EXCHANGE!!
HEE HEE
HA HA HA HA
HA HA HA HA HA
WHAT IN THE WORLD ARE YOU DOING?
Oh.
MR. KUSE...
fwip
fwip
THESE KIDS WERE TRESPASSING AND PLAYING ON THE SWING, SO...
Yeee! More!
Yeee! Swing!
I WAS BEING A HUMAN SWING FOR THEM.
I see...
WELL, LET'S HAVE SOME TEA NOW.
Yeee! More! Yeee!
Later!
OH, THERE SURE ARE A LOT OF PICTURES IN HERE.
Wow, can I look?
Go right ahead.
HUH?

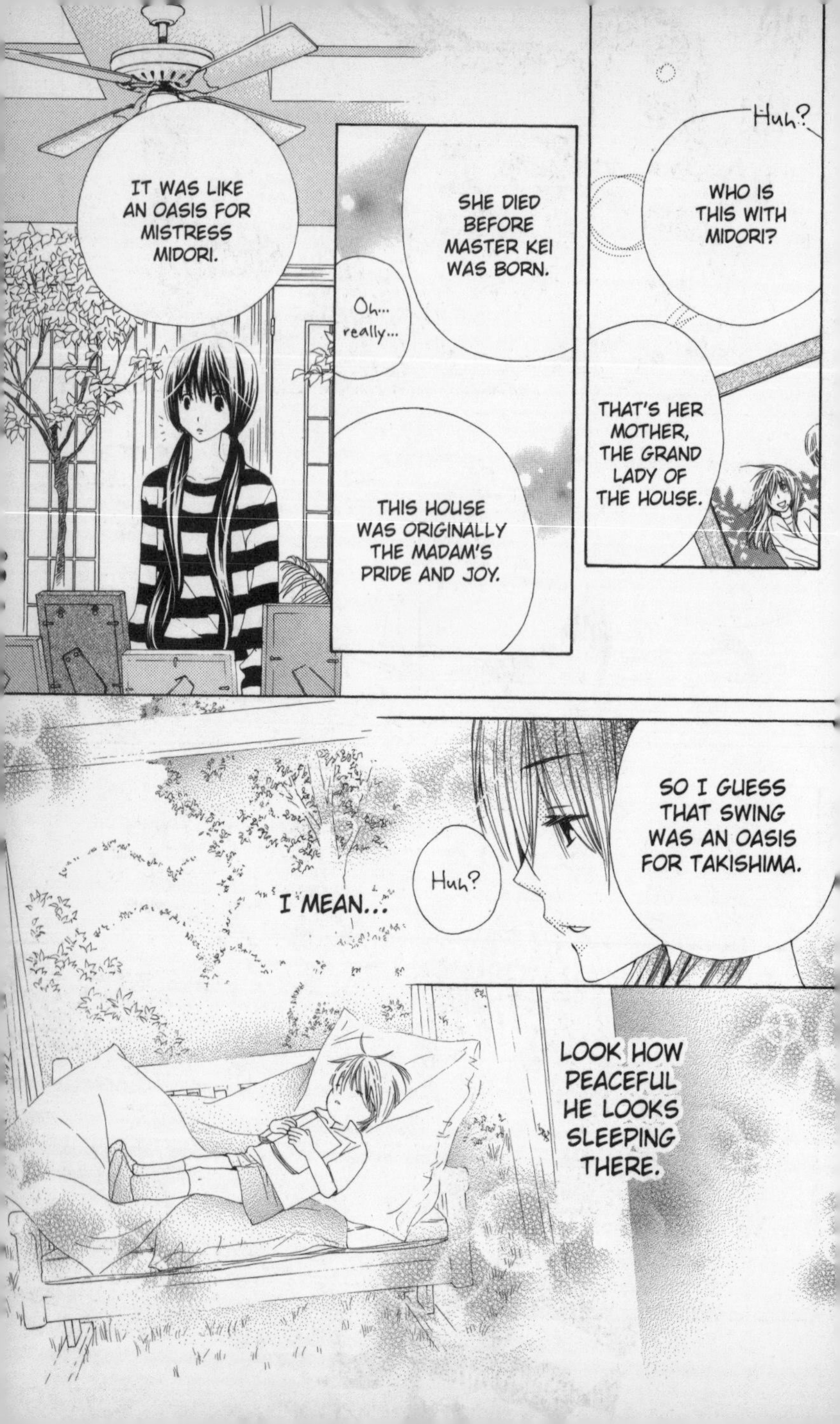
Huh?
WHO IS THIS WITH MIDORI?
THAT'S HER MOTHER, THE GRAND LADY OF THE HOUSE.
SHE DIED BEFORE MASTER KEI WAS BORN.
Oh... really...
THIS HOUSE WAS ORIGINALLY THE MADAM'S PRIDE AND JOY.
IT WAS LIKE AN OASIS FOR MISTRESS MIDORI.
SO I GUESS THAT SWING WAS AN OASIS FOR TAKISHIMA.
Huh?
I MEAN...
LOOK HOW PEACEFUL HE LOOKS SLEEPING THERE.

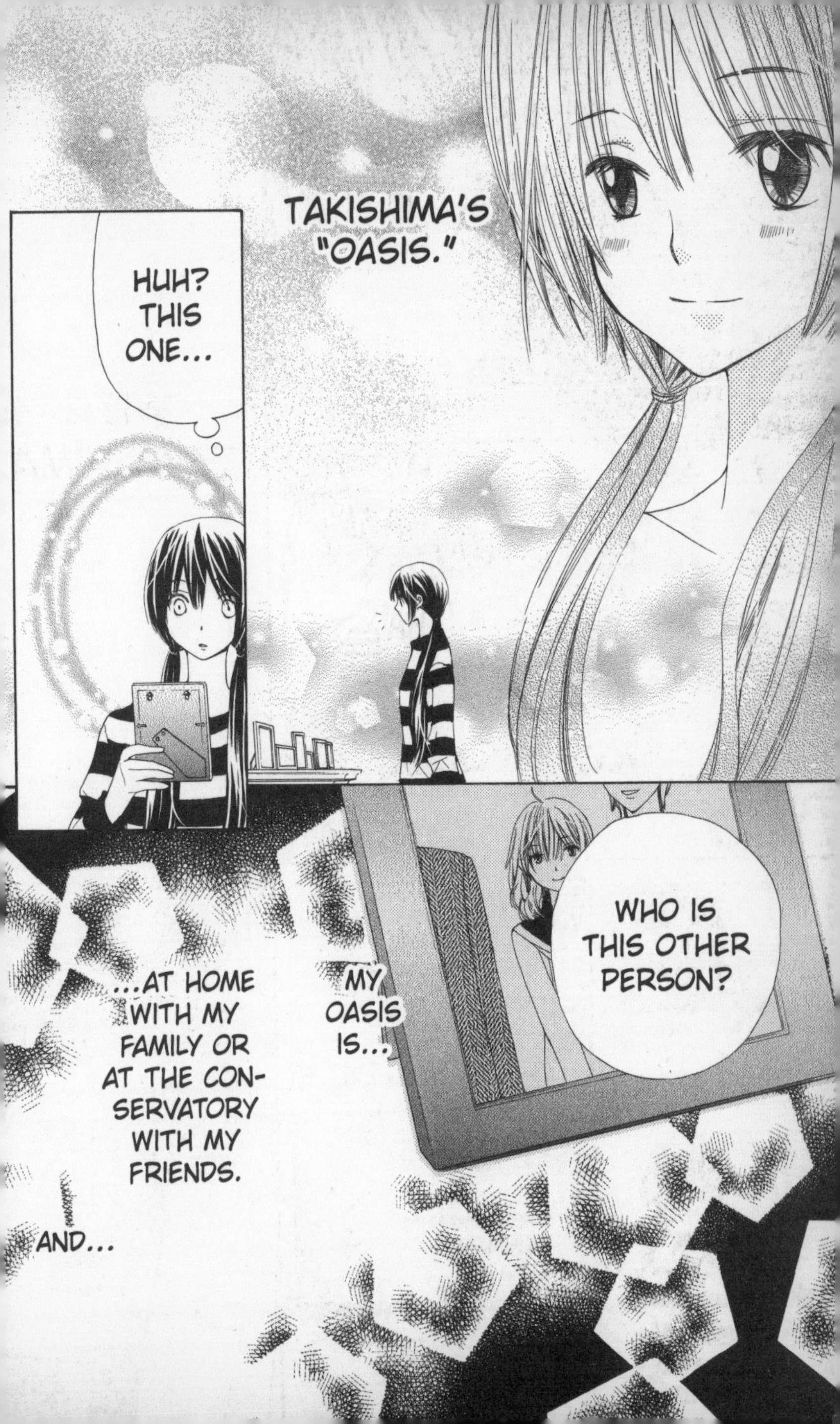
TAKISHIMA'S "OASIS."
HUH? THIS ONE...
WHO IS THIS OTHER PERSON?
MY OASIS IS...
...AT HOME WITH MY FAMILY OR AT THE CONSERVATORY WITH MY FRIENDS.
AND...

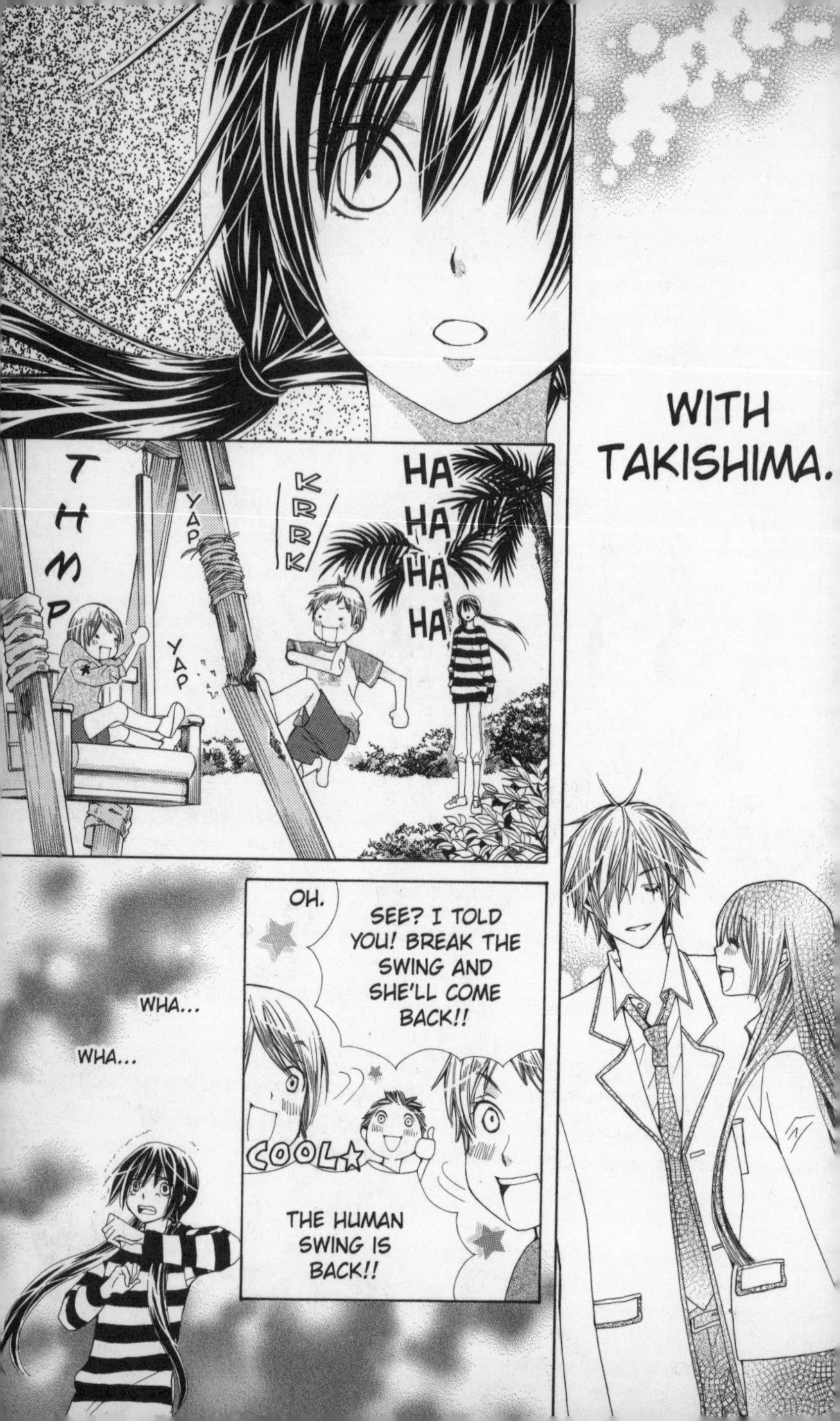
WITH TAKISHIMA.
HA HA HA HA
KRRK
YAP YAP
THMP
OH.
SEE? I TOLD YOU! BREAK THE SWING AND SHE'LL COME BACK!!
COOL☆
THE HUMAN SWING IS BACK!!
WHA...
WHA...

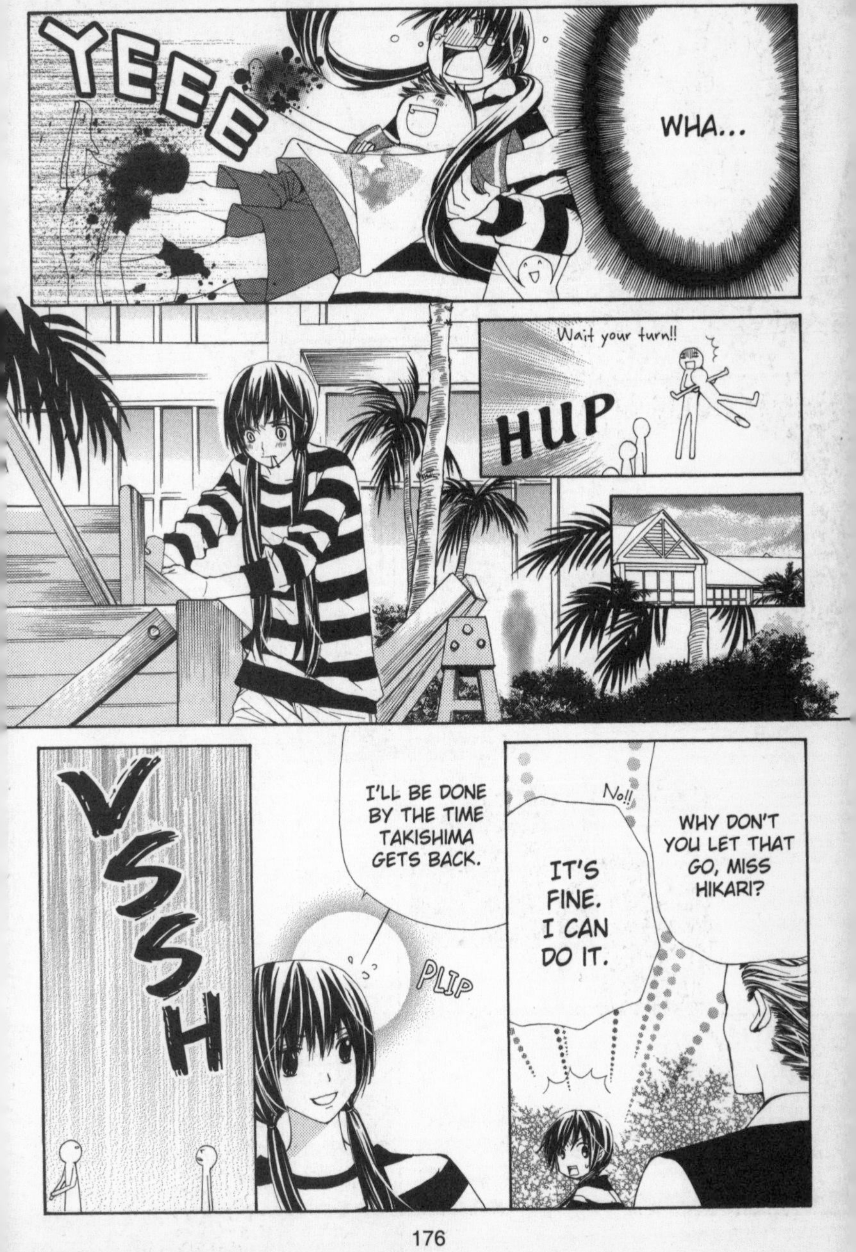
WHA...
YEEE
Wait your turn!!
HUP
WHY DON'T YOU LET THAT GO, MISS HIKARI?
No!!
IT'S FINE. I CAN DO IT.
I'LL BE DONE BY THE TIME TAKISHIMA GETS BACK.
PLIP
VSSH

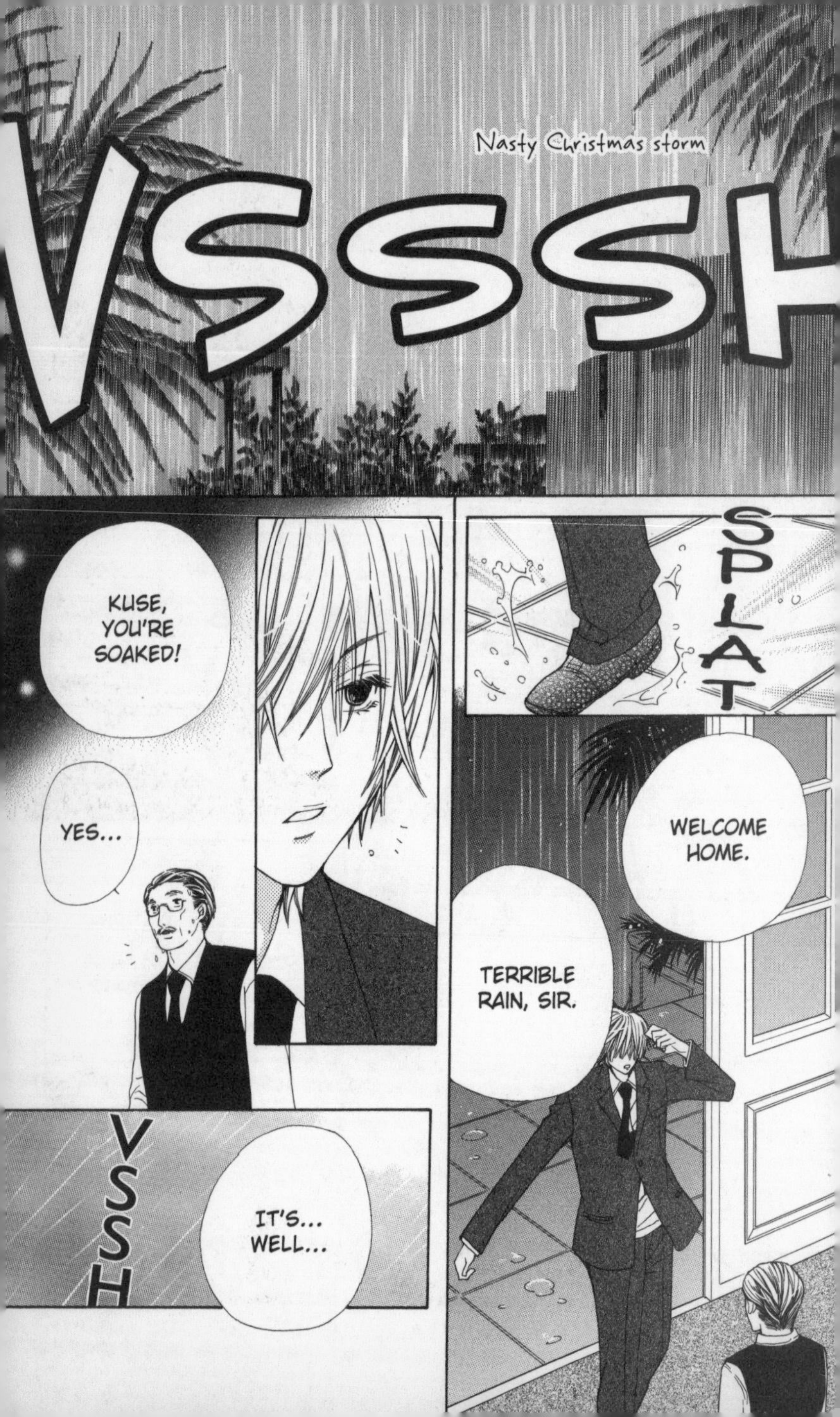
Nasty Christmas storm
VSSSH
SPLAT
WELCOME HOME.
TERRIBLE RAIN, SIR.
KUSE, YOU'RE SOAKED!
YES...
VSSH
IT'S... WELL...

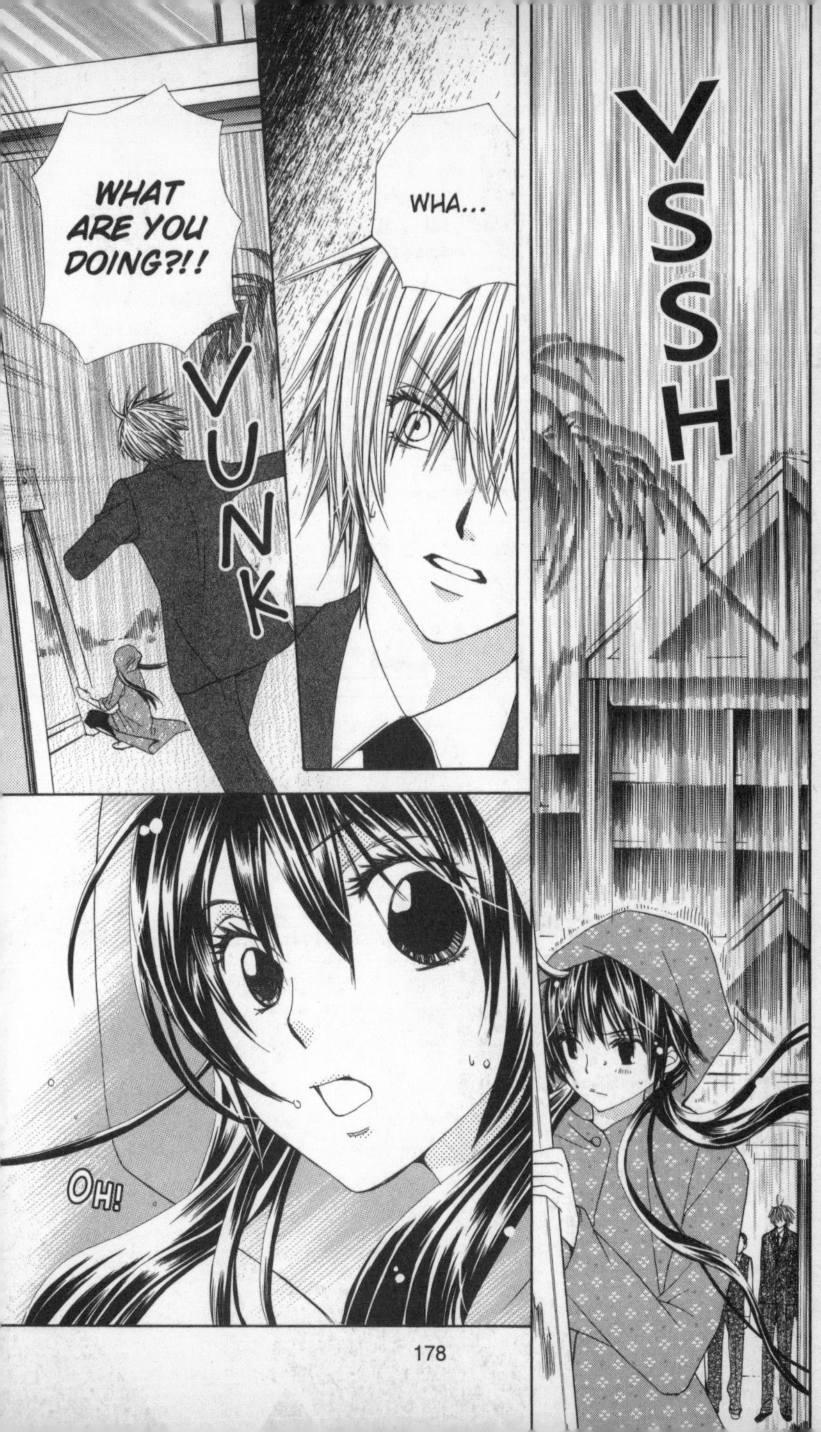
VSSH
WHA...
WHAT ARE YOU DOING?!!
VUNK
OH!

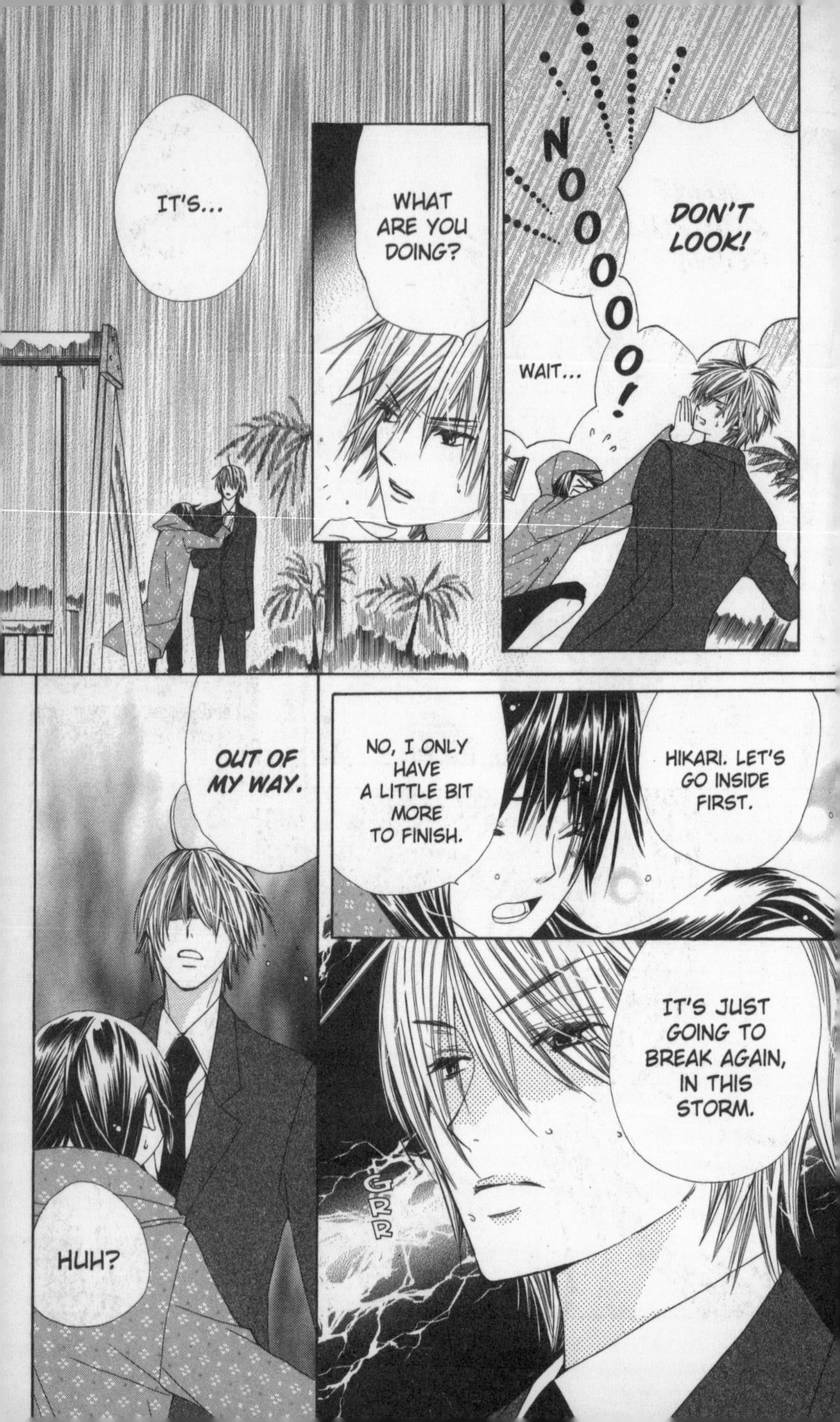
DON'T LOOK!
NOOOOOO!
WAIT...
WHAT ARE YOU DOING?
IT'S...
HIKARI. LET'S GO INSIDE FIRST.
NO, I ONLY HAVE A LITTLE BIT MORE TO FINISH.
IT'S JUST GOING TO BREAK AGAIN, IN THIS STORM.
GRR
OUT OF MY WAY.
HUH?

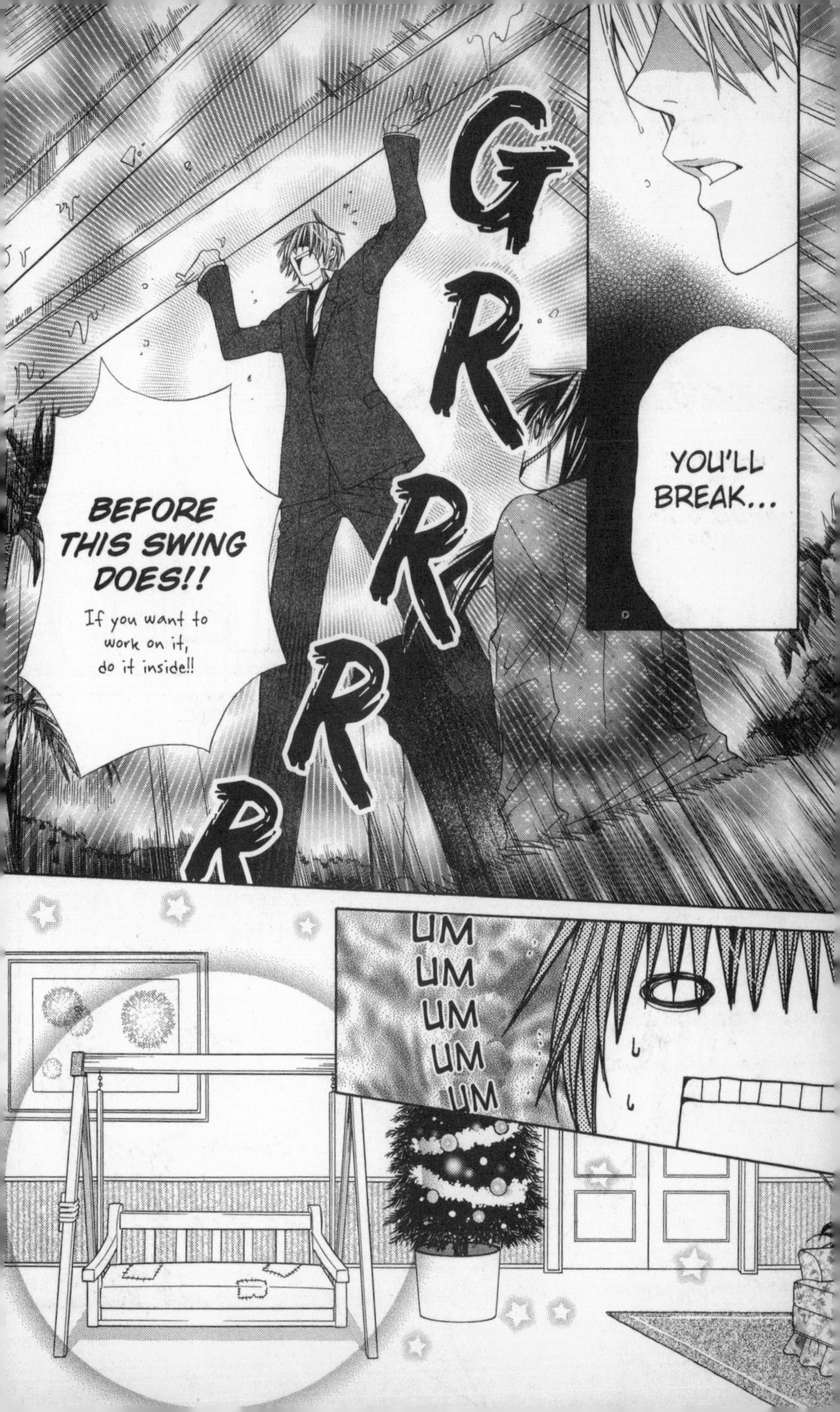
YOU'LL BREAK...
GRRRRR
BEFORE THIS SWING DOES!!
If you want to work on it, do it inside!!
UM UM UM UM UM

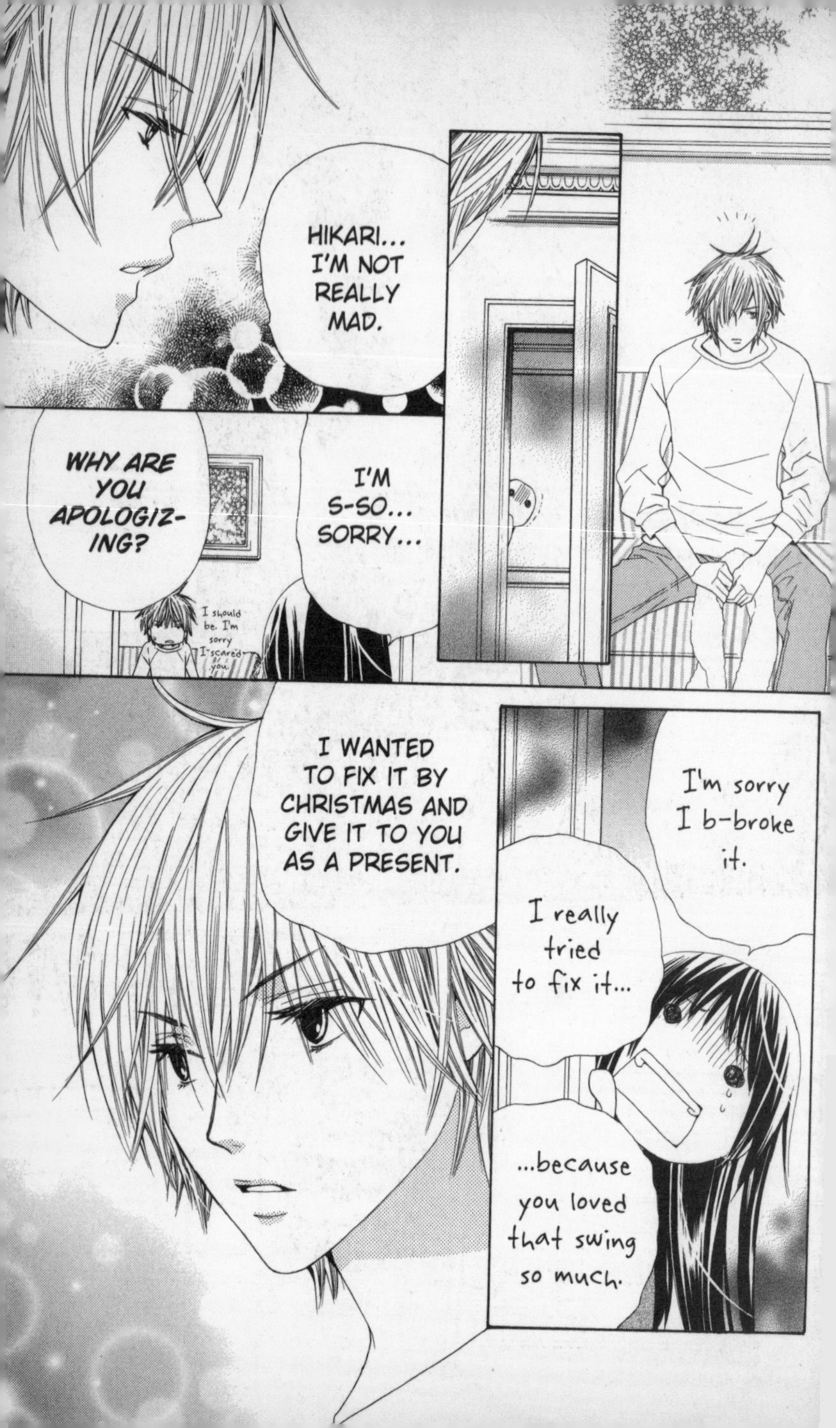
HIKARI... I'M NOT REALLY MAD.
I'M S-SO... SORRY...
WHY ARE YOU APOLOGIZ-ING?
I should be. I'm sorry I scared you.
I'm sorry I b-broke it.
I really tried to fix it...
...because you loved that swing so much.
I WANTED TO FIX IT BY CHRISTMAS AND GIVE IT TO YOU AS A PRESENT.

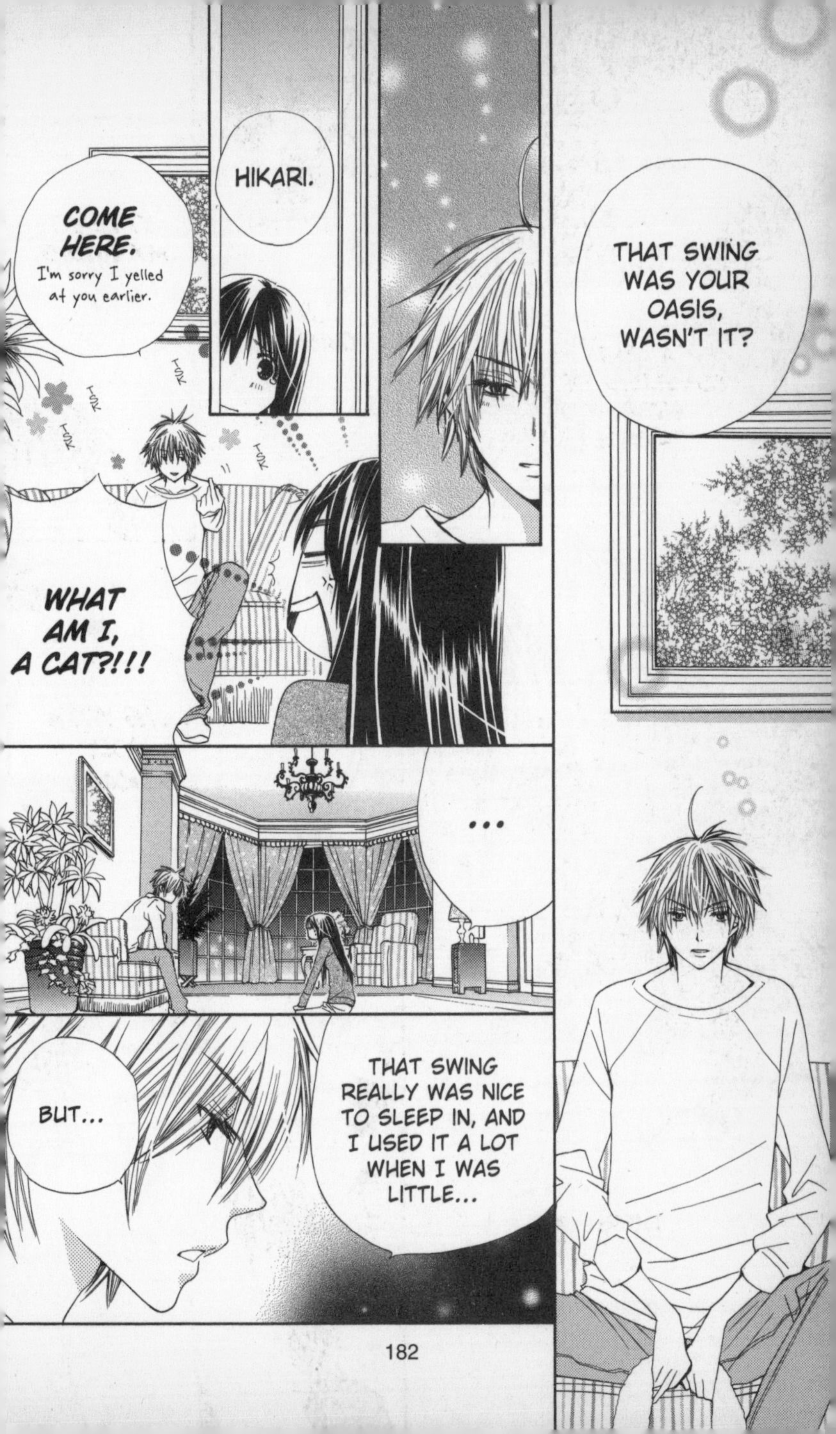
THAT SWING WAS YOUR OASIS, WASN'T IT?
HIKARI.
COME HERE.
I'm sorry I yelled at you earlier.
TSK
TSK
TSK
TSK
WHAT AM I, A CAT?!!!
...
THAT SWING REALLY WAS NICE TO SLEEP IN, AND I USED IT A LOT WHEN I WAS LITTLE...
BUT...

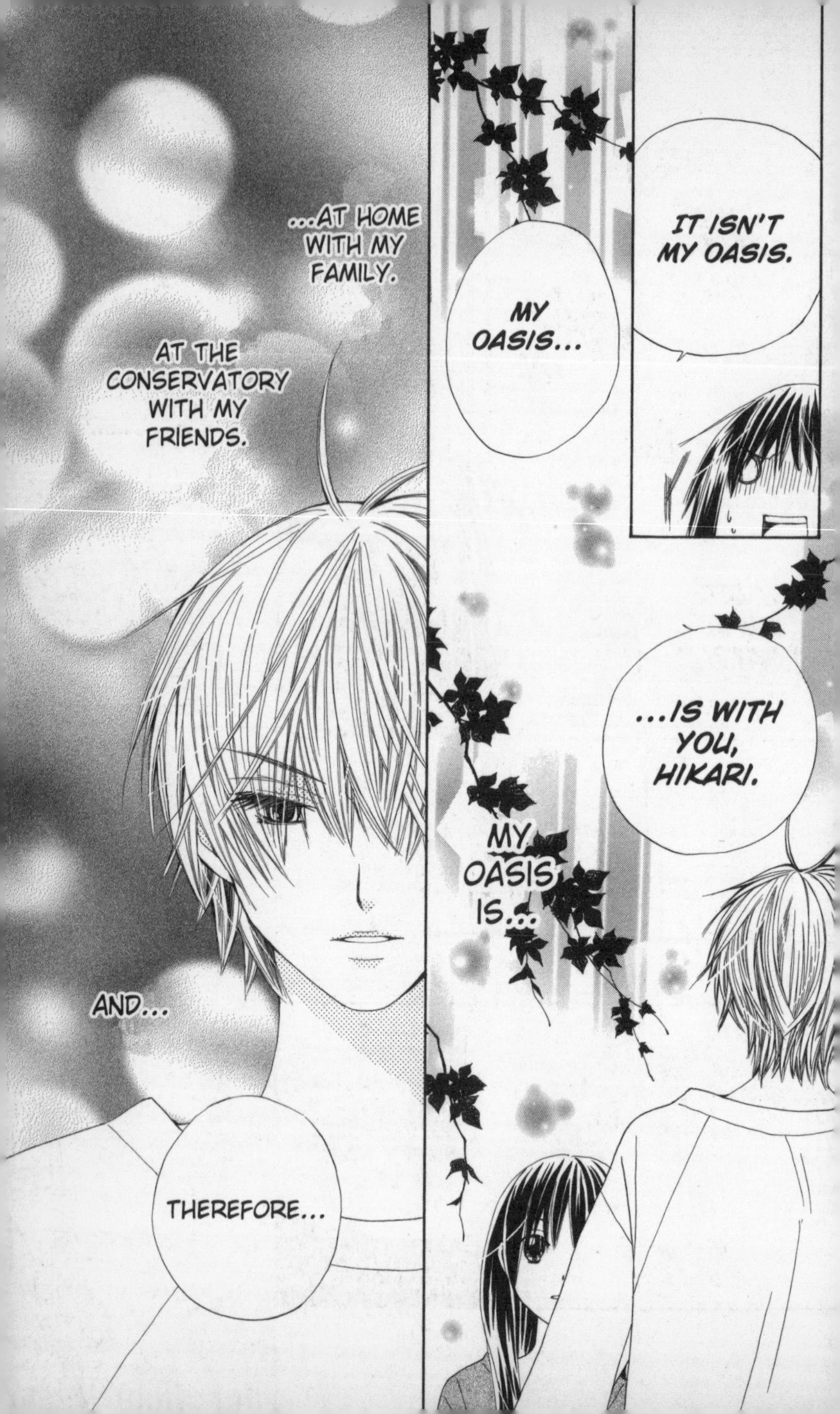
IT ISN'T MY OASIS.
MY OASIS...
MY OASIS IS...
...IS WITH YOU, HIKARI.
...AT HOME WITH MY FAMILY.
AT THE CONSERVATORY WITH MY FRIENDS.
AND...
THEREFORE...

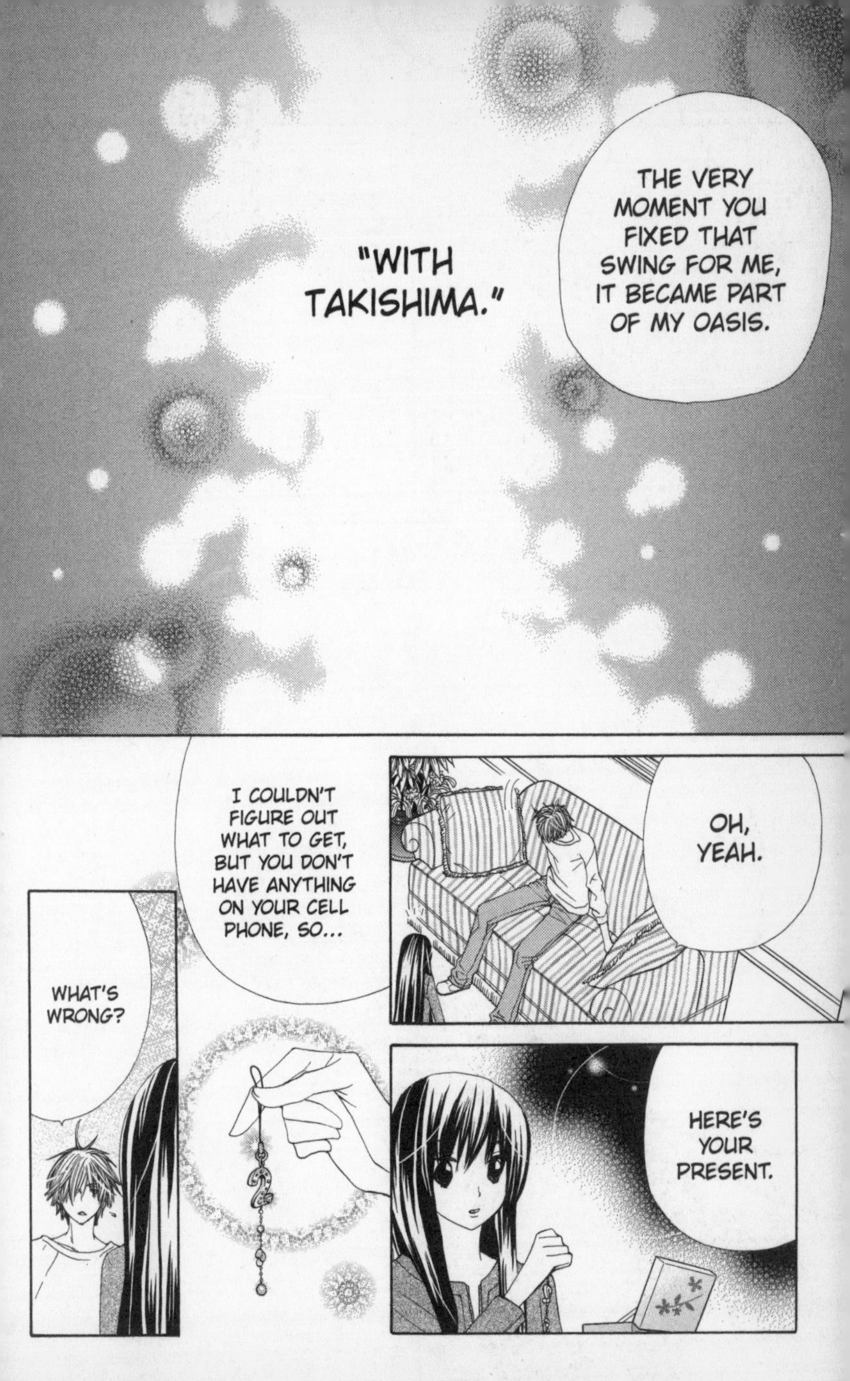
THE VERY MOMENT YOU FIXED THAT SWING FOR ME, IT BECAME PART OF MY OASIS.
"WITH TAKISHIMA."
OH, YEAH.
HERE'S YOUR PRESENT.
I COULDN'T FIGURE OUT WHAT TO GET, BUT YOU DON'T HAVE ANYTHING ON YOUR CELL PHONE, SO...
WHAT'S WRONG?

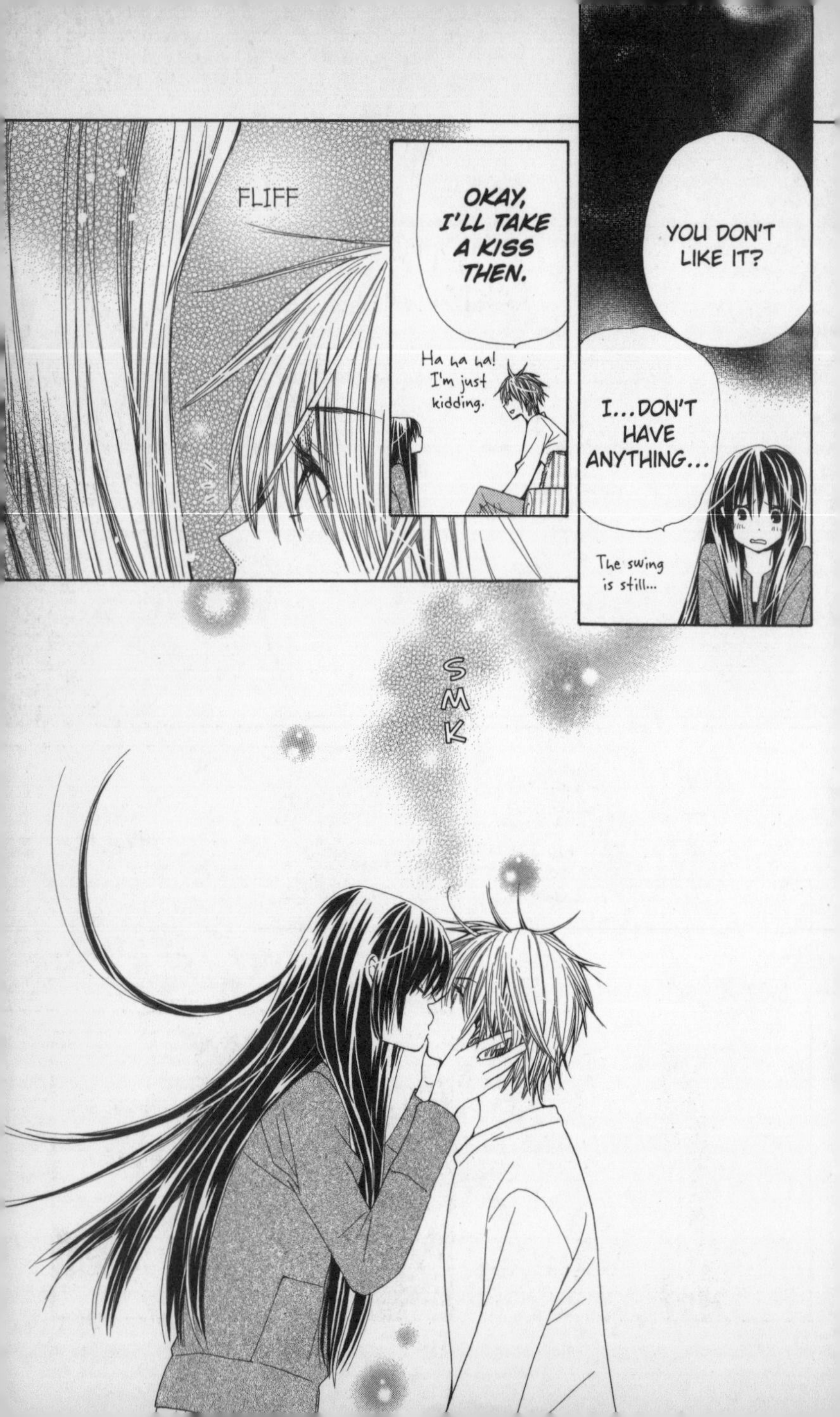
YOU DON'T LIKE IT?
I...DON'T HAVE ANYTHING...
The swing is still...
OKAY, I'LL TAKE A KISS THEN.
Ha ha ha! I'm just kidding.
FLIFF
SMK

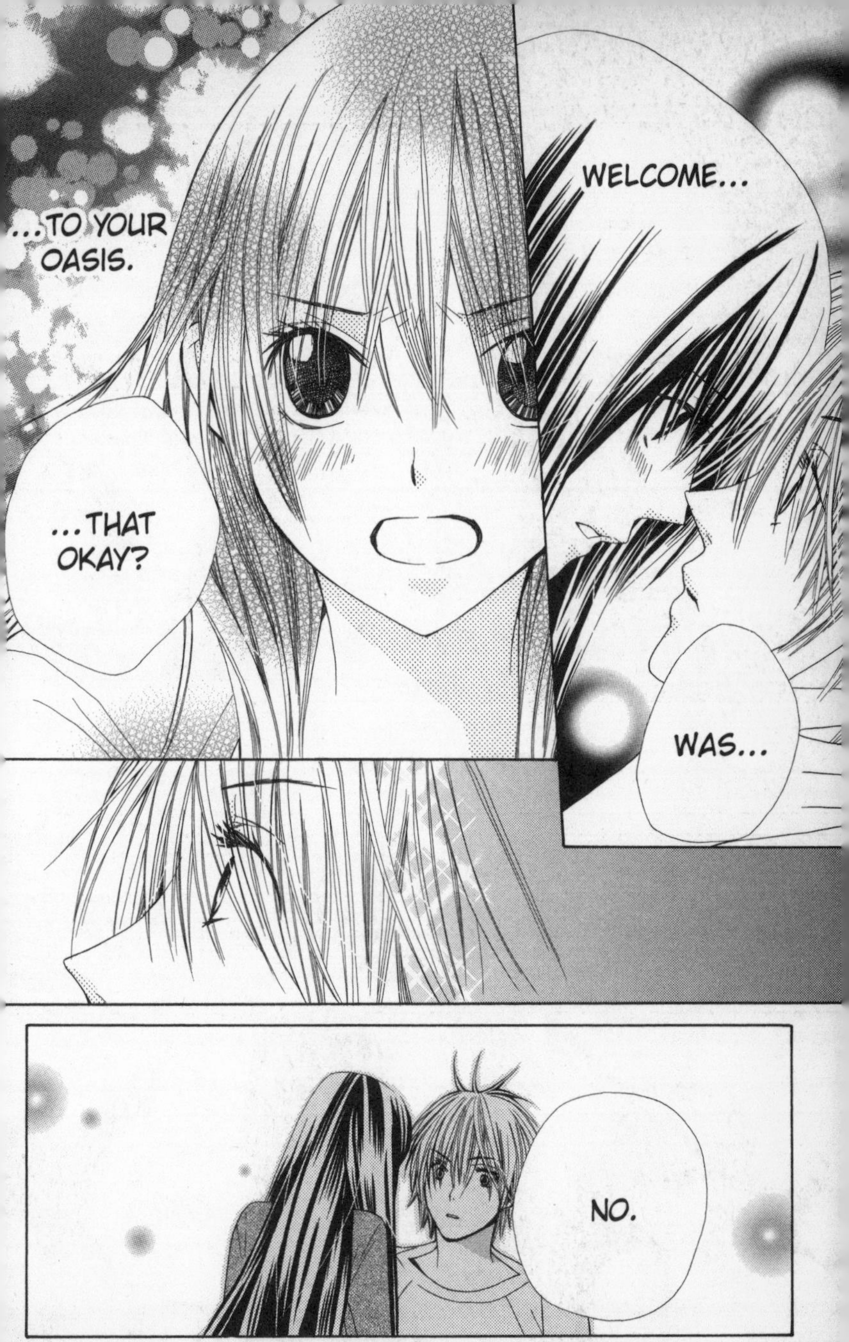
WELCOME...
...TO YOUR OASIS.
WAS...
...THAT OKAY?
NO.

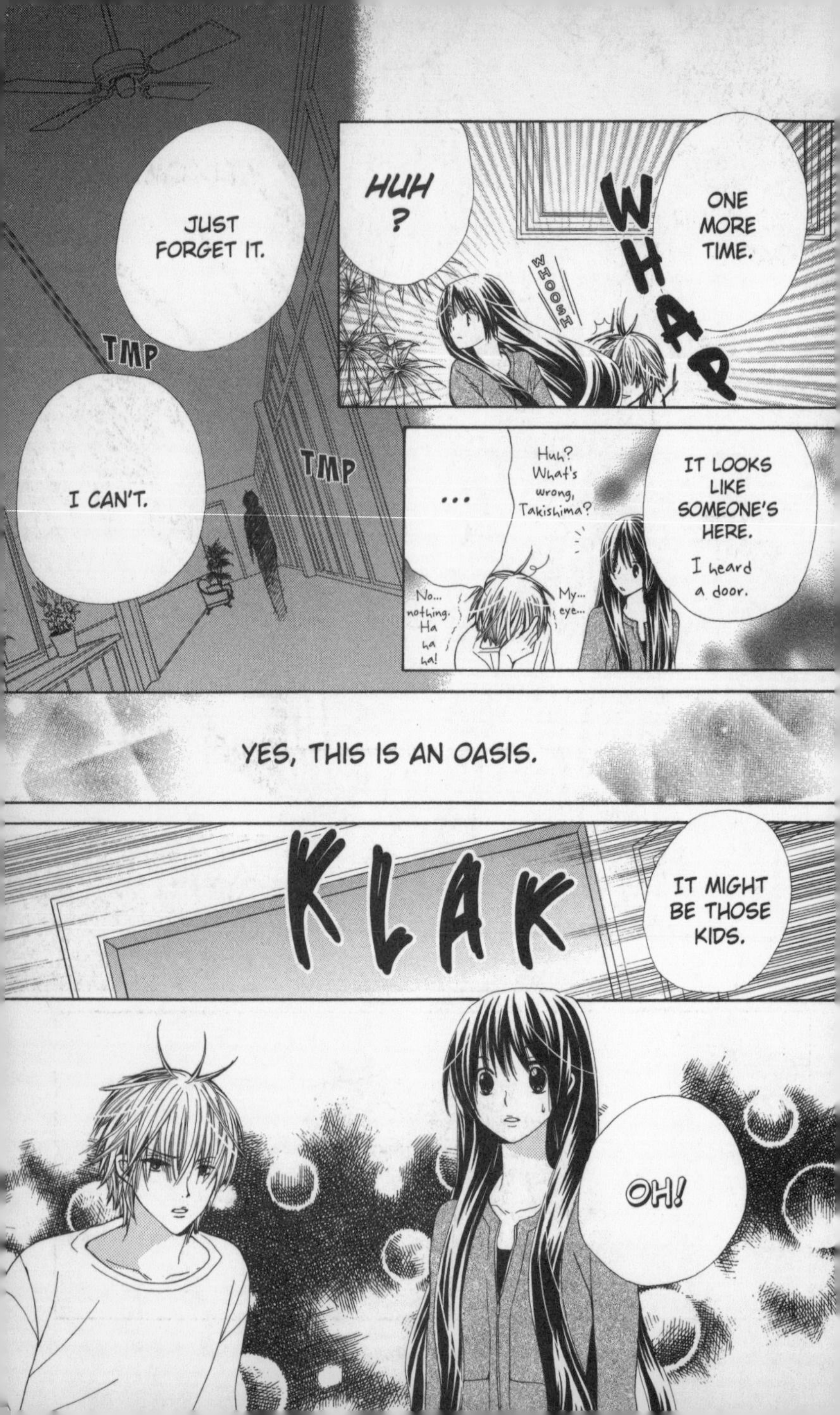
ONE MORE TIME.
WHAP
WHOOSH
HUH?
IT LOOKS LIKE SOMEONE'S HERE.
I heard a door.
Huh? What's wrong, Takishima?
...
My... eye...
No... nothing. Ha ha ha!
JUST FORGET IT.
TMP
I CAN'T.
TMP
YES, THIS IS AN OASIS.
IT MIGHT BE THOSE KIDS.
KLAK
OH!

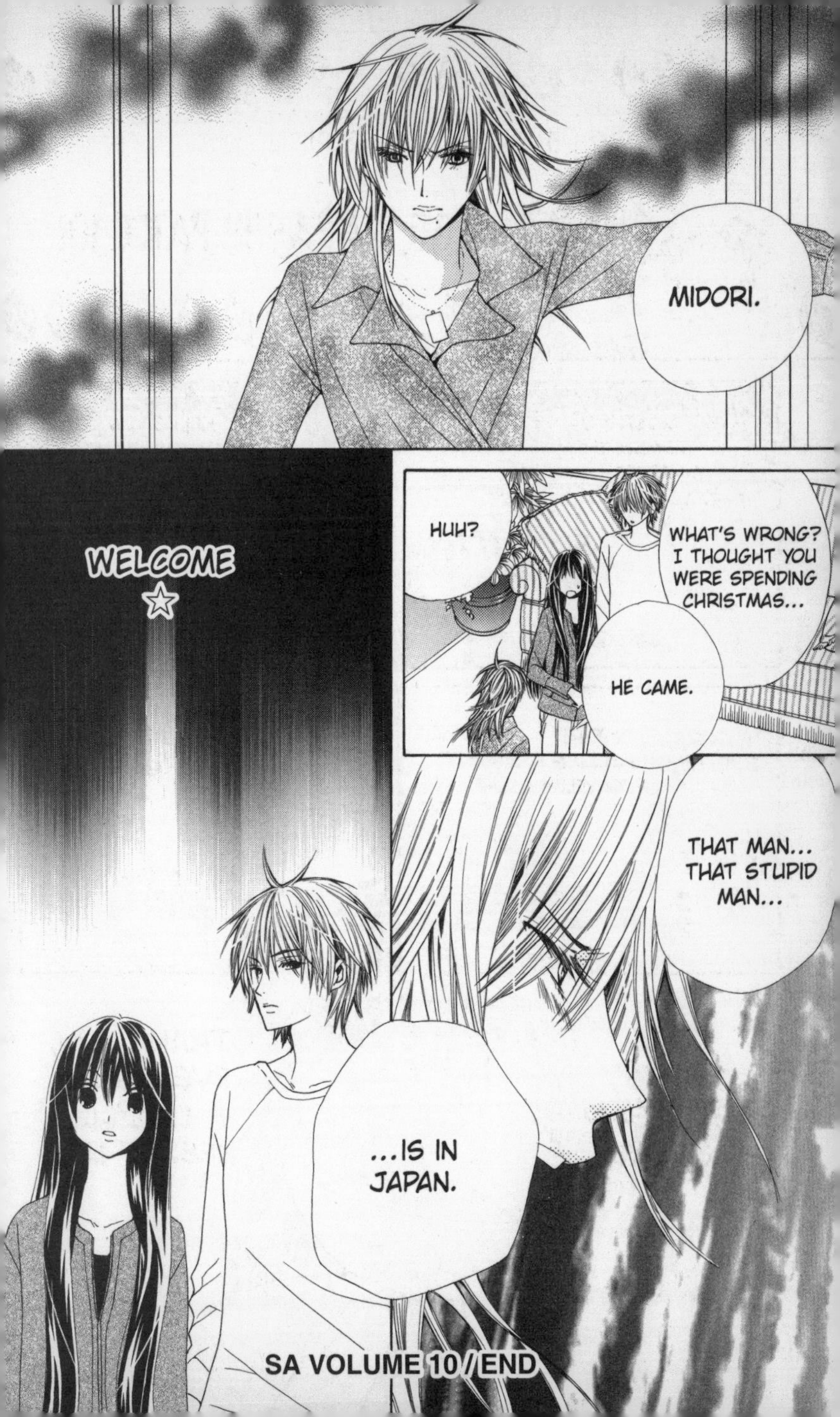
MIDORI.
WHAT'S WRONG? I THOUGHT YOU WERE SPENDING CHRISTMAS...
HUH?
HE CAME.
THAT MAN... THAT STUPID MAN...
...IS IN JAPAN.
WELCOME ☆

SA VOLUME 10 / END

Without warning, a two-page manga.

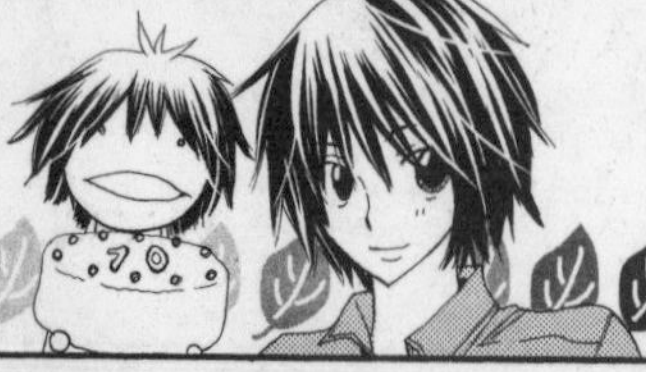

GO, TADASHI! PART 10!

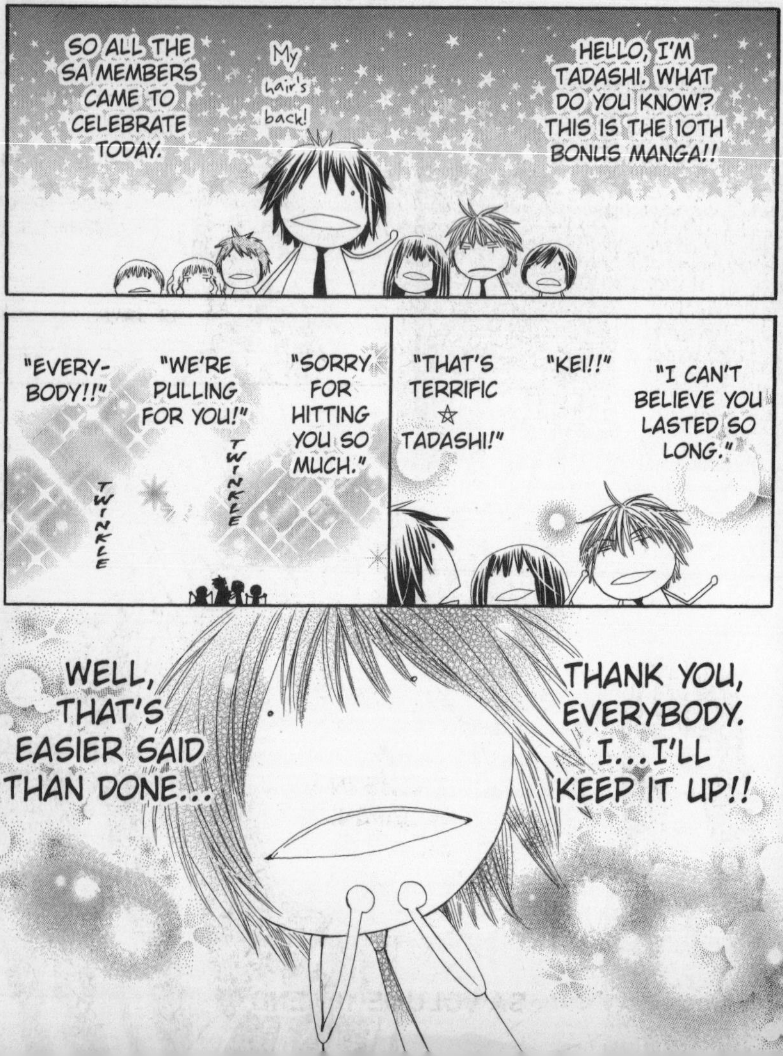
HELLO, I'M TADASHI. WHAT DO YOU KNOW? THIS IS THE 10TH BONUS MANGA!!
My hair's back!
SO ALL THE SA MEMBERS CAME TO CELEBRATE TODAY.
"I CAN'T BELIEVE YOU LASTED SO LONG."
"KEI!!"
"THAT'S TERRIFIC ☆ TADASHI!"
"SORRY FOR HITTING YOU SO MUCH."
TWINKLE
"WE'RE PULLING FOR YOU!"
TWINKLE
"EVERYBODY!!"
THANK YOU, EVERYBODY. I...I'LL KEEP IT UP!!
WELL, THAT'S EASIER SAID THAN DONE...

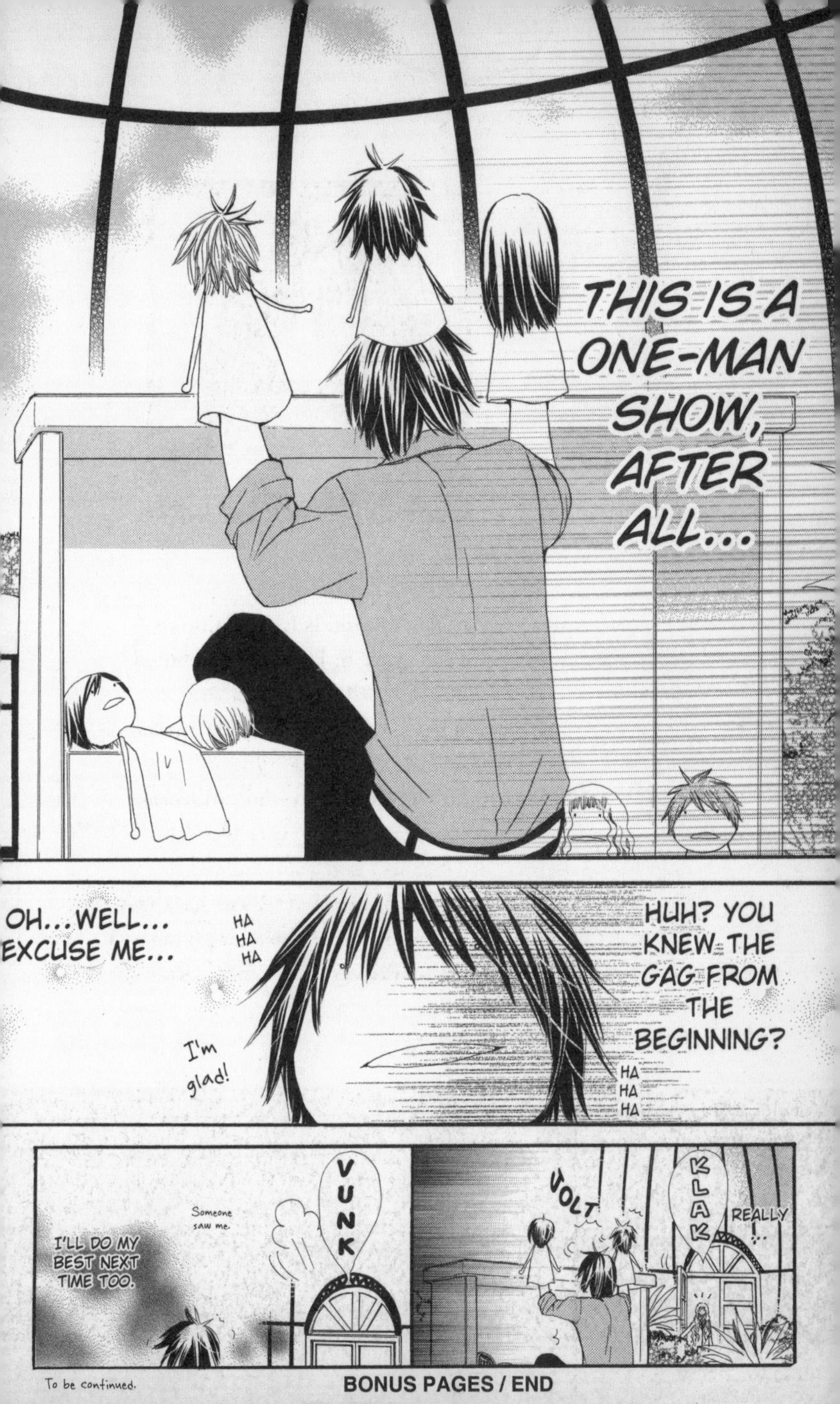
THIS IS A ONE-MAN SHOW, AFTER ALL...
HUH? YOU KNEW THE GAG FROM THE BEGINNING?
HA HA HA
I'm glad!
HA HA HA
OH... WELL... EXCUSE ME...
KLAK
REALLY...
VOLT
VUNK
Someone saw me.
I'LL DO MY BEST NEXT TIME TOO.

To be continued.

BONUS PAGES / END

Maki Minami is from Saitama Prefecture in Japan. She debuted in 2001 with *Kanata no Ao* (Faraway Blue). Her other works include *Kimi wa Girlfriend* (You're My Girlfriend), *Mainichi ga Takaramono* (Every Day Is a Treasure) and *Yuki Atataka* (Warm Winter). *S•A* was serialized in Japan's *Hana to Yume* magazine and made into an anime in 2008.

S•A
Vol. 10
The Shojo Beat Manga Edition

STORY & ART BY
MAKI MINAMI

English Adaptation/Amanda Hubbard
Translation/JN Productions
Touch-up Art & Lettering/HudsonYards
Design/Deirdre Shiozawa
Editor/Jonathan Tarbox

Editor in Chief, Books/Alvin Lu
Editor in Chief, Magazines/Marc Weidenbaum
VP, Publishing Licensing/Rika Inouye
VP, Sales & Product Marketing/Gonzalo Ferreyra
VP, Creative/Linda Espinosa
Publisher/Hyoe Narita

Printed in Canada

Published by VIZ Media, LLC
P.O. Box 77010
San Francisco, CA 94107

Shojo Beat Manga Edition
10 9 8 7 6 5 4 3 2 1
First printing, May 2009